CHANNELING
BLACKNESS

CHANNELING BLACKNESS

Studies on Television and Race in America

Edited by
DARNELL M. HUNT

New York • Oxford
OXFORD UNIVERSITY PRESS
2005

Oxford University Press

Oxford   New York
Auckland   Bangkok   Buenos Aires   Cape Town   Chennai
Dar es Salaam   Delhi   Hong Kong   Istanbul   Karachi   Kolkata
Kuala Lumpur   Madrid   Melbourne   Mexico City   Mumbai   Nairobi
São Paulo   Shanghai   Taipei   Tokyo   Toronto

Copyright © 2005 by Oxford University Press, Inc.

Published by Oxford University Press, Inc.
198 Madison Avenue, New York, New York 10016
www.oup.com

Oxford is a registered trademark of Oxford University Press

Library of Congress Cataloging-in-Publication Data

Hunt, Darnell M.
  Channeling blackness : studies on television and race in America / edited by Darnell M. Hunt.
    p. cm.—(Media and African Americans)
  Includes bibliographical references and index.
  ISBN-13: 978-0-19-516763-4 (alk. paper)—ISBN-13: 978-0-19-516762-7 (pbk. : alk. paper)
  ISBN 0-19-516763-5 (alk. paper)—ISBN 0-19-516762-7 (pbk. : alk. paper)
    1. African Americans on television. I. Title. II. Series.

PN1992.8.A34H86 2005
791.45′652996073—dc22   2004053115

Printing number: 9 8 7 6 5 4 3 2 1

Printed in the United States of America
on acid-free paper

CONTENTS

PREFACE

In 1988, fresh out of business school, I found myself working in the newsroom of a network affiliate in our nation's capital. A twenty-something black male, I had received a fellowship from the network to attend graduate school as part of a program established to help increase the abysmally low number of minorities in television management.

It was a racially tense time in Washington, D.C. Republican George Herbert Walker Bush had successfully won election to the presidency by, among other tactics, circulating television advertisements with the image of a convicted black murderer and rapist, Willie Horton, who had years earlier been furloughed by Michael Dukakis, former governor of Massachusetts and Bush's Democratic challenger. Because Horton had brutalized a Maryland man and raped the man's fiancée while on furlough, Bush's media advisors were able to effectively establish Dukakis's furlough decision as evidence that the Democrat was soft on crime. America, the media informed us, had turned to the Right. Crime, and the associated War on Drugs, had become major campaign issues. So the people turned over the White House to the incumbent vice president, who had served for the past eight years under Republican Ronald Reagan, "The Great Communicator."

The television newsroom in which I worked was caught up in the crime frenzy. We produced countless segments on Washington's drug scene, including some segments in which our camera crews accompanied police officers to black-occupied housing projects where the officers employed paramilitary force to bust up drug operations. We were also engaged—as were most of the competing stations in the market—in a related campaign to dig up information that might out the incumbent black mayor of D.C., Marion Barry, as a drug abuser and incompetent administrator. Barry, who enjoyed enormous support among the city's majority black population, was caught smoking crack cocaine in a federal drug sting two years later.

My time spent in the newsroom proved quite eye-opening when it came to matters of race and perception. A position at the assignment desk permitted me access to morning editorial meetings, where we discussed each day's news agenda in detail—including which stories would be covered, the relevant story angles, and which reporters would staff the assignments. One of the first things I noticed as a newcomer to the newsroom was a rather pronounced staffing pattern that might be described as a "racial division of labor." While the public face of the newsroom—the news anchors and a few of the more popular reporters—were blacks who reflected the city's racial demographics, behind-the-scenes decision makers were almost uniformly white. With one exception, all of the producers were white. The news director and assistant news director were both white. The station manager was white.

Over time, I began to see that this behind-the-scenes racial division of labor had a very real effect on what we placed on the screen. While the newsroom embraced a culture saturated in the journalistic ideal of objectivity, I began to understand the subtle ways in which the subjective perceptions of my seemingly well-intentioned white colleagues who ran the newsroom framed the "news." At editorial meetings, for example, some of these white colleagues would erroneously depict solidly middle-class black neighborhoods—some of the most affluent black communities in the nation—as "bad," crime-ridden areas. These perceptions, it seemed, complemented the decision makers' tendencies to *not* recognize or cover "positive" news stories in those communities. When we did cover "uplifting" stories, we typically selected ones emanating from white communities.

Five years later, having left the network affiliate and the nation's capital, I was wrapping up doctoral research exploring many of the racial issues that had confronted me in the newsroom. The recent election of Democrat William Jefferson Clinton to the White House had ended twelve years of Republican administrations and signaled, for many, the nation's shift back toward the center. Los Angeles, where I was then enrolled in graduate school, had just endured the nation's costliest urban uprisings to date. In an attempt to better understand the racial tensions underlying these 1992 events, the United States Commission on Civil Rights opted to hold a Los Angeles hearing. The commission sent a team of staffers to collect data and to interview elected officials and other community leaders as part of its preparation for the hearings. Observers inside and outside the commission speculated that media images may have had something to do with the racial tensions underlying the events. And because the commission's last comprehensive study of media and race—*Window Dressing on the Set*—had been conducted back in the late 1970s, the decision was made to revisit questions of race in Hollywood and in local Los Angeles television news as part of the hearing. By chance, a city official who had provided me with some background information for my doctoral research on media and race was contacted by the commission to assist with data collection. This mutual contact ultimately led to me working directly with the commission on the Hollywood issues.

As had been my experience in the D.C. newsroom, my staff position with the commission provided me with a firsthand look at how race and media are intertwined. I was paired with a staff attorney, a holdover from the Bush administration, who quickly made it clear to me that he was not overly sympathetic to complaints that the media industry was closed to people of color or that it misrepresented them and their interests. Over a period of months, we collected dozens of statements from network and studio executives, local news directors, reporters, producers, actors, writers, and representatives of media advocacy groups. We also engaged in a low-level struggle with one another over how to frame what these people told us.

My colleague seemed satisfied by the statements of industry insiders, which typically explained industry practices solely in terms of the market: race had nothing to do with it. Moreover, he was impressed by their description of a few industry diversity programs—programs not all that different from the one that had sent me to business school and to work in television—that they assured him signaled industry goodwill on questions of minority inclusion. Meanwhile, I was more impressed by the statements of the nonwhite actors, reporters, writers, and media advocates with whom I spoke. (With the exception of a Latino news director at a local television station, there were no nonwhite executives among our interviewees.) These nonwhite informants painted an image of an incredibly insular and racially homogenous industry that had scarcely changed since the days of *Window Dressing on the Set.*

The Los Angeles public hearing was held amid much fanfare in June of 1993. A divided group of eight Republican- and Democrat-appointed commissioners listened to testimony from several witnesses who had been carefully selected from our list of interviewees. *Racial and Ethnic Tensions in American Communities: Poverty, Inequality, and Discrimination—Los Angeles Hearing* endured an unusually long delay before finally being released with little publicity more than five years later, in November of 1998. Breaking convention with other reports of its type, the report was little more than a summary of testimony before the commission. It contained none of the general conclusions and policy recommendations featured in earlier reports like *Window Dressing on the Set.* It all but guaranteed that serious scrutiny of the industry status quo would have to wait for another day.

Business-as-usual in the television industry, despite claims to the contrary, has always had much to do with race. *Channeling Blackness: Studies on Television and Race in America* represents an attempt to examine this television industry status quo, particularly as it has shaped the inclusion and portrayal of black Americans over the years. I am particularly indebted to the scholars behind the thirteen classic and contemporary studies that form the bulk of this volume. Their analytical skills and cogent writings document in compelling ways the complex, yet basic, relationship between popular television and America's racial order.

I would like to acknowledge the contributions of several individuals who helped me think through and produce my own entries in the volume: Robert Baker, III, Nzinga Blake, Eddie Comeaux, Ryan Ford, Efrain Garibay, Angela James, John Kilgore, Zachariah Mampilly, Raquel Monroe, Lisa Nevins, Tianna Paschel, Samantha Pinto, Erin Randolph, Danny Slu, Zara Taylor, Michaele Turnage, Kelvin White, Jakobi Williams, and Nancy Yuen. I would also like to thank the countless individuals who offered me feedback during earlier presentations of the work, as well as my anonymous reviewers at Oxford University Press. And last, but certainly not least, I would like to express my gratitude to Candace Moore at the Bunche Center for her masterful editing of the manuscript and to Peter Labella at Oxford for his support of the project over the years.

Darnell M. Hunt
Los Angeles

CHANNELING
BLACKNESS

1

MAKING SENSE OF BLACKNESS
ON TELEVISION

Darnell M. Hunt

Blackness remains. In a time when the U.S. population is diversifying at a dizzying rate, when popular accounts of race present it as an anachronistic concern, when color-blind ideology shapes much of our public policy, and when the affirmation of cultural hybridity and multiple subjectivities is all the rage, blackness remains a curious, palpable presence in our land.

Blackness has always been a fundamental *signified* in U.S. culture, one dependent upon an institutionalized complex of prototypical *signifiers:* the African's dark skin; his coarse and curly hair; her earthy and unrestrained culture; his brute physicality. To be sure, this important signified permeated American consciousness even before the nation formally came into existence. It was an essential idea, not necessarily a valid one but a cornerstone nonetheless, in the foundation on which a dominant society would be erected, supported, and stabilized over the years.

But what began four centuries ago as an agrarian society characterized by small-scale, face-to-face interactions has now morphed into an information society marked by a proliferation of media images, messages, and encounters. Today, most of us spend most of our waking hours in the torrential presence of media[1]—newspapers, magazines, billboards, film, radio, CDs, DVDs, the Internet.

And, of course, popular television.

Popular television is a key medium, one that circulates images and messages around the clock on hundreds of broadcast, cable, and satellite channels. While network television has steadily lost viewers to cable and other media alternatives over the years, in 2003 the top-rated network programs still attracted between 20 million to 30 million viewers each—a figure considerable larger than those for the most popular cable programs.[2] Entertainment? Yes. Television titillates us with its slate of situation comedies, dramas, sports, "reality," and "news" programs. Big business? Most definitely. The five media conglomerates that owned the broadcast networks also owned the largest cable outlets in 2001, combining for more than $240 billion in revenue.[3]

But, for better or worse, popular television also functions as a central cultural forum in our society.[4] It serves as social space for the mediated encounters that distinguish the lived experiences of today from those of old, as a place for us to vicariously sample our fondest desires or our most dreaded fears, as a comfort zone from which we can identify with our heroes (particularly in episodic programs) or affirm our differences from undesirable Others.

It is also a medium where blackness permeates every channel. This volume explores why and how.

What follows are fifteen classic and contemporary studies of the shifting, complex relationship between popular television and blackness. All but the present chapter and the final one have appeared in print elsewhere. I selected these studies for reprint because of the unique insights each provides for considering the role blackness plays on American television. I have arranged them roughly in chronological order, based on their original appearance in print. They represent a variety of approaches to studying the matter at hand—from an official government report, to critical essays, to close analyses conducted more in line with the social scientific or cultural studies traditions.

In contrast, the present chapter and the final one constitute my own attempt to bring a sense of coherence to the volume. The final chapter applies insights about race and representation from the other chapters to a detailed case study of prime-time television at the dawn of the new millennium. The present chapter establishes a backdrop of four issues and themes against which we might engage the rest of the volume: the legacy of the black-white binary; the power of media; distinguishing "positive" television images from "negative" ones; and the relative importance of markets versus racial motives in television outcomes.

BLACK AND WHITE

In her critical analysis of American literature, *Playing in the Dark,* Toni Morrison demonstrates how the presence of the African has always been there—sometimes front and center, other times more shadowy—as a foil necessary for situating whiteness in American consciousness. She writes:

> What became transparent were the self-evident ways that Americans choose to talk about themselves through and within a sometimes allegorical, sometimes metaphorical, but always choked representation of an Africanist presence.[5]

The African, as we shall see, has served and continues to serve a comparable function on popular television. From the early days of *Amos 'n' Andy, Beulah,* and the *Nat "King" Cole Show,* through the civil rights era of *I Spy, Julia,* and *CBS Reports,* to the "color-blind" age of *The Cosby Show, Oprah,* and *Survivor,* blackness has been profoundly present on popular television, usually at the service of whiteness. In order to understand this special connection between black and white, its apparent ubiquity in American cultural production, we must first confront the more general issue of *meaning.*

Meaning is relational. The simplicity of this three-word phrase belies the wealth of insight contained within it. It is shorthand for the rather complex notion that the social and cultural meaning of a given object is always determined in relation to other objects; meaning does not flow from some essence within the object itself. Binary oppositions like "black" and "white" most perfectly express this idea, as the perceived location of each concept at an opposing end of the meaning spectrum, by default, anchors the meaning of the other. What is "black" is "not white." What is "white" is "not black." Sociologist Stuart Hall and others have shown how this positioning sets the stage for the emergence of fundamental "chains of equivalence"[6]—for example:

white = European = civilized = rational = superior = free = good

versus

black = African = savage = emotional = inferior = slave = bad

These basic equations have worked to reinforce, at the level of ideology, the relative positioning of persons considered "black" and "white" throughout American history.

Race-as-Representation

But race, of course, does not exist in nature. There is often as much phenotypical difference within so-called racial groups as there is between them. Instead, history has presented us with the *idea* of race; it has presented us with an irresistible *social representation*[7] or naturalized mental framework that works to order the way we see the world before us. We notice otherwise arbitrary differences on the surface of the human body and imbue these differences with social meaning. These social meanings, in turn, reinforce the significance of the otherwise nonessential construct of race, giving it a certain gravitas, a rather objective weight. As philosopher Charles Mills explains:

> Because people come to think of themselves *as* "raced" [emphasis in original], as black and white, for example, these categories, which correspond to no natural kinds, attain a social reality. Intersubjectivity creates a kind of objectivity.[8]

Key cultural forums like television today play a crucial role in this ongoing meaning-making process. Elsewhere I have discussed in some detail the relationship between media texts, discourses, representations, and ideology.[9] If this relationship is imagined as a pyramid, where *ideology* (background assumptions, commonsense definitions, and taken-for-granted justifications) forms the base, then *representations* like race occupy the next level of the structure, followed by *discourses* (networks of ideas and statements constructed out of key representations), and finally media *texts* (relatively bounded packages of images, words, and/or sounds constructed by their creators to convey certain discursive meanings), which form the capstone.

Race-*as-representation* is so central to American culture that we each rely upon it on a day-to-day basis as we attempt to establish meaning in the countless media texts that vie for our attention. Much of this meaning-making activity is wrapped up in our own ongoing efforts to establish who we are, who we are not, and who we hope to be. As a consequence, we each regularly affirm and police the boundaries of race, in our own little ways, as a means of bringing necessary order to our social experiences. As anthropologist Mary Douglas so cogently put it:

> It is only by exaggerating the difference between within and without, about and below, male and female, with and against, that a semblance of order is created.[10]

The black-white binary is particularly powerful because it is so efficient and effective in exaggerating racial difference, in helping to establish order—a *racial order*, if you will. To be sure, those who have a "possessive investment in whiteness"[11] have a fundamental need for blackness. It is no accident that "race" in the contemporary sense emerged with

European colonization of the "New World," and that the "black" and "white" races were created in tandem around the same time that Europeans identified Africans as the group best suited for slavery.[12] This "racial project" is but one of many that have worked over the years to (re)distribute power and resources along racial lines in America.[13]

Today's racial order is supported by racial projects that are more subtle in nature, that typically substitute culture for explicit invocations of biology in their efforts to reproduce the racial status quo. In place of explicit references to the black body and the use of overtly derogatory terms like "nigger," we are now more likely to find the casual use of *code words* like "crime," "welfare," and "quotas" to invoke images of a black culture that breeds dangerous, lazy, and ignorant blacks.[14] Whiteness, in contrast, has become an unspoken proxy for goodness. "Good" schools and "good" neighborhoods are "good" directly in relation to the presence of whiteness—the more the better. Whiteness represents the cultural norm, the implicit standard from which blackness deviates. As Sut Jhally and Justin Lewis (Chapter 6) and Christopher P. Campbell (Chapter 8) demonstrate, popular television works to reinforce this newer, "enlightened racism" through its representations of race. It works to divert our attention away from the underlying social structures that have always privileged white Americans, that continue to subordinate nonwhite Others.

So it goes without saying that black America—white America's most perfect foil—has been severely handicapped by these structures. Blacks, for example, graduate from high school at rates comparable to whites, but are only half as likely as whites to receive a bachelor's degree or more. Blacks are twice as likely as whites to be unemployed, they are nearly three times as likely to live below the poverty line,[15] and they are even more disadvantaged relative to whites in their efforts to accumulate wealth.[16] Meanwhile, black males and females are both heavily overrepresented among the nation's growing prison population. Indeed, in 2001, black men accounted for more than 45 percent of all men in prison, despite making up only about 12 percent of the overall male population.[17]

The Binary Trap

Because the black-white binary is so fundamental to our way of thinking in America, it creates something of a trap both for those who attempt to construct less stereotypical representations of blackness and for those who consume these representations. That is to say, those who attempt to *avoid* "binary thinking" in their production and/or consumption of representations of blackness necessarily do so *against* a cultural milieu that is saturated with the binary. In their efforts to overcome the commonsense, natural, taken-for-granted status that the binary and its chain of equivalences have achieved in our culture, they are forced to expend considerable amounts of effort. Sometimes this effort involves overcompensating for the tremendous social weight of the binary by ignoring race altogether. The "assimilationist" discursive position that Herman Gray (Chapter 9) critiques in his discussion of television representational practices might be thought of as one manifestation of this overcompensation. This position consciously strives to avoid the chains of equivalence that have defined blackness in America through a strategy of *(e)racing*. A black character, for example, is cast into a fictional world with other (mostly white) characters where race is apparently not a concern. But in an attempt to contain all of the racial meanings signified by the actor's *already raced* body, the character is sketched as everything that "blacks are not"—as civilized, rational, superior, good—as "white." The binary thus enters again through the back door: the countless other texts in circulation that are steeped in the binary's chains of equivalence have already informed the practices of those who created the "progressive" representation, just as they will undoubtedly inform the viewers who read it.

In the final analysis, race is a social construction in America that does double duty. It is an expedient ideological device, a social wedge that the racially privileged exploit in calculated ways to divide and conquer those beneath them; but it is also a potent social representation that people, both dominant and subordinate, routinely embrace and (re)circulate in their attempts to understand the actions of others and in their own ongoing rituals of identity affirmation. In the United States, the concepts of black and white have always functioned as social anchors in this continuous process of racial formation. Ideologically charged representations of blackness and whiteness have, for this reason, always dominated American popular culture.

I am not trying to argue here that *other raced* positions in our society are unimportant. Recent scholarship has convincingly made the case for the *relational* nature of racial formation in America.[18] Following this basic insight, however, I *am* arguing that the meanings of other raced positions in a white supremacist America are continually defined and redefined anew in relation to black and white poles, particularly to the chains of equivalence to which the binary gives rise. This volume focuses on the black-white binary in order to explore this racial meaning-making process in depth, which facilitates, for example, a consideration of the class and gender dynamics at work *within* blackness and whiteness. In an effort to make sense of blackness on television, this volume re-centers the fundamental relationship between blackness and whiteness that studies of racial diversification and hybridity often obscure.

Blackness and Ambivalence

The psychology of the black-white binary plays a particularly salient role in this ongoing meaning-making process. Numerous scholars have revealed how representations of the black Other simultaneously provoke attraction and aversion in whites. While the chains of equivalence associated with blackness and whiteness establish European culture as the hallmark of civilization and African culture as the epitome of backwardness, while they represent the essence of white personhood in terms of the mind and black personhood in terms of the body, and while they ultimately work to exalt the humanity of the European over that of the African, a profound ambivalence about blackness, it seems, persists in American culture. Exploring the realm of sexuality in his classic treatise *Black Skin, White Masks,* Frantz Fanon reveals how black male and female bodies work to signify racial inferiority at the same time that they are fetishized by whites as objects of desire:

> For the majority of white men the Negro represents the sexual instinct (in its raw state). The Negro is the incarnation of a genital potency beyond all moralities and prohibitions. The women among the whites, by a genuine process of induction, invariably view the Negro as the keeper of the impalpable gate that opens into the realm of orgies, of bacchanals, of delirious sexual sensations.[19]

In another classic text, *The White Man's Burden,* historian Winthrop Jordan examines American attitudes toward the African from the mid-fifteenth century through the beginning of the nineteenth century.[20] His analysis similarly suggests that the ambivalence white

Americans feel regarding blackness is rooted in a profound sense of loss among whites. That is to say, as whites, in an all-out effort to affirm the superiority of European (particularly English) civilization, projected their worst fears about themselves onto Africans, blackness inadvertently became the repository for all of the *prohibited* qualities that signify communion with nature, that oppose the (English) ideal of civilization. (Recall the chains of equivalence discussed earlier.)

Over the years, of course, this equating of the African with primal sexuality has evoked an ongoing literary, scientific, and popular preoccupation with the bodies of black men and women. From Shakespeare's *Othello,* the raping of black female slaves by white masters, the lynching of black men accused/suspected of raping white women, studies correlating body part measurements and intelligence, to stereotypes of the black athlete, Internet pornography, and the images saturating hip-hop videos, the bodies signifying blackness have been both reviled and revered. John Fiske's (Chapter 7) textual analysis of the Anita Hill–Clarence Thomas hearings, for example, reveals the ways in which representations of hypersexual black bodies—male and female—were recirculated between live television and fictional programming, effectively harnessing the spectacle in the service of competing gender, class, and racial projects. In their study of race as spectacle in college sport, C. Richard King and Charles Springwood (Chapter 11) show that the bodies of black athletes also are potent meaning vehicles; they are both the signifiers of black mental inferiority and the objects of desire for whites, evoking a profound ambivalence that fuels white consumption of the representations.

But African Americans also consume representations of blackness as they navigate the nation's racial waters. bell hooks has argued, for example, that some black men embrace a "phallocentric" masculinity based, in part, on fetishized representations of the hypersexual black male. Black male consumption and affirmation of these representations amount to a form of identity negotiation; they constitute an ongoing performance ritual, usually rebellious, that provides the men with a measure of respect and self-esteem often denied black men because of their disadvantaged status in the racial order.[21] Not surprisingly, these *self*-representations are legion in hip-hop culture and certain competitive sports (e.g., basketball and football[22]), televised expressive realms that feature the bodies of black men and attract large white audiences. The commodification of an exoticized and dangerous black masculinity within these arenas, it seems, is but a contemporary manifestation of the black "buck" stereotype[23] that has long titillated the white imagination.[24] As hooks reminds us, "Within white supremacist capitalist patriarchy, rebel black masculinity has been idolized and punished, romanticized yet vilified."[25]

Similar tensions and contradictions frame recent self-representations of black women. Rana Emerson's (Chapter 12) analysis of music videos featuring black women performers, for example, suggests that the performers often exploit age-old stereotypes of the hypersexual black female in order to celebrate their own sexual agency in a society (and industry) dominated by men. She further argues that the videos' representations of the aggressive and sexually independent black woman provide black female viewers with a space for communion with the performers, which often involves shifting the traditionally patriarchal gaze on the female body to one that centers the black male body as an object of female pleasure.

I should note here that a debate of sorts has emerged in the hip-hop era concerning the degree of control black Americans have over images of blackness. Some have argued that blacks have achieved unprecedented levels of control over black images, while others question whether this apparent control is meaningful. In *Am I Black Enough for You? Popular*

Culture from the 'Hood and Beyond, Todd Boyd seems to adopt the former perspective on the matter. He argues that blackness is an "excessive" image that sells directly in proportion to its excessiveness,[26] and ultimately advances a market-based argument to explain this phenomenon. As new technologies have multiplied the number of available representational channels, he argues, more and more images are required "to fill the ever-expanding visual space" (p. 5). Boyd suggests that this new media reality provides black Americans with an unprecedented amount of control over images of blackness, as they can exploit the related market demand by supplying ever more "excessive" self-representations (e.g., of "phallocentric" black masculinity or sexually free black femininity). But this conceptualization, it seems, erases a crucial point. While blacks clearly enjoy some agency in constructing and marketing the representations of blackness that circulate today, the "increased control" view fails to acknowledge the underlying consumer needs that make black "excess" a viable commodity in the first place. These needs, of course, likely constrain the domain of representational options, which raises pressing questions about the meaning of black "control."

In a racial order such as our own, and in a society where white Americans are the largest single audience segment, we would expect to find images of whiteness dominating a key cultural forum like television. But it is particularly telling that we find blackness, in all its profound ambiguity, *also* permeating the images on every channel. In fact, blackness is *overrepresented* in prime-time television fiction. While television insiders were extremely selective in their representation of blacks in the early days of the medium, studies have shown since at least the late 1990s that black television characters have accounted for a significantly larger proportion of the characters on television than blacks do of the nation's population. Males, of course, are also significantly overrepresented on the small screen— for *both* black and white characters. All other nonwhite groups, it is worth noting, have been significantly *underrepresented* on television throughout its history (see Chapter 15).

In their analysis of a wildly popular beer commercial featuring four black male friends, Eric Watts and Mark Orbe (Chapter 13) suggest that it is white ambivalence toward blackness that fuels its rampant commodification on the small screen today. This ambivalence appears to be rooted in the enduring threat represented by blackness, on the one hand, and in the sense of mastery (superiority) associated with taming "authentic blackness," with incorporating it into the (white) mainstream, on the other. Another manifestation of this ambivalence, Greg Tate suggests, is the seeming disconnect between the "ceaseless parade of troublesome Black stereotypes still proffered and preferred by Hollywood" and "the American music industry's reverberating quest for a white artist who can competently perform a Black musical impersonation."[27] Blackness *as threat* is attractive, it seems, as long as it can be controlled and whiteness can be affirmed. As we shall see, the interplay of the ever-present representations of blackness and whiteness is riddled with tensions and contradictions related to this basic tenet. This is particularly true on popular television, where the resulting discursive work has been and continues to be absolutely fundamental to the functioning of the American racial order.

THE POWER OF MEDIA

Focusing on the "discursive work" performed by television representations of blackness and whiteness necessarily presumes that these messages have some impact on us, that they are more than mere audio and visual apparitions that momentarily arouse our interest before evaporating from consciousness into thin air. Indeed, a long-standing debate exists among media researchers on this very issue that might be crudely divided into three camps: the "media-powerful," "audience-powerful," and "in-between" perspectives.

The "Media-Powerful" Perspective

The first camp grew out of early twentieth-century concerns about the apparent success of propaganda campaigns in mobilizing the masses during the meteoric rise of Hitler's Nazi Germany. These campaigns successfully exploited the relatively new media technologies of film and radio. An infamous example of the implementation of this new technology was Leni Riefenstahl's electrifying film *Triumph of the Will* (1934). The film's potent imagery of a godlike Hitler descending from the clouds to address the huge Nuremberg rally, many felt, exemplified the power of the new media to manufacture popular support for the growing Nazi movement. Motivated by these political developments, Frankfurt School scholars produced a number of alarming studies of media impact during this period that underscored the media's power to cultivate in audiences a dominant understanding of reality.[28] "Mass culture," a key concept associated with these studies, was described as a manufactured culture, one fabricated and circulated by the "culture industries" to serve the political and economic needs of the powerful. An important tenet of orthodox Marxism informed the formulation: "The ideas of the ruling class in every epoch are the ruling ideas."[29]

The "Audience-Powerful" Perspective

Meanwhile, across the Atlantic, similar concerns were being raised about the possible negative effects of comic books and movies, for example, on the moral fiber of American youth.[30] Many of these early studies would produce mixed findings about the impact of media, despite a concern that continues to this day about the possible harmful effects of violent images on children.[31] Nonetheless, it was the rise of radio and television as key platforms for America's transformation into the world's leading consumer society that eventually established a dominant view. The interests behind radio and television technology were invested in ensuring public acceptance of the new media, whose unprecedented power to market consumer goods was just coming into focus. It was essential that notions of consumer choice, metaphorically equated with notions of democracy and freedom, be emphasized in public discourse about the new media. If it appeared that media messages (e.g., commercials) actually manufactured audience responses (as Frankfurt School scholars argued), then cherished American ideals about freedom and democratic participation would be threatened.

So it follows that the most prominent media studies of the period were commissioned by industry insiders—entities who had a clear stake in demonstrating the new technology's congruence with the American Way of Life. This ideological bias, of course, had shaped the design and execution of important "administrative" studies of so-called media effects.[32] Findings such as the "two-step flow" of communication, for example, challenged the "hypodermic" model implied by the Frankfurt School's work, concluding that media messages are filtered through contacts with important others (e.g., opinion leaders) rather than injected directly into the brains of helpless, socially atomized audience members. Other period studies suggested further that the most significant variables in the communication process were those concerning the uses people have for media. Media can have no effect on those who have no use for them, it was argued.[33]

In short, media messages, in themselves, were conceived to have a limited effect at best, while other social variables like personal contacts and audience member needs were held to be more significant.[34] This "dominant paradigm" neatly resolved a potentially vexing contradiction throughout the 1940s and 1950s.[35] It supported the agenda of a media industry striving to be seen as a fount of freedom—an industry that, at the same time, enjoyed soaring profits precisely because of its perceived power to influence choice.

The "In-Between" Perspective

But the 1960s and early 1970s, in many respects, paved the way for an unraveling of the resolution. In addition to the Vietnam War, and a host of other related crises that challenged the nation at home and abroad, the period encompassed what sociologists Michael Omi and Howard Winant have referred to as a "Great Transformation" in American society—a fundamental paradigm shift from a largely uncritical acceptance of individual rights in America to the recognition of the importance of group-based rights, particularly as they legitimated appeals for social remedies (like affirmative action) made in their name.[36] At the center of this storm, of course, was the past, present, and future role of race in the United States, an issue thrust into the national limelight by politicized minority groups who increasingly sought access to media in order to voice their opposition to the nation's racial status quo.

A number of scholars, operating from different locales, produced media studies that began to revisit some of the assumptions inherent in the earlier, largely "administrative" research. Maxwell McCombs and Donald Shaw, for example, found that while media are not very effective in telling us what to think—as the "dominant paradigm" studies of previous decades assured us—they are nonetheless quite powerful in telling us what to think about.[37] To be sure, several of the chapters in this volume offer indirect support for this "agenda-setting" function of media as they explore media depictions of blackness. For example, the National Advisory Commission Report on Civil Disorders (Chapter 2) suggests that captivating news coverage of the urban riots of the 1960s focused national attention on escalating racial tensions in America, even if the information provided was lacking in its accuracy or comprehensiveness. Similarly, Sasha Torres's (Chapter 14) analysis of television and the civil rights movement demonstrates the central role network news and dramatic visuality played in keeping the movement front and center in public discourses about race.

In the United Kingdom, Stuart Hall and his colleagues at the Centre for Contemporary Cultural Studies (CCCS) were grappling with slippery questions of culture, power, and ideology. These scholars had been inspired by neo-Marxist intellectual Antonio Gramsci, whose writings on *hegemony* offered an explanation for how the powerful were often able to maintain their dominance over the masses without the use of direct force. Gramsci understood hegemony as an unstable equilibrium in which culturally promoted yet seemingly commonsense ideas served the function of winning consent from the masses, which relegated the need for coercive force to the background. Nevertheless, Gramsci did not rule out the possibility of *resistance*. Ideologies, while coercive, were not understood to be coherent. As a consequence, "organic" ideologies rooted in everyday consciousness and popular thought had the potential, at least, to displace more dominant ones from time to time. The outcome of the ongoing struggle between everyday consciousness and hegemonic ideas, Gramsci maintained, was always an open question.

In the spirit of this conceptualization, Stuart Hall (Chapter 3) produced a seminal theoretical piece that provided a resolution for a pressing problem in media studies: how to account for the empirical observation that audience members often interpret media messages in unintended ways, without completely dismissing critical perspectives suggesting that media messages ultimately work to reinforce dominant or hegemonic understandings of the world (e.g., Frankfurt School concerns). Hall's *encoding/decoding* model proposed that the creators of media messages encode in them a preferred or "dominant" meaning, but that audience members might decode these messages in accordance with any of three different codes: the "dominant" code, which would produce the preferred or dominant reading intended by the message's creator; a "negotiated" code, which would produce a reading that adjusted, in any number of ways, the intended meaning of the message to suit important needs or predispositions of the audience member; or an "oppositional" code, which challenged fundamental assumptions embedded in the meanings intended by the message creator. Molefi Asante's (Chapter 4) analysis of black consciousness during the civil rights era provides us with a concrete example of what Hall means by negotiated and oppositional reading. Vivid television coverage of confrontations between black protesters and authorities, Asante argues, had the unintended consequence of radicalizing black consciousness, of galvanizing black support for more invasive struggle tactics.

While some have used insights from Hall's model to celebrate a "semiotic democracy" in which audience members are free to do what they will with the intended meanings of media messages,[38] Hall was clear that the domain of possible interpretations is necessarily circumscribed by the social and cultural patterns in which people are embedded, which include the constraints imposed on us by shared linguistic systems. In the long run, these limits on alternative reading possibilities might work to support dominant views despite the negotiated and oppositional readings that we empirically know occur.

Indeed, by the early 1980s, George Gerbner's findings from his Cultural Indicators Project were beginning to show support for media "cultivation" and "mainstreaming" effects.[39] Gerbner observed that heavy exposure to media messages cultivated in audience members a "TV view of the world," a process that worked to pull the views of audience members who may otherwise occupy a variety of social and political vantage points toward a standardized middle or "mainstream" perspective on important issues. In the tradition of this work, Paula Matabane (Chapter 5) found that television fiction tends to downplay the difficulties black Americans encounter in all-white settings, and that heavy television viewing is associated with beliefs among blacks and whites that racial integration is more prevalent than it actually is.

Although the smoking gun of causation is often difficult to locate in media studies, the weight of the evidence suggests that media do indeed matter. Ongoing public debates about representations of blackness confirm the degree to which this idea has permeated and continues to occupy our popular consciousness. Few such debates have raged more hotly than those concerning "negative" and "positive" images.

"NEGATIVE" OR "POSITIVE"?

KINGFISH: Dat's right Madame Awber, I bringin' my motha-in-law into yo beauty parlor here dis afternoon, fo a complete overhaul job.
MADAME AWBER: Well, you make it sound like a big project.

KINGFISH: Well, Madame Awber, I gonna give you da problem wit my motha-in-law. . . . Has you ever been down to the beach and seen a grapefruit washed up on the sand. (*laughter*) One dat been in da water for three or fo weeks—and den washed up n left ta dry in the sun fo a few days?

MADAME AWBER: (*hesitantly*) Yes . . .

KINGFISH: Well, if you can git her lookin dat good, I'll be satisfied. (*laughter*)

—From "Getting Momma Married," *Amos 'n' Andy*

FRIEND 1: Where were we on the agenda?

CLAIR: Oh, yes, Professor Capel's testimonial. Now listen to this. (*fumbling with papers*) I had it written down. That's okay. I know it by heart. "Professor Gene Capel is one of America's foremost philosophical minds. She has written six books. She was very active in the civil rights movement. But she always had time for her nineteen-year-old students."

FRIEND 2: Boring.

FRIEND 3: Nap time. (*laughter*)

FRIEND 1: Besides, Clair. It doesn't say anything about what the woman is really like.

FRIEND 2: Right. If you wanna describe Professor Capel, first you gotta start with the hat.

FRIEND 4: The hat!

CLAIR: She wore that hat everyday!

FRIEND 2: That old yellow felt thing with the wire brim. She could shape that thing sixteen different ways! (*laughter*)

—From "Clair's Reunion," *The Cosby Show*

These excerpts come from two of the most talked about and studied television shows of all time. Both shows are notable for their predominantly black casts. Both were tremendously popular situation comedies. The first show was the creation of two white men who were inspired by the minstrel tradition, a tradition long associated with demeaning, stereotypical depictions of blacks; the other was the brainchild of two black men who were determined to counter the black images circulated by shows like the first. Despite the fact that *Amos 'n' Andy* and *The Cosby Show* are of two different eras—or perhaps *because* of this fact—considering them in tandem provides us with a revealing vantage point from which to consider debates about "negative" and "positive" images of blackness on television.

"The Finest Television Has Ever Produced"

Amos 'n' Andy originated on radio in the late 1920s. Two white actors, Freeman Gosden and Charles Correll, mimicked so-called black dialect as they enacted, with over-the-top gusto, the humorous exploits of the Uncle Tom–like Amos Jones and his gullible associate Andrew "Andy" Brown. The radio show was so successful with white audiences that it endured for decades. In 1951, amid much anticipation, Gosden and Correll brought *Amos 'n' Andy* to television. "At last," a Blatz beer advertisement for the new CBS show proclaimed, "you can see America's most heartwarming cast of comedians in the finest television has ever produced."

Instead of following the minstrel tradition of having white actors perform in blackface, the show's creators assembled an accomplished, all-black cast—television's first (and there would not be another for more than a decade)—after an extensive national search.[40] Because most of the actors eventually chosen for the show were veterans of the stage, their delivery was highly stylized, exaggerated, and larger than life. These qualities often combined with clever writing to produce outlandishly funny sequences, particularly those involving the conniving George "Kingfish" Stevens, his shrew of a wife, Sapphire, the crooked lawyer, Calhoun, and the dim-witted janitor, Lightning. The popularity of the television version of *Amos 'n' Andy* quickly approached that of the radio show.

But this is precisely what troubled the National Association for the Advancement of Colored People (NAACP). In a legal suit against CBS, the NAACP leveled several serious charges against the show:

1. It tends to strengthen the conclusion among uninformed and prejudiced people that Negroes are inferior, lazy, dumb and dishonest.

2. Every character in this one and only show with an all-Negro cast is either a clown or a crook.

3. Negro doctors are shown as quacks and thieves.

4. Negro lawyers are shown as slippery cowards, ignorant of their profession and without ethics.

5. Negro women are shown as cackling, screaming shrews, in big-mouth close-ups using street slang, just short of vulgarity.

6. All Negroes are shown dodging work of any kind.

7. Millions of white Americans see this Amos N Andy picture and think the entire race is the same.[41]

Amos 'n' Andy hit the small screen at a pivotal moment in U.S. race relations, when many believed the nation was close to turning the corner in efforts to integrate society. Established in 1909, the NAACP throughout much of its existence had focused on eradicating media images of black Americans that seemed to work against the movement for racial integration in America. Indeed, more than a generation earlier the civil rights organization had attacked D. W. Griffith's highly popular, groundbreaking film *Birth of a Nation* (1915). The film, the NAACP had charged, promoted white supremacy by circulating distorted images of lazy, ignorant, and dangerous blacks alongside those of noble white victims and heroic Ku Klux Klansmen. Implicit in these critiques, of course, was the assumption that popular media are more than mere entertainment. Echoing Frankfurt School concerns about the power of media to shape perceptions, critics of "negative" black images feared that white acceptance of and belief in the images would stall efforts for increased racial inclusion. That is to say, critics were concerned that whites would be mistakenly led to believe that blacks were not deserving of integration into (white) society.

The NAACP eventually succeeded in its campaign against *Amos 'n' Andy*. CBS cancelled the show in 1953, at the height of its popularity.[42] The timing of the show's cancellation is significant, of course, because a year later the NAACP would also play a major role in the landmark *Brown v. Board of Education* decision, which ended legalized segregation in America and gestured toward an integrated future. *Amos 'n' Andy* continued to run in syndication on television until the early 1960s, when it left the airwaves for good. While the show's depictions of blacks clearly seemed to resonate with the more regressive racial projects of the period, no known audience studies of the show exist to corroborate the corrosive effect the NAACP claimed it had on the movement toward racial inclusion. Moreover, anecdotal accounts suggest that many black viewers actually derived pleasure from the show, even as other (mostly middle-class) blacks regarded its cancellation as a civil rights victory.

The Cosby Mission

In contrast, studies of *The Cosby Show* provide us with considerably more evidence about its probable impact on U.S. race relations. *The Cosby Show* made its debut on NBC in 1984, a year marked by Ronald Reagan's landslide reelection to the White House. Reagan's initial victory over incumbent Jimmy Carter had already signaled a major shift in U.S. politics. Amid growing threats abroad and increasing economic problems at home, Reagan first won the presidency by successfully encouraging and exploiting a backlash movement among relatively affluent white Republicans and less affluent, disaffected whites—the so-called Reagan Democrats. This movement blamed the racial policies of the civil rights era for the current problems plaguing America, particularly those that working-class and middle-class whites felt acutely. Because Reagan had an impeccable record of opposing every major civil rights initiative of the previous two decades, he was the ideal candidate to promote this theme.[43] The former actor's communication skills also helped him in his campaign efforts, as his appeals to white voters were often more dependent on style than substance.

The two black men behind *The Cosby Show,* however, were on a different mission. While 1980s America was taking a turn to the right, away from a commitment to racial justice and progressive reform, these men were determined to fashion a new type of popular television series, one that would work to "recode" blackness. In practical terms, their goal was to provide "positive" and uplifting images of blackness that would correct the distorted images circulated in years past, beginning with stereotypical shows like *Amos 'n' Andy* and moving through the ghetto-centric situation comedies of the 1970s (e.g., *Sanford and Son, Good Times,* etc.; see Chapters 9 and 15). Implicit in this project, of course, was a concern not all that dissimilar from earlier NAACP fears about the power of negative black images to undermine efforts for racial justice.

Bill Cosby was well positioned to undertake this mission. He was a popular comedian and veteran television actor who had starred in several previous series. He was the first black American to star in a television drama when *I Spy* made its debut on NBC in 1965, the same year that racial tensions led to the infamous Watts riots in Los Angeles. Most important, perhaps, a 1966 TVQ study revealed that Cosby was one of the most popular figures on television, a rather momentous finding given the previous history of blacks on the small screen.[44] Cosby's ability to comfort and amuse white audiences would soon be exploited by advertisers like Jello pudding, who sought his services as a commercial pitchman. Cosby also became the first black executive producer on a television show in 1969, when his short-lived situation comedy, *The Bill Cosby Show,* made its debut (see Chapter 15). So when the opportunity arose in the 1980s to create a new type of black image for television, Cosby was more than prepared. In addition to hiring several young black writers and assistants who would later go on to create their own shows (a rare breed in television),[45] he brought black Harvard psychiatrist Alvin Poussaint aboard *The Cosby Show* team in order to ensure that the psychological impact of the black images circulated by the show was carefully considered.

In accordance with their mission, Cosby and his team created a solidly upper-middle-class black family—the Huxtables—who lived in a comfortable Brooklyn brownstone adorned with African and African American art, interspersed among classy, traditional furnishings. Jazz music was typically featured in the opening credits and as a transition device throughout each episode to help establish a sophisticated mood not traditionally associated with situation comedies (or blacks on television). The husband, Cliff, was played by Bill Cosby himself and sketched as a gynecologist/obstetrician. This was a rather bold choice in light of traditional media tropes about the hypersexual black male, particularly given that scenes from the series would eventually show Cosby's character seeing white female patients. Cliff's wife, Clair, was written as a high-powered New York attorney who somehow managed to attend to the needs of her husband and five children with loving care and maternal concern. The children, teenage son Theo and daughters Sondra, Denise, Vanessa, and Rudy, were good kids who seemed to welcome their parents' words of wisdom and generally avoided the kinds of serious trouble news media of the day associated with black youth (see Chapter 9). The Huxtables presented an image of the black family that had truly overcome.

Shortly after its introduction, *The Cosby Show* shot to the top of the ratings, where it remained throughout most of its eight-year run. Audiences would increasingly abandon the networks for cable and other media options during this period, prompting *Entertainment Weekly* to proclaim *The Cosby Show* as "the last show everyone watched." [46] The show was indeed a ratings phenomenon. Its finale was scheduled to air in April of 1992, on an evening that coincided with ongoing coverage of the Los Angeles uprisings. While most of the nation would be permitted to watch the farewell episode as scheduled, the Los Angeles NBC affiliate, KNBC-TV, planned to preempt the episode in favor of local news coverage of the fires. But as Los Angeles mayor Tom Bradley worked to restore order to a violence-torn Los Angeles, he offered, perhaps, the greatest testament to the social power of the series: he successfully lobbied KNBC-TV to broadcast the final episode as originally scheduled. To the degree that viewer attention would be drawn to the screen, authorities surmised, it would be diverted away from the streets.

Despite the apparent success of *The Cosby Show* in circulating "positive" images of blackness, the series was not without its critics. Some observers described the show as a 1980s version of the 1950s white sitcom *Father Knows Best* and the Huxtables as a white family in blackface. Indeed, John Fiske's (Chapter 7) textual analysis of the show suggests that it often worked to celebrate many of the middle-class "family values" that 1980s-era conservatives admired in the earlier nuclear family sitcoms. These were the same values, of course, that conservatives claimed non-nuclear (and black) families generally lacked.

Sut Jhally and Justin Lewis (Chapter 6) conducted an audience analysis of *The Cosby Show* that sheds much light on how real viewers likely made sense of the program. The results reflect a key insight provided by Stuart Hall (Chapter 3) in his important encoding/decoding model: the message sent is not necessarily the message received. While black viewers tended to embrace the show for the "positive" portrayals of blackness Cosby strived to create, some expressed misgivings about the Huxtables' unrealistic failure to regularly interact with less affluent blacks. Meanwhile, the show seemed to "strike a deal" with white viewers, absolving them of responsibility for racial inequality in the United States in exchange for welcoming the affluent black family into their living rooms every Thursday night. Ideologically, this white reading resonated nicely with the Right's claim about the arrival of a color-blind America, with conservative efforts to dismiss the need for racial reforms like affirmative action. Black Americans who had not achieved the American Dream had only themselves to blame.

Beyond "Positive" and "Negative"

Two black situation comedies. One created in the early 1950s, loaded with "negative" black stereotypes, at a time when America was moving in the direction of racial integration. The other created in the mid-1980s, loaded with "positive" black images, at a time when America was reconsidering many of the racial reforms that had transformed the intervening three decades. Together these two cases demonstrate some of the pitfalls associated with conceiving of black images as *inherently* "positive" or "negative."

Rana Emerson's (Chapter 12) analysis of music videos featuring black women performers further underscores these difficulties. Are the music videos' representations of sexually free and independent black women merely repackaged stereotypes of the hypersexual black woman, a potent foil against which wholesome (and docile) white womanhood has been defined since slavery? Or are they appropriated *self*-representations that work to empower black women viewers, a group doubly subordinated in a racist and sexist America?

Criticism of black images has typically been leveled on two fronts: either the images are denounced as *distorted,* or they are attacked for being *damaging* in some way. While the concept of "negative" image obviously joins the two understandings, the understandings are predicated on very different assumptions. In the first case, the criticism is rooted in an acceptance of "mimetic realism," the assumption that images should reflect some underlying reality.[47] Although the second, "damaging" understanding often involves the judgment that the images in question are inaccurate, it sometimes refers to images that are quite accurate but considered to be counterproductive nonetheless. This second basis for criticizing black images is rooted more in an acceptance of "simulacral realism," the assumption that media, for better or worse, have the power to engineer social outcomes.[48]

Stuart Hall's discussion of the "reflective" and "constructionist" approaches to representation map rather neatly onto these two approaches to realism. Noting that the reality we see—that we respond to—is socially constructed through the representations of the world constantly in circulation, Hall argues for the analytical value of the second approach.[49] A "circuit of culture," he argues, necessarily links *representation* to *identity, production, consumption,* and *regulation*—interconnected factors that together fashion the world we experience. Herman Gray's (Chapter 9) analysis of the politics of black representation on television underscores the importance of this insight. Gray shows that "assimilationist," "pluralist," and "multiculturalist" discursive positions have shaped the representations of blackness circulating on television over the years; he also reveals the ways in which these discursive positions have connected with important, underlying social, political, and economic factors—factors that continue to shape racial politics in America.

In short, the ideological impact of shows like *Amos 'n' Andy* and *The Cosby Show* cannot be understood without also considering the social context in which the texts are embedded, as well as audience needs, interests, and proclivities. "Positive" or "negative" means very little in isolation. Meaning is indeed relational, and representational consequences are often a double-edged sword. Coming to terms with the *text/context/audience* triad, as the studies throughout this volume collectively demonstrate, is essential to making sense of the ideological work performed by blackness on television. The consideration of markets and motives is a fundamental component of this exercise.

MARKETS AND MOTIVES

If we are to believe the people who control television in America, then we should accept the claim that the invisible hand of the marketplace governs media industry outcomes. Race has nothing to do with it. After all, the powers behind television are first and foremost in business to attract viewers whose attention is then sold to advertisers; their primary *motive* is to maximize profits. This logic suggests that concerns about the social impact of racial representations are misplaced—the market will make it all work out in the end. It is viewers, industry insiders insist, who ultimately determine the content of what remains on the schedule. If viewers find certain representations problematic, then they are free to vote with their remotes by changing the channel. The resulting drop in ratings for the unpopular programming would eventually result in its cancellation. Moreover, as some have claimed, technological change has presented an unprecedented diversity of choices for viewers, an explosion of new cable channels and time-shifting options (e.g., videotape, DVDs, TiVo) that has revolutionized the television viewing experience.[50] Viewer sovereignty is guaranteed!

But this rather common "viewer democracy" trope suffers from a core faulty assumption: the "invisible hand" metaphor hardly fits with modern media markets. Adam Smith's eighteenth-century formulation envisions markets composed of a multitude of small buyers and sellers who are free to shop around and haggle over products and prices. With this scenario in mind, Smith proposed that market competition between agents acting in their own self-interest is more effective at promoting the overall public good than altruistic attempts to engineer specific market-level outcomes.[51] The contemporary media industry, of course, looks nothing like the market of Smith's day. It is controlled by a handful of multinational media conglomerates whose market power overrides virtually all other forces in shaping the programming choices that confront viewers.[52] Indeed, the five entities that owned the U.S. broadcast networks in 2001 (Disney/ABC; Viacom/CBS/UPN; General Electric/NBC; NewsCorp/Fox; and AOL Time Warner/WB) controlled vertically integrated, global operations combining for more than $240 billion in revenues. Much of the so-called diversity of options available across the cable expanse consists of a deceptively small menu of recycled programming originating with the same handful of media conglomerates. In this sense, it hardly seems as if the public good is being served.

Prime Time in Black and White

To be sure, so-called viewer choice has very little to do with what we see on prime-time television. As a study by sociologists William and Denise Bielby demonstrates,[53] the increasing concentration of media ownership leads to a reduction in the diversity of network programming options available to viewers. Recent government deregulation of the industry has allowed the owners of networks to enter the programming production business. The networks, in turn, have increasingly favored programs produced by their conglomerate-related suppliers. In 2002, for example, subsidiaries of the "Big 5" media conglomerates accounted for nearly 81 percent of the programs on the schedule. And most of these programs aired on networks and were produced by production companies owned by the same conglomerate. That is to say, 68.4 percent of ABC's programs were developed by Disney; 50 percent of CBS's programs were developed by five production companies owned by Viacom; 52.4 percent of Fox's programs were developed by two production companies owned by Fox/NewsCorp; 38.5 percent of NBC's programs were developed by NBC Studios; 77.8 percent of UPN's programs were developed by four production companies owned by Viacom; and 50 percent of WB's programs were developed by five production companies owned by AOL Time Warner.[54]

It should also be noted that network programmers are motivated by a desire to protect their jobs in a highly ambiguous market environment. Thus they tend to invoke *imitation* (which favors already dominant programming practices), *genre* (which favors the traditional sitcom and drama formats), and the *reputation* of producers (which favors those who already have power in the industry) as rhetorical strategies to rationalize and justify their programming decisions.[55] Together, these tendencies have effectively crowded out smaller and/or newer suppliers of programming and virtually ensured that the domain of programming choices available to viewers is severely truncated. Indeed, while viewer "choice" results in more than 70 percent of all new shows being canceled within the first season, viewers are regularly confronted with more of the same, cloaked in different garb, in subsequent seasons.

Moreover, and perhaps most directly related to the matter at hand, far from being race neutral, media markets are actually the direct product of *raced* processes. That is to say, network television continues to be defined by a highly insular industry in which white decision makers typically reproduce themselves by hiring other whites who share similar experiences and tastes. White males, in particular, have traditionally occupied nearly all of the industry "green-lighting" positions—the positions from which it is decided which projects will be made, with what size budget, and by whom. Similarly, on the production side, white executive producers or "showrunners" have a stranglehold on the development and day-to-day creation of television programs. Once these insiders have a hit program under their belt, they can generally rely upon a revolving door of opportunities to develop other programs.

Nonwhites who aspire to these lucrative positions, however, face a vicious employment cycle. Because nonwhites perennially account for such an infinitesimally small portion of those assigned to run a show, opportunities for nonwhites to develop hit series have been few and far between. And because the credential of having a hit series to one's credit has been the surest way to show running assignments, few nonwhites are seriously considered for opportunities when they arise. In other words, the revolving door of opportunity has never really turned for nonwhites, and business as usual in the industry has resulted in a process that smacks of institutional discrimination.[56]

Similar exclusionary processes have also been the norm over the years for nonwhite television directors and writers. Although white males made up only about 34 percent of the U.S. population in 2000, they accounted for about 80 percent of the television directors from the Top 40 shows in the 2000–2001 season. Women (composed primarily of white women) accounted for 11 percent of television directors, while nonwhites—31 percent of the U.S. population—combined for just 6 percent (3 percent black, 2 percent Latino, and 1 percent Asian). In 2001, nonwhites were similarly underrepresented among prime-time television writers, combining for only 9 percent of the total (6.2 percent black, 1.4 percent Latino, 1.3 percent Asian, 0.1 percent Native American).

These observations about white control of television fiction are significant because racial control has a direct bearing on racial content. Just as showrunners are more likely than not to develop show concepts that resonate with their own experiences or fantasies, television writers tend to fashion stories and characters with which they are familiar. To the degree that African Americans have been crowded out of this creative process, black *self-*representation has been conspicuously absent on the small screen (see Chapter 15). In its place, we have traditionally found representations of blackness created by whites—industry insiders who unconsciously (and sometimes consciously) invoke the black-white binary and the chains of equivalence associated with it in their work.

Alongside this traditional industry pattern, it is worth noting, exists a relatively new phenomenon that we might describe as "televisual ghettoization." Recent years have witnessed the production of several new black-themed situation comedies, concentrated on the newer, smaller networks—Fox, WB, and most notably, UPN (see Chapter 15). Nearly all of the black showrunners working in television during the first few years of the twenty-first century worked on these shows, which featured black self-representations rarely seen on the larger networks. Kristal Brent Zook's (Chapter 10) analysis of why one 1990s black-produced show succeeded on the Fox network while two others failed sheds much light on this new phenomenon. It reveals how racial considerations factor into network marketing decisions; it also documents how white decision makers' imposition of industry conventional wisdom works to contain the counter-hegemonic potential of black self-representation. "The biggest fights with networks were not about money or ratings," one of Brent Zook's black informants notes. "They were about different ways of seeing the world."

Black Threat, White Surveillance

Not surprisingly, we find comparable raced processes at work in television news. While news operations couch their claims to legitimacy in Fourth Estate concerns about balancing government power, in concerns about providing the public with an independent source of information, other less altruistic considerations determine how news is actually constructed. First, the line between news and entertainment, particularly on television, has blurred over the years. Understood largely as a public service in the early days of television, news programming has become an audience attraction in its own right. The emphasis on short sound bites, action, and visuals—as opposed to more in-depth analysis of events and their causes—is an important component of practices designed to maximize audience ratings and advertising revenue.

Moreover, far from serving as a real check on government power, mainstream media and the state are locked in a symbiotic relationship that significantly constrains adversarial possibilities. State officials depend on media to reach the public, and media depend on state officials for access to official government information. This fundamental relationship, enacted at press conferences and marked by newsworkers' heavy reliance on the accounts of official sources, shapes the tenor of news by crowding out alternative accounts of developments.[57]

Because race was so central to the founding of our republic, and because it continues to play a central role in the functioning of every state institution, racial implications are always embedded (if not explicitly referenced) in the accounts of official sources. Numerous studies have shown that the net effect of these privileged accounts is that mainstream news primarily supports a "white reality." [58] Just as the images in television fiction have been crafted to comfort the dominant white audience, television news has routinely served the security needs of this "white reality" by keeping the threat of nonwhite Others under constant surveillance. The Report of the National Advisory Commission on Civil Disorders (Chapter 2) presents a case in point. A somewhat problematic, official account of the urban riots that rocked America in the mid-1960s, it nonetheless provides us with a revealing glimpse at how a shared media and state investment in (white) order shaped (and continues to shape) the news construction process. To be sure, this symbiosis has at times prompted news media to cooperate with officials by censoring stories that might embarrass civil authorities or by discrediting spokespersons that represent causes at odds with state interests.

Another, more notorious, example of this government-media symbiosis is documented in *The Cointelpro Papers: Documents from the FBI's Secret Wars Against Dissent in the United States.* Ward Churchill's and Jim Vander Wall's text provides evidence of television news collusion with the FBI and its counterintelligence operations that targeted the black liberation movement during the 1960s and 1970s. One document—a 1968 Miami field office report to FBI headquarters about tactics employed at an area television station— describes how "a carefully planned television show can be extremely effective in showing these extremists for what they are." In addition to selecting black nationalist interviewees "for either their inability to articulate or their simpering and stupid appearance," the document notes, newsworkers "had the leaders seated, ill at ease, in hard chairs. Full-length camera shots showed each movement as they squirmed about in their chairs, resembling rats trapped under scientific observation."[59]

In a hegemonic order, however, forces sometimes align to produce outcomes that run counter to expectation. Indeed, Sasha Torres (Chapter 14) shows that in the earliest days of television, network news operations were engaged in a symbiotic relationship with what might appear to be the most unlikely suspects: black civil rights leaders. While black leaders recognized the power of the emerging medium and effectively exploited it as a platform to draw attention to the moral contradictions inherent in a segregated "democracy," television newsworkers were invested in winning a prime seat for the new medium at the table of national politics. The raw visuality and immediacy of television news coverage of the civil rights movement would serve both interests well.

Of course, it goes without saying that the people who control television news—as we saw with television fiction—are overwhelmingly white. Decisions about which stories are newsworthy and how the chosen stories are to be framed are routinely made with little or no input from nonwhites. In 2001, for example, it was projected that minorities (31 percent of the U.S. population) accounted for only 18 percent of the television news workforce and an abysmally low 8 percent of news directors.[60] Returning to the example of the 1960s riots, the absence of black journalists during the period slanted coverage in ways that likely alienated blacks and kept whites in the dark about the true state of American race relations (see Chapter 2). Combined with the reliance upon mostly white official sources, the relative paucity of nonwhites in the newsworker corps results in a whitewashed depiction of reality—a reality populated by nonwhite Others who are often rendered in ways that reflect the black-white binary and its related chains of equivalence.

Indeed, recent studies document the attractiveness of the crime story as a local television news staple; they also identify the racial imagery of black and brown suspects as an important part of the "scripts" used to construct crime stories.[61] The intersection of these popular news practices with the small but visible presence of black reporters and anchors in local television news, Christopher Campbell argues (Chapter 8), produces a troubling paradox: while the *absence* of black newsworkers virtually guarantees problematic black representation in news, their *presence* may actually support an important myth undergirding "enlightened racism." That is to say, the juxtaposition of televised news images of poor and/or menacing blacks with those of accomplished black reporters and anchors may work—as did similar juxtapositions in *The Cosby Show* case—to reassure white viewers that society is now color-blind. If the black reporters and anchors can succeed in America, the logic suggests, then poor and criminal blacks have only themselves to blame.

Blackness and Consumption

Transcending all of these industry patterns, in the end, is a fundamental axiom: popular television is a medium that exists to sell. Broadcasters rely on programming to attract the attention of viewers. These viewers are in turn sold to advertisers who strive to imbue their products with qualities that would—if the products were purchased—make the consumers feel better about themselves. These qualities are often conveyed rather concretely, as in the proverbial fast-food commercial that attempts to address the immediate need of satisfying hunger. At other times they are conveyed more abstractly, through metaphor and connotation, as in a luxury car commercial that appeals to latent desires for increased status. Race has always factored into this marketing process in a fundamental way, shaping the content of not only fictional and news programming but also the commercials that support it. Indeed, research reveals that whiteness dominates in commercials just as it does in popular television programming. White characters not only are *overrepresented* in commercials but also are more likely than other-raced characters to be *featured* in commercials[62]— particularly when the advertising appeals are predicated on consumer needs for status.

A *New York Times* article from the 1980s is rather revealing vis-à-vis the history of black representation in commercials. Quoting a William Morris Agency executive who described the company's advertising practices as "colorblind," the Article reports that "nobody ever calls and says they want black actors unless they're going after the black market." [63] Today, when television commercials include black actors, they are likely to be cast as background figures. When black actors are *featured,* however, it is often as objects of sexual desire. Moreover, contact between blacks and other characters (e.g., speaking, hugging, caressing, kissing) is "nearly taboo" in prime-time commercials, which rather effectively works to disconnect images of black sexuality from romance ideals.[64] The immensely popular Budweiser commercial discussed in Chapter 13 is a notable exception to this rule. Nonetheless, as is true with most commercials featuring black actors, the origin of what is being bought and sold can be traced squarely back to the black-white binary, which always activates politically potent chains of equivalence.

The America of the early twenty-first century, of course, is not the America of the 1950s. The racial order of the earlier period, which routinely permitted the circulation of explicitly racist representations of blackness, has been replaced by a more "enlightened" racism that exerts its influence through code and connotation. As Herman Gray's (Chapter 9) analysis shows us, popular television has continually adjusted to shifts in the racial order over the years. But these adjustments, I would submit, are more akin to remodeling one's old house than to moving into another home. The same underlying structure remains.

Because media markets in the United States are so profoundly raced, it is not necessary to invoke overtly racist motives in order to explain the ideological work performed by today's representations of blackness. To be sure, the politics of industry insiders often appear to be more progressive than those of the general population. But the racial order is remarkably redundant. Just by adhering to industry conventions and by acting on their own understandings of market demand, industry insiders all but guarantee the centrality of the black-white binary in televised representations. Just by doing their jobs, they help reproduce the racial status quo.

CHANNELING RACE

Economically, culturally, and politically, popular television remains firmly in white control. Black Americans account for nearly 13 percent of the nation's population and spend more time watching television than any other group,[65] but own only about 1 percent of the nation's seven hundred television stations—twenty stations concentrated in smaller media markets.[66] There has never been black majority ownership of a major television network in the United States. Bill Cosby's attempts to purchase NBC in 1993 were quickly and rather quietly dismissed.[67] The network, whose acronym was sometimes derisively translated as the "Nigger Broadcasting Company" during the civil rights era and "Nothing But Cosby" during the heyday of *The Cosby Show,* remains in white hands.

Indeed, the closest the nation has come to a significant black-owned television outlet is cable's Black Entertainment Television (BET). But BET has relied primarily upon the rotation of music videos and other low-cost, recycled programming in order to offset relatively low subscriber and advertising rates in its bid for profits—hardly a comparable alternative to mainstream networks that feature original programming and global news operations. Moreover, following the industry trend toward increasing consolidation of ownership, BET was sold to Viacom for $3 billion in 2000.[68] At the time, the multi-billion-dollar media conglomerate also owned CBS, UPN, Showtime, and countless other media companies that routinely circulated representations of blackness under white control.

Perhaps it is easy to downplay the significance of these observations because America's racial order is a *hegemonic* order. While white control and the threat of coercive force always reside in the background, the dream of opportunity and the quiet of consent keep the nation suspended in unstable equilibrium. Much of American history, however, has revolved around struggles over defining the terms on which consent would be predicated, over who might realistically expect to live the dream. When the nation was a "racial dictatorship,"[69] blacks were officially designated as less than citizens. Rationalizing myths of black racial inferiority supported unabashed white dominance and exploitation of raced Others, while also helping whites to, as Stuart Hall has so cogently put it,[70] "sleep comfortably in their beds at night." But nonwhite demands for inclusion, coupled with changing political and material conditions at home and abroad, led to a legitimation crisis. A new unstable equilibrium and hegemonic order emerged that officially recognized the rights of blacks and nonwhite Others. New spaces opened, if only momentarily, for the circulation of black self-representation and for black resistance. The black-white binary and associated chains of equivalence, nonetheless, remained intact in the background, quietly animating a newer, "enlightened" racism.

Only time will tell how America's racial concerns and related projects play out in forging future unstable equilibriums. But one thing seems quite certain: popular television will continue to play a pivotal role in the process. As a medium barely sixty years old, television matured with the civil rights movement. It served then, and continues to serve now, as a key cultural forum in which we imagine the nation and negotiate our places in it. Its propensity to circulate racial understandings, to channel race in the service of racial projects—particularly hegemonic ones—has often been masked, but it is always profound. Each of the studies that follow has something to say about these representational dynamics. Considered in tandem, they provide us with essential insights for making sense of blackness on television.

NOTES

1. For example, see Todd Gitlin, *Media Unlimited: How the Torrent of Images and Sounds Overwhelms Our Lives* (New York: Owl Books, 2002).
2. "Prime-Time TV Rankings," *Los Angeles Times,* October 22, 2003, E12.
3. Darnell M. Hunt, "Prime Time in Black and White: Making Sense of the 2001 Fall Season," *CAAS Research Report* 1, no. 1 (2002), UCLA Center for African American Studies.
4. For a detailed discussion of the role of television as a cultural forum, see Horace Newcomb and Paul M. Hirsch, "Television as a Cultural Forum," in *Television: The Critical View,* 5th ed., ed. H. Newcomb (New York: Oxford University Press, 1994).
5. Toni Morrison, *Playing in the Dark: Whiteness and the Literary Imagination* (New York: Vintage, 1990), 17.
6. Stuart Hall, "Race, the Floating Signifier," videotaped lecture, Northhampton, MA: Media Education Foundation, 1996.
7. See Robert M. Farr and Serge Moscovici, *Social Representations* (Cambridge: Cambridge University Press, 1984).
8. Charles Mills, *Blackness Visible: Essays on Philosophy and Race* (Ithaca, NY: Cornell University Press, 1998), 48.
9. See Darnell M. Hunt, *Screening the Los Angeles "Riots": Race, Seeing, and Resistance* (Cambridge: Cambridge University Press, 1997), 181, Figure 2.
10. Mary Douglas, *Purity and Danger: An Analysis of the Concepts of Pollution and Taboo* (London: Routledge, 1966), 4.
11. George Lipsitz, *The Possessive Investment in Whiteness: How White People Benefit from Identity Politics* (Philadelphia: Temple University Press, 1998).
12. Michael Omi and Howard Winant, *Racial Formation in the United States: From the 1960s to the 1990s* (New York: Routledge, 1994).
13. Ibid.
14. Ibid.
15. U.S. Bureau of the Census, *The Black Population in the United States: March 2002,* Washington, DC, 2002.
16. For example, see Melvin L. Oliver and Thomas M. Shapiro, *Black Wealth, White Wealth: A New Perspective on Racial Inequality* (New York: Routledge, 1997).
17. U.S. Bureau of Justice Statistics, "Prisoners in 2002, NC 200248," Table 13, Washington, DC, 2002.
18. For example, see Omi and Winant, *Racial Formation.*
19. Frantz Fanon, *Black Skin, White Masks* (New York: Grove Weidenfeld, 1967), 177.
20. Winthrop Jordan, *The White Man's Burden: Historical Origins of Racism in the United States* (London: Oxford University Press, 1974).

21. bell hooks, *Black Looks: Race and Representation* (Boston: South End Press, 1992).

22. For a discussion of the potent role media representations of black male athletes play in American culture, see Laurel R. Davis and Othello Harris, "Race and Ethnicity in US Sports Media," in *Media Sport,* ed. L. Wenner (London: Routledge, 1998).

23. For a more detailed discussion of the "buck" stereotype, see Donald Bogle, *Toms, Coons, Mulattoes, Mammies & Bucks: An Interpretive History of Blacks in American Films* (New York: Continuum, 2001).

24. See Todd Boyd, *Am I Black Enough for You? Popular Culture from the 'Hood and Beyond* (Bloomington: University of Indiana Press, 1997). Boyd's conception of the "Nigga" echoes important elements of the black "phallocentric" masculinity and "buck" stereotype so prominent in hip-hop culture and certain sports spectacles today. For Boyd, the "Nigga" is an "in your face" persona of "excessive" blackness that reflects a "world of chaos and nihilism"; it is a black masculinity that is certainly not trying to live up to or surpass white standards (17). He argues that commodification of this representation grows out of the 1992 Los Angeles uprisings and the rise of gangsta rap—a musical genre that regularly valorizes the types of violence white media associate with black males. (See Chapter 15 for a more detailed discussion of the relationship between changing social contexts and representations of blackness.)

25. hooks, *Black Looks,* 96.

26. Boyd, *Am I Black Enough For You?*

27. Greg Tate, *Everything But the Burden: What White People Are Taking from Black Culture* (New York: Harlem Moon, 2003), 4.

28. See Theodor Adorno, "The Schema of Mass Culture," in *The Culture Industry: Selected Essays on Mass Culture,* ed. J. M. Bernstein (London: Routledge, 1991).

29. Karl Marx, "The German Ideology," in *The Marx and Engels Reader,* ed. R. Tucker (New York: W. W. Norton, 1972).

30. Shearon Lowery and Melvin L. DeFleur, *Milestones in Mass Communication Research* (New York: Longman, 1983).

31. Karen Sternheimer, *It's Not the Media: The Truth About Pop Culture's Influence on Children* (Boulder, CO: Westview Press, 2003).

32. Todd Gitlin, "Media Sociology: The Dominant Paradigm," *Theory and Society* 6, no. 2 (1978): 205–53.

33. See Lowery and DeFleur, *Milestones.*

34. For example, see Joseph Klapper, *The Effects of Mass Communication* (New York: Free Press, 1960).

35. See Gitlin, "Media Sociology."

36. See Omi and Winant, *Racial Formation.*

37. Maxwell McCombs and Donald L. Shaw, "The Agenda-Setting Function of Mass Media," *Public Opinion Quarterly* 36 (1972): 176–87.

38. See John Fiske, *Television Culture* (London: Routledge, 1987).

39. George Gerbner, Larry Gross, Michael Morgan, and Nancy Signorielli, "Living with Television: The Dynamics of the Cultivation Process," in *Perspectives on Media Effects,* ed. J. Bryant and D. Zillman (Hillsdale, NJ: Lawrence Erlbaum, 1986).

40. See J. Fred MacDonald, *Blacks and White TV: African Americans in Television Since 1948* (Chicago: Nelson-Hall, 1992). See also Pamela S. Deane, "Amos 'n' Andy Show," in *Encyclopedia of Television,* ed. H. Newcomb (Chicago: Fitzroy Dearborn, 1997).

41. Reprinted in MacDonald, *Blacks and White TV,* 29–30.

42. Other factors included an increasing advertiser aversion to controversy of any sort and concerns about southern media markets. The combination of these factors made it easier for CBS to simply cut its losses (see Deane, "Amos 'n' Andy Show").

43. See Omi and Winant, *Racial Formation.*

44. Donald Bogle, *Prime Time Blues: African Americans on Network Television* New York: Farrar, Straus and Giroux, 2001).

45. See Chapter 10.

46. Cited in Bogle, *Prime Time Blues,* 303.

47. Philip Brian Harper, "Extra-Special Effects: Televisual Representation and the Claims of the 'Black Experience,'" in *Living Color: Race and Television in the United States,* ed. S. Torres (Durham, NC: Duke University Press, 1998).

48. Ibid.

49. Stuart Hall, Introduction to *Representation: Cultural Representations and Signifying Practices,* ed. S. Hall (London: Sage, 1997).

50. FCC chairman Michael Powell, for example, has advocated this position (see www. usatoday.com/money/media/2003-04-20-media-ownership-rules_x.htm).

51. Adam Smith, *The Wealth of Nations* (1776; repr., Chicago: University of Chicago Press, 1976).

52. For a detailed discussion of this trend, see Ben H. Bagdikian, *The Media Monopoly* (Boston: Beacon Press, 1992).

53. William T. Bielby and Denise D. Bielby, "Controlling Primetime: Organizational Concentration and Network Television Programming Strategies," *Journal of Broadcasting and Electronic Media,* forthcoming.

54. Data from Writers Guild of America, West.

55. William T. Bielby and Denise D. Bielby, "'All Hits are Flukes': Institutional Decision Making and the Rhetoric of Network Prime-Time Program Development," *American Journal of Sociology* 99, no. 5 (1994): 1287–1313.

56. By "institutional discrimination," I mean the use of unjustified requirements or prerequisites in routine practice that result in the disproportionate exclusion of minority groups from participation in institutions.

57. For example, see David L. Altheide and Robert P. Snow, *Media Logic* (Beverly Hills: Sage, 1979).

58. See Herbert Gans, *Deciding What's News* (New York: Pantheon, 1979).

59. Ward Churchill and Jim Vander Wall, *The Cointelpro Papers: Documents from the FBI's Secret Wars Against Dissent in the United States* (Boston: South End Press, 1990), 119.

60. Statistics provided by Vernon Stone, Missouri School of Journalism.

61. Franklin D. Gilliam and Shanto Iyengar, "Prime Suspects: The Influence of Local Television News on the Viewing Public," *American Journal of Political Science* 44, no. 3 (July 2000): 560–73.

62. R. Wilkes and H. Valencia, "Hispanics and Blacks in Television Commercials," *Journal of Advertising* 18 (1989).

63. Cited in Jannette Dates and William Barlow, *Split Image: African Americans in the Mass Media* (Washington, DC: Howard University Press, 1990), 436.

64. See Robert M. Entman and Andrew Rojecki, *The Black Image in the White Mind: Media and Race in America* (Chicago: University of Chicago Press, 2000).

65. *Variety,* June 22, 2003.

66. Data from National Association of Black Owned Broadcasters (NABOB).

67. "Bid for NBC Confirmed by Wussler," Variety.com, July 14, 1993, www. variety.com/index.asp?layout=upsell_article&articleID=VR008667&cs=1.

68. "Viacom Completes BET Deal," *Washington Business Journal,* January 23, 2001, www. bizjournals.com/washington/stories/2001/01/22/daily11.html.

69. Omi and Winant, *Racial Formation.*

70. Hall, "Race, the Floating Signifier."

2

THE NEWS MEDIA
AND THE DISORDERS

Report of the National Advisory Commission on Civil Disorders

INTRODUCTION

The President's charge to the Commission asked specifically; "What effect do the mass media have on the riots?"

The question is far reaching and a sure answer is beyond the range of presently available scientific techniques. Our conclusions and recommendations are based upon subjective as well as objective factors; interviews as well as statistics; isolated examples as well as general trends.

Freedom of the press is not the issue. A free press is indispensable to the preservation of the other freedoms this nation cherishes. The recommendations in this chapter have thus been developed under the strong conviction that only a press unhindered by government can contribute to freedom.

To answer the President's question, the Commission:

- Directed its field survey teams to question government officials, law enforcement agents, media personnel, and ordinary citizens about their attitudes and reactions to reporting of the riots;
- Arranged for interviews of media representatives about their coverage of the riots;
- Conducted special interviews with ghetto residents about their response to coverage;
- Arranged for a quantitative analysis of the content of television programs and newspaper reporting in 15 riot cities during the period of the disorder and the days immediately before and after;
- From November 10–12, 1967, sponsored and participated in a conference of representatives from all levels of the newspaper, news magazine, and broadcasting industries at Poughkeepsie, New York.

Finally, of course, the Commissioners read newspapers, listened to the radio, watched television, and thus formed their own impressions of media coverage. All of these data, impressions, and attitudes provide the foundation for our conclusions.

The Commission also determined, very early, that the answer to the President's question did not lie solely in the performance of the press and broadcasters in reporting the riots

Reprinted from the *Report of the National Advisory Commission on Civil Disorders* (New York: E. P. Dutton, 1968).

proper. Our analysis had to consider also the overall treatment by the media of the Negro ghettos, community relations, racial attitudes, urban and rural poverty—day by day and month by month, year in and year out.

On this basis, we have reached three conclusions:

First, that despite incidents of sensationalism, inaccuracies, and distortions, newspapers, radio and television, on the whole, made a real effort to give a balanced, factual account of the 1967 disorders.

Second, despite this effort, the portrayal of the violence that occurred last summer failed to reflect accurately its scale and character. The overall effect was, we believe, an exaggeration of both mood and event.

Third, and ultimately most important, we believe that the media have thus far failed to report adequately on the causes and consquences of civil disorders and the underlying problems of race relations.

With these comments as a perspective, we discuss first the coverage of last summer's disturbances. We will then summarize our concerns with overall coverage of race relations.

Coverage of the 1967 Disturbances

We have found a significant imbalance between what actually happened in our cities and what the newspaper, radio, and television coverage of the riots told us happened. The Commission, in studying last summer's disturbances, visited many of the cities and interviewed participants and observers. We found that the disorders, as serious as they were, were less destructive, less widespread, and less a black-white confrontation than most people believed.

Lacking other sources of information, we formed our original impressions and beliefs from what we saw on television, heard on the radio, and read in newspapers and magazines. We are deeply concerned that millions of other Americans, who must rely on the mass media, likewise formed incorrect impressions and judgments about what went on in many American cities last summer.

As we started to probe the reasons for this imbalance between reality and impression, we first believed that the media had sensationalized the disturbances, consistently overplaying violence and giving disproportionate amounts of time to emotional events and "militant" leaders. To test this theory, we commissioned a systematic, quantitative analysis, covering the content of newspaper and television reporting in 15 cities where disorders occurred. The results of this analysis do not support our early belief. Of 955 television sequences of riot and racial news examined, 837 could be classified for predominant atmosphere as either "emotional," "calm," or "normal." Of these, 494 were classified as calm, 262 as emotional, and 81 as normal . Only a small proportion of all scenes analyzed showed actual mob action, people looting, sniping, setting fires, or being injured, or killed. Moderate Negro leaders were shown more frequently than militant leaders on television news broadcasts.

Of 3,779 newspaper articles analyzed, more focused on legislation which should be sought and planning which should be done to control ongoing riots and prevent future riots than on any other topic. The findings of this content analysis are explained in greater detail in Section I. They make it clear that the imbalance between actual events and the portrayal of those events in the press and on the air cannot be attributed solely to sensationalism in reporting and presentation.

We have, however, identified several factors which, it seems to us, did work to create incorrect and exaggerated impressions about the scope and intensity of the disorders.

First, despite the overall statistical picture, there were instances of gross flaws in presenting news of the 1967 riots. Some newspapers printed "scare" headlines unsupported by the mild stories that followed. All media reported rumors that had no basis in fact. Some newsmen staged "riot" events for the cameras. Examples are included in the next section.

Second, the press-obtained much factual information about the scale of the disorders—property damage, personal injury, and deaths—from local officials, who often were inexperienced in dealing with civil disorders and not always able to sort out fact from rumor in the confusion. At the height of the Detroit riot, some news reports of property damage put the figure in excess of $500 million.[1] Subsequent investigation shows it to be $40 to $45 million.[2]

The initial estimates were not the independent judgment of reporters or editors. They came from beleaguered government officials. But the news media gave currency to these errors. Reporters uncritically accepted, and editors uncritically published, the inflated figures, leaving an indelible impression of damage up to more than ten times greater than actually occurred.

Third, the coverage of the disorders—particularly on television—tended to define the events as black-white confrontations. In fact almost all of the deaths, injuries and property damage occurred in all-Negro neighborhoods, and thus the disorders were not "race riots" as that term is generally understood.

Closely linked to these problems is the phenomenon of cumulative effect. As the summer of 1967 progressed, we think Americans often began to associate more or less neutral sights and sounds (like a squad car with flashing red lights, a burning building, a suspect in police custody) with racial disorders, so that the appearance of any particular item, itself hardly inflammatory, set off a whole sequence of association with riot events. Moreover, the summer's news was not seen and heard in isolation. Events of these past few years— the Watts riot, other disorders, and the growing momentum of the civil rights movement— conditioned the responses of readers and viewers and heightened their reactions. What the public saw and read last summer thus produced emotional reactions and left vivid impressions not wholly attributable to the material itself.

Fear and apprehension of racial unrest and violence are deeply rooted in American society. They color and intensify reactions to news of racial trouble and threats of racial conflict. Those who report and disseminate news must be conscious of the background of anxieties and apprehension against which their stories are projected. This does not mean that the media should manage the news or tell less than the truth. Indeed, we believe that it would be imprudent and even dangerous to down-play coverage in the hope that censored reporting of inflammatory incidents somehow will diminish violence. Once a disturbance occurs, the word will spread independently of newspapers and television. To attempt to ignore these events or portray them as something other than what they are, can only diminish confidence in the media and increase the effectiveness of those who monger rumors and the fears of those who listen.

But to be complete, the coverage must be representative. We suggest that the main failure of the media last summer was that the totality of its coverage was not as representative as it should have been to be accurate. We believe that to live up to their own professed standards, the media simply must exercise a higher degree of care and a greater level of sophistication than they have yet shown in this area—higher, perhaps, than the level ordinarily acceptable with other stories.

This is not "just another story." It should not be treated like one. Admittedly, some of what disturbs us about riot coverage last summer stems from circumstances beyond media control. But many of the inaccuracies of fact, tone and mood were due to the failure of reporters and editors to ask tough enough questions about official reports, and to apply the most rigorous standards possible in evaluating and presenting the news. Reporters and editors must be sure that descriptions and pictures of violence, and emotional or inflammatory sequences or articles, even though "true" in isolation, are really representative and do not convey an impression at odds with the overall reality of events. The media too often did not achieve this level of sophisticated, skeptical, careful news judgment during last summer's riots.

The Media and Race Relations

Our second and fundamental criticism is that the news media have failed to analyze and report adequately on racial problems in the United States and, as a related matter, to meet the Negro's legitimate expectations in journalism. By and large, news organizations have failed to communicate to both their black and white audiences a sense of the problems America faces and the sources of potential solutions. The media report and write from the standpoint of a white man's world. The ills of the ghetto, the difficulties of life there, the Negro's burning sense of grievance, are seldom conveyed. Slights and indignities are part of the Negro's daily life, and many of them come from what he now calls "the white press"—a press that repeatedly, if unconsciously, reflects the biases, the paternalism, the indifference of white America. This may be understandable, but it is not excusable in an institution that has the mission to inform and educate the whole of our society.

■ ■ ■

Our criticisms, important as they are, do not lead us to conclude that the media are a cause of riots, any more than they are the cause of other phenomena which they report. It is true that newspaper and television reporting helped shape people's attitudes toward riots. In some cities people who watched television reports and read newspaper accounts of riots in other cities later rioted themselves. But the causal chain weakens when we recall that in other cities, people in very much the same circumstances watched the same programs and read the same newspaper stories but did not riot themselves.

The news media are not the sole source of information and certainly not the only influence on public attitudes. People obtained their information and formed their opinions about the 1967 disorders from the multiplicity of sources that condition the public's thinking on all events. Personal experience, conversations with others, the local and long-distance telephone are all important as sources of information and ideas and contribute to the totality of attitudes about riots.

No doubt, in some cases, the knowledge or the sight on a television screen of what had gone on elsewhere lowered inhibitions or kindled outrage or awakened desires for excitement or loot—or simply passed the word. Many ghetto residents we interviewed thought so themselves. By the same token, the news reports of riots must have conditioned the response of officials and police to disturbances in their own cities. The reaction of the authorities in Detroit was almost certainly affected in some part by what they saw or read of Newark a week earlier. The Commission believes that none of these private or official reactions was decisive in determining the course of the disorders. Even if they had been more significant than we think, however, we cannot envision a system of governmental restraints that could successfully eliminate these effects. And an effort to formulate and impose such restraints would be inconsistent with fundamental traditions in our society.

The failings of the media must be corrected and the improvement must come from within the media. A society that values and relies on a free press as intensely as ours, is entitled to demand in return responsibility from the press and conscientious attention by the press to its own deficiencies. The Commission has seen evidence that many of those who supervise, edit, and report for the news media are becoming increasingly aware of and concerned about their performance in this field. With that concern, and with more experience, will come more sophisticated and responsible coverage. But much more must be done, and it must be done soon.

The Commission has a number of recommendations designed to stimulate and accelerate efforts toward self-improvement. And we propose a privately organized, privately funded Institute of Urban Communications as a means for drawing these recommendations together and promoting their implementation.

I. NEWS COVERAGE OF CIVIL DISORDERS—SUMMER 1967

The Method of Analysis

As noted, the Commission has been surveying both the reporting of disorders last summer and the broader field of race relations coverage. With respect to the reporting of disorders, we were trying to get a sense of content, accuracy, tone, and bias. We sought to find out how people reacted to it and how reporters conducted themselves while carrying out their assignments. The Commission used a number of techniques to probe these matters and to provide cross checks on data and impressions.

To obtain an objective source of data, the Commission arranged for a systematic, quantitative analysis of the content of newspapers, local television, and network coverage in 15 cities for a period from three days before to three days after the disorder in each city.[3]

The cities were chosen to provide a cross-section in terms of the location and scale of the disorders and the dates of their occurrence.

Within each city, for the period specified, the study was comprehensive. Every daily newspaper and all network and local television news films were analyzed, and scripts and logs were examined. In all, 955 network and local television sequences and 3,779 newspaper articles dealing with riot and race relations news were analyzed. Each separate analysis was coded and the cards were cross-tabulated by computer to provide results and comparisons for use by the Commission. The material was measured to determine the amount of space devoted to news of riot activity; the nature of the display given compared with other news coverage; and the types of stories, articles, and television programming presented. We sought specific statistical information on such matters as the amount of space or time devoted to different kinds of riot stories, the types and identities of persons most often depicted or interviewed, the frequency with which race relations problems were mentioned in riot stories or identified as the cause of riot activity.

The survey was designed to be objective and statistical. Within its terms of reference, the Commission was looking for broad characterizations of media tone and content.

The Commission is aware of the inherent limitations of content analysis techniques. They cannot measure the emotional impact of a particular story or television sequence. By themselves, they provide no basis for conclusions as to the accuracy of what was reported. Particular examples of good or bad journalistic conduct, which may be important in themselves, are submerged in a statistical average. The Commission therefore sought through staff interviews and personal contact with members of the press and the public to obtain direct evidence of the effects of riot coverage and the performance of the media during last summer's disturbances.

Conclusions About Content[4]

Television

1. Content analysis of television film footage shows that the tone of the coverage studied was more calm and "factual" than "emotional" and rumor-laden. Researchers viewed every one of the 955 television sequences and found that twice as many "calm" sequences as "emotional" ones were shown. The amount and location of coverage were relatively limited, considering the magnitude of the events. The analysis reveals a dominant, positive emphasis on control of the riot and on activities in the aftermath of the riot (53.8 percent of all scenes broadcast) rather than on scenes of actual mob action, or people looting, sniping, setting fires, or being injured or killed (4.8 percent of scenes shown). However, according to participants in our Poughkeepsie conference, coverage frequently was of the postriot or interview variety because newsmen arrived at the scene after the actual violence had subsided. Overall, both network and local television coverage was cautious and restrained.

2. Television newscasts during the periods of actual disorder in 1967 tended to emphasize law enforcement activities, thereby overshadowing underlying grievances and tensions. This conclusion is based on the relatively high frequency with which television showed and described law enforcement agents, police, national guardsmen, and army troops performing control functions.

Television coverage tended to give the impression that the riots were confrontations between Negroes and whites rather than responses by Negroes to underlying slum problems. The control agents were predominantly white. The ratio of white male adults[5] to Negro male adults shown on television is high (1:2) considering that the riots took place in predominantly Negro neighborhoods. And some interviews with whites involved landlords or proprietors who had lost property or suffered business losses because of the disturbances and thus held strongly antagonistic attitudes.

The content analysis shows that by far the most frequent "actor" appearances on television were Negro male adults, white male adults, law enforcement agents, and public officials. We cannot tell from a content analysis whether there was any preconceived editorial policy of portraying the riots as racial confrontations requiring the intervention of enforcement agents. But the content analysis does present a visual three-way alignment of Negroes, white bystanders, and public officials or enforcement agents. This alignment tended to create an impression that the riots were predominantly racial confrontations between black and white citizens.

3. About one-third of all riot-related sequences for network and local television appeared on the first day following the outbreak of rioting, regardless of the course of

development of the riot itself. After the first day there was, except in Detroit, a very sharp decline in the amount of television time devoted to the disturbance. In Detroit, where the riot started slowly and did not flare out of control until the evening of July 24, 48 hours after it started, the number of riot-related sequences shown increased until July 26, and then showed the same sharp drop-off as noted after the first day of rioting in the other cities.[6] These findings tend to controvert the impression that the riot intensifies television coverage, thus in turn intensifying the riot. The content analysis indicates that whether or not the riot was getting worse, television coverage of the riot decreased sharply after the first day.

4. The Commission made a special effort to analyze television coverage of Negro leaders. To do this, Negro leaders were divided into three categories: (a) celebrities or public figures, who did not claim any organizational following (e.g., social scientist Dr. Kenneth B. Clark, comedian Dick Gregory); (b) "moderate" Negro leaders, who claim a political or organizational following; and (c) "militant" Negro leaders who claim a political or organizational following. During the riot periods surveyed, Negro leaders appeared infrequently on network news broadcasts and were about equally divided among celebrity or public figures, moderate leaders, and militant leaders. On local television, Negro leaders appeared more often. Of the three categories, "moderate" Negro leaders were shown on local stations more than twice as often as Negro leaders identified primarily as celebrities or public figures, and three times more frequently than militant leaders.

Newspapers

1. Like television coverage, newspaper coverage of civil disturbances in the summer of 1967 was more calm, factual and restrained than outwardly emotional or inflammatory. During the period of the riot there were many stories dealing exclusively with nonriot racial news. Considering the magnitude of the events, the amount of coverage was limited. Most stories were played down or put on inside pages. Researchers found that almost all the articles analyzed (3,045 of 3,770) tended to focus on one of 16 identifiable subjects. Of this group, 502 articles (16.5 percent) focused primarily on legislation which should be sought and planning which could be done to control ongoing riots and prevent future riots. The second largest category consisted of 471 articles (15.5 percent) focusing on containment or control of riot action. Newspaper coverage of the disorders reflects efforts at caution and restraint.

2. Newspapers tended to characterize and portray last summer's riots in national terms rather than as local phenomena and problems, especially when rioting was taking place in the newspaper's own city. During the actual disorders, the newspapers in each city studied tended to print many stories dealing with disorders or racial troubles in other cities. About 40 percent of the riot or racial stories in each local newspaper during the period of rioting in that city came from the wire services. Most newspaper editors appear to have given more headline attention to riots occurring elsewhere than to those at home during the time of trouble in their own cities.

Accuracy of the Coverage

We have tested the accuracy of coverage by means of interviews with local media representatives, city and police officials, and residents of the ghettos. To provide a broad base, we used three separate sources for interview data: the Commission's field survey teams, special field teams, and the findings of a special research study.

As is to be expected, almost everyone had his own version of "the truth," but it is note-worthy that some editors and reporters themselves, in retrospect, have expressed concern about the accuracy of their own coverage. For example, one newspaper editor said at the Commission's Poughkeepsie conference:

> We used things in our leads and headlines during the riot I wish we could have back now, because they were wrong and they were bad mistakes . . . We used the words "sniper kings" and "nests of snipers." We found out when we were able to get our people into those areas and get them out from under the cars that these sniper kings and these nests of snipers were the constituted authorities shooting at each other, most of them. There was just one con-firmed sniper in the entire eight-day riot and he was . . . drunk and he had a pistol, and he was firing from a window.

Television industry representatives at the conference stressed their concern about "live" coverage of disorders and said they try, whenever possible, to view and edit taped or filmed sequences before broadcasting them. Conference participants admitted that live television coverage via helicopter of the 1965 Watts riot had been inflammatory, and net-work news executives expressed doubts that television would ever again present live cov-erage of a civil disorder.

Most errors involved mistakes of fact, exaggeration of events, overplaying of particu-lar stories, or prominently displayed speculation about unfounded rumors of potential trou-ble. This is not only a local problem; because of the wire services and networks, it is a national one. An experienced riot reporter told the Commission that initial wire service reports of a disturbance tend to be inflated. The reason, he said, is that they are written by local bureau men who in most cases have not seen a civil disorder before. When out-of-town reporters with knowledge in the field, or the wire services' own riot specialists arrive on the scene, the situation is put into a more accurate context.

Some examples of exaggeration and mistakes about facts are catalogued here. These examples are by no means exhaustive. They represent only a few of the incidents discov-ered by the Commission and, no doubt, are but a small part of the total number of such inaccuracies. But the Commission believes that they are representative of the kinds of errors likely to occur when, in addition to the confusion inherent in civil disorder situa-tions, reporters are rushed and harried or editors are superficial and careless. We present these as examples of mistakes that we hope will be avoided in the future.

In particular, we believe newsmen should be wary of how they play rumors of impend-ing trouble. Whether a rumor is reliable and significant enough to deserve coverage is an editorial decision. But the failure of many headlined rumors to be borne out last summer suggests that these editorial decisions often are not as carefully made as the sensitivity of the subject requires.

- In Tampa, Florida, a deputy sheriff died in the early stages of the disturbance, and both national wire services immediately bulletined the news that the man had been killed by rioters. About 30 minutes later, reporters discovered that the man had suf-fered a fatal heart attack.

- In Detroit, a radio station broadcast a rumor, based on a telephone tip, that Negroes planned to invade suburbia one night later; if plans existed, they never materialized.

- In Cincinnati, several outlets ran a story about white youths arrested for possessing a bazooka; only a few reports mentioned that the weapon was inoperable.

- In Tampa a newspaper repeatedly indulged in speculation about impending trouble. When the state attorney ruled the fatal shooting of a Negro youth justifiable homicide, the paper's news columns reported: "There were fears today that the ruling would stir new race problems for Tampa tonight." The day before, the paper quoted one "top lawman" as telling reporters "he now fears that Negro residents in the Central Avenue Project and in the West Tampa trouble spots feel they are in competition, and are trying to see which can cause the most unrest—which area can become the center of attraction."

- A West Coast newspaper put out an edition headlined: "Rioting Erupts in Washington, D.C. / Negroes Hurl Bottles, Rocks at Police Near White House." The story did not support the headline. It reported what was actually the fact: that a number of teenage Negroes broke store windows and threw bottles and stones at police and firemen near downtown Washington, a mile or more from the White House. On the other hand, the same paper did not report unfounded local rumors of sniping when other news media did.

Television presents a different problem with respect to accuracy. In contrast to what some of its critics have charged, television sometimes may have leaned over too far backward in seeking balance and restraint. By stressing interviews, many with whites in predominantly Negro neighborhoods, and by emphasizing control scenes rather than riotous action, television news broadcasts may have given a distorted picture of what the disorders were all about.

The media—especially television—also have failed to present and analyze to a sufficient extent the basic reasons for the disorders. There have, after the disorders, been some brilliant exceptions.[7] As the content analysis findings suggest, however, coverage during the riot period itself gives far more emphasis to control of rioters and black-white confrontation than to the underlying causes of the disturbances.

Ghetto Reactions to the Media Coverage

The Commission was particularly interested in public reaction to media coverage; specifically, what people in the ghetto look at and read and how it affects them. The Commission has drawn upon reports from special teams of researchers who visited various cities where outbreaks occurred last summer. Members of these teams interviewed ghetto dwellers and middle-class Negroes on their responses to news media. In addition, we have used information from a statistical study of the mass media in the Negro ghetto in Pittsburgh.[8]

These interviews and surveys, though by no means a complete study of the subject, lead to four broad conclusions about ghetto, and to a lesser degree middle-class Negro, reactions to the media.

Most Negroes distrust what they refer to as the "white press." As one interviewer reported:

> The average black person couldn't give less of a damn about what the media say. The intelligent black person is resentful at what he considers to be a totally false portrayal of what goes on in the ghetto. Most black people see the newspapers as mouthpieces of the "power structure."

These comments are echoed in most interview reports the Commission has read. Distrust and dislike of the media among ghetto Negroes encompass *all* the media, though in general, the newspapers are mistrusted more than the television. This is not because television is thought to be more sensitive or responsive to Negro needs and aspirations, but because ghetto residents believe that television at least lets them see the actual events for themselves. Even so, many Negroes, particularly teenagers, told researchers that they noted a pronounced discrepancy between what they saw in the riots and what television broadcast.

Persons interviewed offered three chief reasons for their attitude. First, they believed, as suggested in the quotation above, that the media are instruments of the white power structure. They thought that these white interests guide the entire white community, from the journalists' friends and neighbors to city officials, police officers, and department store owners. Publishers and editors, if not white reporters, supported and defended these interests with enthusiasm and dedication.

Second, many people in the ghettos apparently believe that newsmen rely on the police for most of their information about what is happening during a disorder and tend to report much more of what the officials are doing and saying than what Negro citizens or leaders in the city are doing and saying. Editors and reporters at the Poughkeepsie conference acknowledged that the police and city officials are their main—and sometimes their only—source of information. It was also noted that most reporters who cover civil disturbances tend to arrive with the police and stay close to them—often for safety, and often because they learn where the action is at the same time as the authorities—and thus buttress the ghetto impression that police and press work together and toward the same ends (an impression that may come as a surprise to many within the ranks of police and press).

Third, Negro residents in several cities surveyed cited as specific examples of media unfairness what they considered the failure of the media:

- To report the many examples of Negroes helping law enforcement officers and assisting in the treatment of the wounded during disorders;
- To report adequately about false arrests;
- To report instances of excessive force by the National Guard;
- To explore and interpret the background conditions leading to disturbances;
- To expose, except in Detroit, what they regarded as instances of police brutality;
- To report on white vigilante groups which allegedly came into some disorder areas and molested innocent Negro residents.

Some of these problems are insoluble. But more first-hand reporting in the diffuse and fragmented riot area should temper easy reliance on police information and announcements. There is a special need for news media to cover "positive" news stories in the ghetto before and after riots with concern and enthusiasm.

A multitude of news and information sources other than the established news media are relied upon in the ghetto. One of our studies found that 79 percent of a total of 567 ghetto residents interviewed in seven cities[9] first heard about the outbreak in their own city by word of mouth. Telephone and word of mouth exchanges on the streets, in churches, stores, pool halls, and bars, provide more information—and rumors—about events of direct concern to ghetto residents than the more conventional news media.

Among the established media, television and radio are far more popular in the ghetto than newspapers. Radios there, apparently, are ordinarily listened to less for news than for music and other programs. One survey showed that an over-whelmingly large number of Negro children and teenagers (like their white counterparts) listen to the radio for music alone, interspersed by disc jockey chatter. In other age groups, the response of most people about what they listen to on the radio was "anything," leading to the conclusion that radio in the ghetto is basically a background accompaniment.

But the fact that radio is such a constant background accompaniment can make it an important influence on people's attitudes, and perhaps on their actions once trouble develops. This is true for several reasons. News presented on local "rock" stations seldom constitutes much more than terse headline items which may startle or frighten but seldom inform. Radio disc jockeys and those who preside over the popular "talk shows" keep a steady patter of information going over the air. When a city is beset by civil strife, this patter can both inform transistor radio-carrying young people where the action is, and terrify their elders and much of the white community. "Burn, baby, burn," the slogan of the Watts riot, was inadvertently originated by a radio disc jockey.

Thus, radio can be an instrument of trouble and tension in a community threatened or inundated with civil disorder. It can also do much to minimize fear by putting fast-paced events into proper perspective. We have found commendable instances, for example, in Detroit, Milwaukee, and New Brunswick, of radio stations and personalities using their air time and influence to try to calm potential rioters. In Section II, we recommend procedures for meetings and consultations for advance planning among those who will cover civil disorders. It is important that radio personnel, and especially disc jockeys and talk show hosts, be included in such pre-planning.

Television is the formal news source most relied upon in the ghetto. According to one report, more than 75 percent of the sample turned to television for national and international news, and a larger percentage of the sample (86 percent) regularly watched television from 5 to 7 p.m., the dinner hours when the evening news programs are broadcast.

The significance of broadcasting in news dissemination is seen in Census Bureau estimates that in June 1967, 87.7 percent of nonwhite households and 94.8 percent of white households had television sets.

When ghetto residents do turn to newspapers, most read tabloids, if available, far more frequently than standard size newspapers and rely on the tabloids primarily for light features, racing charts, comic strips, fashion news and display advertising.

Conduct of Press Representatives

Most newsmen appear to be aware and concerned that their very physical presence can exacerbate a small disturbance, but some have conducted themselves with a startling lack of common sense. News organizations, particularly television networks, have taken substantial steps to minimize the effect of the physical presence of their employees at a news event. Networks have issued internal instructions calling for use of unmarked cars and small cameras and tape recorders, and most stations instruct their cameramen to film without artificial light whenever possible. Still, some newsmen have done things "for the sake of the story" that could have contributed to tension.

Reports have come to the Commission's attention of individual newsmen staging events, coaxing youths to throw rocks and interrupt traffic, and otherwise acting irresponsibly at the incipient stages of a disturbance. Such acts are the responsibility of the news organization as well as of its individual reporter.

Two examples occurred in Newark. Television cameramen, according to officials, crowded into and in front of police headquarters, interfering with law enforcement operations and "making a general nuisance of themselves." In a separate incident, a New York newspaper photographer covering the Newark riot repeatedly urged and finally convinced a Negro boy to throw a rock for the camera. Pushing and crowding may be unavoidable, but deliberate staging of events is not.

We believe every effort should be made to eliminate this sort of conduct. This requires the implementation of thoughtful, stringent staff guidelines for reporters and editors. Such guidelines, carefully formulated, widely disseminated, and strictly enforced, underlie the self-policing activities of some news organizations already, but they must be universally adopted if they are to be effective in curbing journalistic irresponsibility.

The Commission has studied the internal guidelines in use last summer at the Associated Press, United Press International, the Washington Post, and the Columbia Broadcasting System. Many other news organizations, large and small, have similar guidelines. In general, the guidelines urge extreme care to ensure that reporting is thorough and balanced and that words and statistics used are appropriate and accurate. The AP guidelines call for broad investigation into the immediate and underlying causes of an incident. The CBS guidelines demand as much caution as possible to avoid the danger of camera equipment and lights exacerbating the disturbance.

Internal guidelines can, and all those studied do, go beyond problems of physical presence at a disturbance to the substantive aspects of searching out, reporting, and writing the story. But the content of the guidelines is probably less important than the fact that the subject has been thoughtfully considered and hammered out within the organization, and an approach developed that is designed to meet the organization's particular needs and solve its particular problems.

We recommend that every news organization that does not now have some form of guidelines—or suspects that those it has are not working effectively—designate top editors to (a) meet with its reporters who have covered or might be assigned to riots, (b) discuss in detail the problems and procedures which exist or are expected and (c) formulate and disseminate directives based on the discussions. Regardless of the specific provisions, the vital step is for every news-gathering organization to adopt and implement at least some minimal form of internal control.

II. A RECOMMENDATION
TO IMPROVE RIOT COVERAGE

A Need for Better Communication

A recurrent problem in the coverage of last summer's disorders was friction and lack of cooperation between police officers and working reporters. Many experienced and capable journalists complained that policemen and their commanding officers were at best apathetic and at worst overtly hostile toward reporters attempting to cover a disturbance. Policemen, on the other hand, charged that many reporters seemed to forget that the task of the police is to restore order.

After considering available evidence on the subject, the Commission is convinced that these conditions reflect an absence of advance communication and planning among the people involved. We do not suggest that familiarity with the other's problems will beget total amity and cooperation. The interests of the media and the police are sometimes necessarily at variance. But we do believe that communication is a vital step toward removing the obstacles produced by ignorance, confusion, and misunderstanding of what each group is actually trying to do.

Mutual Orientation

What is needed first is a series of discussions, perhaps a combination of informal gatherings and seminar-type workshops. They should encompass all ranks of the police, all levels of media employees, and a cross-section of city officials. At first these would be get-acquainted sessions—to air complaints and discuss common problems. Working reporters should get to know the police who would be likely to draw duty in a disorder. Police and city officials should use the sessions for frank and candid briefings on the problems the city might face and official plans for dealing with disturbances.

Later sessions might consider procedures to facilitate the physical movement of personnel and speed the flow of accurate and complete news. Such arrangements might involve nothing more than a procedure for designating specific locations at which police officers would be available to escort a reporter into a dangerous area. In addition, policemen and reporters working together might devise better methods of identification, communication, and training.

Such procedures are infinitely variable and depend on the initiative, needs, and desires of those involved. If there is no existing institution or procedure for convening such meetings, we urge the mayor or city manager to do so in every city where experience suggests the possibility of future trouble. To allay any apprehension that discussions with officials might lead to restraints on the freedom to seek out and report the news, participants in these meetings should stipulate before-hand that freedom of access to all areas for reporters will be preserved.

Designation of Information Officers

It is desirable to designate and prepare a number of police officers to act as media information officers. There should be enough of these so that, in the event of a disturbance, a reporter will not have to seek far to find a policeman ready and able to give him information and answer questions. Officers should be knowledgeable, of high enough rank within the police department to have ready access to information, and be at ease with reporters.

Creation of Central Information Center

A nerve center for reliable police and official government information should be planned and ready for activation when a disturbance reaches a predetermined point of intensity. Such a center might be located at police headquarters or city hall. It should be directed by an experienced, high-ranking information specialist with close ties to police officials. It is imperative, of course, that all officials keep a steady flow of accurate information coming into the center. Ideally, rooms would be set aside for taping and filming interviews with public officials. Local television stations might cut costs and relieve congestion by pooling some equipment at this central facility. An information center should not be thought of as replacing other news sources inside and outside the disturbance area. If anything, our studies suggest that reporters are already too closely tied to police and officials as news sources in a disorder. An information center should not be permitted to intensify this dependence. Properly conceived, however, a center can supplement on-the-spot reporting and supply news about official action.

Relations with Out-of-Town Reporters

Much of the difficulty last summer apparently revolved around relations between local law enforcement officials and out-of-town reporters. These reporters are likely to be less sensitive about preserving the "image" of the local community.

Still, local officials serve their city badly when they ignore or impede national media representatives instead of welcoming them, informing them about the city, and cooperating with their attempts to cover the story. City and police officials should designate liaison officers and distribute names and telephone numbers of police and other relevant officials, the place they can be found if trouble develops, and other information likely to be useful.

National and other news organizations, in turn, could help matters by selecting a responsible home office official to act as liaison in these cases and to be accessible by phone to local officials who encounter difficulty with on-the-spot representatives of an organization.

General Guidelines and Codes

In some cases, if all parties involved were willing, planning sessions might lead to the consideration of more formal undertakings. These might include: (a) agreements on specific procedures to expedite the physical movement of men and equipment around disorder areas and back and forth through police lines; (b) general guidelines on the behavior of both media and police personnel, and (c) arrangements for a brief moratorium on reporting news of an incipient disturbance. The Commission stresses once again its belief that though each of these possibilities merits consideration, none should be formulated or imposed by unilateral government action. Any procedure finally adopted should be negotiated between police and media representatives and should assure both sides the flexibility needed to do their respective jobs. Acceptance of such arrangements should be frankly based on grounds of self-interest, for negotiated methods of procedure can often yield substantial benefits to each side—and to the public which both serve.

At the request of the Commission, the Community Relations service of the Department of Justice surveyed recent experiences with formal codes. Most of the codes studied: (a) set forth in general terms common sense standards of good journalistic conduct, and (b) establish procedures for a brief moratorium (seldom more than 30 minutes to an hour) on reporting an incipient disturbance.

In its survey, the Community Relations Service described and analyzed experiences with codes in eleven major cities where they are currently in force. Members of the CRS staff conducted interviews with key citizens (newsmen, city officials, and community leaders) in each of the eleven cities, seeking comments on the effectiveness and practicality of the codes and guidelines used. CRS's major findings and conclusions are:

- All codes and guidelines now in operation are basically voluntary arrangements usually put forward by local authorities and accepted by the news media after consultation. Nowhere has an arrangement or agreement been effected that binds the news media without their assent.

- No one interviewed in this survey considered the code or guidelines in effect in his city as useless or harmful. CRS thought that, where they were in effect, the codes had a constructive impact on the local news media. Observers in some cities, however, thought the increased sense of responsibility manifested by press and television was due more to experience with riot coverage than to the existence of the codes.

- The more controversial and often least understood aspect of guidelines has been provision for a brief voluntary moratorium on the reporting of news. Some kind of moratorium is specified in the codes of six cities surveyed (Chicago, Omaha, Buffalo, Indianapolis, Kansas City, and Toledo), and the moratorium was invoked last summer in Chicago and Indianapolis. In each case, an effort to prevent quite minor racial incidents from escalating into more serious trouble was successful, and many thought the moratorium contributed.

- The confusion about a moratorium, and the resulting aversion to it, is unfortunate. The specific period of delay is seldom more than 30 minutes. In practice, under today's conditions of reporting and broadcasting, this often will mean little if any delay before the full story gets into the paper or on the air. The time can be used to prepare and edit the story and to verify and assess the reports of trouble. The only loss is the banner headline or the broadcast news bulletin that gets out prematurely to avoid being beaten by "the competition." It is just such reflexive responses that can lead to sensationalism and inaccuracy. In cities where a moratorium is part of the code, CRS interviewers detected no discontent over its presence.

- The most frequent complaint about shortcomings in existing codes is that many of them do not reach the underpinnings of crisis situations. Ghetto spokesmen, in particular, said that the emphasis in the codes on conduct during the crisis itself tended to lead the media to neglect reporting the underlying causes of racial tension.

At the Poughkeepsie Conference with media representatives, there was considerable criticism of the Chicago code on grounds that the moratorium is open ended. Once put into effect it is supposed to be maintained until "the situation is under control." There were doubts about how effective this code had been in practice. The voluntary news blackout in Detroit for part of the first day of the riot—apparently at the request of officials and civil rights groups—was cited as evidence that suppression of news of violence does not necessarily de-fuse a riot situation.

On the basis of the CRS survey and other evidence, the Commission concludes that codes are seldom harmful, often useful, but no panacea. To be of any use, they must address themselves to the substance of the problems that plague relations between the press and officialdom during a disorder, but they are only one of several methods of improving those relations. Ultimately, no matter how sensitive and comprehensive a code or set of guidelines may be, efficient, accurate reporting must depend on the intelligence, judgment, and training of newsmen, police, and city officials together.

III. REPORTING OF RACIAL PROBLEMS
IN THE UNITED STATES

A Failure to Communicate

The Commission's major concern with the news media is not in riot reporting as such, but in the failure to report adequately on race relations and ghetto problems and to bring more Negroes into journalism. Concern about this was expressed by a number of participants in our Poughkeepsie conference. Disorders are only one aspect of the dilemmas and difficulties of race relations in America. In defining, explaining, and reporting this broader, more complex and ultimately far more fundamental subject, the communications media, ironically, have failed to communicate.

They have not communicated to the majority of their audience—which is white—a sense of the degradation, misery, and hopelessness of living in the ghetto. They have not communicated to whites a feeling for the difficulties and frustrations of being a Negro in the United States. They have not shown understanding or appreciation of—and thus have not communicated—a sense of Negro culture, thought, or history.

Equally important, most newspaper articles and most television programming ignore the fact that an appreciable part of their audience is black. The world that television and newspapers offer to their black audience is almost totally white, in both appearance and attitude. As we have said, our evidence shows that the so-called "white press" is at best mistrusted and at worst held in contempt by many black Americans. Far too often, the press acts and talks about Negroes as if Negroes do not read the newspapers or watch television, give birth, marry, die, and go to PTA meetings. Some newspapers and stations are beginning to make efforts to fill this void, but they have still a long way to go.

The absence of Negro faces and activities from the media has an effect on white audiences as well as black. If what the white American reads in the newspapers or sees on television conditions his expectation of what is ordinary and normal in the larger society, he will neither understand nor accept the black American. By failing to portray the Negro as a matter of routine and in the context of the total society, the news media have, we believe, contributed to the black-white schism in this country.

When the white press does refer to Negroes and Negro problems it frequently does so as if Negroes were not a part of the audience. This is perhaps understandable in a system where whites edit and, to a large extent, write news. But such attitudes, in an area as sensitive and inflammatory as this, feed Negro alienation and intensify white prejudices.

We suggest that a top editor or news director monitor his news production for a period of several weeks, taking note of how certain stories and language will affect black readers or viewers. A Negro staff member could do this easily. Then the staff should be informed about the problems involved.

The problems of race relations coverage go beyond incidents of white bias. Many editors and news directors, plagued by shortages of staff and lack of reliable contacts and sources of information in the city, have failed to recognize the significance of the urban story and to develop resources to cover it adequately.

We believe that most news organizations do not have direct access to diversified news sources in the ghetto. Seldom do they have a total sense of what is going on there. Some of the blame rests on Negro leaders who do not trust the media and will not deal candidly with representatives of the white press. But the real failure rests with the news organization themselves. They—like other elements of the white community—have ignored the ghettos for decades. Now they seek instant acceptance and cooperation.

The development of good contacts, reliable information, and understanding requires more effort and time than an occasional visit by a team of reporters to do a feature on a newly-discovered ghetto problem. It requires reporters permanently assigned to this beat. They must be adequately trained and supported to dig out and tell the story of a major social upheaval—among the most complicated, portentous and explosive our society has known. We believe, also, that the Negro Press—manned largely by people who live and work in the ghetto—could be a particularly useful source of information and guidance about activities in the black community. Reporters and editors from Negro newspapers and radio stations should be included in any conference between media and police-city representatives, and we suggest that large news organizations would do well to establish better lines of communication to their counterparts in the Negro press.[10]

In short, the news media must find ways of exploring the problems of the Negro and the ghetto more deeply and more meaningfully. To editors who say "we have run thousands of inches on the ghetto which nobody reads" and to television executives who bemoan scores of underwatched documentaries, we say: find more ways of telling this story, for it is a story you, as journalists, must tell—honestly, realistically, and imaginatively. It is the responsibility of the news media to tell the story of race relations in America, and with notable exceptions, the media have not yet turned to the task with the wisdom, sensitivity, and expertise it demands.

Negroes in Journalism

The journalistic profession has been shockingly backward in seeking out, hiring, training, and promoting Negroes. Fewer than 5 percent of the people employed by the news business in editorial jobs in the United States today are Negroes. Fewer than 1 percent of editors and supervisors are Negroes, and most of them work for Negro-owned organizations. The lines of various news organizations to the militant blacks are, by admission of the newsmen themselves, almost nonexistent. The plaint is, "We can't find qualified Negroes." But this rings hollow from an industry where, only yesterday, jobs were scarce and promotion unthinkable for a man whose skin was black. Even today, there are virtually no Negroes in positions of editorial or executive responsibility and there is only one Negro newsman with a nationally syndicated column.

News organizations must employ enough Negroes in positions of significant responsibility to establish an effective link to Negro actions and ideas and to meet legitimate employment expectations. Tokenism—the hiring of one Negro reporter, or even two or three—is no longer enough. Negro reporters are essential, but so are Negro editors, writers and commentators. Newspaper and television policies are, generally speaking, not set by reporters. Editorial decisions about which stories to cover and which to use are made by editors. Yet, very few Negroes in this country are involved in making these decisions, because very few, if any, supervisory editorial jobs are held by Negroes. We urge the news media to do everything possible to train and promote their Negro reporters to positions where those who are qualified can contribute to and have an effect on policy decisions.

It is not enough, though, as many editors have pointed out to the Commission, to search for Negro journalists. Journalism is not very popular as a career for aspiring young Negroes.

The starting pay is comparatively low and it is a business which has, until recently, discouraged and rejected them. The recruitment of Negro reporters must extend beyond established journalists, or those who have already formed ambitions along these lines. It must become a commitment to seek out young Negro men and women, inspire them to become—and then train them as—journalists. Training programs should be started at high schools and intensified at colleges. Summer vacation and part-time editorial jobs, coupled with offers of permanent employment, can awaken career plans.

We believe that the news media themselves, their audiences and the country will profit from these undertakings. For if the media are to comprehend and then to project the Negro community, they must have the help of Negroes. If the media are to report with understanding, wisdom and sympathy on the problems of the cities and the problems of the black man—for the two are increasingly intertwined—they must employ, promote and listen to Negro journalists.

The Negro in the Media

Finally, the news media must publish newspapers and produce programs that recognize the existence and activities of the Negro, both as a Negro and as part of the community. It would be a contribution of inestimable importance to race relations in the United States simply to treat ordinary news about Negroes as news of other groups is now treated.

Specifically, newspapers should integrate Negroes and Negro activities into all parts of the paper, from the news, society and club pages to the comic strips. Television should develop programming which integrates Negroes into all aspects of televised presentations. Television is such a visible medium that some constructive steps are easy and obvious. While some of these steps are being taken, they are still largely neglected. For example, Negro reporters and performers should appear more frequently—and at prime time—in news broadcasts, on weather shows, in documentaries, and in advertisements. Some effort already has been made to use Negroes in television commercials. Any initial surprise at seeing a Negro selling a sponsor's product will eventually fade into routine acceptance, an attitude that white society must ultimately develop toward all Negroes.

In addition to news-related programming, we think that Negroes should appear more frequently in dramatic and comedy series. Moreover, networks and local stations should present plays and other programs whose subjects are rooted in the ghetto and its problems.

IV. INSTITUTE OF URBAN COMMUNICATIONS

The Commission is aware that in this area, as in all other aspects of race relations, the problems are great and it is much easier to state them than to solve them. Various pressures—competitive, financial, advertising—may impede progress toward more balanced, in-depth coverage and toward the hiring and training of more Negro personnel. Most newspapers and local television and radio stations do not have the resources or the time to keep abreast of all the technical advances, academic theories, and government programs affecting the cities and the lives of their black inhabitants.

During the course of this study, the Commission members and the staff have had many conversations with publishers, editors, broadcasters, and reporters throughout the country.

The consensus appears to be that most of them would like to do much more but simply do not have the resources for independent efforts at either training or coverage.

The Commission believes that some of these problems could be resolved if there were a central organization to develop, gather and distribute talent, resources, and information and to keep the work of the press in this field under review. For this reason, the Commission proposes the establishment of an Institute of Urban Communications on a private, non-profit basis. The Institute would have neither governmental ties nor governmental authority. Its board would consist in substantial part of professional journalists and, for the rest, of distinguished public figures. The staff would be made up of journalists and students of the profession. Funding would be sought initially from private foundations. Ultimately, it may be hoped, financial support would be forthcoming from within the profession.

The Institute would be charged, in the first instance, with general responsibility for carrying out the media recommendations of the Commission, though as it developed a momentum and life of its own it would also gain its own view of the problems and possibilities. Initial tasks would include:

1. *Training and education for journalists in the field of urban affairs.* The Institute should organize and sponsor, on its own and in cooperation with universities and other institutions, a comprehensive range of courses, seminars and workshops designed to give reporters, editors and publishers the background they need to cover the urban scene. Offerings would vary in duration and intensity from weekend conferences to grants for year-long individual study on the order of the Nieman Fellowships.

All levels and all kinds of news outlets should be served. A most important activity might be to assist disc jockeys and commentators on stations that address themselves especially to the Negro community. Particularly important would be sessions of a month or more for seasoned reporters and editors, comparable to middle management seminars or mid-career training in other callings. The press must have all of the intellectual resources and background to give adequate coverage to the city and the ghetto. It should be the first duty of the Institute to see that this is provided.

2. *Recruitment, training and placement of Negro journalists.* The scarcity of Negroes in responsible news jobs intensifies the difficulties of communicating the reality of the contemporary American city to white newspaper and television audiences. The special viewpoint of the Negro who has lived through these problems and bears their marks upon him is, as we have seen, notably absent from what is, on the whole, a white press. But full integration of Negroes into the journalistic profession is imperative in its own right. It is unacceptable that the press, itself the special beneficiary of fundamental constitutional protections, should lag so far behind other fields in giving effect to the fundamental human right to equality of opportunity.

To help correct this situation, the Institute will have to undertake far-ranging activities. Providing educational opportunities for would-be Negro journalists is not enough. There will have to be changes in career outlooks for Negro students and their counselors back to the secondary school level. And changes in these attitudes will come slowly unless there is a change in the reality of employment and advancement opportunities for Negroes in journalism. This requires an aggressive placement program, seeking out newspapers, television and radio stations that discriminate, whether consciously or unconsciously, and mobilizing the pressures, public, private and legal, necessary to break the pattern. The Institute might also provide assistance to Negro newspapers, which now recruit and train many young journalists.

3. *Police-press relations.* The Commission has stressed the failures in this area, and has laid out a set of remedial measures for action at the local level. But if reliance is placed exclusively on local initiative we can predict that in many places—often those that need it most—our recommended steps will not be taken. Pressure from the federal government for action along the lines proposed would be suspect, probably, by both press and local officials. But the Institute could undertake the task of stimulating community action in line with the Commission's recommendations without arousing local hostility and suspicion. Moreover, the Institute could serve as a clearing house for exchange of experience in this field.

4. *Review of Media Performance on Riots and Racial Issues.* The Institute should review press and television coverage of riot and racial news and publicly award praise and blame. The Commission recognizes that government restraints or guidelines in this field are both unworkable and incompatible with our Constitution and traditions. Internal guidelines or voluntary advance arrangements may be useful, but they tend to be rather general and the standards they prescribe are neither self-applying nor self-enforcing. We believe it would be healthy for reporters and editors who work in this sensitive field to know that others will be viewing their work and will hold them publicly accountable for lapses from accepted standards of good journalism. The Institute should publicize its findings by means of regular and special reports. It might also set a series of awards for especially meritorious work of individuals or news organizations in race relations reporting.

5. *An urban affairs service.* Whatever may be done to improve the quality of reporting on urban affairs, there always will be a great many outlets that are too small to support the specialized investigation, reporting and interpreting needed in this field. To fill this gap, the Institute could organize a comprehensive urban news service, available at a modest fee to any news organization that wanted it. The Institute would have its own specially trained reporters, and it would also cull the national press for news and feature stories of broader interest that could be reprinted or broadcast by subscribers.

Continuing Research

Our own investigations have shown us that academic work on the impact of the media on race relations, its role in shaping attitudes, and the effects of the choices it makes on people's behavior, is in a rudimentary stage. The Commission's content analysis is the first study of its type of contemporary riot coverage, and it is extremely limited in scope. A whole range of questions needs intensive scholarly exploration, and indeed the development of new modes of research and analysis. The Institute should undertake many of these important projects under its own auspices and could stimulate others in the academic community to further research.

▪ ▪ ▪

Along with the country as a whole, the press has too long basked in a white world, looking out of it, if at all, with white men's eyes and a white perspective. That is no longer good enough. The painful process of readjustment that is required of the American news media must begin now. They must make a reality of integration—in both their product and personnel. They must insist on the highest standards of accuracy—not only reporting single events with care and skepticism, but placing each event into meaningful perspective. They must report the travail of our cities with compassion and in depth.

In all this, the Commission asks for fair and courageous journalism: commitment and coverage that are worthy of one of the crucial domestic stories in America's history.

NOTES

1. As recently as February 9, 1968, an Associated Press dispatch from Philadelphia said "damage exceeded $1 billion" in Detroit.
2. Michigan State Insurance Commission Estimate, December, 1967. See also *Meeting the Insurance Crisis of Our Cities,* a Report by the President's National Advisory Panel on Insurance in Riot-Affected Areas, January, 1968.
3. Detroit, Michigan; Milwaukee, Wisconsin; Cincinnati, Ohio; Dayton, Ohio; Tampa, Florida; Newark, New Jersey; Plainfield, New Jersey; Elizabeth, New Jersey; Jersey City, New Jersey; East Orange, New Jersey; Paterson, New Jersey; New Brunswick, New Jersey; Englewood, New Jersey; New Haven, Connecticut; Rochester, New York.
4. What follows is a summary of the major conclusions drawn from the content analysis conducted for the Commission.
5. The white male adult category in this computation does *not* include law enforcement agents or public officials.
6. Detroit news outlets substantially refrained from publicizing the riot during the early part of Sunday, the first day of rioting.
7. As examples, less than a month after the Detroit riot, the *Detroit Free Press* published the results of a landmark survey of local Negro attitudes and grievances. *Newsweek* Magazine's November 20, 1967 special issue on "The Negro American—What Must Be Done" made a significant contribution to public understanding.
8. The Commission is indebted, in this regard, to M. Thomas Allen for his document on *Mass Media Use Patterns and Functions in the Negro Ghetto in Pittsburgh.*
9. Detroit, Newark, Atlanta, Tampa, New Haven, Cincinnati, Milwaukee.
10. We have not, in this report, examined the Negro press in detail. The thrust of our studies was directed at daily mass circulation, mass audience media which are aimed at the community as a whole.

3

ENCODING AND DECODING
IN THE TELEVISION DISCOURSE

Stuart Hall

Two themes have been cited for this Colloquy: the highly focussed theme concerning the nature of the "televisual language," and the very general and diffused concern with "cultural policies and programmes." At first sight, these concerns seem to lead in opposite directions: the first towards formal, the second towards societal and policy questions. My aim, however, is to try to hold both concerns within a single framework. My purpose is to suggest that, in the analysis of culture, the inter-connection between societal structures and processes and formal or symbolic structures is absolutely pivotal. I propose to organize my reflections around the question of the encoding/decoding moments in the communicative process: and, from this base, to argue that, in societies like ours, communication between the production elites in broadcasting and their audiences is necessarily a form of "systematically distorted communication." This argument then has a direct bearing on "cultural policies," especially those policies of education, etc. which might be directed towards "helping the audience to receive the television communication better, more effectively." I therefore want, for the moment, to retain a base in the semiotic/linguistic approach to "televisual language": to suggest, however, that this perspective properly intersects, on one side, with social and economic structures, on the other side with what Umberto Eco has recently called "the logic of culture."[1] This means that, though I shall adopt a semiotic perspective, I do not regard this as indexing a closed formal concern with the immanent organization of the television discourse alone. It must also include a concern with the "social relations" of the communicative process, and especially with the various kinds of "competences" (at the production and receiving end) in the use of that language.[2]

In his paper[3] Professor Halloran has properly raised the question of studying "the whole mass communication process," from the structure of the production of the message at one end to audience perception and "use" at the other. This emphasis on "the whole communicative process" is a comprehensive, proper and timely one. However, it is worth reminding ourselves that there is something distinctive about the product, and the practices of production and circulation in communications which distinguishes this from other types of production. The "object" of production practices and structures in television is the production of a *message*: that is, a sign-vehicle, or rather sign-vehicles of a specific kind organized, like any other form of communication or language, through the operation of codes,

Reprinted from Stuart Hall, "Encoding and Decoding in the Television Discourse," Centre for Contemporary Cultural Studies Working Paper, University of Birmingham (Birmingham, England: 1973).

within the syntagmatic chains of a discourse. The apparatus and structures of production issue, at a certain moment, in the form of a symbolic vehicle constituted within the rules of "language." It is in this "phenomenal form" that the circulation of the "product" takes place. Of course, even the transmission of this symbolic vehicle requires its material substratum—video-tape, film, the transmitting and receiving apparatus, etc. It is also in this symbolic form that the reception of the "product," and its distribution between different segments of the audience, takes place. Once accomplished, the translation of that message into societal structures must be made again for the circuit to be completed. Thus, whilst in no way wanting to limit research to "following only those leads which emerge from content analysis,"[4] we must recognize that the symbolic form of the message has a privileged position in the communicative exchange: and that the moments of "encoding" and "decoding," though only "relatively autonomous" in relation to the communicative process as a whole, are *determinate* moments. The raw historical event cannot in that form be transmitted by, say, a television news-cast. It can only be signified within the aural-visual forms of the televisual language. In the moment when the historical event passes under the sign of language, it is subject to all the complex formal "rules" by which language signifies. To put it paradoxically, the event must become a "story" before it can become a *communicative event*. In that moment, the formal sub-rules of language are "in dominance," without, of course, subordinating out of existence the historical event so signified, or the historical consequences of the event having been signified in this way. The "message-form" is the necessary form of the appearance of the event in its passage from source to receiver. Thus the transposition into and out of the "message-form" or the meaning-dimension (or mode of exchange of the message) is not a random "moment," which we can take up or ignore for the sake of convenience or simplicity. The "message-form" is a determinate moment, though, at another level, it comprises the surface-movements of the communications system only, and requires, at another stage, to be integrated into the essential relations of communication of which it forms only a part.

From this general perspective, we may crudely characterise the communicative exchange as follows. The institutional structures of broadcasting, with their institutional structures and networks of production, their organized routines and technical infrastructures, are required to produce the programme. Production, here, initiates the message: in one sense, then, the circuit begins here. Of course, the production process is framed throughout by meanings and ideas: knowledge-in-use concerning the routines of production, technical skills, professional ideologies, institutional knowledge, definitions and assumptions, assumptions about the audience, etc. frame the passage of the programme through this production structure. However, though the production structures of television originate the television message, they do not constitute a closed system. They draw topics, treatments, agendas, events, personnel, images of the audience, "definitions of the situation" from the wider socio-cultural and political system of which they are only a differentiated part. Philip Elliott has expressed this point succinctly in his discussion of the way in which the audience is both the source and the receiver of the television message. Thus circulation and reception are, indeed, "moments" of the production process in television, and are incorporated, via a number of skewed and structured "feed-backs," back into the production process itself. The consumption or reception of the television message is thus itself a "moment" of the production process, though the latter is "predominant" because it is the "point of departure for the realization" of the message. Production and reception of the television message are, not, therefore, identical, but they are related: they are differentiated moments within the totality formed by the communicative process as a whole.

At a certain point, however, the broadcasting structures must yield an encoded message in the form of a meaningful discourse. The institution-societal relations of production must pass into and through the modes of a language for its product to be "realized." This initiates a further differentiated moment, in which the formal rules of discourse and language operate. Before this message can have an "effect" (however defined), or satisfy a "need" or be put to a "use," it must first be perceived as a meaningful discourse and meaningfully de-coded. It is this set of de-coded meanings which "have an effect," influence, entertain, instruct or persuade, with very complex perceptual, cognitive, emotional, ideological or behavioural consequences. In a determinate moment, the structure employs a code and yields a "message": at another determinate moment, the "message," via its decodings, issues into a structure. We are now fully aware that this re-entry into the structures of audience reception and "use" cannot be understood in simple behavioural terms. Effects, uses, "gratifications" are themselves framed by structures of understanding, as well as social and economic structures which shape its "realization" at the reception end of the chain, and which permit the meanings signified in language to be transposed into conduct or consciousness.

Clearly, what we have called Meanings I and Meanings II may not be the same [see Figure 3.1]. They do not constitute an "immediate identity." The codes of encoding and decoding may not be perfectly symmetrical. The degrees of symmetry—that is, the degrees of "understanding" and "misunderstanding" in the communicative exchange depend *both* on the degrees of symmetry/a-symmetry between the position of encoder-producer and that of the decoder-receiver: and *also* on the degrees of identity/non-identity between the

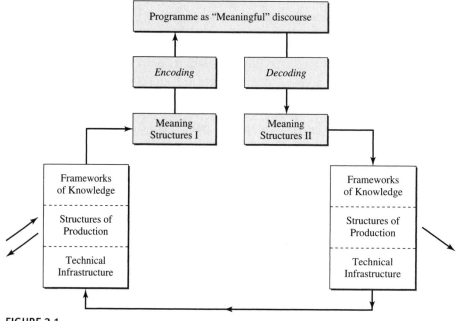

FIGURE 3.1

codes which perfectly or imperfectly transmit, interrupt or systematically distort what has been transmitted. The lack of "fit" between the codes has a great deal to do with the structural differences between broadcasters and audiences: but it also has something to do with the a-symmetry between source and receiver at the moment of transformation into and out of the "message-form." What is called "distortion" or "misunderstandings" arise precisely from the lack of equivalence between the two sides in the communicative exchange. Once again, this defines the "relative autonomy" but "determinateness" of the entry and exit of the message in its linguistic/meaning form.

The application of this rudimentary paradigm has already begun to transform our understanding of television "content": and we are just beginning to see how it might also transform our understanding of audience reception and response as well. Beginnings and endings have been announced in communications research before, so we must be cautious. But there seems some ground for thinking that a new and exciting phase in audience research, of a quite new kind, may be opening up. At either end of the communicative chain, the use of the semiotic paradigm promises to dispel the lingering behaviourism which has dogged mass media research for so long. Though we know the television programme is not a behavioural input, like a tap on the knee-cap, it seems to have been almost impossible for researchers to conceptualize the communicative process without lapsing back into one or other variant of low-flying behaviourism. We know, as Gerbner has remarked, that representations of violence on the TV screen "are not violence but messages about violence"[5]: but we have continued to research the question of violence as if we were unable to comprehend the epistemological distinction.

Let us take an example from the drama-entertainment area in television and try to show how the recognition that television is *a discourse,* a communicative not simply a behavioural event, has an effect on one traditional research area, the television/violence relation.[6] Take the simple-structure, early (and now children's) TV Western, modelled on the early Hollywood B-feature *genre* Western: with its clear-cut, good/bad Manichean moral universe, its clear social and moral designation of villain and hero, the clarity of its narrative line and development, its iconographical features, its clearly-registered climax in the violent shoot-out, chase, personal show-down, street or bar-room duel, etc. For long, on both British and American TV, this form constituted the predominant drama-entertainment *genre.* In quantitative terms, such films/programmes contained a high ratio of violent incidents, deaths, woundings, etc. Whole gangs of men, whole troops of Indians, went down, nightly, to their deaths. Researchers—Himmelweit among others—have, however, suggested that the structure of the early TV/B-feature Western was so clear-cut, its action so conventionalized, stylized, that most children (boys rather earlier than girls, an interesting finding in itself) soon learned to recognize and "read" it like a "game": a "cowboys-and-Injuns" game. It was therefore further hypothesized that Westerns with this clarified a structure were less likely to trigger the aggressive imitation of violent behaviour or other types of aggressive "acting-out" than other types of programmes with a high violence ratio which were not so stylized. But it is worth asking what this recognition of the Western as a "symbolic game" means or implies.

It means that a set of extremely tightly-coded "rules" exist whereby stories of a certain recognizable type, content and structure can be easily encoded within the Western form. What is more, these "rules of encoding" were so diffused, so symmetrically shared as between producer and audience, that the "message" was likely to be decoded in a manner highly symmetrical to that in which it had been encoded. This reciprocity of codes is, indeed, precisely what is entailed in the notion of stylization or "conventionalization," and the presence of such reciprocal codes is, of course, what defines or makes possible the existence of a *genre*. Such an account, then, takes the encoding/decoding moments properly into account, and the case appears an unproblematic one.

But let us take the argument a little further. Why and how do areas of conventionalization arise (and disappear)? The Western tale, of course, arose out of—though it quickly ceased to conform to—the real historical circumstances of the opening up of the American West. In part, what the production of the Western *genre*-codes achieved was the transformation of a real historical West, selectively, into the symbolic or mythical "West." But why did this transformation of history into myth, by the intervention of a stylized set of codes, occur, for our societies and times, in relation to just this historical situation. This process, whereby the rules of language and discourse intervene, at a certain moment, to transform and "naturalize" a specific set of historical circumstances, is one of the most important test-cases for any semiology which seeks to ground itself in historical realities. We know, and can begin to sketch, the elements which defined the operation of codes on history. This is *the* archetypal American story, America of the frontier, of the expanding and unsettled West, the "virgin land" before law and society fully settle in, still closer to Nature than to Law and order. It is the land of *men,* of independent men, isolated in their confrontations with Nature or Evil: and thus stories of masculine prowess, skill power and destiny: of men "in the open air," driven to their destinies by inner compulsion and by external necessity— by Fate, or by "the things a man just has to do": and thus a land where morality is inner-centered, and clarified—i.e. fully objectivated not in speech but in the facticities of gesture, gait, dress, "gear," appearance. A land where women are either subordinate (whether as "little homebodies" or ladies from "back East"): or, if somewhat more liberated—e.g. good/bad saloon girls—destined to be inadvertently and conveniently shot or otherwise disposed of in the penultimate reel: and so on. If we wanted to make a strict semiological analysis, we could trace the specific *codes* which were used to signify these elements within the surface-structures of particular films, plots, programmes. What is clear is that, from this deep-structured set of codes, extremely limited in its elements, a great number of surface strings and transformations were accomplished: for a time, in film and television, this deep-structure provided the taken-for-granted story-of-all-stories, the paradigm action-narrative, the perfect myth.

In the semiotic perspective, of course, it is just this surface variety on the basis of limited transformations which would define the Western as an object of study. Nor would the transformations which we have witnessed since the early days be at all surprising. We can see, and follow at least the basic methods which would be required for us to account for the transformation of this simple-structure Western into the psychological Western, the baroque Western (*Left Handed Gun*?), the "end-of-the-West" Western, the comic Western, the "spaghetti" Western, even the Japanese and Hong-Kong Western, the "parody" Western (*Butch Cassidy*?), paradoxically, the return-of-violence Western (*The Wild Bunch*), or the domestic, soap-opera Western (the TV *Virginian* series) or the Latin-American revolution Western. The opening sequence of a film like *Hud*—one of the moment when the "heroic" West begins to pass into the "decline of the West," in which the "hero" appears driving through that familiar landscape in a Cadillac, or where the horse appears in the back of an Oldsmobile truck, far from indexing the break-up of the code, shows precisely how an opposite meaning can be achieved by the *reversal* of a limited number of "lexical items" in the code, in order to achieve a transformation in the meaning.

From this perspective, the prolonged preoccupation of mass media researchers with the issue of violence in relation to the Western film appears more and more arbitrary, bizarre. If we refuse, for a moment, to bracket and isolate the issue of violence, or the violent episode from its matrix in the complex codes governing the *genre*, how many other crucial kinds of meaning were in fact transmitted whilst researchers were busy counting the bodies. This is not to say that violence was not an element in the TV Western, nor to suggest that there were not quite complex codes regulating the ways in which violence could be signified. It is to insist that what audiences were receiving was not "violence" but messages about violence. Once this intervening term has been applied, certain consequences for research and analysis follow: ones which irrevocably break up the smooth line of continuity offering itself as a sort of "natural logic," whereby connections could be traced between shoot-outs at the OK Corral, and delinquents knocking over old ladies in the street in Scunthorpe.

The violent element or string in the narrative structure of the simple-structure Western—shoot-out, brawl, ambush, bank-raid, fist-fight, wounding, duel or massacre, like any other semantic unit in a structured discourse cannot signify anything on its own. It can only signify in terms of the structured meanings of the message as a whole. Further, its signification depends on its relation—or the sum of the relations of similarity and difference—with other elements or units. Burgelin[7] has long ago, and definitively, reminded us that the violent or wicked acts of a villain only mean something in relation to the presence/absence of good acts.

> we clearly cannot draw any valid inferences from a simple enumeration of his vicious acts (it makes no difference whether there are ten or twenty of them) for the crux of the matter obviously is: what meaning is conferred on the vicious acts by the fact of their juxtaposition with the single good action ... one could say that the meaning of what is frequent is only revealed by opposition to what is rare ... The whole problem is therefore to identify this rare or missing item. Structural analysis provides a way of approaching this problem which traditional content analysis does not.

Indeed, so tightly constructed was the rule-governed moral economy of the simple-structure Western, that one good act by a "villain" not only could, but apparently *had to* lead to some modification or transformation of his end. Thus, presence of numerous bad-violent acts (marked) / absence of any good-redeeming act (unmarked) = unrepentant villain: can be shot down, without excuse, in the final episode and makes a brief and "bad" or undistinguished death (provided the hero does not shoot the villain in the back, or unawares, and does not draw first). *But,* presence of bad-violent acts (marked) / presence of single good-redeeming act (marked) = possible salvation or regeneration of the villain, death-bed reconciliation with hero or former cronies, restitution to wronged community, at the very least, lingering and "good" death. What, we may now ask, is the meaning of "violence" when it only appears and signifies anything within the tightly-organized moral economy of the Western?

We have been arguing (a) the violent act or episode in a Western cannot signify in isolation, outside the structured field of meanings which is the film or programme; (b) it signifies only in relation to the other elements, and in terms of the rules and conventions which govern their combination. We must now add (c) that the meaning of such a violent act or episode cannot be fixed, single and unalterable, but must be capable of signifying different values depending on how and with what it is articulated. As the signifying element, among other elements, in a discourse, it remains *polysemic*. Indeed, the way it is structured in its combination with other elements serves to delimit its meanings within that specified field, and effects a "closure," so that a *preferred meaning* is suggested. There can never be only one, single, univocal and determined meaning for such a lexical item, but, depending on how its integration within the code has been accomplished, its possible meanings will be organized within a scale which runs from *dominant* to *subordinate*. And this of course has consequences for the other—the reception—end of the communicative chain: there can be no law to ensure that the receiver will take the preferred or dominant meaning of an episode of violence in precisely the way in which it has been encoded by the producer.

Typically, the isolation of the "violent" elements from the Western by researchers was made on the presumption that all the other elements—setting, action, characters, iconography, movement, conduct and appearance, moral structure, etc.—were present as so many inert supports for the violence: in order to warrant or endorse the violent act. It is now perfectly clear that the violence might be present only in order to warrant or endorse the character. We can thus sketch out more than one possible path of meaning through the way in which the so-called "content" is organized by the codes. Take that ubiquitous semantic item of the simple Western: *hero draws his gun, faster than anyone else (he seems always to have known how), and shoots the villain with bull's-eye aim.* To use Gerbner's term,[8] what norm, proposition or cultural signification is here signified? It is possible to decode this item thus: "The hero figure knows how to draw his gun faster, and shoot better than his enemy: when confronted by the villain, he shoots him dead with a single shot." This might be called a "behavioural" or "instrumental" interpretation. But—research suggests—this directly behavioural "message" has been stylized and conventionalized by the intervention of a highly organized set of codes and *genre*-conventions (a code-of-codes, or meta-code). The intervention of the codes appear to have the effect of neutralizing one set of meanings, while setting another in motion. Or, to put it better, the codes effect a transformation and *displacement* of the same denotative content-unit from one reference-code to another, thereby effecting a transformation in the signification. Berger and Luckmann[9] have argued that "habitualization" or "sedimentation" serves to routinize certain actions or meanings, so as to free the foreground for new, innovative meanings. Turner[10] and others have shown how ritual conventions redistribute the focus of ritual performances from one domain (e.g. the emotional or personal) to another (e.g. the cognitive, cosmological or social) domain. Freud,[11] both in his analysis of ritualization in symptom-formation and in the dream-work, has shown the pivotal position of condensation and displacement in the encoding of latent materials and meanings through manifest symbolizations. Bearing this in mind, we may speculatively formulate an alternative connotative "reading" for the item. "To be a certain kind of man (hero) means the ability to master all contingencies by the demonstration of a practised and professional 'cool.'" This reading transposes the same (denotative) content from its instrumental-behavioural connotative reference to that of decorum, conduct, the idiom and style of (masculine) action. The "message" or the "proposition," now, would be understood, not as a message about "violence" but as a message about conduct, or even about professionalism, or perhaps even about the relation of professionalism to character. And here we recall Robert Warshow's intuitive observation, that, fundamentally, the Western is not "about" violence but about codes of conduct [see Figure 3.2].

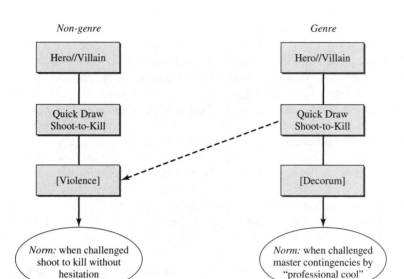

FIGURE 3.2

I have been trying to suggest—without being able to take the example very far—how an attention to the symbolic/linguistic/coded nature of communications, far from boxing us into the closed and formal universe of signs, precisely opens out into the area where cultural content, of the most resonant but "latent" kind, is transmitted: and especially the manner in which the interplay of codes and content serve to displace meanings from one frame to another, and thus to bring to the surface in "disguised" forms the repressed content of a culture. It is worth, in this connection, bearing in mind Eco's observation that[12] "Semiology, shows us the universe of ideologies arranged in codes and sub-codes within the universe of signs." My own view is that, if the insights won by the advances in a semiotic perspective are not to be lost within a new mind of formalism, it is increasingly in this direction that it must be pushed.[13]

Let us turn, now, to a different area of programming, and a different aspect of the operation of codes. The televisual sign is a peculiarly complex one, as we know. It is a visual sign with strong, supplementary aural-verbal support. It is one of the iconic signs, in Peirce's sense, in that, whereas the form of the written sign is arbitrary in relation to its signified, the iconic sign reproduces certain elements of the signified in the form of the signifier. As Feirce says, it "possesses some of the properties of the thing or object represented."[14] Actually, since the iconic sign translates a three dimensional world into two representational planes, its "naturalism" with respect to the referent lies not so much at the encoding side of the chain, but rather in terms of the learned perceptions with which the viewer decodes the sign. Thus, as Eco has convincingly argued, iconic signs "look like objects in the real world," to put it crudely (e.g. the photograph or drawing of a /cow/, and the animal /cow/), because they "reproduce the conditions of perception in the receiver."[15] These conditions of "recognition" in the viewer constitute some of the most fundamental perceptual codes which all culture-members share. However, because these perceptual codes are so widely shared, denotative visual signs probably give rise to less "misunderstandings" than linguistic ones. A lexical inventory of the English language would throw up thousands of words which the ordinary speaker could not denotatively comprehend: but provided enough "information" is given, culture-members would be able or competent to decode, denotatively, a much wider range of visual signifiers. In this sense, and at the denotative level, the visual sign is probably a more universal one than the linguistic sign. Whereas, in societies like ours, linguistic competence is very unequally distributed as between different classes and segments of the population (predominantly, by the family and the education system), what we might call "visual competence," at the denotative level, is more universally diffused. (It is worth reminding ourselves, of course, that it is not, in fact, "universal," and that we are dealing with a spectrum: there are kinds of visual representation, short of the "purely abstract," which create all kinds of visual puzzles for ordinary viewers: e.g. cartoons, certain kinds of diagrammatic representation, representations which employ unfamiliar conventions, types of photographic or cinematic cutting and editing, etc.). It is also true that the iconic sign may support "mis-readings" simply because it is so "natural," so "transparent." Mistakes may arise here, not because we as viewers cannot literally decode the sign (it is perfectly obvious what it is a picture of), but because we are tempted, by its very "naturalisation" to "misread" the image for the thing it signifies.[16] With this important proviso, however, we would be surprised to find that the majority of the television audience had much difficulty in literally or denotatively identifying what the visual signs they see on the screen refer to or signify. Whereas most people require a lengthy process of education in order to become relatively competent users of the language of their speech community, they seem to pick up its visual-perceptual codes at a very early age, without formal training, and are quickly competent in its use.

The visual sign is, however, also a connotative sign. And it is so pre-eminently within the discourses of modern mass communication. The level of connotation of the visual sign, of its contextual reference, of its position in the various associative fields of meanings, is precisely the point where the denoted sign intersects with the deep semantic structures of a culture, and takes on an ideological dimension. In the advertising discourse, for example, we might say that there is almost no "purely denotative" communication. Every visual sign in advertising "connotes" a quality, situation, value or inference which is present as an implication or implied meaning, depending on the connotational reference. We are all probably familiar with Barthes' example of the /sweater/, which, in the rhetoric of advertising and fashion, always connotes, at least, "a warm garment" or "keeping warm," and thus by further elaboration, "the coming of winter" or "a cold day." In the specialized sub-codes of fashion, /sweater/ may connote "a fashionable style of *haute couture*," or, alternatively, "an informal style of dress." But, set against the right background, and positioned in the romantic sub-code, it may connote "long autumn walk in the woods."[17] Connotational codes of this order are, clearly, structured enough to signify, but they are more "open" or "open-ended" than denotative codes. What is more, they clearly contract relations with the universe of ideologies in a culture, and with history and ethnography. These connotative codes are the "linguistic" means by which the domains of social life, the segmentations of culture, power and ideology are made to signify. They refer to the "maps of meaning" into which any culture is organized, and those "maps of social reality" have the whole range of social meanings, practices and usages, power and interest "written in" to them. Connoted signifiers, Barthes has reminded us, "have a close communication with culture, knowledge, history, and it is through them, so to speak, that the environmental world invades the linguistic and semantic system. They are, if you like, the fragments of ideology."[18]

The denotative level of the televisual sign may be bounded within certain, very complex but limited or "closed" codes. But its connotative level, though bounded, remains open, subject to the formation, transformation and decay of history, and fundamentally polysemic: any such sign is potentially mappable into more than one connotative configuration. "Polysemy" must not, however, be confused with pluralism. Connotative codes are not equal among themselves. Any society/culture tends, with varying degrees of closure, to impose its segmentations, its classifications of the social and cultural and political world, upon its members. There remains a *dominant cultural order,* though it is neither univocal nor uncontested. This question of the "structure of dominance" in a culture is an absolutely crucial point. We may say, then, that the different areas of social life appear to be mapped out into connotative domains of *dominant or preferred meanings.* New, problematic or troubling things and events, which breach our expectancies and run counter to our "common-sense constructs," to our "taken-for-granted" knowledge of social structures, must be assigned to their connotational domains before they can be said to "make sense": and the most common way of "mapping them" is to assign the new within some domain or other of the existing "maps of problematic social reality." We say *dominant,* not "determined," because it is always possible to order, classify, assign and decode an event within more than one "mapping." But we say "dominant" because there exists a pattern of "preferred readings," and these mappings both have the institutional/political/ideological order imprinted in them, and have themselves become institutionalized.[19] The domains of "preferred mappings" have the whole social order embedded in them as a set of meanings: practices and beliefs, the everyday knowledge of social structures, of "how things work for all practical purposes in this culture," the rank order of power and interest, and a structure of legitimations and sanctions. Thus, to clarify a "misunderstanding" at the denotative level, we need primarily to refer to the immanent world of the sign and its codes. But to clarify and resolve "misunderstandings" at the level of connotation, we must refer, *through* the codes, to the rules of social life, of history and life-situation, of economic and political power, and, ultimately, of ideology. Further, since these connotational mappings are "structured in dominance" but not closed, the communicative process consists, not in the unproblematic assignment of every visual item to its position within a set of prearranged codes, but of *performative rules*—rules of competence and use, of logics-in-use—which seek to *enforce* or *pre-fer* one semantic domain over another, and rule items into and out of their appropriate meaning-sets. Formal semiology has too often neglected this level of *interpretive work,* though this forms in fact the deep-structure of a great deal of broadcast time in television, especially in the political and other "sensitive areas" of programming. In speaking of *dominant meanings,* then, we are not simply talking about a one-sided process, which governs how any event will be signified (we might think, for example, of the recent *coup* in Chile): it also consists of the "work" required to enforce, with plausibility for and command as legitimate a *de-coding* of the event within the dominant definition in which it has been connotatively signified. Dr. Terni remarked, in his paper[20] that, "By the word *reading* we mean not only the capacity to identify and decode a certain number of signs, but also the subjective capacity to put them into a creative relation between themselves and with other signs: a capacity which is, by itself, the condition for a complete awareness of one's total environment." Our only quarrel here is with the notion of "subjective capacity," as if the denotative reference of the televisual sign is an objective process, but the connotational and connective level is an individualized and private matter. Quite the opposite seems to us to be the case. The televisual process takes "objective" (i.e. systemic) responsibility precisely for the relations which disparate signs contract with one another, and thus continually delimits and prescribes into what "awareness of ones total environment" these items are arranged.

This brings us, then, to the key question of "misunderstandings" between the encoders and decoders of the television message: and thus, by a long but necessary detour, to the matter of "cultural policies" designed to "facilitate better communication," to "make communication more effective." Television producers or "encoders," who find their message failing to "get across" are frequently concerned to straighten out the kinks in the communicative chain, and thus to facilitate the "effectiveness" of their messages. A great deal of research has been devoted to trying to discover how much of the message the audience retains or recalls. At the denotative level (if we can make the analytic distinction for the moment), there is no doubt that some "misunderstandings" exist, though we have no real idea how widespread this is. And we can see possible explanations for it. The viewer does not "speak the language," figuratively if not literally: he or she cannot follow the complex logic of argument or exposition: or the concepts are too alien: or the editing (which arranges items within an expository logic or "narrative," and thus in itself proposes connections between discrete things) is too swift, truncated, sophisticated; etc. At another level, encoders also mean that their audience has "made sense" of the message in a way different from that intended. What they really mean is that viewers are not operating within the dominant or preferred code. The ideal is the perfectly transparent communication. Instead, what they have to confront is the fact of "systematically distorted communication."

In recent years, discrepancies of this kind are usually accounted for in terms of individually "aberrant" readings, attributed to "selective perception." "Selective perception" is the door via which, in recent research, a residual pluralism is reserved within the sphere of a highly structured, a-symmetrical cultural operation. Of course, there will always be individual, private, variant readings. But my own tentative view is that "selective perception" is almost never as selective, random, or privatized, as the concept suggests. The patterns exhibit more structuring and clustering than is normally assumed. Any new approach to audience studies, via the concept of "de-coding" would have to begin with a critique of "selective perception" theory.

Eco has recently pointed to another, intermediary, level of structuration, between competence in the dominant code, and "aberrant" individual readings: that level provided by sub-cultural formations. But, since sub-cultures are, by definition, differentiated articulations within a culture, it is more useful to specify this mediation within a somewhat different framework.[21]

The very general typology sketched below is an attempt to reinterpret the notion of "misunderstandings" (which we find inadequate) in terms of certain broadly-defined societal perspectives which audiences might adopt towards the televisual message. It attempts to apply Gramsci's work on "hegemonic" and "corporate" ideological formations[22] and Parkin's recent work on types of meaning systems. I should like now (adapting Parkin's schema) to put into discussion four "ideal-type" positions from which decodings of mass communications by the audience can be made: and thus to re-present the common-sense notion of "misunderstandings" in terms of a theory of "systematically distorted communication."[23]

Literal or denotative "errors" are relatively unproblematic. They represent a kind of noise in the channel. But "misreadings" of a message at the connotative or contextual level are a different matter. They have, fundamentally, a societal, not a communicative, basis.

They signify, at the "message" level the structural conflicts, contradictions and negotiations of economic, political and cultural life. The first position we want to identify is that of the *dominant or hegemonic code*. (There are, of course, many different codes and subcodes required to produce an event within the dominant code.) When the viewer takes the connoted meaning from, say, a television newscast or current affairs programme, full and straight, and decodes the message in terms of the reference-code in which it has been coded, we might say that the viewer is operating inside the dominant code. This is the ideal-typical case of "perfectly transparent communication," or as close as we are likely to come to it "for all practical purposes." Next (here we are amplifying Parkin's model), we would want to identify the *professional code*. This is the code (or set of codes, for we are here dealing with what might be better called meta-codes) which the professional broadcasters employ when transmitting a message which has already been signified in a hegemonic manner. The professional code is "relatively independent" of the dominant code, in that it applies criteria and operations of its own, especially those of a technico-practical nature. The professional code, however, operates within the "hegemony" of the dominant code. Indeed, it serves to reproduce the dominant definitions precisely by bracketing the hegemonic quality, and operating with professional codings which relate to such questions as visual quality, news and presentational values, televisual quality, "professionalism," etc. The hegemonic interpretation of the politics of Northern Ireland, or the Chilean *coup* or the Industrial Relations Bill are given by political elites: the particular choice of presentational occasions and formats, the selection of personnel, the choice of images, the "staging" of debates, etc. are selected by the operation of the professional code.[24] How the broadcasting professionals are able both to operate with "relatively autonomous" codes of their own, while acting in such a way as to reproduce (not without contradiction) the hegemonic signification of events is a complex matter which cannot be further spelled out here. It must suffice to say that the professionals are linked with the defining elites not only by the institutional position of broadcasting itself as an "ideological apparatus,"[25] but more intimately by the structure of *access* (i.e. the systematic "over-accessing" of elite personnel and "definitions of the situation" in television). It may even be said that the professional codes serve to reproduce hegemonic definitions specifically by not overtly biassing their operations in their direction: ideological reproduction therefore takes place here inadvertently, unconsciously, "behind men's backs." Of course, conflicts, contradictions and even "misunderstandings" regularly take place between the dominant and the professional significations and their signifying agencies. The third position we would identify is that of the *negotiated code* or position. Majority audiences probably understand quite adequately what has been dominantly defined and professionally signified. The dominant definitions, however, are hegemonic precisely because they represent definitions of situations and events which are "in dominance," and which are *global*. Dominant definitions connect events, implicitly or explicitly, to grand totalizations, to the great syntagmatic views-of-the-world: they take "large views" of issues: they relate events to "the national interest" or to the level of geo-politics, even if they make these connections in truncated, inverted or mystified ways. The definition of a "hegemonic" viewpoint is (a) that it defines within its terms the mental horizon, the universe of possible meanings of a whole society or culture; and (b) that it carries with it the stamp of legitimacy—it appears coterminous with what is "natural," "inevitable," "taken for granted" about the social order. Decoding within the *negotiated version* contains a mixture of adaptive and oppositional elements: it acknowledges the legitimacy of the hegemonic definitions to make the grand significations, while, at a more restricted, situational level, it makes its own ground-rules, it operates with "exceptions" to the rule. It accords the priveleged position to the dominant definition of events, whilst reserving the right to make a more negotiated application to "local conditions," to its own more *corporate* positions. This negotiated version of the dominant ideology is thus shot through with contradictions, though these are only on certain occasions brought to full visibility. Negotiated codes operate through what we might call particular or situated logics: and these logics arise from the differential position of those who occupy this position in the spectrum, and from their differential and unequal relation to power. The simplest example of a negotiated code is that which governs the response of a worker to the notion of an Industrial Relations Bill limiting the right to strike, or to arguments for a wages-freeze. At the level of the national-interest economic debate, he may adopt the hegemonic definition, agreeing that "we must all pay ourselves less in order to combat inflation," etc. This, however, may have little or no relation to his willingness to go on strike for better pay and conditions, or to oppose the Industrial Relations Bill at the level of his shop-floor or union organization. We suspect that the great majority of so-called "misunderstandings" arise from the disjunctures between hegemonic-dominant encodings and negotiated-corporate decodings. It is just these mis-matches in the levels which most provoke defining elites and professionals to identify a "failure in communications." Finally, it is possible for a viewer perfectly to understand both the literal and connotative inflection given to an event, but to determine to decode the message in a globally contrary way. He detotalizes the message in the preferred code in order to retotalize the message within some alternative framework of reference. This is the case of the viewer who listens to a debate on the need to limit wages, but who "reads" ever mention of "the national interest" as "class interest." He is operating with what we must call an *oppositional code*. One of the most significant political moments (they also coincide with crisis-points within the broadcasting organizations themselves for obvious reasons) is the point when events which are normally signified and decoded in a negotiated way begin to be given an oppositional reading.

The question of cultural policies now falls, awkwardly, into place. When dealing with social communications, it is extremely difficult to identify as a neutral, educational goal, the task of "improving communications" or of "making communications more effective," at any rate once one has passed beyond the strictly denotative level of the message. The educator or cultural policy-maker is performing one of his most partisan acts when he colludes with the re-signification of real conflicts and contradictions as if they were simply Kinks in the communicative chain. Denotative mistakes are not structurally significant. But connotative and contextual "misunderstandings" are, or can be, of the highest significance. To interpret what are in fact essential elements in the systematic distortions of a socio-communications system as if they are technical faults in transmission is to misread a deep-structure process for a surface phenomenon. The decision to intervene in order to make the hegemonic codes of dominant elites more effective and transparent for the majority audience is not a technically neutral, but a political one. To "misread" a political choice as a technical one represents a type of unconscious collusion with the dominant interests, a form of collusion to which social science researchers are all too prone. Though the sources of such mystification are both social and structural, the actual process is greatly facilitated by the operation of discrepant codes. It would not be the first time

that scientific researchers had "unconsciously" played a part in the reproduction of hegemony, not by openly submitting to it, but simply by operating the "professional bracket."

NOTES

1. Umberto Eco, "Does the Public Harm Television?" Cyclostyled paper for Italia Prize Seminar, Venice (1973).
2. Cf: Dell Hymes' critique of transformational approaches to language, via concepts of "performance" and "competence" in "On Communicative Competence." In *Sociolinguistics,* ed. Pride & Holmes. Penguin Education (1972).
3. J. D. Halloran, "Understanding Television." Paper for Council of Europe Colloquy, Leicester (1973).
4. Halloran, ibid.
5. Gerbner, et al., *Violence in TV Drama: A Study of Trends & Symbolic Functions.* Annenberg School, Univ. of Pennsylvania (1970).
6. This example is more fully discussed in Part II, "New Approaches to Content," *Violence in the TV Drama-Series.* CCS Report to Home Office Inquiry into TV/Violence, Centre for Mass Comm./Research. Shuttleworth, Carmargo, Lloyd and Hall. Birmingham University (forthcoming).
7. O. Burgelin, "Structural Analaysis & Mass Communications." *Studies in Broadcasting, No. 6.* Nippon Hoso Kyokai (1968).
8. For "proposition-analysis," see Gerbner, "Ideological Perspectives & Political Tendencies in News Reporting," *Jounalism Quarterly* 41 (1964) and E. Sullerot, "Use Etude De Presse . . ." Temps Modernes vol. XX No. 226 (1965). For "norm-analysis," Cf: Gerbner, in *Violence & The Mass Media,* Task Force Report to Eisenhower Commission on Causes & Prevention of Violence, US Printing Office (1969).
9. Berger & Luckmann, *Social Construction of Reality.* Penguin (1971).
10. V. W. Turner, *The Ritual Process.* Routledge & Kegan Paul (1969).
11. Especially in *Interpretation of Dreams.*
12. U. Eco, "Articulations of Cinematic Code," *Cinemantics* 1.
13. Cf: developments of this argument in S. Hall, "Determinations of The News Photograph," *WPCS 3* (CCCS, 1972), and "Open & Closed Uses of Structuralism" (stencilled: CCCS, 1973).
14. C. S. Peirce, *Speculative Grammar.*
15. Eco, op. cit.
16. Cf: S. Hall, "Determinations . . .", op. cit.
17. R. Barthes, "Rhetoric of The Image," in *WPCS 1.* CCCS, B'ham (1971).
18. R. Barthes, *Elements of Semiology.* Cape (1967).
19. Cf: the section on "Codes of Connotation," in S. Hall, op. cit., and more generally, in "Deviance, Politics & The Media," in *Social Control Deviance & Dissent,* ed. McIntosh & Roch. Tavistock (forthcoming).
20. P. Terni, *Memorandum.* Council of Europe Colloquy, Leicester (1973).
21. Eco, "Does The Public Harm Television?" op. cit.
22. Antonio Gramsci, *Selections from Prison Notebooks.* Lawrence & Wishart (1971): F. Parkin, *Class Inequality & Political Order.* McGibbon & Kee (1971).
23. Cf: J. Habermas, "Systematically Distorted Communications." In *Recent Sociology* 2, ed. P. Dretzel. Collier-McMillan (1970).
24. Cf: S. Hall, "External/Internal Dialectic in Broadcasting." In *Fourth Symposium on Broadcasting.* Dept. of Extra Mural Studies, University of Manchester (1972).
25. Cf: L. Althusser, "Ideological State Apparatuses." In *Lenin & Philosophy and Other Essays,* New Left Books (1971).

4

TELEVISION AND
BLACK CONSCIOUSNESS

Molefi Kete Asante
(Arthur L. Smith)

Patterns of messages galvanized the nation in the 1960s and speeded recognition of TV's role as an institution of political education.

Television is a political instrument in the sense that it creates its own territory and its own audiences. Probably at no other time in the history of the communication of ideas did a cause and instrument rally to one another with so much vigor as did the nascent black movement and television in the 1960s (1, p. xii). For television, the black movement could produce a massive demonstration of singing, chanting blacks, frequently attacked by fierce-looking state troopers and policemen. For blacks, television could cover the grievances and abuses of the black masses and send them nationwide, perhaps worldwide. Thus, it helped fan the fires of black discontent by discovering militant black audiences which grew out of a collective will to redress the grievances of the black masses (5, p. 115). Television uncovered the presence of bitterness in the black community and the distaste for marchers and demonstrators in some white communities.

Martin Luther King exercised significant intellectual and moral control over the direction of the early civil rights movement (4, p. vii). In fact, King was the chief reason for television's fascination with the substance of the movement. He was eloquent, capable of high moral pronouncements and dramatic persuasive appeals, and thus became a critical rhetorical figure in television's discourse. In addition, his conception of television had a profound effect on the course of racial history in America. As the first black leader to galvanize thousands with his own rhetoric during television's maturity, his judgment of television's importance for the movement was crucial to black consciousness. No other leader of the black masses before him, e.g., Douglass, Washington, Garvey, Randolph, had such a powerful instrument at his disposal. In effect, King, like John Kennedy and the Vietnam War, was intricately bound to the emergence of television.

Given King's faith in America's inherent moral and spiritual qualities, it is rather easy to understand how his philosophy of television developed from his moral perspective. He argued that laws were just or unjust and, if just, a man had a moral right to obey the law; on the other hand, if the law were unjust, a man had a moral right to disobey the law (2). Segregationist laws

Reprinted from Molefi Kete Asante, "Television and Black Consciousness," *Communication* 26, no. 4 (Autumn 1976): 137–141.

were unjust and thus a person could disobey them as long as he accepted the penalty. Furthermore, all demonstrations were to be non-violent in order to keep morality and dignity on the side of the demonstrators. Persons unable to abide by the strict discipline of the non-violent marchers were not permitted to join the group. These were, in effect, soldiers with only one weapon—King's redemptive love. Television found this confrontation with guns, whips, and electric cattle prods on one side and love and non-violence on the other as the classic drama of black and white, good and evil. By structuring the discourse around traditional dichotomies, television was able to present instantaneous conflict and, there fore, interest.

King's view was based upon two assumptions. First, if the demonstrators were attacked by police and hecklers the nation would be repulsed by the cruelty received by the peaceful marchers. Secondly, he thought that policemen and hecklers who observed their violent behavior toward peaceful demonstrators would, in a moment of reflection, be ashamed (6, p. 148).

Both of these expectations were based upon a particular view toward the power and uses of television. The initial reaction to the violence was often disbelief. Viewers wondered how white people could be so violent and black people so non-violent (7, p. 3). Soon restatement become overkill: viewers became bored with so many demonstrations and so much brutality. As the mass of white viewers turned away from the endless demonstrations, blacks became increasingly politicized. Caught up in the vicarious sufferings of their fellow blacks, the black viewers were radically transformed.

With this background we can now turn to the messages received in an effort to determine the kinds of situations created by the televised images. Several attitudinal clusters contributing to black consciousness are identifiable around televised messages received. Although these clusters fall into recognizable patterns around television messages, they pre-date television in the American value context. The major clusters are (1) *prudence and conscience,* (2) *property rights and human rights,* (3) *public and private interest,* and (4) *separation and integration.* What televised messages created these areas of concern? If we look at the cluster referred to as prudence and conscience (or one might prefer prudence versus *moral* conscience) we see how televised messages received were organized as clusters which influenced black action during the height of the civil rights movement.

With the rise of street demonstrations, boycotts, pray-ins, sit-ins, bombings, political murders, and violent rebellions, television clearly put to the public the question "Where do you stand?" To amplify, television, like radio, is a non-discriminatory mass instrument. In print jounalism, the audiences must know how to read; in radio, audiences must be able to imagine; but in television, audiences do not have to be able to read or to imagine to understand its message and in this respect its politicalization potential is greatly increased. Thus, when black Americans saw the demonstrations the question that came to most was "And what dues have I paid while my brother had his brains knocked out?" To say the least, this was a hard question because prudence sometimes instructed one way and moral conscience another.

But it was television that brought this issue into every black person's home. Historically, blacks had demonstrated, protested, and even rebelled before; but what was different was the fact that the black in California or New York could see and sympathize with the black in Georgia. Black Republicans and Democrats, Methodists, Catholics, Episcopalians, and Baptists marched together singing "We shall overcome some day." And prudence increasingly gave way to the burden of conscience as hundreds of thousands of blacks, politicized via the television demonstration, became participants in the movement.

As prudence and conscience occupy one cluster of messages received, so property rights and human rights form another. The message content of television during the insurrections of the 1960s was frequently of a confrontation between property rights and human rights. Whether it was over privileges of eating at restaurants, walking in parks, or finding lodging, the major conflict was over black human rights and white property rights. By virtue of its power, one group dominated the property; the other group, because of its relative powerlessness, could only appeal to basic human rights. What television made clear to the black community was the extent to which some people would go to protect property. When blacks saw that human life took second place to property in the communities of the South, fundamental political awareness had arrived.

What television did for many humanitarian and relatively religious black people was to shatter their dreams of a humane society. The nation's last massive group of dreamers awakened to a nightmare of reality when people were dragged from lunch counters to "protect business" and others had their houses bombed because their occupancy threatened property values (3). Television once again had created and vigorously, night after night, sustained this attitudinal cluster.

A third cluster around messages received is the concern with private versus public interest. Immediately before the black rebellion of the sixties, a strong anticipation existed that equal rights would serve the public interest. However, the daily fare of television cameras zooming in on whites defending restaurants, clubs, and hotels sent a clear message: private interest is considered a higher good than public interest when it comes to human rights. And if this was not the case with the majority, it frequently appeared so. A society whose highway messages urged motorists to drive safely, not out of public concern but because "the life you save may be your own," was unwilling to substitute public interests for private concerns. What blacks had seen on television was the defeat of rhetoric and the capture of irony as well. Private interest remained king and lesser interests paid the necessary homage.

The fourth cluster is separation and integration, the fundamental choices for black Americans. Manifestations may take several directions but the initial choices are limited. Television had tended to present the alternatives in the form of human drama. Lessons learned from the conflicts and controversies of demonstrations have served as catalytic agents for an awakening rhetoric. Separation or integration were the choices bluntly put to the viewing public. Such hard choices, augmented by recrudescing attacks upon demonstrators attempting to eat sandwiches, became increasingly clarified. In addition to television's intensification of the choices was the generative expanding geographics of the situations created by the messages received. Thus, when share-croppers in Georgia, exhausted and angry, sat before the television and saw blacks beaten in Chattanooga, hosed in Birmingham, and electrified with cattle prods in New Orleans, they entered the fields with a new reality the next morning. Blacks in the North experienced the same changes in purposes when they went to the Ford Plant or simply walked 125th Street the next day. These Northern blacks, especially those who had never been in the South, could hardly believe the manifestations of violence and cruelty perpetrated by whites in the sixties. It was useless to speak of history.

Television is a major partner in the transmission of principal symbols that are unrepresentative of the multi-ethnic composition of the society. In recent years, commercial television has tried to correct the flaws present in earlier programming by including various black leading figures in the regular run of good versus evil dramas, soap operas, and fantasies. While this effort has helped to alleviate some of the racism transmitted through electronic media, it has not been totally successful because the rhetoric of television, like all rhetorics, is dependent upon the audiences. What the Nielsen ratings have demonstrated in the past is that the American public is not to be led too swiftly down the road to human justice and dignity. Thus, television has barely touched its potential in combating the insidious ethnocentricity which is at the heart of the American conundrum.

From the inception of this nation, and possibly before, the circumstances, beliefs, and values that would shape the contemporary society were at work. Conceived as a homogeneous society, yet emerging as a heterogeneous society, the country experienced numerous contradictions in its symbology. But because television had, during the 1960s, educated large portions of the black community in the knowledge of general violence against blacks, it became the primary medium through which black leaders could politicize the black masses. One "Black is Beautiful" by Stokeley Carmichael carried live and in color on national television could do more to alert the black community to self-dignity and pride than a decade of NAACP legal battles.

Turning to the future of television's role in creating consciousness, it is clear that electronic media, with all of their contradictory assumptions, will develop as basic instruments in national socialization. But because television, like the educational system, is an institution, its rhetoric will reflect the mores and values inherent in securing the traditional. Television operates within the same restraining environment as politicians who seek to be successful. To say or do the racial, however valuable as political rhetoric, is to become suspect and dangerous.

This is to say that revolutionary rhetoric will neither hold the novelty for television nor gain the prominence it did in the 1960s. What has emerged from the pattern of starts and stops of a few years ago is largely the acceptance of television as an institution comparable to public education, the church, and the judicial system.

After the conflagrations carried out by black communities in over one hundred and fifty places during the sixties, the Kerner Commission reported that television could, in effect, be incendiary. The immediate impact was a decline in coverage of the black movement. But among the achievements of television was the production of a black population more bent on absolute political and social liberty than ever before.

REFERENCES

1. Bagdikian, Ben H. *The Information Machines: Their Impact on Men and the Media*. New York: Harper and Row, 1971.
2. Bosmajion, Haig. "Rhetoric of Martin Luther King's Letter from a Birmingham Jail." *Midwest Quarterly,* January 1967, pp. 127–43.
3. Cleghorn, Reese. "Martin Luther King, Jr.: Apostle of Crises." *Saturday Evening Post,* June 15, 1963, p. 17.
4. Lincoln, C. Eric. *Martin Luther King, Jr.* New York: Hill and Wang, 1970.
5. Lomax, Louis. *To Kill a Black Man.* Los Angeles: Holloway House, 1968.
6. Meier, August. "The Conservative Militant." In C. Eric Lincoln (Ed.) *Martin Luther King, Jr.* New York: Hill and Wang, 1970.
7. Smith, Arthur L. "Television and the Black Revolution." In D. Parson and W. Linkugel (Eds.) *Television and the New Persuasion*. Lawrence, Kan.: Usher, 1972, p. 3.

5

TELEVISION AND THE
BLACK AUDIENCE
Cultivating Moderate Perspectives on Racial Integration

Paula W. Matabane

Television's influence seems "most evident in isolating pockets of black dissidence among young and better-educated Afro-Americans" and may conceal existing inequalities and injustices in the relations between blacks and whites.

Cultivation research has explored the possible influence of television on viewers' conceptions of a variety of social and political topics (e.g., 11, 16, 17, 24). According to this perspective, television brings to an otherwise heterogeneous audience a single set of values and social descriptions produced to the specifications of the owners of the broadcast industry and their advertising sponsors. One countervailing force for various ethnic and racial groups is their own experience and their desire to maintain their cultural identity in the face of economic, political, and cultural pressures. As the largest and most politically active minority racial group in the United States, Afro-Americans are a critical audience to examine in evaluating how television viewing may shape social perceptions.

Television has provided a conduit for the easy distribution of dominant values and images to groups who in the past were relatively isolated from direct exposure to mainstream ideas and concepts. A white minister of evangelical conservatism who might never be tolerated in the pulpit of a black church can be seriously listened to and even financially supported by members of a black church if he appears on television. Black viewers also consume steady diets of all-white prime-time fiction. According to Nielsen's Television Index (January–February 1987), two all-white comedies set in upscale settings, *Family Ties* and *The Golden Girls,* ranked number two and four, respectively, among black viewers. In both cases, black viewership of these programs exceeded that of white viewers in ratings and shares. Afro-Americans have traditionally reinterpreted (though not necessarily rejected) mainstream beliefs and images, but television viewing directly exposes them to these mainstream values without reflecting their own social experiences and expectations. Black viewers are heavy consumers of all television, including fictional black characters scripted by the white upper stratum. The entire spectrum of black life and racial relations on television is dominated by the same ideological perspectives.

Does television's view of black life influence or contribute to what blacks believe about themselves in society in spite of their own experiences in the real world? This study

Reprinted from Paula W. Matabane, "Television and the Black Audience: Cultivating Moderate Perspectives on Racial Integration," *Journal of Communication* 38, no. 4 (Autumn 1988): 21–31.

looked at the contribution that viewing commercial television fiction may make to black viewers' perceptions of racial integration, which has been a concern central to three decades of mass black political activity. We also examined the role of television in the formation of a new consensus on racial integration among Afro-Americans.

Television fiction establishes the social value of an integrated setting while omitting the social negatives that many blacks may experience in real-life all-white circumstances. A review of content analyses of fictional black television characters suggests that they make the following explicit statements about black social reality: Black characters tend to be cast either in all-black settings or as lone black persons in an otherwise all-white setting (3). Black settings tend to be low income, with few socially productive persons concerned about social problems; blacks in white settings tend to be upscale and productive (2). Black English is generally used by low-income characters in all-black settings (6). Racism is rarely discussed or portrayed (3).

When this study was conducted in late 1984, twelve fictional programs (excluding soap operas or movies) starring or costarring black characters were available on the over-the-air commercial stations to the local viewing audience in Washington, D.C. The three programs set in all-black neighborhoods portrayed low-income characters; the other nine programs had integrated and economically upscale settings. Since white settings are consistently represented as upscale and hence preferred (3), viewers who preferred black character programs would nonetheless primarily be exposed to racial values similar to those encountered by viewers of programs where black persons are seldom or never seen. This consistent and repetitive representation of race and social class across most television content may teach black viewers dominant values about the prevalence of racial integration. As Morgan (15) observed, heavy television viewing was associated with a reduction in variance in racial attitudes across regions in the United States. And Gerbner et al. (10) observed a more racially conservative attitude among heavy viewers.

Because the amount of exposure to television is an important predictor of what viewers believe about real-world social relations (e.g., 8, 9, 10, 11), we expected heavy television viewers to report higher estimations of the prevalence of racial integration than light viewers. Although across-the-board contributions might logically be expected in all cases, we suspected that the degree of influence would vary based on differing social experience. We expected that television would contribute more to the thinking of groups with relatively more "extreme" attitudes toward racial integration than to those groups with more moderate views. This "mainstreaming" process would lead to an overall moderation of beliefs among heavy viewers regardless of previous social experience.

An ongoing debate in the interpretation of cultivation research has centered on whether observed relationships are a function of social experience (4, 12, 13, 15). Potter (18) has concluded that the cultivation of beliefs by television is highly contingent upon viewers' preexisting attitudes and beliefs, but he did not reject the cultivation hypothesis. His research and that of others suggests the need to further refine the specification of important social experiences. In their refinement of the mainstreaming model, Gerbner et al. (10) looked at relatively homogeneous subgroups in order to isolate the influence of television from other factors. They argued that political distinctions and working class consciousness become blurred among heavy television viewers.

In order to specify television's contribution to black viewers' perceptions of racial integration, we included some social experiences that are theoretically important in the socialization of Afro-Americans. These factors included age (as a reflection of different racial experiences), religious participation, community participation, and subjective social class, as well as gender, education, and home ownership. Allen and Bielby (1) suggest that those experiences that shape black people's racial and self-perceptions are significant in their relationship to television. They observed that alienation from the dominant society produced the single largest effect on perceptions of television bias among black viewers. Tan and Vaughn (23) found an inverse relationship between support for black nationalism and use of the mass media.

Our main hypothesis was that differences in social perceptions of racial integration among light television viewers will be diminished or absent for heavy television viewers. Data were obtained by a telephone survey of 161 adult Afro-Americans in Washington, D.C., conducted between October 1, 1984 and November 7, 1984. Interviews were conducted by seven trained interviewers in four census tracts (neighborhoods), selected on the basis of income and racial composition, that ranged from 20 percent to 90 percent black. The first available adult per household was interviewed. Telephone numbers were obtained from the reverse street directory and randomly assigned a calling order. The response rate was 22 percent. This included disconnects and non-sample households, which were highest in the predominantly white neighborhoods. Out of 726 calls made, there were only 91 outright refusals.

One result of the low response rate was that the distribution of the obtained sample's socioeconomic characteristics was skewed somewhat higher than that of the total black population of Washington, D.C. This was particularly true of education, income, and home ownership. Nearly half of the sample were home owners. The mean income was $25,000 per year. The mean level of education was 14 years, with professionals comprising 39 percent of the respondents. About 65 percent of the sample was female. Thirty-five percent was between 38 and 57, and 25 percent was between 18 and 37. Almost 70 percent of the sample lived in a predominantly black neighborhood. The low number of respondents obtained from white neighborhoods made it impossible to test the variable of race of neighborhood.

Television viewing was measured as viewers' estimation of "about how many hours did you spend viewing television yesterday." Based on their responses, categories of heavy, medium, and light viewing were constructed to maximize as well as equalize cell size. Approximately 20 percent of the sample fell into the medium category, while 40 percent each were in the light and heavy categories.

Respondents used a ten-point scale to evaluate four items about racial integration in Washington, D.C., which were developed from a pretest and evaluated for content validity by five communication experts. These were: "Blacks can easily fit into an all-white setting"; "Blacks are generally no different from whites in the way they act, dress, or socialize"; "Most blacks have achieved middle-class status"; and "Blacks and whites frequently socialize together." Higher scores indicated a higher estimation of the prevalence of integration. Raw scores from the four items were averaged (alpha = .68) to form a single integration index score for each respondent. In a factor analysis using only the principal rotation, the above four items loaded significantly on one factor (.57, .63, .51, and .67) whose eigenvalue was 1.43. These results suggest that the index constituted one underlying dimension, which we called racial integration.

Cross-tabular analysis and one-way analysis of variance (using the Scheffe a posteriori contrast test) were used to test the significance of differences in the percentage of light and heavy viewers whose answers reflected the "television" perspective on racial integration and the significance of differences between light and heavy viewers' mean scores on perceptions of racial integration. The "television" perspective, for this study, was defined as a score above 5 in one's estimation of racial integration on the individual statements and/or the index. We controlled for social and cultural experiences: age, length of neighborhood residency, community participation,[1] membership in a black church denomination,[2] church going, sex, education, income, home ownership, and subjective social class. Findings for the four individual statements are presented in Table 5.1 (some variables were dropped from the analysis due to small cell size); findings for the racial integration index are shown in Table 5.2.

Overall, the data support the cultivation thesis: heavy television viewers more frequently perceived that racial integration is more prevalent, that blacks and whites were more similar, and that more blacks were middle-class. As shown in Tables 5.1 and 5.2, in many cases the differences between light and heavy viewers, as defined by the cultivation differential (CD), are significant. Television seems to be a more important factor in the construction of racial integration perceptions for young respondents, high-income respondents, women, churchgoers, those with low community participation, and those with medium length of residency in one neighborhood.

We predicted that television would be more important among those groups with relatively more "extreme" attitudes. In general, we find that prediction supported by the findings. Although we were surprised, for example, that fewer female light viewers reported the "TV answer" than males, the greater cultivation differential among women than men is consistent with our expectations. Churchgoers and those with a high income have different opportunities for obtaining information independently than those isolated from community participation. Yet, we observe a consistent influence of television among all these groups in the direction of a more mainstream perception of racial integration.

The one group that significantly reports beliefs contrary to our general expectations is the over-57 age group. Heavy viewers in that category report the "television response" less often than light viewers for three out of four questions, and the percent of older heavy viewers overestimating blacks as middle class is significantly lower than the percent of light viewers making that same estimation among older respondents.

Table 5.3 looks at the cultivation process from the perspective of differences in mean scores between light and heavy viewers. The findings show striking across-the-board differences, in many cases statistically significant. Respondents' mean scores, overall, are skewed toward the lower end of the scale even among heavy viewers, indicating lower estimations of racial integration in Washington, D.C. It may be that the predominantly black racial makeup of the city, along with its highly segregated residential patterns (within the city and its suburbs) and strong black political movements (both mainstream and nationalist) contribute to a generally more conservative perception of black integration into the white mainstream.

But the cohorts differ in their perceptions of racial integration based on their amount of television viewing. Again, age was significant. The only light viewers who reported a mean score above 5 (the mid-point on the integration rating scale) were respondents over age 57, for whom amount of television viewing seems to be an inconsequential factor in the formation of some of their racial beliefs. The relationship between beliefs and television viewing is most evident among respondents between 18 and 37 years of age.

TABLE 5.1 Relationship Between Amount of Viewing and Four Beliefs About Racial Integration

	% Saying Blacks Fit In			% Agreeing Blacks and Whites Are Similar			% Over-estimating Black Middle Class			% Agreeing Blacks and Whites Socialize		
	%L	CD	tau[a]	%L	CD	tau[a]	%L	CD	tau[a]	%L	CD	tau[a]
TV viewing overall	21.2	+18.3	17*	25.0	+22.4	24***	32.7	+14.7	14	21.2	+13.0	12
Controlling for:												
Age												
18–37	3.7	+39.2	37*	11.1	+17.5	27*	18.5	+31.5	26*	7.4	+21.2	19*
38–57	28.6	−16.1	−19	35.7	+1.8	03	35.7	+39.3	33*	21.4	+28.6	21
Over 57	54.5	−4.5	−04	45.5	+23.3	21	63.6	−32.3	−33*	54.5	−23.2	23
Education												
No college	25.0	+15.0	14	18.8	+33.2	28*	50.0	+6.0	05	25.0	+7.0	06
College or more	19.4	+19.1	14	27.8	+10.7	20	25.0	+5.8	06	19.4	+19.1	12
Income												
Less than $25,000	33.3	+2.4	02	25.0	+25.0	22*	37.5	+5.4	05	25.0	+10.7	10
$25,000 or more	10.7	+39.3	26**	25.0	+15.0	23*	28.6	+31.4	23*	17.9	+12.1	10
Home owner												
No	15.6	+23.3	21*	18.8	+20.1	24*	21.9	+33.7	26**	12.5	+20.8	17*
Yes	26.3	+13.7	13	36.8	+18.2	17	47.4	−7.4	−07	36.8	−1.8	02
Sex												
Male	27.3	−3.8	−03	31.8	+21.1	21	27.3	+13.9	15	22.7	+12.6	12
Female	16.7	+35.7	32***	20.0	+22.9	24*	36.7	+15.7	12	20.0	+13.3	11

*p < .05   **p < .01   ***p < .001.

%L = Percent who are light viewers.

CD = Cultivation differential: difference between percent of light and heavy viewers.

[a]Tau—decimals dropped.

TABLE 5.2 Relationship Between Amount of Viewing and Racial Integration Index

	% Giving Overall Higher Estimates of Racial Integration				% Giving Overall Higher Estimates of Racial Integration		
	%L	CD	tau[a]		%L	CD	tau[a]
TV viewing overall	26.9	+36.3	33***	Sex			
Controlling for:				Male	36.4	+22.4	22
Age				Female	20.0	+46.7	41***
18–37	7.4	+42.6	38***	Black church			
38–57	42.9	+32.1	23	No	33.3	+38.1	31
Over 57	54.5	+14.3	13	Yes	26.9	+48.1	39***
Education				Neighborhood tenure			
No college	37.5	+30.5	27*				
College or more	22.2	+31.6	21*	Short	13.6	+26.4	19
Income				Medium	18.8	+47.9	45***
Less than $25,000	33.3	+27.4	26*	Long	53.8	+21.2	20
$25,000 or more	21.4	+48.6	21*	Community participation			
Subjective social class				Low	17.2	+47.1	44***
Low	10.5	+43.3	39***	High	39.1	+20.9	12
High	21.4	+48.6	37***	Churchgoer			
Home owner				No	21.4	+18.6	20
No	18.8	+36.8	29***	Yes	28.9	+41.5	36***
Yes	36.8	+33.2	31**				

*p < .05   **p < .01   ***p < .001.

%L = Percent who are light viewers.

CD = Cultivation differential: difference between percent of light and heavy viewers.

[a]Tau—decimals dropped.

TABLE 5.3 Mean Scores of Light and Heavy Television Viewers' Perceptions of Racial Integration

	Light $\bar{x}$	Heavy $\bar{x}$		Light $\bar{x}$	Heavy $\bar{x}$
Integration beliefs overall	3.96	5.33***	Sex		
Controlling for:			Male	3.86	5.19*
			Female	4.03	5.40**
Age			Black church		
18–37	2.99	4.76***	No	4.48	5.69
38–57	4.39	5.30	Yes	3.88	5.57***
Over 57	5.79	5.84	Neighborhood tenure		
Education			Short	3.21	4.52
No college	4.43	5.53	Medium	4.09	5.50*
College or more	3.75	5.06**	Long	4.94	5.80
Income			Community participation		
Less than $25,000	4.36	5.36			
$25,000 or more	3.61	5.28***	Low	3.57	5.17***
Subjective social class			High	4.46	5.59
Low	3.46	4.34	Churchgoer		
High	4.25	5.73***	No	3.87	4.06
Home owner			Yes	3.99	5.59***
No	3.59	5.25***			
Yes	4.44	5.40			

*p < .05   **p < .01   *** p < .001.

Light viewing = 0–2 hours per day; heavy viewing = 4 or more hours per day.

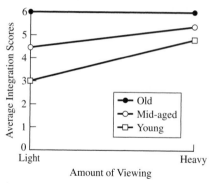

FIGURE 5.1 Mainstreaming by age.

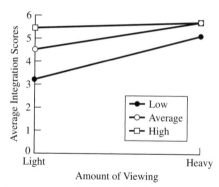

FIGURE 5.2 Mainstreaming by participation.

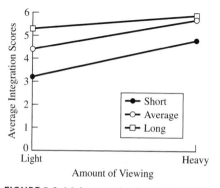

FIGURE 5.3 Mainstreaming by residency.

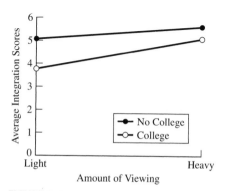

FIGURE 5.4 Mainstreaming by education.

We were also interested in the role of television in creating a new consensus or "moderate majority" among blacks with respect to beliefs about racial integration. Figures 5.1–5.4 present the integration scores of the four relatively homogeneous subgroups whose light viewers held significantly different perspectives on integration. The social experiences derived from community participation, age, education, and length of residency in one neighborhood contributed to these different perceptions; however, in each case, their heavy viewing cohorts report similar perceptions of a greater degree of racial integration than is reported by light viewers. As predicted, heavy television viewing appears to diminish differences generated by social experience.

It is not surprising that age would produce differing perspectives of integration among Afro-Americans. Each generation has had a different social experience in race relations, ranging from segregation to civil rights, and varying modes of protest. Samuels's (20) argument that groups experiencing nationalist struggles are more inclined to be separated by generations could apply to the black power/nationalist movements of the late 1960s. Light-viewing young respondents seem to reflect such a militant, even nationalist, perspective, challenging the moderate mainstream position that understates the existence and problem of racial inequality. But young respondents who are heavy television viewers report perceptions about integration that are more similar to those of older viewers than to their own light-viewing age cohorts. For older respondents, the amount of television viewing appears to be of little consequence in the formation of some of their racial beliefs, but even these distinctions in the perceptions of the degree of integration are blurred or absent for heavy viewers overall (see Table 5.3).

We find similar relationships based on length of neighborhood residence, education, and community participation. In the case of education, the influence of television is most evident upon the perceptions of respondents with at least some college education. Light television viewers in that group think there is significantly less racial integration occurring than do light viewers with less education. Heavy television viewing appears to mold the ideas of the best educated to those of the less educated. From the standpoint of cultural and political hegemony that is a startling observation.

Since the 1950s, Afro-Americans' patterns of voting have been sharply distinguished from those of white voters, particularly in national elections and on issues of racial and social equality. Much of this difference has been attributed to a relatively shared perception of social inequality and injustice for blacks and other peoples of color in the United States. The prospect that television viewing may have long-range influences on black people's political beliefs about themselves is unsettling.

For this sample, the effect of heavy television seems most evident in isolating pockets of black dissidence among young and better-educated Afro-Americans and, to a lesser extent, individuals not active in their communities or in keeping informed about social events. If the "essential mission of the television institution is mass mobilization for consumption" (10, pp. 121–123), then the ideological penetration of Afro-Americans' political perceptions through their leisure activities would be significant. Ewen (5, p. 15) contends that one of the main purposes of corporate advertising (and by extension television programming) is to transform class struggle from an anti-capitalist thrust toward a struggle for consumption of industrial goods. Similarly, the moderation of Afro-Americans' beliefs about the nature and prevalence of integration revealed here might contribute to a transformation of the content of black discontent from an emphasis on racial justice to consumerism and the attainment of middle-class status. This would undoubtedly exacerbate class differences among blacks, eventually affecting their racial and political unity.

Content analyses of television programs suggest that programming since the mid-1980s may further highlight and promote mainstream images of integration (7, 21). The context in which black characters are cast on television appears to be changing from low-income all-black settings to more upscale middle-class ones, as in programs such as *The Cosby Show, 227, Frank's Place, Amen,* and *A Different World.* In these programs issues of racism seem secondary to mainstream quests for middle-class status based on merit and competition.

The Cosby Show, for example, epitomizes the Afro-American dream of full acceptance and assimilation into U.S. society. Both the series and Bill Cosby as an individual represent successful competitors in network television and in attaining a high status. Although this achievement is certainly not inherently negative, we should consider the role television plays in the cultivation of an overall picture of growing racial equality that conceals unequal social relationships and overestimates of how well blacks are integrating into white society (if at all). The illusion of well-being among the oppressed may lead to reduced political activity and less demand for social justice and equality. Although a wealth of research suggests that television viewing may lead to increased political activity and concern (19, 22), the opposite hypothesis should not be automatically rejected.

NOTES

1. Community participation was measured using a revised version of Miller's Scorecard for Community Services Activity (14) (alpha = .75).
2. Churches coded as black were Baptist, A.M.E., Holiness, Pentacostal, Apostolic, Church of God, Church of Christ, and Evangelical Christian.

REFERENCES

1. Allen, Richard L. and William T. Bielby. "Blacks' Attitudes and Behaviors Toward Television." *Communication Research* 6(4), October 1979, pp. 437–462.
2. Banks, Cherry. "A Content Analysis of the Treatment of Black Americans on Television." *Social Education* 41, 1977, pp. 336–339.
3. Baptista-Fernandez, Pilar and Bradley S. Greenberg. "The Context, Characteristics and Communication Behaviors of TV Blacks." In Bradley S. Greenberg (Ed.), *Life on Television: Content Analyses of U.S. TV Drama.* Norwood, N.J.: Ablex, 1980, pp. 13–23.
4. Doob, A. N. and G. E. McDonald. "Television Viewing and Fear of Victimization: Is the Relationship Causal?" *Journal of Personality and Social Psychology* 37, 1979, pp. 170–179.
5. Ewen, Stuart. *Captains of Consciousness.* New York: McGraw-Hill, 1979.
6. Fine, Marlene and Carolyn Anderson. "Dialectical Features of Black Characters in Situation Comedies on Television." *Phylon* 16, 1980, pp. 396–410.
7. Gandy, Oscar and Paula Matabane. "Television and Social Perceptions among African-Americans and Hispanics." In M. K. Asante and W. B. Gudykunst (Eds.), *The Handbook of Intercultural and Development Communication.* Newbury Park, Cal.: Sage, forthcoming.
8. Gerbner, George, Larry Gross, Michael F. Eleey, Marilyn Jackson-Beeck, Suzanne Jeffries-Fox, and Nancy Signorielli. "TV Violence Profile No. 8: The Highlights." *Journal of Communication* 27(2), Spring 1977, pp. 177–180.
9. Gerbner, George, Larry Gross, Nancy Signorielli, and Michael Morgan. "The 'Mainstreaming' of America: Violence Profile No. 11." *Journal of Communication* 30(3), Summer 1980, pp. 11–29.
10. Gerbner, George, Larry Gross, Michael Morgan, and Nancy Signorielli. "Charting the Mainstream: Television's Contribution to Political Orientations." *Journal of Communication* 32(2), Spring 1982, pp. 100–126.
11. Hawkins, Robert and Suzanne Pingree. "Television's Influence on Social Reality." In David Pearl et al. (Eds.), *Television and Behavior: Ten Years of Scientific Progress and Implications for the Eighties,* Volume 2: *Technical Reviews.* Washington, D.C.: U.S. Department of Health and Human Services, 1982, pp. 224–248.
12. Hirsch, Paul. "Distinguishing Good Speculation from Bad Theory: Rejoinder to Gerbner et al." *Communication Research* 8, 1981, pp. 73–95.
13. Hughes, Michael. "The Fruits of Cultivation Analysis: A Reexamination of Some Effects of Television Watching." *Public Opinion Quarterly* 44(3), Fall 1980, pp. 287–302.
14. Miller, Delbert (Ed.). *Handbook of Research Design and Social Measurement.* New York: David McKay, 1977.
15. Morgan, Michael. "Television and the Erosion of Regional Diversity." *Journal of Broadcasting and Electronic Media* 30, 1986, pp. 123–139.
16. Nelville, T. "Television Viewing and the Expression of Interpersonal Mistrust." Unpublished dissertation, Princeton University, 1980.
17. Pingree, Suzanne and Robert Hawkins. "Soap Opera Viewers and Social Reality." Unpublished manuscript, Women's Studies Program, University of Wisconsin–Madison, 1979.

18. Potter, W. James. "Perceived Reality and the Cultivation Hypothesis." *Journal of Broadcasting and Electronic Media* 30, 1986, pp. 159–174.
19. Robinson, John and M. Levy. "Interpersonal Communication and News Comprehension." *Public Opinion Quarterly* 50, 1986, pp. 160–175.
20. Samuels, Richard R. (Ed.). *Political Generations and Political Change.* Lexington, Mass.: Lexington Books, 1977.
21. Stroman, Carolyn, Bishetta Merritt, and Paula Matabane. "Twenty Years Later: The Portrayal of Blacks on Prime-Time Television." Paper presented to the Minorities and Communications Division of the Association for Education in Journalism and Mass Communication, February 1988.
22. Tan, Alexis. "Mass Media Use, Knowledge and Political Involvement." *Public Opinion Quarterly* 44, 1980, pp. 241–248.
23. Tan, Alexis and Percy Vaughn. "Mass Media Exposure, Public Affairs Knowledge, and Black Militancy." *Journalism Quarterly* 53, Summer 1976, pp. 271–279.
24. Volgy, Thomas and John E. Schwartz. "TV Entertainment Programming and Socio-political Attitudes." *Journalism Quarterly* 57, 1980, pp. 150–154.

6

WHITE RESPONSES
The Emergence of "Enlightened" Racism

Sut Jhally
Justin Lewis

THE INSIDIOUS RETURN OF RACISM

Although *The Cosby Show* and others like it seem to persuade some white viewers that black doctors and lawyers have become almost commonplace, most white respondents realized that the Huxtables were, in fact, unusual black people. The role of television in this sense is more complicated than it first appears. Our evidence suggests that shows like *The Cosby Show* cultivate, for white viewers, a curious contradiction: the Huxtables' presence on TV finally proves that "anyone can make it"; yet most people know that the vast majority of black people are not like the Huxtables:

> He's not representing what most blacks are. He's not even representing what most whites are—but especially, he's not representing what most blacks are.

> They [the black people the respondent sees every day] are all lower income and have that jive talk, so that I hardly understand them, whereas this . . .

> [Father and daughter discussing whether class would make a difference] Money would be a big issue at that point. . . . The house is the biggest part of the show. It's a gorgeous, big house. . . . Do you know how much a house in New York goes for, Dad? You know how many typical black families live in those homes?

Despite their statements about how real, average, or regular the Huxtable family is, most white viewers realized that the Huxtables were not a typical black family. Many observed that they were far less typical than the more working class characters in black sitcoms like *The Jeffersons* or *Good Times:*

> It's not a typical black family though. . . . [*The*] *Jeffersons* is typical.

> [Other black shows] are directed more to blacks. . . . That show [*The Jeffersons*] tries to grasp as a family, you know, any black family type of thing.

> The only show that I've watched on a daily basis was *Good Times*. It was so much more realistic than *The Cosby Show*. They were poor, which is easier to make for a black situation considering what the average layman perceives of black people.

Reprinted from Sut Jhally and Justin Lewis, *Enlightened Racism: The Cosby Show, Audiences, and the Myth of the American Dream* (Boulder, CO: Westview Press, 1992).

This contradiction, despite some of the liberal ideas that inform it, leads to a decidedly illiberal conclusion. The only way to explain the failure of most black people to achieve what the Huxtables have achieved is to see most black people as intrinsically lazy or stupid. Few white respondents actually articulated such a nakedly racist attitude, preferring to suppress (publicly, at least) the logical outcome of this contradiction. We can see, nevertheless, that the absence of an awareness of the role of class in sustaining racial inequalities means that this racist conclusion is kept simmering (consciously or unconsciously) beneath the surface. Our study would seem to confirm the fears of Henry Louis Gates (1989: 40):

> As long as *all* blacks were represented in demeaning or peripheral roles, it was possible to believe that American racism was, as it were, indiscriminate. The social vision of "Cosby," however, reflecting the minuscule integration of blacks into the upper middle class, reassuringly throws the blame for black poverty back onto the impoverished.

The Cosby Show, by demonstrating the opportunity for African Americans to be successful, implicates the majority of black people who have, by the Huxtable criterion, failed.

The show's emphasis on education, for all its good intentions, simply compounds this impression. The Huxtables' children are constantly urged by their parents to recognize the importance of educational achievement and to try hard to get good grades. This provides the viewer with an explanation for the comparative failure of most other black people: if they had only tried harder in school, maybe they would have succeeded. As Bill Cosby says of the Huxtables, "This is an American family—an *American* family—and if you want to live like they do, and you're willing to work, the opportunity is there."

The lesson was not lost on most white respondents. Although they happily welcomed the Huxtables into their homes, careful examination of their discussions made it clear that this welcome would not be extended to all black people. What shows like *The Cosby Show* allow, we discovered, was a new and insidious form of racism. The Huxtables proved that black people can succeed; yet in doing so they also prove the inferiority of black people in general (who have, in comparison with whites, failed).

In his study of television news, Robert Entman makes a similar point. He highlights the contradiction between the black people who appear on the news as stories and the increasing number of black anchors and reporters who tell those stories. He suggests that black people in news stories are mainly linked with crime and special interest politics. Entman (1990: 342–343) writes:

> These images would feed the first two components of modern racism, anti-black affect and resistance to blacks' political demands. On the other hand, the positive dimension of the news, the presence of black anchors and other authority figures, may simultaneously engender an impression that racial discrimination is no longer a problem, bolstering the third component of modern racism, an impression that blacks are not inferior and undesirable, working against *old-fashioned racism* [our emphasis].

In other words, there is a distinction to be made between the crude racism of old and its new, more insidious, and apparently enlightened forms. We shall, in this chapter, explore the origin and character of this duplicitous attitude.

DEFINITIONS OF BLACK:
COLOR VERSUS CULTURE

We are used to thinking of racism as an attitude that is crude in its simplicity. The racist discriminates between people purely on the basis of race or color. Although it would be foolish to assume that this kind of prejudice is a thing of the past, we must acknowledge that racism today clothes itself more respectably, allowing a deep-rooted racism to appear to be open-mindedly liberal.

It is easy to forget that race and racial difference involve a great deal more than the categories of physiognomy and skin pigmentation. The differences between a black person and a white person in the United States are deeply rooted in their distinct and separate racial histories, histories encapsulating a host of material and cultural distinctions that render the experience of being black quite different from the experience of being white. Race, in other words, is a social as well as a physical construction.

Racial discrimination, throughout its infamous history, has usually been predicated on a series of perceived symbolic links between skin color and culture. To colonialists, slave owners, and promoters of apartheid, such discrimination meant a straightforward denunciation of black culture as uncivilized, inferior, or threatening. Despite their manifest crudity, these racist attitudes have never been as simple or homogeneous as they sometimes appear. From colonialism onward, the racist discourses within white societies have borne contradictory assumptions about the relation between nature and nurture. Black people have been seen as simultaneously within the reaches of white society and beyond it. The black person's soul was therefore treated, on the one hand, as a changeable commodity open to the influences of missionary zeal and, on the other, as the heart of darkness, inherently irredeemable.

Once placed in the industrial melting pots of the late twentieth century, black people struggling for achievement in an oppressive white world disentangled many of the associations between race and culture. The successes of some black people, against the odds, in a predominantly white environment have made notions of biological determinism decidedly less fashionable. Even limited black success makes white claims to racial superiority difficult to sustain. Although the notion of white racial superiority has certainly not disappeared, it is less common now than ideas of racial equality. But this does not mean the end of racism. Far from it. As an instrument of repression, racism now takes more subtle forms.

In most Western countries, particularly in the United States, the idea that white people and black people are irrevocably tied to discrete cultures has been seriously compromised by the promise of social mobility: the idea that anyone, regardless of race, creed, or class, can change their class. The principle of social mobility is now enshrined within legal structures that, although not guaranteeing racial equality, at least give the idea of equal rights a certain amount of credibility.

Racism is, however, capricious, and it has adapted to this discursive climate by absorbing a number of contradictions. The history of racism, we have demonstrated, is now embedded in an iniquitous capitalist system, where economic rather than racial laws ensure widespread racial segregation and disadvantage. These, in turn, encourage white people, looking around them at the comparative prosperity of whites over blacks, to believe in an imagined cultural superiority and simultaneously to give credence to the idea that we are only what we become.

These beliefs lead to an attitude that separates blackness from the color that defines it. Blackness becomes a cultural notion associated with African Americans, but, from a white perspective, not irredeemably so. It is the same perspective adopted by nineteenth-century missionaries: blackness is seen as a condition from which black people can be liberated.

How is such an apparently archaic attitude sustained in the modern United States? The answer returns us, once again, to the national failure to come to terms with the harsh realities of class barriers. The phenomenon of racism, unlike inequality of wealth and opportunity, is understood not as a consequence of social structures but as the collective sum of individual opinions. If white people as individuals, the thinking goes, stop discriminating against black people, then racial equality is suddenly possible.

We have, we hope, revealed the naïveté of this position. Yet it persists not only among the gullible but throughout mainstream opinion in the United States. Accordingly if, as our study suggests, most white people believe such racism is a thing of the past, then how can we explain the failure of black people, as a group, to achieve parity with white people? In the absence of a class analysis, the answer is to see most black people as culturally inferior. This classless logic says that if most black people fail when there are no individuals discriminating against them, then there must be something wrong with them.

Bill Cosby, whether as himself or as Dr. Heathcliff Huxtable, is easily assimilated into this ideology. He is, as Mark Crispin Miller (1986) argues, visible "proof" of the meritocratic mythology that fuels the American dream, a black person who has achieved success beyond the confines of a racially defined culture. He has, in this sense, escaped from the shackles of his racial origins. It is as if racial disadvantage is something that black people are born with rather than something imposed upon them.

This is racism masquerading as liberalism. White people are willing to accept that black and white people can be equal, and their enjoyment of *The Cosby Show* is testimony to this. They can accept the Huxtables as people who are "just like us." Beneath this progressive attitude, however, lies an implicit and unstated rejection of the majority of black people, who are not like the Huxtables and, by implication, not "like us."

How does this apparently liberal racism manifest itself among the white groups in our audience study? The answer, we shall suggest, reveals a great deal about the ambivalent way many white people *really* feel about black people.

THE BLACK AND WHITE *COSBY SHOW*

One criticism that black people have made of *The Cosby Show* is that the Huxtable family behaves, as Gates has put it, "just like white people." Although this statement is more complex than it sounds at first, it raises an interesting possibility. Perhaps white people do not actually see the Huxtables as a black family at all. Perhaps they see them as white—or as some shade of gray in between.

We discovered that many white people do not view the Huxtables as only black. Just as people were able to see *The Cosby Show* as both realistic and unrealistic, most members of our white audience saw the Huxtable family as simultaneously black *and* white. Before we describe this ambiguous perception in more detail, it is useful to clarify what it means.

Most white people—certainly those who watch *The Cosby Show*—no longer see skin color as a barrier to liking someone or treating them as an equal. Unimpeded by such all-encompassing prejudice, they are able to discriminate between black people, some of whom have succeeded, some of whom have not. However, they quietly (and perhaps unconsciously) retain the association of blackness as an indicator of cultural inferiority, albeit one from which African Americans, if they are talented enough or hard working enough, can escape. This position is arrived at not through malice but through a failure to adequately recognize the disadvantaged position black people occupy in the class structure. This failure is extremely significant because, without such a recognition, there is no nonracist way to resolve the disparity between the Huxtables (and other successful black TV characters) and the majority of comparatively unsuccessful black people. Television, we have suggested, is culpable, albeit unwittingly, at every stage in this process.

This argument explains why many white viewers express considerable ambivalence about issues of race on *The Cosby Show.* The Huxtables are, on the one hand, undeniably black, proving the just nature of the brave, new, nonracist world. They are, on the other, unlike most other black people because they fit neatly into the privileged middle class world of television. Because this world has traditionally been the preserve of white people, the Huxtables' entry into it does indeed make them appear to be "just like white people." It is hardly surprising, in this context, if many of the whites' responses were confused: the Huxtables represent the compromise between black and white culture that is unconsciously seen as a prerequisite of black success.

The degree to which the color was seen to fade from the show varied. Some respondents insisted that, as one person put it, "You can't notice it [the Huxtables' race] at all." This statement is itself revealing. It does not refer to variations in skin tone; rather, it demonstrates the perception of blackness as a function of culture (in its general sense) rather than skin color. Their color is, after all, no more or less noticeable than is that of any other group of African Americans. It is their culture, the way they speak and behave, that makes their color less noticeable.

Respondents were asked whether they felt *The Cosby Show* would be very different if the characters were white rather than black. . . . [A] number of respondents felt that the Huxtables' assimilation into a white televisual world was complete enough to say, as these respondents did:

> If they were carrying off the thing the same way, you know, really making a satire of life the way they're doing it, average everyday things that happen every day, then I don't think it would be that much different, you know. Because what they do is they really carry it off and say these are the things that can happen to anybody, I don't care if you're white, black, pink, yellow, or green, this happens to everybody in everyday life. That's what they do. They just satirize everything that happens in normal life.

> I don't think it would be all that different; they seem to come across . . . I think it is generic enough so that anyone could watch it and appreciate it. Like they acknowledge their own heritage and they happen to be black.

> I think at the beginning you would notice it more because it is an all-black show and it was something different. . . . I don't think it makes a difference if they are black or white if it's funny.

> You can't [notice color], really! I mean, it wouldn't be any different if they were white.

> I would imagine there's some kind of subtlety there that I'm missing, that I'm not picking up on right away. It would have to be different, I would think; but I can't see in what capacity. . . . They don't seem to make any reference to their race.

This last comment is particularly interesting. The respondent feels sure that there must be some difference, yet she is unable to detect anything identifiably "black" about the Huxtables.

There is an underlying tension beneath these apparently liberal statements. The fact that "you just think of them as people," praise for which *The Cosby Show* is singled out, does not prove that race is no longer an issue. Quite the contrary: these particular black people are unusual because they have *transcended* their racial origin and, in so doing, have become normal.

The notion of "average," "everyday," or "generic" that these respondents refer to, although it appears to be ethnically neutral, is actually racially specific. The statement that they are "just like any other family" or "just like us" is specific to the Huxtables; it does not refer to black people in general. As one respondent put it:

> I like the fact that they're black and they present a whole other side of what you tend to think black families are like.

The Huxtables may be thought to be normal or average, but they are unlike most black families. The everyday world of the Huxtables is the everyday, generic world of white television. One respondent made this point directly:

> What they're trying to do here is portray a black family in a white family atmosphere.

Most other group members preferred to make this point by implication, referring to a notion of "normality" that is clearly white. So, for example, when one respondent suggested that, unlike most black TV characters, "they just act like people," he was implying a separation between ordinary people and black people. So, unlike most black people, as another respondent put it:

> You can just identify with this family, even if they're a different race.

Similarly, one group member stated:

> I have Jewish friends, that are so good, that I don't know they're Jewish. . . . There is no constant reminder that this is a black family.

He was implying that being white Anglo-Saxon is the norm from which others deviate.

These responses are ambiguous rather than color-blind. The respondents knew that they were watching a black family but "forgot" in the face of its familiarity. "You lose track of it," said one woman, "because it's so average." Another respondent described how the Huxtables' race "just sort of drifted" out of her mind while watching. This forgetfulness is simply a way of sustaining two contradictory interpretations of the same thing. The Huxtables are, in this sense, both black and white. This working class white woman, when asked if she was aware of the Huxtables' race, replied:

> Not at all. But at the same time they don't neglect the black pride which I think is a hard thing to do; and I think they've done it successfully. They've done shows on Martin Luther King and on going down to Washington to do Civil Rights marches when they get together with the grandparents . . . but they do it in a way that's not [too conspicuous or threatening].

Other respondents replied to the same question in the same way:

> It depends on what they are talking about. Again, what issue they are dealing with. If they are dealing with something that pertains to black people in particular, I'm aware of it; but if they are not, it really, I don't think it really comes to mind.

Yes and no. You're aware because at points they make you aware, but you could lose track of it because it's so average.

Their attributes are white—in comparison to *Good Times* or something like that. . . . I'd say it's fifty-fifty, sometimes their culture and attitudes, the things they say, bring you back to the fact that this is an entirely black cast, so I'd say 50 percent of the time I notice, 50 percent I don't.

There's something in Clair's voice. There's something in Clair's voice that is not white American.

NOW YOU SEE IT, NOW YOU DON'T

What makes these ambivalent responses particularly interesting is their particularity to *The Cosby Show.* These respondents were not usually so ambiguous about race. They share a common definition of what blackness is, and they recognize it when they see it. This perception manifested itself when respondents were asked to talk about other, more traditional black TV sitcoms, shows like *Good Times, The Jeffersons, 227,* and *Amen.* While most respondents were able to link these shows under the general category of "black sitcoms," they did not, significantly, include *The Cosby Show* in this category (only one person in the entire white sample made such a link). As one respondent put it, "I think [those shows] are totally different." The difference being that those shows, unlike *The Cosby Show,* involve what is identified as "black humor" in a "black setting."

The black shows that are seen to signify blackness more strongly are, accordingly, compared unfavorably to *The Cosby Show.* These other black sitcoms were often denigrated by white groups for being "slapstick," "loud," "full of yelling and screaming," "stereotypical," and more "black in style and humor":

I don't like them, to be honest with you. They're sarcastic, they're loud, they yell, there's no, they just criticize each other openly.

I think they are more stereotypical black shows than *Cosby.* I don't think *Cosby* is stereotypical black. . . . I mean they really don't make much point to the fact that they're black. And certainly don't do black stereotypical things like *Good Times* used to do. But I think *Amen, 227,* are more that way. They talk the slick black accent, and they work on the mannerisms, and I think they make a conscious effort to act that way like they are catering to the black race in that show. Whereas Cosby, you know, definitely doesn't do that. He's upper middle class and he's not black stereotypical. There's a difference in the tone of those shows, completely.

I think there's a lot of black families out there that are similar to the Cosbys that they're not such a stereotype black. You know, talking like the black slang or that kind of stuff, . . . being portrayed as intelligent, white-collar workers and that kind of thing. I should think, from a black perspective, *The Cosby Show* is more complimentary to blacks than some of the other shows. You know, the *227,* the older woman hanging out of the window watching the neighbors walk by and stuff like that, which is reality in a lot of situations but in terms of. . . . It just seems to be heavy into black stereotyping.

Cosby is much better. . . . The actors are much better, a lot funnier, more stuff you can relate to; they're a lot funnier than the other two. . . . Like *Amen,* the daughter who dates the priest, or whatever he is, you know she's just not realistic, from my point of view anyway. With *227* and Jackie, I don't relate to her or care for her at all as an actress, and she's hardly a realistic person. You can get involved in *The Cosby Show* and feel that you understand it, you're a part of it and can relate to it; while on these other shows there's not even usually a whole plot, it's just kind of there.

If you look at *Good Times,* it's a majority of black. It was very racist the going over the white. The "whitey" down the street, you know.

They [the Huxtables] don't base any humor on black and white kind of thing yet; they let it be known that they are a black family, etc., etc. But the Jeffersons actually made many, many jokes on black-white interaction.

I couldn't picture doing some of those things they did [on *Good Times*] or being so desperate for a new refrigerator.

I don't watch that much TV so I don't watch that many; but I've seen one of them with a black cast and they weren't as funny. Atypical of whatever happens in life and all that.

It's slapstick. It's too noisy for me . . . and I don't remember much about the family, or the interactions, or relationships. Except the slapstick and the volume of it. I'd usually miss half the dialogue. It was all extraneous.

I remember that it [*The Jeffersons*] was a little bit more slapstick, a little bit more . . . stereotypical. Much more stereotypical. They were more concerned with racial issues, blatant racial issues. There was a couple in the building who were mixed race. And it was much more interested in class, and the difference between class, middle class versus working class. So it was a much different show.

Running through these statements is a clear dislike of the kind of blackness these other sitcoms represent. The use of the term *stereotypical* by these respondents is interesting in this respect. Normally the term *stereotypical* implies a critical awareness that the stereotype is, in some important way, misleading. This was not necessarily the case with members of our white groups. On the contrary, a vague awareness of media stereotypes was combined with an equally vague assumption that perhaps these stereotypes were, after all, accurate. So, for example, a show that "seems to be heavy into black stereotyping" may also be "reality in a lot of situations." What makes these shows stereotypical for these white viewers is partly that they are seen as unambiguously black. They remind the viewer of racial issues that *The Cosby Show* allows them to forget. So they are "much more stereotypical" partly because "they were more concerned with racial issues, blatant racial issues." These programs are seen as "black humor" for black people; as one respondent says: "Like they are catering to the black race in that show." This perception is not impartial: the blackness on display here is seen by these respondents, almost universally, as negative.

One respondent made an unusual attempt to pursue the question of stereotyping in relation to news coverage, but even she went on to acknowledge that it was difficult for her to make a critical judgment:

You know how they show, in a courtroom, when they accuse someone, and they would probably always be black. And then the white tend to be left out, I think, in terms of crime.

And I don't know, is that really what's happening? Or is it just the way the media are reporting it? You have no way of knowing. I have no way of knowing.

In other words, in the absence of other information, we have to accept the stereotypical image as the most plausible one. As a consequence, there was, for the white respondents, only a tiny discursive space between an awareness of TV stereotypes of black people and acceptance of those stereotypes. To condemn other black shows for being stereotypical was, therefore, close to condemning them for being too black. *The Cosby Show*, as a corollary to this, is less stereotypical and therefore less black.

Some white respondents (particularly in the upper middle class groups) expressed their dislike for these stereotypical shows by not watching them at all:

> Do you want to know the truth? I tried once, and I couldn't relate to any of it. I don't even know which one I had on. It did not hold my attention at all, and I never turned them back on.

Those who did watch one of these shows appeared to do so without much enthusiasm, particularly when they were compared to the "calm, thought-out" *Cosby Show*. A typical complaint was that they were "less easy to relate to." "They're just not like our family." Just as the absence of race on *The Cosby Show* allows the inclusion of white viewers, the cultural presence of race on other shows serves to alienate the same white viewers. One woman suggested that she was aware of race when watching other black sitcoms, "But you don't think about it with *The Cosby Show*. . . . It doesn't even cross my mind." Or, as another respondent put it, although other black sitcoms exploit identifiably "black humor," with *The Cosby Show* "you just think of them as people."

What do these responses to the Huxtable household signify? In the first instance, it appears that *The Cosby Show* has an appeal among white audiences that other black shows do not. These respondents . . . had few problems relating to or identifying with the Huxtable family. This identification allows them the enjoyment of taking part vicariously in the pleasant lives of the Huxtables "because," as one respondent observed, *The Cosby Show* "relates mostly to usual, regular families and stuff, and their regular problems, and stuff like that."

Would these viewers enjoy the show as much if its blackness was overtly signified? Moreover, is the absence of any discussion or acknowledgment of racism on *The Cosby Show* a prerequisite for these viewers' enjoyment and participation (as viewers)? The answers to these questions reveal the limits of the apparently liberal perception that the Huxtables are less obviously black because they are, for these white viewers, "just like us." On the whole, these respondents want to be reminded neither that the Huxtables are black nor, still less, of the existence of any form of racism.

A number of respondents were aware, when prompted, that black issues were either introduced with the greatest delicacy or entirely absent from *The Cosby Show*. One respondent suggested that, having been accepted by a wide audience, the Huxtables were able to make gentle references to their race:

> The early shows, to the best of my recollection, were devoid [of reminders they were black]. They could have been anybody. They didn't have to be black. It was only after the show maintained its popularity for a while that they—I interpret—that they had the ability to keep reminding people that they were black. . . . Suddenly they would be speaking in a

black idiom. . . . It's just to put a little bit blacker face on what was until then just happened to be a very good comedy, about realistic people who were played by black people.

Although a couple of the more self-consciously liberal respondents were critical of the show's failure to go beyond such gentle reminders, most felt that this restraint was positive. Although one respondent did suggest that *The Cosby Show* had now established enough credibility (among white people) to deal with racial issues, she remained unenthusiastic about the prospect:

They don't want to deal with the issue of interracial. . . . Life is tough enough anyways, and then to get into interracials. . . . I think if the Cosbys did it, though, I don't think they would have any problems. I think it would be all right, you know; people have a lot of trust in them.

Most other respondents rejected the idea much more unequivocally. Some expressed this by saying that they watched the show to enjoy it, not to be preached at; others stated that the introduction of black issues would be "alienating" and that the show would "lose a lot" if it dealt with racism, with the ominous consequence that they would "probably lose the white audience they have":

I think they'd get a lot of mixed publicity for the show. And it would start to alienate some people.

I don't think they want to get into those provocative things . . . you know, controversial subjects which raise race, gayness, grievances, losses, yeah, that stuff. I suppose they think there's enough of that anyway. Let's keep this nice and easy.

I think it was intentional on *The Cosby Show;* they want them, they don't want them to be a racially oriented show. They want it to be just another family.

It's the only show I can ever remember where a black family was shown, and they were upper middle class, professional family, having situations that were familiar to most people—well, familiar to that type of person. And race is never an issue.

I think it's low. It would diminish their show. I wouldn't want to see them, you know, doing the black and white thing. Yeah, I don't like that. I really don't think they need to do that.

Other respondents expressed a similar sentiment in relation to Bill Cosby's support for black causes and politicians. Such support made them distinctly uneasy:

But why did Bill Cosby go after this [Tawana Brawley case]? There are plenty of children on the streets of New York that have been raped. And why is he not, as a parent, going after these? . . . Excuse me, but does he also support Jesse Jackson? That really upsets me, about Bill Cosby. . . . So in terms of principles and stuff, I really question Cosby. . . . But then I have to question Bill Cosby's philosophy and principles and everything, if he can stand behind someone like Jesse Jackson. I don't see Bill Cosby in the pure sense that I saw him years ago.

Then you read about him giving money to the Negro College Fund and you wonder, you don't want to watch a show that's against you, you know . . . against the white race.

Bill Cosby is, in these responses, removed from the comfortable sanctity of *The Cosby Show* and placed in a context that emphasizes his blackness. Our respondents reflect here the accuracy of TV producer Norman Lear's assessment of white viewers when he says: "I don't think there's any question that white America is uncomfortable with victim-ization, or however you want to term the black experience, that which makes you feel guilty, feel uncomfortable" (quoted in Riggs, 1991).

To introduce black issues would transform the Huxtables from a celebrated Every-family into a *black* family, an identity these respondents would prefer to avoid. One respon-dent illustrated this perspective thus:

> My speculation is that they're trying to present a family who's just a normal American fam-ily. And that, as white people don't talk about racial issues all the time, or confront them, or deal with them, then neither would this family. They're trying to get the point across that it's not an all-consuming issue in their lives.

To be "normal" here means, as we have seen, to be part of the dominant culture, which is white and, on television, middle or upper middle class. Class is therefore seen as a signifier of race: to be working class and black is seen as being *more* black.

One manifestation of this entangling of perceptions of class and race occurred during a discussion with an upper middle class white group. The group, having complained that the Huxtables, as working professionals, could not possibly cope without some form of domestic help, were asked if such a character should be introduced into the show. Their response was equivocal because, for them, the presence of class differences automatically signaled *racial* tensions:

> A loaded issue. If they bring in help, what's the color going to be? Are they going to be treated as a second-class citizen? . . . It would take some courage because it makes it trickier.

Questions of class are not seen as generally difficult; they are "tricky" in this case only because the Huxtables are black. The Huxtables' perceived universality is, therefore, partly a function of their privileged class position.

This reaction to class differences is compounded by the nature of contemporary tele-vision. The middle class world of television is one without struggle. To admit a black fam-ily to this world without disrupting it, the family must, like white TV characters, rise to this social position effortlessly. As far as most viewers in the study were concerned, to include class or racial issues would have made *The Cosby Show* seem less "normal" and ironically, less "realistic."

We can see, in this respect, how television has created a form of doublethink in which it becomes necessary for black characters to deny the realities that distinguish black expe-rience in order to appear credible and realistic.

The general resistance of most white viewers in our study to the possibility of trans-forming the Huxtables into a blue-collar family suggests that this perception is wide-spread. The Huxtables, having risen to the comfortable upper middle class world, have, for many white viewers, thereby disentangled themselves from their racial origin. They did not want to see the show, as one respondent put it, "stoop down to another cultural level." To be a blue-collar family, in the media world, would emphasize their "blackness"; as professionals, contrarily, they merge into the "normal" white world of TV. Social mobility, in this sense, becomes a form of sanctity from more unpleasant reminders of racial difference.

BIOLOGY VERSUS CULTURE

The significance of this ambiguity about the Huxtables' race becomes a little clearer when we examine the responses of whites who did *not* articulate it. For these viewers, the Huxtables' race, their blackness, formed a nonnegotiable part of the show. Although such responses were less common among white viewers than some variation of the more color-blind response, they took a number of different tones ranging from progressive to reactionary. These differences originated in quite different attitudes toward black people and race relations.

Viewers who held a number of overtly racist assumptions or were antagonistic in some way toward *all* black people seemed unable to ignore the Huxtables' color. This inability made it difficult for them to identify with the show, and watching it was less enjoyable. Such responses in this study were present only in glimpses. The reactions noted by one interviewer while recruiting participants suggested that some people with strongly held racist views would dislike *The Cosby Show* simply because it was black. One person, refusing to take part in the study, remarked that the show was "stupid, stupid, stupid." Because the respondents were only people who watched *The Cosby Show,* we were less likely to hear this kind of response. Whenever an overtly racist judgment was made, it was fairly blatant. One interview group, for example, was interrupted toward the end of the session by friends, who castigated *The Cosby Show* for being "too black":

The show is too black. . . . It's too black, centered around the black race.

A more subtle articulation of this reaction came from a viewer who, unlike all the other white interviewees, put *The Cosby Show* in the same category as other black shows. Though he enjoyed some aspects of these shows, he criticized them for excluding white people from their casts. In an inverse version of the discourse of racial stereotyping (used by most black respondents), he argued that the only white people who appeared on the show were "fat and stupid"—this being evidence of what he saw as *The Cosby Show*'s pro-black, anti-white position.

The differences between this kind of reading and the more ambiguous view of *The Cosby Show*'s race is instructive. The more overtly racist viewer is less able to distinguish between blackness as a physical and a cultural category. It is more difficult for those expressing a more overt form of racism to forget that the Huxtables are black because skin color is seen to bear an inevitable cultural message. It is a discourse of biological determinism that can only work to amplify the signifier "black." The ability of other respondents to disentangle the physical from the cultural is, by the same token, a prerequisite for their apparently enlightened failure to identify *The Cosby Show* as a black show.

A few respondents articulated racial awareness in quite a different way. These people also rejected the idea that the Huxtables could be white but saw their "blackness" as enjoyable. This idea, though perhaps deeply felt, was expressed only tentatively. As one woman put it, "It wouldn't be as funny if it was white. . . . They have a way about them—I don't know what it is." The inexplicable appeal of the Huxtables' blackness—the idea that the show would lose an ineffable something if it became white—was, for some respondents, clearly more difficult to articulate than the idea that "you forget that they're black." If nothing else, this tells something about the nature of the dominant white culture, and, in particular, what that culture allows white people, or makes it easy for white people, to say about black people. It is easier, in other words, to celebrate the absence of blackness than its presence.

Only the viewers who were most positive about *The Cosby Show* as a *black* show were able to offer any explanation. One referred to her enjoyment of black culture, while another felt it was more "fun" and "colorful" because it was a black show ("Black moms are cooler"). These people tended to be the most progressive in their racial attitudes, and they usually had considerable experience of black people in their own lives.

THE CONSEQUENCES OF CLASSLESSNESS

There is a sense in which *The Cosby Show* does appear, for a number of white viewers, to cultivate a liberal attitude toward black people and racial equality. The lapses into moments of color-blindness that characterized so many white responses is, in this sense, a major step forward. The series does, as Dyson suggests, allow white North Americans "to view black folks as *human beings.*" *The Cosby Show* proves that black people can be just like white people or, as one respondent put it, "that black people are just like us." The inevitabilities of crude racism have been disentangled; the color of someone's skin can, indeed, signify nothing.

Before we hurl our hats into the air proclaiming *The Cosby Show* to be the vision of the racially tolerant society to come, we should reflect that this victory in race relations is a rather hollow one, achieved at an extremely high price. For many white respondents, the Huxtables' class position distinguishes them from other black people, making it possible for white audiences to disentangle them from preconceived (white) notions of black culture (they're "upper middle class," not "black"). The Huxtables, in this sense, look like most white families on television. If it is necessary for black people to become upper middle class to be spared the prejudice of whites, then it is a price most cannot afford to pay. The acceptance of the Huxtables as an Everyfamily did not dislodge the generally negative associations white viewers have of "black culture," attitudes quickly articulated when other black TV sitcoms were discussed. *The Cosby Show* caters to a need for familiarity, and, in this sense, the price it pays for acceptance is that the Huxtables do appear "just like white people."

For many white respondents in our study, the Huxtables' achievement of the American dream leads them to a world where race no longer matters. This attitude enables white viewers to combine an impeccably liberal attitude toward race with a deep-rooted suspicion of black people.

They are, on the one hand, able to welcome a black family into their homes; they can feel an empathy with them and identify with their problems and experiences. They will, at the same time, distinguish between the Huxtables and most other black people, and their welcome is clearly only extended as far as the Huxtables. If *The Cosby Show* were about a working class family, it would be an unpleasant reminder of the class-based inequalities that support our racially divided society. *The Cosby Show* thus allows white people the luxury of being both liberal and intolerant. They reject bigotry based upon skin color, yet they are wary of most (working class) black people. Color difference is okay, cultural difference is not.

This tells us something about the nature of modern racism. The blackness that many white people fear or regard as inferior is no longer simply a function of skin pigmentation; blackness is seen, instead, as the cultural category that appears to bind most black people to certain class positions, to stunt their capacity for upward mobility. As we have suggested, in a culture that makes it difficult to talk in terms of social and class barriers, this neoracism is the only way to explain why the Huxtables have made it in a United States where most black people have not.

At the same time, *The Cosby Show* panders to the limits of white liberalism, allowing white audiences the sanctimonious pleasure of viewing the world through rose-tinted spectacles. Although we disagree with Shelby Steele's general analysis of race, we concur with his description of the relationship between *The Cosby Show* and white audiences when he says:

> [The] success of this handsome, affluent black family points to the fair-mindedness of whites who, out of their essential goodness, changed society so that black families like the Huxtables could succeed. Whites can watch *The Cosby Show* and feel complimented on a job well done. . . . On Thursday nights, Cosby, like a priest, absolves his white viewers, forgives and forgets the sins of the past (Steele, 1990: 11).

REFERENCES

Aronowitz, Stanley. 1989. "Working Class Culture in an Electronic Age." In *Cultural Politics in Contemporary America,* edited by I. Angus and S. Jhally. New York: Routledge.

Bourdieu, Pierre. 1984. *Distinction.* Cambridge, Mass.: Harvard University Press.

Bowles, Sam. 1986. "Schooling and Inequality." In *The Capitalist System,* edited by R. Edwards, M. Reich, and T. Weisskopf. Englewood-Cliffs, NJ: Prentice-Hall.

Center for Popular Economics. 1986. *Economic Report of the People.* Boston: South End Press.

DeMott, Benjamin. 1990. *The Imperial Middle: Why Americans Can't Think Straight About Class.* New York: William Morrow and Co.

Downing, John. 1988. *"The Cosby Show* and American Racial Discourse." In *Discourse and Discrimination,* edited by Geneva Smitherman-Donaldson and T. van Dijk. Michigan: Wayne State University Press.

Dyson, Michael. 1989. "Bill Cosby and the Politics of Race." *Zeta,* September.

Entman, Robert. 1990. "Modern Racism and the Images of Blacks in Local Television News." *Critical Studies in Mass Communication 7* (no. 4, December).

Gates, Henry Louis. 1989. "TV's Black World Turns—But Stays Unreal." *New York Times,* November 12.

Gramsci, Antonio. 1971. *Selections from the Prison Notebooks.* London: Lawrence and Wishart.

Hartsough, Denise. 1989. *"The Cosby Show* in Historical Context: Explaining its Appeal to Middle-Class Black Women." Paper presented to the Ohio University Film Conference.

Katz, Elihu and Tamar Liebes. 1985. "Mutual Aid in the Decoding of *Dallas.*" In *Television in Transition,* edited by P. Drummond and R. Paterson. London: British Film Institute.

Lewis, Justin. 1991. *The Ideological Octopus: An Exploration of Television and Its Audience.* New York: Routledge.

Miller, Mark Crispin. 1986. "Deride and Conquer." In *Watching Television: A Pantheon Guide to Popular Culture,* edited by Todd Gitlin. New York: Pantheon.

Morgan, Michael. 1989. "Television and Democracy." In *Cultural Politics in Contemporary America,* edited by I. Angus and S. Jhally. New York: Routledge.

Morley, David. 1986. *Family Television.* London: Comedia.

Press, Andrea. 1991. *Women Watching Television.* Philadelphia: University of Pennsylvania Press.

Real, Michael. 1991. "Bill Cosby and Recoding Ethnicity." In *Television Criticism,* edited by Leah R. Vande Berg and L. A. Wenner. New York: Longman.

Reed, Ishmael. 1991. "Tuning out Network Bias." *New York Times,* OP-ED, Tuesday, April 9.

Riggs, Marlon. 1991. *Color Adjustment* (a film produced, directed, and written by Marlon Riggs). San Francisco, Calif.: California Newsreel.

Rosen, Ruth. 1986. "Soap Operas: Search for Yesterday." In *Watching Television: A Pantheon Guide to Popular Culture,* edited by Todd Gitlin. New York: Pantheon.

Steele, Shelby. 1990. *The Content of Our Character.* New York: Harper Perennial.

United States Department of Commerce. 1991. *Statistical Abstract of the United States, 1990.* Washington, D.C.: U.S. Government Printing Office.

Walton, Anthony. 1989. "Willie Horton and Me." *The New York Times Magazine,* August 20.

Williams, Raymond. 1961. *The Long Revolution.* New York: Columbia University Press.

Wilson, W. J. 1980. *The Declining Significance of Race.* 2d ed. Chicago: University of Chicago Press.

———. 1987. *The Truly Disadvantaged.* Chicago: University of Chicago Press.

7

HEARING ANITA HILL
(AND VIEWING BILL COSBY)

John Fiske

The Senate Judiciary Committee's hearings into Anita Hill's allegations that Clarence Thomas, Bush's nominee to fill the Supreme Court seat vacated by Thurgood Marshall, had sexually harassed her when he was her boss at the Equal Employment Opportunity Commission caused some of the greatest cultural and political turbulence of the early 1990s. They stirred up all the murkiest currents of race, gender, class, and party politics into a maelstrom that involved a multiaxial complex of struggles in which defeats could be turned into victories, ground gained could be lost and regained, and the only certainties were instability, fluidity, and contestation.

The two Black figures at the center of the storm were put into white discourse most vividly and dangerously by racialized and sexualized metonyms. Anita Hill accused Clarence Thomas of, among other things, making two sexually offensive remarks to her: he compared his own penis to that of Long Dong Silver, a Black porn star, and he claimed to have discovered a pubic hair on his can of Coke. Because the Republican strategy was to focus the hearings not upon what Clarence Thomas *did,* but upon who Anita Hill *was,* the politics of the female pubic hair were, in this case, more decisive than those of the male penis. In other cases, such as that of Willie Horton . . . , the Black male is cast as the sexualized racial threat to the white social order and its "family values," and we must note here how eagerly white discourse circulated these metonyms of both male and female versions of the always already sexualized Black body. In one sense this pubic hair was as hyperreal as Murphy Brown's baby, for both existed only in discourse, but that discourse was material in both its presence and its applications. In another sense, however, its hyperreality was intensified because it could sink its taproots into a figure that is deeply engraved and deeply hidden in the white imagination—that of the hypersexualized Black female.

Hypersexuality, like hyperreality, gathers into itself the conceptualization of both "reality" and its representations, both the real and the imaginary, and becomes a concept whose power is greater than the sum of its components. Hypersexuality condenses into itself both racial-sexual differences and the white imaginations of them: it is hyperreal, not just because it is unreal and surreal (which it is), but because it it is super-real, more than real, for its affective reality is magnified and accelerated, and so its material effects, or effective materiality, are more intensively condensed and extensively dispersed. It is a

Reprinted from John Fiske, *Media Matters: Everyday Culture and Political Change* (Minneapolis: University of Minnesota Press, 1994).

HYPERREALITY HYPERSEXUALITY

The Senate Judiciary Committee

Statement of Anita Hill: One of the oddest episodes I remember was an occasion in which Thomas was drinking a Coke in his office. He got up from the table at which we were working, went over to his desk to get the Coke, looked at the can and asked, "Who has put pubic hair on my Coke?" On other occasions he referred to the size of his own penis as being larger than normal and he also spoke on some occasions of the pleasure he had given to women with oral sex. (October 11, 1991)

Cross Examination 1

ANITA HILL: I recall at least one instance in his office at the EEOC when he discussed, er, some pornographic material, and he brought up the substance, of the content, of the pornographic material.

JOSEPH BIDEN: Again, it's difficult, but for the record, what substance did he bring up in this instance in the EEOC in his office? What was the content of what he said?

ANITA HILL: This was a reference to an individual who, er, had a very large penis, and he used the name that he had

been referred to in the pornographic material, er . . .

JOSEPH BIDEN: Do you recall what it was?

ANITA HILL: Yes I do, the name that was referred to was Long Dong Silver.

Cross Examination 2

ORRIN HATCH (referring to Anita Hill's testimony): That's a gross thing to say, isn't it? Whether it's said by you or by someone else, it's a gross thing to say, isn't it?

CLARENCE THOMAS: As far as I am concerned, Senator, it is. And it's something I did not, nor would I, say.

ORRIN HATCH (holding up a copy of *The Exorcist*): Ever read this book?

CLARENCE THOMAS: No.

ORRIN HATCH: *The Exorcist?*

CLARENCE THOMAS: No, Senator. . . .

ORRIN HATCH: You said you never did say, "Who has put pubic hair on my Coke?" You never did talk to her about Long Dong Silver. I submit those things were found. On page 70 of this particular version of *The Exorcist,* [he reads] "'Oh Burke,' sighed Sharon. In a guarded tone she described an encounter between the senator and the director, 'Denny remarked to him in passing,' said Sharon, 'that there appeared to be—quote—an alien pubic hair floating around in my gin—unquote.'" Do you think that was spoken by happenstance? And she would have us believe that you were saying these things because you wanted to date her!

Designing Women: The Strange Case of Clarence and Anita

BERNICE: Well, I don't see what all this fuss is about, anyway, even if these things did happen. I've eaten at Long John Silver's a number of times and I've never gotten a hair in my Coke, but I'll tell you if I did, I wouldn't hesitate to send it back! And it wouldn't be ten years later, either! . . .

JULIA: It shows they've learned their lesson well.

CHARLENE: What lesson is that?

JULIA: The one that says, all men are created equal.

MARY JO: Evidently, they haven't seen Long Dong Silver.

LAWRENCE SHILES, a student of Anita Hill's at Oral Roberts University: "Sitting next to me [in class] were fellow students Jeffrey Landoff and Mark Stewart. Upon opening the assignments and reviewing our grades and comments made by Anita Hill, I found ten to twelve short black pubic hairs in the pages of my assignment. I glanced over at Jeff Landoff's assignment and saw similar pubic hairs in his work. At that time I made the statement to Landoff that either she had a low opinion of our work or she had graded our assignment in the bathroom. Mark Stewart overheard the conversation and said he had similar pubic hairs in his assignment also. This became the standing joke among many students for the remainder of the year in her classes" (quoted in David Brock, "The Real Anita Hill," *American Spectator,* March 1992, 27).

powerful concept that should be approached with caution by those who wish to weaken it rather than deploy it. Both bell hooks and Paula Giddings (see below) warn that any reference to the hypersexualized Black woman can be dangerous to Black women, and it is difficult for a critic such as I to refer to it without increasing that danger. But if we leave the figure undisturbed we can never dislodge it from its centrality, nor weaken its grasp: a critical analysis of the way it is used should be able to turn it against its users. As this figure became the prime weapon in the white Republican battle to discredit Anita Hill, we must fight back to discredit both it and those who use it.

The pubic hair became a resonant sign by which this hyperreal figure was put into public discourse, and therefore became a site of discursive struggle. Orrin Hatch, the Republican senator, was the first into the fray: a few short hours after Anita Hill's testimony, he brandished a copy of *The Exorcist* and remade the pubic hair into a sign not of Clarence Thomas's sexuality but of Anita Hill's fantasy, and thus a symptom of her pathologized hypersexuality (see *Sidebar: Hyperreality Hypersexuality*). He then located this white construction of Black female hypersexuality in William Peter Blatty's fiction of the horrific threat of the unknown and the uncontrollable. Linda Bloodworth-Thomason did not let him get away with that for long. In her sitcom *Designing Women* she fought back and attempted to reclaim the gender politics of the pubic hair (as well as of the penis), if not its racial ones, by turning it away from masculine horror and into a feminized dirty joke (see *Sidebar: Hyperreality Hypersexuality*). The dirty joke is normally a male way of controlling women, not only in its content but also in the act of telling it. Thomas's original remark, "Who put the pubic hair on my Coke can?" was a dirty joke of this conventional, sexist type. But giving it a feminine accent trivializes not only the man's pride in his sexuality and performance but also his need to exert its power in public discourse, and thus attempts to reclaim, momentarily at least, not just the meaning of the pubic hair but the gender politics of the dirty joke.

This episode of *Designing Women* charts the movement of gender politics from the private to the public as it passes through the domains of the body, of personal conversation, of the workplace, and of the state. The show closes on the public end of the continuum with a shot of George Bush flanked by the victorious Clarence Thomas proclaiming to the press assembled in the White House rose garden that Thomas's confirmation proves that, in the United States at least, "all men are created equal." This is turned against him twice: once jokingly by Mary Jo pointing out that the men who believe that "evidently haven't seen Long Dong Silver," and once seriously by the shot of Anita Hill's exhausted face as he speaks, which showed all too painfully that, whatever equality there may be, it was certainly men's.

The meanings of "men" and "equal" become prizes to be vied for, and, when won, the reclaimed meaning has to be stabilized by being allied with other meanings, or articulated with them. Articulation involves the process of forming linkages among meanings by which they are made politically usable. Three articulations are at work here, making three differently usable meanings of "men" and "equal": the first articulation of "men" is with Clarence Thomas's Blackness (in which case men = human beings), the second is with Anita Hill's femaleness (men = males), and the third is with men's sense of the phallus (men = the penis). With each rearticulation of "man" there is an equivalent rearticulation of "equal."

RACIAL-SEXUAL ARTICULATIONS

Designing Women's rearticulations of "men" and "equal" were white, and in advancing gender politics they could be seen to put back or at least repress racial ones. Many whites did not perceive how the racial politics of the hearings might appear to African Americans, at least not initially. We discussed them ardently and at length, but, until African Americans pointed it out to us, many of us failed to realize clearly enough that allegations of Black sexual harassment made public on white media differed significantly from similar allegations in an all-white workplace, despite their important similarities. When race did enter our discussions, the issue that we saw most clearly was Thomas's strategic turning of the explicit politics of the hearings from gender to race in his now-famous description of them as "a high-tech lynching of an uppity Black man." And we dismissed this as a misuse of racial politics, for we saw only half the issue—we understood well enough that no Black man had ever been lynched for abuse of a Black woman, but not that the hearings and their televising might have been, through their treatment of Anita Hill as well as Clarence Thomas, a symbolic lynching of African Americans in general. Our focus on gender politics was, to an extent, justified: the official topic of the hearings was, after all, sexual harassment, and race was rarely mentioned by any of the protagonists or media commentators. But the television camera showed racial difference clearly in shot after shot of white questioners, Black respondents, and white listeners. The white skin of Thomas's wife was as vivid in the visual discourse as it was silenced in the verbal.

I don't wish to suggest either that all white discussions of the hearings were color-blind (I'm sure they were not) or that my circle of friends is a representative sample of whites in general. But I do want to point out that our comparative neglect of the racial dimension was widely reproduced in the public discourse of the white media, and that our discussions could be legitimately described as "white" in that they differed significantly from those that, as we later learned, were taking place among Black Americans. During and immediately after the hearings, these Black responses were confined largely to the Black community and received little public circulation. This can be attributed in part to the whiteness of the media, but partly, too, to the difficulty for African Americans of reaching any consensus about an appropriate response to the hearings' complex and contradictory mix of race and gender, particularly in front of a white audience.

One widespread Black meaning was that the parade of Black sexuality by and for whites on white media could only damage Black interests: only whites had anything to gain by it. To whites, the imagined large Black penis symbolizes the sexualization of the Black threat to the white social order. The Black male body out of control, whether on the streets of Los Angeles or in the bedrooms of the suburbs, incarnates the white fear of the fragility of the white social order and the racial power it exercises. And as throughout the 1980s Reaganomics widened the gaps between whites and Blacks and depressed African Americans even further, it increased the white fear that this sharpened sense of difference might cause the body of Black America to break out of control and erupt. The power of the Black male body has always figured centrally in the nightmare that forms the dark side of the American dream: it was the product and the target of lynchings, and in late Reaganism this figure loomed even larger—Willie Horton, Rodney King, Mike Tyson, and, as its obverse, Clarence Thomas and Bill Cosby.

The White House put Ken Duberstein in charge of its campaign to secure the confirmation of Clarence Thomas to the Supreme Court.[1] His previous job for Bush had been in the 1988 election, when he masterminded the advertising campaign that included the Willie Horton commercial. . . . Clarence Thomas's strategic and, in the short run, decisive charge that the hearings had become a "high-tech lynching of an uppity Black man" shows the Duberstein hallmark in its button-pushing appeal to this sexual/racial figure in the white imagination. At the immediate instrumental level, the charge put the white Democrats discursively into the category of the lynch mob and tapped into the anxieties that characterize the post-civil rights United States to disable their criticism by coloring it in advance with overt racism, and thus to discredit it in a society whose racism must be covert. By making overt the figuring of Thomas as the overpotent Black stud, this strategy made that figuring impossible. He was thus turned into the category waiting to receive him with open arms, that of the tamed Black man. This Clarence Thomas offered himself to white America as the seductively reassuring obverse of Willie Horton, Rodney King, and Mike Tyson.

If, in these white Republican politics, Thomas was the reassuringly tamed Black man, then Anita Hill had to be turned into the female equivalent of what Thomas no longer was. The uncontrolled sexuality of the Black woman may not loom as large in white fear as her male counterpart, but it is always there, serving as an alibi for the white male use of the Black woman as his sexual property and, at the same time, as a threat to his sexual competence. Orrin Hatch was no fool when he used the horrific world of *The Exorcist* as the ground wherein to locate this threatening Anita Hill.

Some months later, when women, both Black and white, were demonstrably turning Anita Hill's local defeat into a series of broader victories, David Brock in the *American Spectator* tried to recover lost ground by simultaneously pathologizing and hypersexualizing Anita Hill.[2] He recruited to his strategy male students, presumably white and certainly conservative, at Oral Roberts University (whose law school had been bought by Pat Robertson's right-wing Christian organization): one, Lawrence Shiles, claimed that he had found pubic hairs in an assignment returned to him by Anita Hill (see *Sidebar: Hyperreality Hypersexuality*); another, when asked how he knew that the hair was pubic, replied with the cliché, "You just know it when you see it." The cliché, which more commonly serves to turn the conservative reaction to pornography into a definition of it, together with the laughter of these adolescent fundamentalist youths, would seem to locate these pubic hairs in a white imagination every bit as fevered as William Peter Blatty's rather than on a can of Coke or in the pages of an assignment. No one would corroborate the affidavit, so the Republicans were unable to use it in the hearings. David Brock, however, felt no such constraint, and used it imaginatively to demonstrate that the "real" Anita Hill was as "real" as the fictional character in Blatty's horror novel, and thus unwittingly revealed that the Black pubic hair's only "reality" lay in the fearful imagination of white men.

In his lengthy and detailed article (which he later turned into a book), Brock cites evidence that leads him to conclude that Anita Hill's accusations stemmed from a combination of professional ineptitude and sexual frustration. His figuring of her as the pathologically sexual woman reproduces that of Senator John Danforth, who, on the morning after Anita Hill's initial testimony, went before the TV cameras to accuse her of "erotomania," a sexual disorder in which a repressed and unsatisfied desire for a man produces delusions in the woman. This obscure disorder was brought into the debate by Bush's nephew, Jamie. He told the White House of a dinner-table conversation in which a Dr. Satinover, a psychiatrist, had described its symptoms. Within hours, the doctor was in Danforth's offices, and shortly after, Danforth went public with the "erotomania theory." He was, however, not allowed to go unchallenged: Alessandra Stanley in the *New York Times* was quick to charge him with "erotomonomania," or the "male delusion that attractive young women are harboring fantasies about them." And Mary Jo, on *Designing Women,* retaliated that the only delusions were those of aging white male senators "if they think American women are gonna continue to reelect them after they get on TV and say stuff like that."

Apart from Mary Jo's one-word recognition of Danforth's whiteness, race was largely repressed from the surface of this argument, conducted as it was between white women and white men. But repressing it did not erase it, and traces of it were always visible although generally seen less clearly by whites than by Blacks. The threat of the sexually uncontrolled woman is intensified when racialized, and, when racial and sexual politics are simultaneous, the stakes for African Americans are much higher than for Caucasians. In these conditions, the politics of the reclaimed dirty joke becomes much more problematic.

Mary Jo's and Bernice's ability to joke about Long Dong Silver and the importance men give to inequality below the waist does not extend to Black women, certainly not when the penis is Black and the audience is white. In a PBS documentary screened on the anniversary of the hearings, some Black women took the opportunity to express their anxiety in public: as one put it, with horror in her voice, "There was this Black, I mean really Black, dark, dark Black man, and here they're going to put his penis all over the screen!"[3] The history of African Americans tells them unequivocally that any white attention to Black sexuality is likely to result in rape or lynching: Black survival depends upon keeping Black sexuality out of the sight of whites. On the same program, Paula Giddings explained this fear:

> Sexuality is taboo in the Black community, in terms of public revelation, for reasons that are very obvious if you know anything about Black history. Racism has always been based, for our community, upon sexual difference in many ways and in many cases—not just racial difference, not just color difference, but Black people were defined by being sexually different from whites in this society. So anything that seems to confirm that view, especially when revealed in public, gives us a lot of ambivalence, makes us very, very nervous. Historically, in the late nineteenth century, for example, that kind of difference got people lynched, that kind of difference got women raped.

bell hooks has traced in detail how whites have historically constructed Black women as "sexual savages" as a racial-sexual strategy of power.[4] She is sympathetic to Black women such as Tina Turner, who attempt to turn this construction to their own advantage, but her final conclusion is that its politics are so oppressive as to make it unreclaimable. Senators Danforth and Hatch, therefore, had a powerful weapon at hand in their assault on Anita Hill in particular and Black women in general. And in their immediate arena, it was effective: not only was the Judiciary Committee unconvinced by Anita Hill, but polls taken immediately after the hearings showed that the majority of Americans, both white and Black, shared their disbelief. In the wider arena of racism-sexism, their invocation of the Black female sexual savage was also effective. bell hooks gives evidence that the anxieties recognized by Paula Giddings were justified:

> Many black folks can testify that the Thomas hearings seemed to have a profound impact on many white Americans. . . . A number of black females I know have said they have been the objects of unprecedented assaults both verbal and physical by white males since the Thomas hearings. Concurrently, the Thomas hearings exacerbated overall social bashing of black females, and professional black females in particular.[5]

It is, therefore, not surprising that many African Americans saw the televising of the hearings in terms of lynching and raping, not so much of Clarence Thomas and Anita Hill in particular as of African Americans in general. Television and the white senators worked together to continue this sexualization of white supremacy: Trellie Jeffers, for instance, felt that "black women were raped on national television, and black men were doused with gasoline in front of one million viewers."[6] Charles Lawrence saw the hearings as a continuation of "a history of black men lynched and castrated, of black women raped—with no fear of consequences."[7] U.S. Representative Charlie Hayes considered that both Thomas and Hill were lynched by the hearings, and that "if one or both parties were Caucasian the scenario would have been drastically different, Americans would not have been privy to such a spectacle."[8] The Rodney King beating was in one sense a lower-class replay of the hearings. The widely replayed video showed a Black man being beaten by four white cops while between nineteen and twenty-three others looked on.[9] Rodney King's beating was physical, Anita Hill's and Clarence Thomas's verbal: the batons and boots of the four cops replayed the words of the Judiciary Committee; the circle of watching cops stood for the Senate; and the white media made a national spectacle of each event.[10]

Many African Americans saw the hearings as further evidence of their "total subordination in the political machinations of a tiny calculating elite."[11] They argued that Anita Hill was used by white Democrats and white feminists to advance their own agendas, but not that of Black people, in the same way Clarence Thomas was used by white Republicans to advance theirs. A Black woman told me that she and her friends discussed the similarities between the hearings and the Marion Barry case: both involved the white use of Black female sexuality to bring down a powerful Black man.[12] There were, of course, crucial differences: Barry's position of power resulted from Black votes, Thomas's from white patronage. Consequently, different white agendas were advanced in each case, but both were white. It was tragically easy to see the hearings as a contest between a Black man and white feminists,[13] and even moderate Black women were often critical of the feminist performance, Kimberle Crenshaw for one:

> Content to rest their case on a raceless tale of gender subordination, white feminists missed an opportunity to span the chasm between feminism and anti-racism. Indeed, feminists actually helped maintain the chasm by endorsing the framing of the event as a race versus a gender issue.[14]

For other Black women, however, putting gender second to race advanced Black patriarchy, for it defined the interests of the race as masculine and thus continued the double oppression of Black women. As Barbara Smith put it: "The Hill-Thomas confrontation reinforced the perception that any Black woman who raises the issue of sexual oppression in the African American community is somehow a traitor to the race, which translates into being a traitor to Black men."[15] Calvin Hernton made the point forcefully when he wrote:

> The ideology of race first and sex second fosters both white supremacy and male supremacy, and it underpins the racial oppression of black women and men. At the same time it underpins the sexual oppression of both black and white women. . . .
>
> Because it is impossible to separate their sex from their race, and since they are at once sexually and racially oppressed, the primary target of the ideology of race first and sex second are black women. . . . the ideology of race first and sex second verifies and denies that sexual oppression exists, and it prohibits and penalizes anyone who says that sexism and racism are intertwined and that they should be fought as one.[16]

In this light, Anita Hill's decision to break the silence imposed by the ideology of "race first" could be seen as a victory. The hearings allowed a Black woman and her oppression to be heard by millions across the nation, and that, according to Julianne Malveaux, is no small matter:

> But here is the bottom line. Supreme Court Justice Clarence Thomas was confirmed because he invoked the image of a black man hanging. They don't make ropes for black women's lynchings or destroy us with high drama. Instead, it is the grind of daily life that wears us slowly down, the struggle for a dignified survival. Black women work the same endless day white women do, but when we juggle work and family, we also bear the burden of the racism that shapes the composition of our households. We are not lynched, just chipped at by the indignity swallowed, the harassment ignored, the gossamer thread of job security frayed by last hired, first fired. We have been taught silence, and Anita Hill's lifted voice is evidence that she finally found the Sojourner within her.[17]

In 1981, bell hooks had pointed out that "no other group in America has so had their identity socialized out of existence as have black women,"[18] and now, ten years later, Black feminists were still having to make the same point. For Kimberle Crenshaw, for example, Anita Hill showed Americans "the place where African-American women live, a political vacuum of erasure and contradiction . . . existing within the overlapping margins of race and gender discourse and in the empty spaces between, it is a location whose very nature resists telling."[19] But Anita Hill told it, and her story was the spur for Black women to form a grassroots organization called African American Women in Defense of Ourselves. Their manifesto, signed by more than 1,600, was published in a full-page advertisement in the *New York Times*[20] and reprinted widely. These Black women continued the public speech that Anita Hill began. Barbara Smith calls this a "watershed in black feminist organizing." "Never before," she writes, "have so many black women publicly stated their refusal to pit racial oppression against sexual oppression," and she goes on to record the continued outpouring of support and the organizers' intention to create a mechanism for organizing and speaking out.[21]

The importance for African Americans of overcoming their silencing by Caucasian America comes to the surface again in the Los Angeles uprisings. Many used looting and arson as public speech, the only Black speech that whites would listen to. . . . For them, the media attention was their victory over silencing. But, when multiaxial oppression works as fluidly as it does, such victories may not be claimed by all, may not be recognized by all. For some, Anita Hill's public speech was so effective because her quiet steadfastness appeared to disarticulate her and therefore Black women from the category of "the sexual savage." For others, however, her calmness fitted her into the category of the "enduring woman" in a way that undercut the positive aspects of her speaking out. bell hooks identifies the contradictory effects of her way of speaking:

> To many viewers, her calm demeanor was a sign of her integrity, that she had chosen the high moral ground. Yet to some of us, it was yet another example of black female stoicism in the face of sexist/racist abuse. While it may not have changed the outcome of the hearings in any way, had Hill been more strategic and passionate, and dare I say it, even angry at the assault on her character, it would have made the hearings less an assault on the psyches of black females watching and on women viewers in general.
>
> Contrary to those who wish to claim that the hearings were in some way a feminist victory, it was precisely the absence of either a feminist analysis on Hill's part or a feminist response that made this spectacle more an example of female martyrdom and victimization than of a constructive confrontation with patriarchal male domination. Black women have always held an honored place in the hall of female martyrdom. As Anita Hill's friend Ellen Wells declared in a passionate defense of Hill not initiating a case against Thomas when the harassment first occurred, "Being a black woman, you know you have to put up with a lot so you grit your teeth and do it." With this comment, Wells evoked a tradition of female martyrdom and masochism.[22]

For *Ebony,* however, Anita Hill's speaking out helped Black women to throw off their cloak of invisibility and silence. Twelve months later, the magazine dubbed 1992 "The Year of the Black Woman": "For this year . . . the power and presence of Black women is being felt in politics, literature, sports, entertainment, science, education and religion."[23] The magazine led its account of Black women's achievements with that of Carol Moseley Braun, the Illinois Democrat and first Black woman to be elected to the Senate. Her success was attributed to the alliance that she forged among inner-city Blacks, women, and other Democrats; the most influential factor in making this alliance possible was Anita Hill. Braun is not alone. Black women challenged for seats in either the House of Representatives or the Senate in at least ten states.[24] Johnetta B. Cole, the first Black woman president of Spelman College, summarizes "The Year of the Black Woman":

> What dynamics have come into play to make this possible? Surely it is a complex of factors, but among them must be: The role of law professor Anita Hill in bringing the issue of sexual harassment before the eyes of millions of Americans: the fact that large numbers of Americans are tired of the antics of so many politicians and are interested in seeing if women can do any better; and the coming of age of Black feminism as a connector between the modern Black Liberation and Women's movements.[25]

GENDER ARTICULATIONS

In the public domain, these Black contestations over the hearings came after the female ones. This may be because white women immediately united around the more straightforward gender politics of the hearings, whereas African America was far more conflicted about their racial ones. It may also be because the white media allowed readier access to white female voices than to Black ones. But whatever the reasons, the women's fight to regain the ground lost by the confirmation was the one that first gained public recognition. This struggle was so successful that nine months later, the *New York Times* could run a front-page story that began,

Sexual harassment complaints to the Equal Employment Opportunities Commission are up sharply [by over 50%], Congress and the White House have responded to complaints of sexual abuse in the military in ways that would have been unimaginable nine months ago. Employers are scurrying to hire sensitivity trainers to teach men how to treat women. And men are wondering how they failed to notice the anger of their female colleagues. This change in American attitudes, experts of both sexes and all political persuasions agree, is a direct result of last fall's nationally televised colloquium on sexual harassment, the Anita Hill-Clarence Thomas hearings.[26]

The article could have added that donations to the Women's Campaign Fund have run at double their prehearings rate, that more women than ever before stood for election in 1992, that enrollments in women's studies courses in universities surged, and that for months after the hearings women were wearing lapel buttons proclaiming, "I believe Anita Hill." Anita Hill herself has had a hectic schedule of public lectures in which she used her "defeat" to continue women's struggles against harassment at work, and *60 Minutes* ran a sympathetic portrait of her. *Designing Women* joined in women's reclamation of the defeat, and, in the episode in which its characters watched the hearings on TV, gave a national voice to women's pride in Anita Hill's courage, to their anger at her treatment, to their dismay at the verdict, and to their determination not to take it lying down. The episode climaxed with a passionate outcry by Mary Jo:

> I'm sorry! Your time is up. Listen, I don't mean to be strident and overbearing; I used to be nice, but quite frankly, nice doesn't cut it. We want to be treated equally and with respect. Is that too much to ask? Like a lot of women around this country tonight I'm mad! I'm mad because we're 51 percent of the population and only 2 percent of the United States Senate. I'm mad because 527 men in the House of Representatives have a pool, a sauna, a gym and we have six hair dryers and a Ping-Pong table. I'm mad because in spite of the fact that we scrub America's floors, wash her dishes, commit very little of the crime, and have all of the babies, we still make 58 cents on the dollar. As a matter of fact, I don't know about the rest of the women out there, but I don't give a damn anymore if you call me a feminist or a fruitcake—I just know I am so mad I am going to get in my car and drive to the centermost point of the United States of America and climb to the top of a tower and shout, "Don't get us wrong, we love you, BUT . . . who the hell do you men think you are?"

A graduate student of mine held long telephone conversations with women about this episode.[27] Two of the words used most frequently by those with whom she spoke were "validation" and "vindication"; these were combined with a sense of solidarity among all women, and a sharp sense of how rare it was for women's point of view to gain public circulation. Typical comments included the following: "It was powerful and validating—on prime-time TV! I get so tired of the male media." "You know, the show made me feel vindicated, like I knew I was right. I know she was right, the show reminded me of that." "She made me proud to be who I am. The program was healing for me, I was finally able to laugh about this." "What really sticks out for me was that this was on mainstream TV, and I didn't feel alone." This sense of validation and solidarity could extend into the politics of personal behavior, and women reported they felt emboldened to stand up against harassment at work or to answer back to the jerk at the bus stop.

It is interesting to note that many of these women considered *Designing Women* to act as a corrective not only to masculine power in the workplace, but also to the masculine bias of TV. In this, it joined *Murphy Brown* (which ran immediately before it in the schedule). Despite including Anthony, a nonthreatening Black male, among its characters, *Designing Women* did focus on gender, rather than racial, issues. Indeed, the script for this particular episode contained only four explicit references to race, and of those, only two survived the editing deck to reach the screen. Both these shows appear to me to repress racial discourse. Some of *Designing Women*'s viewers, however, disagree with me; they considered that racial differences were not repressed, but transcended by emphasis on gender. One, for instance, a half-Irish, half-Cherokee woman, said of Anita:

> Her color had nothing to do with it—she represented all women and what is happening to all women. I was angry, but also proud to be a woman. . . . We talked about this at work, too. Does it matter if all the women I work with are Black? I don't think it does, we all watch the show and we all watched the hearings. We all work together all day, and we keep bringing up points that piss us off: everybody's got stories on sexual harassment—the color of the man isn't the important thing, though it was funny to hear these women talk about how common it is for Black men to be so arrogant and into their own sexuality. The biggest thing is that no one believes you. They don't take you seriously, you know, you're the one overreacting. Nobody takes you seriously, even some women. We all felt good about this episode, though, and we were all proud of her. We felt bad for her, too, but she did it for all of us. She'll be remembered for what she did, she's a very courageous woman to do that.

We must note, however, that this woman is not Black, and, for her Black co-workers, gender solidarity did not overcome racial difference altogether; they experienced a specifically Black dimension to sexual harassment that whites did not.

On the other side of the gender battlefront, conservatives mobilized to hold the ground the vote had given them. Rush Limbaugh and Phyllis Schlafly, for instance, quickly recognized that the conservative victory in the hearings was temporary at best. Both of them have radio shows, and Schlafly is as tireless as Anita Hill on the lecture circuit. Limbaugh claims that the liberal media (most of his examples of which are mainstream TV) have combined to show "how far America is being dragged into the cloud-cuckoo-land of feminism,"[28] and that feminists didn't care if Anita Hill was telling the truth, the airing of her charges was what they wanted: "Anita Hill was nothing more than a football to be kicked around to score points for feminism."[29] Interestingly, his charges are almost identical to those made by some Black women, but similar accusations articulated differently in different alliances have quite different politics: Limbaugh's advance dominant conservative male interests, the Black women's those of a minority oppressed by both gender and race.

Phyllis Schlafly, who came to fame as leader of the successful "Stop ERA" campaign in the early 1980s, has never flagged in her campaign against women's rights. She, too, believes that radical feminists used Anita Hill and the hearings to push their views, through the liberal media, upon the American public. The feminists' use of the sexual harassment issue is, Schlafly claims, an example of "trying to have it both ways: they want to be a macho man and they want to be a victim someone will protect."[30] Like Rush Limbaugh, Schlafly sees Hillary Rodham Clinton as promoting the same agenda, and her argument moves back and forth between Anita Hill and Hillary Clinton as easily as does Quayle/Buchanan's between Murphy Brown and Hillary Clinton. She also sets herself against the gains made by women in increasing their political representation in 1992. Despite, or maybe because of, three failed attempts to be elected, she advises most women to stay out of politics because it is just not in their nature: "Women don't like to do what you have to do to get to Congress. Life isn't worth that kind of commitment to the majority of women."[31]

ARTICULATIONS OF CLASS

If, on the gender front, the victory was uncertain, on a class or populist one, Washington lost. There was a widespread belief that regardless of the outcome, the hearings gave the U.S. public a clear view of how badly politicians could behave. On the front of "them" versus "us," of "Washington" versus "everyday America," television inflicted grievous damage upon the credibility of "the power structure." Not only fictional programs refused to let the verdict be the last word: typical of many responses was that of WXYZ-TV in Detroit. An interview of Orrin Hatch by Bill Bonds, one of the station's news anchors, ended with Hatch storming out of the studio in a fury (see *Sidebar: Bonds and Hatch*). The antagonism was neither racial nor gendered, but a populist one between the people and Washington. The call for change behind which Clinton rallied his electoral forces included, besides changes in policy, changes in the relationship between politicians and the people. He managed to position his team as part of "us" and Bush's as "them," and in these populist sentiments to activate both class and age politics.

Populism, as a way of inflecting class difference, has uncertain and risky politics. In recent history, the right has generally been more effective than the left in claiming the class resentment that fuels it. Clinton succeeded in tapping into some of it, but there is no fixed relationship between populist sentiments and party affiliation, and Rush Limbaugh consistently gives populist resentment a right-wing accent. His constant attacks on today's women—Murphy Brown, Hillary Rodham Clinton, and Anita Hill—recode class resentment into gender antagonism, a strategy also used by Peggy Noonan, a white speechwriter for Reagan and Bush, who argued that the hearings revealed "class division" between the "chattering classes" who supported Anita Hill and the "normal humans" who believed Thomas. She figured the difference between them by analyzing the character witnesses for each: Susan Hoerchner, one of today's women supporting Anita Hill, was characterized as "professional, movement-y, and intellectualish," with an "unmakeupped face." But Clarence Thomas was validated by J. C. Alvarez, who was "Maybellined," "straight shooting," and "the voice of the real, as opposed to the abstract, America." Noonan read Anita Hill's professional behavior as a marker of class difference: a "real American" (that is, a blue-collar one), when faced with the harassment Hill suffered, "would kick him in the gajoobies and haul him straight to court."[32] The mobility of class difference is astonishing: lower-class resentment is here mobilized for Clarence Thomas (the boss) against Anita Hill (the subordinate)! Class power, when taken up by currents of masculinism and Republicanism, can be turned and made to flow "upstream," against its normal social topography. Nellie McKay recognized a similar resentment among lower-class Black women of Hill's ineptitude at handling Thomas's dirty remarks: they would have put their hands on their hips and given him a good tongue-lashing, and, if that failed, a well-aimed kick would have followed.[33]

Nancy Fraser gives an insightful class analysis of the currents and countercurrents swirling around the hearings. She cites a *New York Times* article that also reported that blue-collar women (we presume white) were put off by Anita Hill's soft-spokenness and, in their eyes, failure to deal with Thomas on the spot. The article contrasted this

BONDS AND HATCH

BILL BONDS: I have to say to you, sir, as an American from the Midwest, that frankly—that was kind of an embarrassing spectacle. Do you regret that that went on?

ORRIN HATCH: It was a tense, difficult process, as it should be. And it was made worse because of one dishonest senator who leaked raw FBI data—

BONDS: Senator, you guys leak all the time.

HATCH: No we don't.

BONDS: Who are you trying to kid? You guys leak stuff all the time.

HATCH: Let me just say something, that's not true.

BONDS: Yes, it is.

HATCH: No, not FBI reports from the Judiciary Committee. I've been here fifteen years. I have not seen leaks of FBI reports, because they contain raw data—

BONDS: Okay, your conduct was great. You guys all looked terrific; 250 million Americans are really proud of Senator Orrin Hatch and all the rest of you guys.

HATCH: I'm not, I'm not—

BONDS: You did a marvelous job. You never made the country look better. Let me ask you something: What are you going to do if you find out six months from now that Clarence Thomas—who you've just about made into a saint—is a porno freak?

HATCH: Don't worry, we won't. But I'll tell you this: If you're going to interview us in the future, you ought to be at least courteous. You're about as discourteous a person as I've ever interviewed with. I don't like it, and I don't like what you're doing. I go through enough crap back here, I don't have to go through it with you. Let me tell you something—

BONDS: No, let me tell you something—

HATCH: No, you tell yourself something. I'm tired of talking to you. [Removes microphone and steps off-camera.]

BONDS: Okay, fine. I'm tired of talking to you. See you later.

(Interview transcript in *Washington Journalism Review,* December 1991, and reprinted in *Harper's,* February 1992, 18.)

"blue-collar" view (in which, incidentally, we can hear an echo of bell hooks's race-gender based strictures) with those of the professional classes who strongly supported and believed Anita Hill. Nancy Fraser's analysis grants this class resentment a degree of validity, but points to its limitations: "Working-class people who felt that Hill should simply have told Thomas off and quit and found another job were not attuned to professional career structures, which require cultivation of one's reputation in the profession via networking and long-term maintenance of relationships."[34]

In the *Frontline* documentary screened by PBS to mark the first anniversary of the hearings, a similar pattern of gendered class difference was given a racial inflection. Most of the Black women that it showed supporting Anita Hill were ones with professional careers; the criticism of her was voiced by women with lower-class jobs, such as hairdressing, and, of course, by some men. Race, gender, and class differences are each structured and experienced in terms of the others, and the multiaxiality of power as it is both exerted and resisted results in a fluidity and multiplicity of positions from which any event may be viewed. Cornel West, for instance, laments that from the point of view of most Black leaders, class seemed to be invisible. With passionate clarity he shows the racism of economic policies:

> For example, both Thomas and Hill would be viewed as two black conservative supporters of some of the most vicious policies to besiege black working and poor communities since Jim and Jane Crow segregation. Both Thomas and Hill supported an unprecedented redistribution of wealth from working people to well-to-do people in the form of regressive taxation, deregulation policies, cutbacks and slowdowns in public service programs, take-backs at the negotiation table between workers and management, and military buildups at the Pentagon. Both Thomas and Hill supported the unleashing of unbridled capitalist market forces on a level never witnessed before in this country that have devastated black working and poor communities. These market forces took the form principally of unregulated corporative and financial expansion and intense entrepreneurial activity. This tremendous ferment in big and small businesses—including enormous bonanzas in speculation, leveraged buy-outs and mergers, as well as high levels of corruption and graft—contributed to a new kind of culture of consumption in white and black America.[35]

Here, he prefigures some of the more radical explanations of the "looting" in the L.A. uprisings: that the real looters were the unregulated corporate capitalists of Reaganomics and that those carrying boxes of Pampers and Nikes from the stores of South-Central were minuscule imitations of the corporate model.

When class power and economic inequality are interwoven with race, gender, and age distinctions, no alliances can be relied upon as structurally determined or taken as self-evident: they have to be consciously and laboriously forged and maintained in a social order characterized by the fluidity of alliances, the multiaxiality of power, and the instability of meanings.

ARTICULATIONS AND ALLIANCES

Articulation is the discursive equivalent of forming social alliances, for making meanings and making allies are part of the same process of putting meanings into social circulation, giving them an effectivity and thus a politics.

Anita Hill was articulated so differently because she was pulled into so many different and often contradictory alliances in which gender, race, class, party politics, and a sort of populism were pulled together in multiple and, at times, surprising configurations. The hearings were so significant and controversial partly because their politics were so complex and so contradictory. They could be understood in a number of different ways, according to how the social axes involved were articulated: party political thought articulated them around the axis of Democrat versus Republican, progressive versus conservative, left versus right; in gender politics they showed a lone woman up against ranks of men wielding immense institutional power; in racial politics they showed white against Black; in more populist politics they showed one of "us" against "them," the ordinary person against "Washington"; and in class politics they showed the professional classes fighting over what lower classes often saw as trivial.

Each of these axes of power could be, and in many cases were, articulated with and disarticulated from any or all of the others. Each point where these different axes were brought to intersect was a point of articulation: it was a hinge point from which one could speak and thus identify oneself, one's allies, and one's enemies. The multiaxiality of speech and alliance is a multiaxiality of social identity. Each articulation changes the meanings carried by each power axis. The meanings of femininity, for instance, depend upon their racial articulations and on their class ones: femininity may be an axis of unity among all women, but its intersections with the axes of race and class produce differences that may disrupt that unity. Being a Black woman in the United States is necessarily different from being a white woman because of the different histories that lie behind each social identity or point of intersection, but alliances can be formed across these differences if *both* parties consent to the repression of difference involved. And the intersections of class or age with gender and race bring other points of difference into the picture, so that Murphy Brown (white/middle-class/mature/feminine) differs multiaxially from the figure of the unmarried Black teenage mother, despite the commonality of single motherhood by which Dan Quayle linked Murphy Brown to the L.A. "riots." Unities and alliances along some axes necessarily repress the differences of others, and, for the alliance to be effective, any repression of difference must be consented to by all, particularly by those for whom the axis of difference is one of subordination. A social identity formed at any one point of intersection can always be shifted to another by reconfiguring the play of similarity and difference that is central to the multiaxial politics of identity. The concept of identity here is not essentialist or individualistic but relational, for it forms the point from which social alliances are entered: the social identity of Anita Hill, who she was or could be made to be, was important because it determined which alliances she could be pulled into and therefore which political ends she could be made to serve. But not all social axes are brought into play in every point of identification or alliance: for instance, I heard little evidence from those speaking as Black/female/lower-class that party politics mattered much at all. For those speaking as white/female/upper-class, however, the Republican-Democrat axis was salient, because it was determinate in the abortion rights issue that mattered so intensely to them.

This multiaxiality of discursive and social alliances means that the identities it produces are as fluid as the process. Because Anita Hill came into Washington as unmarried, Black, female, successful, and quietly self-assured, the Beltway had no pigeonhole to fit her into. Who she *was* appeared an open question, and the politicians rushed to answer it. A year later, Anita Hill gave her perception of this process:

> Not only did the Senate fail to understand or to recognize me, because of my lack of attachment to certain institutions, like marriage and patronage, they failed to relate to my race, my gender, my race and gender combined, and in combination with my education, my career choice and my demeanor. . . .
>
> Because I and my reality did not comport with what they accepted as their reality, I and my reality had to be reconstructed by the Senate committee members with assistance from the press and others. In constructing an explanation for my marital status as single, I became unmarriageable or opposed to marriage, the fantasizing spinster or the man hater. An explanation of my career success had to be introduced which fit with their perceptions about the qualifications of people of color, women and the myth of the double advantage enjoyed by women of color.

I thus became aloof, ambitious, an incompetent product of affirmative action and an ingrate who betrayed those who had worked for my success.[36]

These hearings provided a clear example of the problems facing the analyst in post-structural politics when the social categories have lost the fixity of their relations to each other. In them, progressive women who supported Anita Hill formed a tactical alliance with Senator Edward Kennedy, whose personal sexual politics, like those of most of the Kennedy men, are ones they would vehemently oppose. But the intersection here of the gender politics of the workplace (sexual harassment) with the gender politics of the law (Thomas was believed to want to overturn *Roe v. Wade*) and with progressive social policies in general not only allied them *on this issue* with a male chauvinist but against an African American who was about to maintain the only nonwhite presence on the Supreme Court (an objective they would normally applaud). For them, Thomas's conservatism and maleness were articulated more emphatically than his Blackness; on other issues the articulations may have been reversed. Some Black women, however, saw the Anita Hill-Democrat-feminist alliance as a white one that worked against them: at the articulation of the categories of the "haves" and the "have-nots" with those of gender and race they saw Anita Hill being swept up into the "haves" by whites, and thus being taken out of the "have-nots" in which most Black women are firmly positioned. Other African Americans, both men and women, allied themselves with Clarence Thomas because they saw him as a Black man about to break through the glass ceiling and the Democrats as whites trying to stop him: his conservatism, in racial as other matters, was relegated to the margins. Equally contradictorily, white Democrats and feminists formed their alliance around a conservative woman who, previously, had supported "that man with the notoriously racist and sexist reputation, Judge Robert Bork, in his unsuccessful campaign for a seat on the Supreme Court,"[37] and had taught at the right-wing Christian fundamentalist Oral Roberts University. (Anita Hill claims to have been misunderstood on her support for Bork.)[38] Similarly, racist Republican supporters would have had to ally themselves with Democrats, feminists, and a Black woman to maintain the glass ceiling and "keep Blacks in their place." So it is not surprising if, on this issue, some progressive nonsexist Black men gave highest priority to the racial axis and allied themselves with white Republicans whom normally they would oppose. Robert Staples gives his account of the tactical and strategic fluidity and the consequent apparent contradictions of the alliances involved:

> And old alliances meant nothing. The former segregationists, the current perpetuators of racial buzzwords (eg, quotas, welfare, crime) found themselves supporting a black man, with a white wife. Anita Hill's most visible supporters were middle-class white women, who identified with the issue—if not with her. Most non-southern white Democratic males sided with Hill and Republican white males overwhelmingly supported Thomas. Since people claimed it was impossible to tell who was telling the truth, they came down on the side of their racial, gender or political preferences and interest—at least the whites did. Blacks were almost divided down the middle over Thomas (about 60% supported him after the hearings).[39]

Politics that are fought on a multiaxial terrain, politics that are fought around perceived social interests in which gains often have to be paid for with losses, politics that involve tactical alliances formed for occasions and issues, are politics of fluidity, contradiction, and uncertainty: difficult though they may be, they are the politics with which we have to cope in late capitalism. The struggles that these fluidities make possible and necessary are well illustrated in the aftermath of the hearings. On its own turf, in front of its own crowd, the power bloc won, and Clarence Thomas took his seat on the Supreme Court. But, as the Rodney King case also demonstrated, verdicts in the courtroom or the Senate do not necessarily carry over into the streets and workplaces of everyday life. A verdict that closes the argument in one setting may stimulate it in another.

If the Anita Hill case can indeed be made to forge alliances between the Black liberation and the women's movements and to bridge the gaps that have sometimes separated them, then this may prove in the long term to be the most politically significant victory of all. Nellie McKay believes that it can; she is confident in her belief that Anita Hill is the best thing that has happened to the feminist movement for the past twenty-five years.[40] The electoral success of Carol Moseley Braun is a welcome indicator that the possibility can be realized.

The struggles to reclaim the verdict of the hearings were as contradictory and multiaxial as the alliances formed around them. But we must recognize that this analysis of their multiaxiality comes with the benefit of hindsight and from outside the battleground: those who engaged in the struggle at the time did not fight on all axes, but tended to give high priority to one or two, and to minimize others. It would appear that effective engagement requires a focus of energy that reduces the fronts on which one fights and therefore the alliances one forms, whereas long-term coalition building requires a much broader grasp of the contradictions that may, in the short term, make effective action harder to organize. It is difficult to fight on all fronts at once without dispersing one's energy, and a tightly focused struggle may, in its immediate effects, appear more likely to succeed. But if the alliances formed to fight it make other potential allies feel excluded, then the outcome may be hostility where there ought to be friendship.

The complications of these multiaxial politics, however, produce opportunities as well as difficulties: their multiplicity means that the position of every social formation will overlap to some extent with that of others, that every alliance will have social axes along which it can reach out to others. Sexual harassment, for example, whether in the workplace, on the streets, or in the home, is a common experience for all women in our society: although the experience of it will be inflected by racial and class positions—African American women and blue-collar women, for example, will experience it quite differently from Murphy Brown—it retains a gender commonality that may facilitate interracial and interclass alliances. Black and white women in lower-class positions, to give another example, held very similar views of Anita Hill's method of coping with Thomas's harassment, which offered an opportunity, unfortunately not taken, to form an interracial alliance along the axis of class.

These opportunities for alliance building, or, in Gramsci's terms, bloc formation, are not offered equally to all: our history of dominations has seen to that. The dominant alliances that characterize the power bloc have a long history of effectiveness. The result of this is that whiteness, masculinity, the upper classes, and older ages can be so effortlessly articulated together that the alliance appears natural. The history of applied and effective power has smoothed any rough edges between their different axes with the result that their mutuality of interests makes them so interwoven that, in effect, their multiaxiality becomes monoaxiality. But there are more ways of being subordinated than of dominating. As a result, subordinated social formations are more varied and more numerous than dominant ones. Their histories are more varied, too, and have developed fewer means of smoothing out the differences between them. Consequently, alliances between subaltern social formations are harder to form and maintain than are those within the power bloc. Opportunities to form them, however, do occur, and if the politics of a post-structural world are to be progressive rather than oppressive, we must learn to develop our skills of alliance building and maintenance. If we do not, the danger of a one-superpower world will become a national as well as a global reality.

BLACK FIGURES:
CLARENCE THOMAS AND BILL COSBY

The battles around Anita Hill and Clarence Thomas were as strong as they were because both figured wide and deep conflicts in U.S. culture. Fast-flowing and deep cultural currents, such as those bearing meanings of race, sexuality, and the family, will surface in different places and in different configurations. If the hearings were a maelstrom, *The Cosby Show* appears a calm backwater in comparison. Yet its benign surface is precisely that, for only just below it similar currents and countercurrents muddy its waters.

The Cosby Show is relevant to my analysis for a number of reasons. The conservative strategy in the hearings was, though not explicitly, to join Clarence Thomas with Bill Cosby/Cliff Huxtable to figure the "tamed Black male": its corollary, therefore, was to figure Anita Hill as the sexual savage, the opposite of Clair Huxtable. Figures can always be positive or negative, they can always be written with a plus or a minus. So, if x = the Black male and y = the Black female (in white figuring), then $+x$ = Clarence Thomas and Bill Cosby/Cliff Huxtable, and $-x$ = Willie Horton and Rodney King. Similarly $+y$ = Clair Huxtable, $-y$ = Anita Hill. It was thus an appropriate calculation for Tom Bradley, the Black mayor of Los Angeles ($+x$), to advise people to stay at home and watch the final episode of *The Cosby Show* ($+x$) rather than go out on the streets to participate in the uprisings ($-x$). The fact that the final episode coincided with the uprisings is one of those noncoincidences of history. If, in the realm of family values, *Married . . . with Children* (see below) was known by Fox executives as "not *The Cosby Show*," so, in the realm of race relations, the events on the streets of South-Central Los Angeles could be known nationally as "very definitely not *The Cosby Show*."

The Cosby Show grew and flourished alongside Reaganism: indeed, Henry Louis Gates has called the 1980s "the Cosby decade."[41] First screened in 1984, it headed the ratings from 1985 to 1989, dropped to second place in 1989–90, to fifth in 1990–91, and ended on the second night of the L.A. uprisings in 1992. On the surface it promoted pure Reaganism (and, indeed, Ronald was one of its fans), celebrating as it did the achievement, happiness, and harmony of a professional nuclear family, who happened to be Black. It invited us to watch parents coping cheerfully and successfully with common family problems in raising their kids and adapting traditional gender roles to the changed, if only slightly, conditions of the eighties. Cliff Huxtable/Bill Cosby (the figure merged the fictional and real just as thoroughly as Murphy does) was a gynecologist, Clair a lawyer, and their children, Theo, Sondra, Denise, Vanessa, and Rudi, grew up into and through their teens into young adulthood. Murphy Brown may suffer from the hollowness at the heart of yuppiedom, but for Cliff and Clair the core was solid and satisfying. White conservatives loved what they showed. William Buckley, for instance, thought that "it is simply not correct . . . that race prejudice is increasing in America. How does one know this? Simply, by the ratings of Bill Cosby's television show and the sales of his books. A nation simply does not idolize members of a race which that nation despises."[42] The confirmation of Clarence Thomas could, in the same discourse, be used to prove exactly the same point.

Others have claimed that Bill Cosby is a contemporary Uncle Tom, or Afro-Saxon, who provides white racism with the alibi that it needs in order to continue working in the post–civil rights United States. But, wherever we stand in the debate, Bill Cosby was a central figure in the way that Americans struggled over meanings of race, gender, class, and the family throughout the Reagan and Bush administrations.

In their book on the show and its audiences, Sut Jhally and Justin Lewis carefully add up the positives and negatives and calculate that, for whites at least, Bill Cosby is finally a figure of "enlightened racism."[43] A key calculation in their analysis, as in one account of Clarence Thomas, is the effectiveness of "bootstrapping." The concept continues the conservative strategy of laying the responsibility for failure upon the weak, not the powerful; upon the individual, not the social order. Everyone, bootstrappers would have us believe, can rise up through the system by their own efforts, and those who fail have simply not made the necessary effort. The bootstrap offers the conservative comfort of knowing that the means of overcoming contemporary racial inequalities lie in the attitudes and abilities of individual African Americans: white society need only provide the opportunity and leave the rest to them. The laws of physics may prove the physical impossibility of lifting oneself up by one's own bootstraps, but the conservative imagination is not hampered by such inconveniences as gravity: so in it Clarence and Cosby can easily demonstrate the effectiveness of the bootstrap as an elevator.

Welfare is the opposite of bootstrapping. In conservative discourse, welfare not only rewards those who have failed to grasp their opportunities but produces in them a dependency mentality that ensures they will never even look for their bootstraps, let alone tug on them. Clarence Thomas had previously castigated his sister, Emma Mae Martin, for welfare dependency; at a convention of Black conservatives he told a reporter, "She gets mad when the mailman is late with her welfare check, that's how dependent she is. What's worse is that now her kids feel entitled to the check too. They have no motivation for doing better or getting out of that situation."[44] (This was his account of her; others painted a quite different picture—see below. By the time of his nomination, she was supporting her family.) This "welfare mentality" lay, according to Bush and Quayle, at the heart of L.A.'s problems. Their white imagination saw it given form in the body of the Black unwed teenage mother, easily recoded as "the welfare mother," whose "poverty of values" was endorsed by Murphy Brown's fatherless baby. The fear is that welfare will replace the father with the state (it was, we recall, the "irrelevance of fathers" that worried Rush Limbaugh so much) and will thus undermine the traditional "family values" to which the Republicans had hitched their campaign wagon. Such beliefs are well rooted in the Republican imagination: in 1986, for example, Gary Bauer opined that "the values taught on *The Cosby Show* would do more to help low-income and minority children than a bevy of new federal programs. [A] lot of research indicates that values are much more important than, say, the level of welfare payments."[45] Views like that cannot have hindered his appointment to head the family planning office within the Education Department. Republicans will always reward those who tax their intelligence rather than their wallets. Bauer later expanded on these views, and underscored the masculinism he shared with both Limbaugh and Quayle, by explaining that what he found most edifying about the show was its depiction of a family where "the children respect the father."[46] Dan Quayle used the same opposition between masculinist family values and welfare in his account of the causes of the L.A. "riots": "A welfare check is not a husband," he explained gravely. "The state is not a father." . . . For him, there would have been no riots in South-Central L.A. if it had been populated by bootstrapping, family-centered Clarence Thomases and Bill Cosbys instead of Cripps, Bloods, and welfare mothers.

Much of Clarence Thomas's statement to the Senate Judiciary Committee consisted of his personal story of bootstrapping, in which his individual history was used to authenticate a Republican version of social history. Time and again he returned to his humble origins in Pin Point, Georgia, and his disadvantaged family background (he was raised by his grandparents). This individual history of a man improving his life by struggling up from rural poverty to Yale to the Supreme Court in only forty years was used by him and his conservative supporters to validate not only his own character, but also implicitly their own racial policies, particularly that affirmative action is demonstrably unnecessary. In their critical analysis of the racist effects of *The Cosby Show* within white America, Budd and Steinman cite a 1988 poll showing that 83 percent of whites saw no need for affirmative action, and one in 1991 showing that only 35 percent of whites believed that Congress should do anything to help the position of African Americans.[47]

Many white viewers read the same message in *The Cosby Show*. Typical was one who said while discussing it, "I think there really is room in the United States for minority people to get ahead, without affirmative action,"[48] and Jhally and Lewis's study gives many examples of whites using the show to validate their often passionate belief that affirmative action is unfair to whites. Judge Thomas's opposition to affirmative action policies, like that of some other successful conservative African Americans, speaks indirectly through these readings of Bill Cosby.

However antiracist in intention and origins, affirmative action has all too often been co-opted into white policy, for its implementation remains under the control of white employers, admissions officers, and the courts. Affirmative action was a product of multiracial struggles, and many formations of color still struggle to claim it as theirs, for it is one of the few institutionalized antiracist strategies to which they have access. But white power over the ways in which it is implemented often produces effects that countervene its original intentions. One, which is widely recognized in Black if not in white America, is that the social formation that has gained most from the policy is that of white women, particularly professional ones. From this viewpoint, Murphy Brown and "today's women" appear to have made their progress at the expense of African Americans. Another, equally distressing, has been the increase in class differences within African America. In general, the middle-class Blacks who are least threatening to white society have benefited most from the policy, and their benefit has widened the gap between them and the blue-collar and underclasses. Michael Eric Dyson identifies another effect of this class divisiveness: "With black track from the inner cities mimicking earlier patterns of white flight, severe class changes have negatively affected black ghettos. Such class changes have depleted communities of service establishments, local business and stores that . . . could provide full-time employment."[49] Black track offers one partial explanation for the influx of Korean store owners to Black neighborhoods that proved so incendiary in South-Central L.A. . . . The *Oprah Winfrey Show* on the L.A. uprisings . . . provided a glimpse of this intraracial conflict between the "haves" and the "have-nots" in action. Long-term white interests are thus served by the selective and strategic implementations of the policy that contradicts its explicit intention. The solution to the problems that selective affirmative action has caused within African America lies in taking white power and strategy out of its implementation. Clarence Thomas, however, used his version of his history to argue the opposite, that universal opportunity exists and that affirmative action, however implemented, is neither necessary nor beneficial. In opposing his nomination, the Congressional Black Caucus pointed to the way he himself had benefited from affirmative action both at Yale and in his subsequent career in Washington, and thus to the racist effects of his denying that he was selected as a beneficiary.

African Americans opposing Clarence Thomas, then, had to rewrite his individual history to refigure him in the political debate. By figuring in the role of affirmative action they showed that his rejection of it was also a rejection of the majority of African Americans whom it was intended to benefit. The NAACP stated:

> While we appreciate the fact that Judge Thomas came up in the school of hard knocks and pulled himself up by his own bootstraps—as many other black Americans have—our concern is for the millions of blacks who have no access to bootstraps, theirs or others. It is particularly disturbing that one who has himself so benefitted from affirmative action now denigrates it and would deny those opportunities to other blacks.[50]

In a candidly worded open letter to Clarence Thomas, Justice Leon Higginbotham also reminded him of how much he owed, not only to affirmative action, but to the long Black struggles that produced it.[51] Thomas's criticism of past and present Black leaders in the civil rights movement raised Higginbotham to some of his sternest language, for their work, which Thomas belittled, had made his success possible.

This distance between Thomas and much of African America is authenticated by the rewriting of his individual history. A friend of his family contradicted Thomas's account of the closeness between him and his grandfather, and between him and the Black community of Pin Point (see *Sidebar: Pinpointing Clarence*).

Clarence Thomas, too, had to rewrite his family history to turn his sister into the welfare scrounger who was hardly fit to polish his bootstraps. Nell Irvin Painter tells a different story of Emma Mae Martin:

> It turns out that she was only on welfare temporarily and that she was usually a two-job-holding, minimum-wage-earning mother of four. Unable to afford professional help, she had gone on welfare while she nursed the aunt who had suffered a stroke but who normally kept her children when Martin was at work.[52]

Thomas had to erase this part of her story because it showed all too clearly that lack of effort and poverty of values were in no way to blame for her "failure," but that the absence of welfare was.

Emma Mae Martin had to be distorted by her brother to fit the stereotype of "the lazy Black welfare scrounger." Her case reveals the degree to which counterevidence has to be repressed for stereotyping to be an effective discursive strategy. The L.A. uprisings gave the inhabitants of South-Central the chance to plead in public for jobs, but Dan Quayle repressed these pleas in order to fit them into his stereotype of "people who are dependent on drugs or the narcotic of welfare." . . . This black dependency figures powerfully in the white conservative imagination, but one has to look hard to find it in African America.

PINPOINTING CLARENCE

A scene from the PBS *Frontline* documentary, *Clarence Thomas and Anita Hill: Public Hearing, Private Pain* showing an interview with Tim Williams, a friend and business partner of Thomas's grandfather in Pin Point, Georgia, intercut with shots of Thomas's statement to the Senate Judiciary Committee:

CLARENCE THOMAS: I've always carried in my heart the world, the life, the people, the values of my youth.

TIM WILLIAMS: Down here, all we only had at that time was the NAACP. . . . we had lawyers that we couldn't even pay. And he, er, he had in mind that Clarence could help us out like that, and he went so far as to get him through school, and train him and all, like that. I think that's what he had in

his mind more than anything else—to help us out—the awful things we were in down here.

INTERVIEWER: And Clarence did not?

TIM WILLIAMS: No, he didn't. Even after he got out of school—as a civil rights—under Reagan, there. No, he didn't do anything for us.

CLARENCE THOMAS: I watched as my grandfather was called "boy," I watched as my grandmother suffered the indignity of being denied the use of a bathroom, but through it all they remained fair, decent, good people.

INTERVIEWER: Thomas cried when he talked about his grandfather.

TIM WILLIAMS: I know he did. But I really didn't buy that.

INTERVIEWER: You didn't?

TIM WILLIAMS: No, I didn't, because his grandfather was disappointed in him.

CLARENCE THOMAS: I can still hear my grandfather, "You all going to have more of a chance than me." And he was right.

TIM WILLIAMS: I don't know whether he changed or not, but the only thing he had was a Black skin, Clarence: everything else was as white as a sheet.

As Dan Quayle used the inhabitants of South-Central Los Angeles to advance his agenda, so Clarence Thomas used Emma Mae Martin. The gap between brother and sister is evidence of the divisive effects within African America that the selective implementation of affirmative action may have, particularly when it is turned into bootstrapping. A painful paradox underlies the widely differing attitudes of African Americans to Clarence Thomas: he exemplifies both the good and the bad effects of affirmative action.

On the surface, Bill Cosby/Cliff Huxtable seems a much less contradictory figure than Clarence Thomas. Under the surface, however, currents and countercurrents disturb the waters in much the same way. In particular, the cross-currents between the figures of the few successful Blacks and the majority firmly held at the bottom of white society make for muddy waters in which no truths can be clearly seen. For many whites, as we have noted, the few successful African Americans act as an index of the decline of white racism, and they therefore extend this into their understanding of the "failure" of the majority. White television shows both the successful Black (Cosby, Oprah, Magic Johnson, Clarence Thomas) and, on the news particularly, the unsuccessful—the criminal, the teenage mother, the drug abuser, the welfare leech, the homeless man.[53] The two are opposite sides of the same figure.

There were Black viewers of Cosby, however, for whom the figure's double-sidedness meant something different. Jhally and Lewis's study showed that Black audiences of Cosby were much more likely to point to the contrasts between the two sides of the figure than were whites. They were so pained by the constantly negative pictures of Blacks on the news that they welcomed any representation of the successful Black, because of both its rarity and its contradiction of the more normal public image of Black failure. Michael Eric Dyson makes a similar point when he claims that Bill Cosby undercut the dominant stereotype of the Black male and that the show "permitted America to view black folk as *human beings.*"[54] John Downing (who is white) also contrasts the news's negative portrayal of African Americans with Cosby's: "*The Cosby Show* may operate as a reinstatement of black dignity and culture in a racist society where television culture has generally failed to communicate these realities and has often flatly negated them."[55] Similar arguments were made about the way the hearings showed dignified Blacks to white America. *New Yorker* magazine, for example, thought that "the nation was treated to a parade of blacks who—for once—weren't crack dealers, athletes, welfare mothers, or any of the other stereotypes, but solid citizens, fine friends and excellent character witnesses for the two principals."[56]

Such representations can have quite different political circulations in white and Black America. Whereas for whites, the Huxtables' success could demonstrate the death of racism, for many African Americans it offered a rare affirmative and inspiring image: precisely those features that enabled whites to deny racism allowed Blacks some hope that they might prosper despite it. Cosby provided a source of hope and energy to counter the far more numerous sources of despair. Similarly, some African Americans were pleased that Cosby showed them to whites in a way that they could be proud of. They understood how racism could be justified and made legitimate to whites by constantly negative representations of Blacks.

Being Black in the United States today necessarily produces a double consciousness of one's identity: Blacks have to be as aware of how they appear to whites as of how they appear to themselves. This dual consciousness is characteristic of subordinated social formations in general, whose very survival can depend upon their ability to see how they and their actions appear to the alliances that dominate them. Dominant formations, however, rarely acquire this duality, for they have little need of it. So women are much more conscious of how they appear to men than vice versa, and workers see more clearly how their behavior looks to bosses than bosses see how theirs may look to their employees; and, of course, whites are not good at looking at their actions through the eyes of Blacks, whereas, from the slave auction onward, Blacks have always had to understand how whites see them. Much of the Black criticism of Anita Hill's allegations was based upon this knowledge of what whites would make of them, not upon their truth, or upon their gender politics within African America. The knowledge that both Bill Cosby and Clarence Thomas were viewed positively by powerful formations within white America led many African Americans to support them in the absence of any more positive figure of the Black man. If, in current conditions, Cosby and Thomas are the best that is available, then it may appear to make tactical good sense to make the best possible use of them. The problem, of course, is that in the longer term and the larger arena the strategic values of these figures to conservative whites is likely to outweigh their short-term tactical value to Blacks.

This absence of any more positive figure must be contextualized by the looming presence of a much more negative one. When the alternative to Clarence Thomas is Willie Horton . . . , the positives of Thomas may justly seem to outweigh the negatives. The racial-sexual threat of the untamed Black male in the white imagination has had such devastating effects in the white treatment of Blacks that any contradiction of it can be seen as a step in the right direction. Sadly, this is not the case. The figure of the tamed Black male is at least as likely to serve, in the white imagination, to justify the intensified oppression of his untamed obverse and to provide an alibi against the charge of racism: if we love Bill Cosby and seat Clarence Thomas on the Supreme Court, then we cannot be charged with either racism or injustice in the beating of Rodney King.

RACE AND "TODAY'S WOMAN": CLAIR HUXTABLE, ANITA HILL, AND MURPHY BROWN

The struggle to figure Clarence Thomas with either Bill Cosby or Willie Horton was not a racially balanced one: whites stood to gain from either figuration, Blacks only from the former, and even there, any gain could be achieved only at considerable cost. The conflict between Anita Hill and Clarence Thomas presented whites with clear choices, and generally they made them unequivocally and unhesitatingly; for African Americans, however, the issues were less clear-cut, the choices harder to make, and unequivocality very difficult to achieve.

The struggle over Anita Hill was as difficult to engage in as that over Thomas. White opponents figured her as the female equivalent of Willie Horton and the opposite of Clair Huxtable. White supporters put her alongside Murphy Brown as an example of "today's woman." For her Black supporters she could be another Sojourner Truth; for Black opponents, Delilah or Jezebel, a betrayer of men's strength.

Different meanings of today's woman and of her relations to men and to the family swirl around the figures of Anita Hill, Clair Huxtable, and Murphy Brown. In the Murphy Brown–Anita Hill–Clair Huxtable configuration, racial difference comes into the picture as it does not in the Murphy Brown–Zoë Baird–Hillary Rodham Clinton one. Despite racial difference, however, it is worth noting that all of these women, except Murphy, are lawyers, and that the legal profession has been good to today's women, who have increased their numbers within it from 8 percent to 21 percent during the past twelve years (another of them, incidentally, is Marilyn Quayle, Dan's wife). It was appropriate, then, for the American Bar Association to honor Anita Hill, and for Hillary Rodham Clinton to present the award. . . .

But my point here is a different one. This configuration of Anita-Clair-Murphy carries hot issues in the debate around family values, single motherhood, and race: Murphy the white single mother, Anita the hypersexual Black woman or the oppressed raceless one, and Clair the Black opposite of both, the embodiment of every possible family value. The visible currents and countercurrents within this configuration of professional women barely mask the powerful subcurrent into which Clarence tossed Emma Mae Martin—that of the Black welfare mother. Dan Quayle tapped into it, too, in his attack on Murphy

Brown: in emphasizing the statistics that demonstrated the disintegration of the Black family, he made the Black single mother into the key figure of this "disintegration." The issue of William Buckley's *National Review* discussing the causes of the L.A. "riots" contains a cartoon that all too neatly brings together the different Black "family values" of the Cosbys and South-Central: it shows a Black man watching a television on which an announcer is saying, "Tonight, the final episode with the Huxtable family"; beside the viewer on the couch is a newspaper with a headline that reads, in a direct reference to Dan Quayle's speech, "63% of children live with a single parent"; a balloon shows the Black man thinking, "What's a family?"[57]

The statistics do show a dramatic increase in Black single motherhood; they also show that sex, race, and marital status are important elements in poverty—families headed by a single woman, particularly if nonwhite, are more likely to live below the poverty line than those with both parents, particularly if white. But statistics have to be given meaning, they do not come equipped with it: to be made to mean, they have to be articulated with other facts. One articulation is to relate these statistics to economic ones, particularly the sharp decline in the employment of young Black males over the past twenty years, which has paralleled closely the increase in Black single motherhood. When the dominant discourses define fatherhood primarily by the economic ability to be a breadwinner and then economic alliances within the dominant classes export millions of the jobs that used to make this definition achievable, then Quayle and Limbaugh have to work hard to submerge the articulations among an unregulated economy, job loss, and the absence of fathers, and to create new ones that articulate the absent father to absent values.

The interests that produced unregulated economic policies also produced the welfare policies of the 1980s and, in them, as in employment, discourse and economics work together. Like single motherhood, "welfare" does not contain its own prescription of how to understand it. In Dan Quayle's discourse, welfare causes the family to disintegrate by producing a dependency mentality and by substituting a government check for a male breadwinner. The policies of his alliance underwrote this meaning: the regulations of AFDC (Aid to Families with Dependent Children) for most of the 1980s were such as to have made it almost impossible for a woman married to an unemployed man to qualify for welfare—she had to be single to receive the check. This was compounded by the economic conditions in which even a fully employed man on the minimum wage, rare though even he be in South-Central L.A., could not lift her and her two children even close to the poverty line, let alone above it. Whether her man was employed or unemployed, the poor woman was economically better off without him. It is not surprising, then, that many African Americans see the undermining of the Black family by unemployment and welfare regulations as part of a white racist strategy that amounts to genocide: racism is recoded, and racial power applied along the axis of economics. In its effects, then, welfare can be similar to affirmative action: both appear to promote the interests of disadvantaged African Americans, but their implementation can all too easily ensure that any Black advantage is controlled and directed by whites.

Herman Gray criticizes a CBS documentary called *The Vanishing Family: Crisis in Black America* because of its blaming of the victims for their own situation.[58] In telling the stories of "typical" Black families in Newark, New Jersey, it showed image after image of Black men "irresponsibly" hanging out on the streets while women, many of them single, struggled to raise their children. The documentary was screened in January

1985, at the period when *The Cosby Show* was steadily climbing in the ratings. At one point the documentary's host, Bill Moyers, implicitly brought the two programs together:

> There are successful strong black families in America. Families that affirm parental author-ity and the values of discipline, work and achievement. But you won't find many who live around here.[59]

Although Moyers is publicly seen as a liberal, neither Reagan, Bush, nor Quayle would have been provoked into any liberal bashing by a comment like that. Quayle, too, would have enjoyed the way that Moyers predicted his "Murphy Brown" speech:

> A whole lot of white families are in trouble too. Single parent families are twice as com-mon in America today as they were 20 years ago. But for the majority of white children, family still means a mother and a father. This is not true for most black children. For them, things are getting worse. Today black teenagers have the highest pregnancy rate in the industrialized world, and in the black inner city practically no teenage mother gets married. That's no racist comment. What's happening goes far beyond race.[60]

As a liberal, Moyers does not blame the victims for their own victimization quite as explicitly as does Dan Quayle. But by submerging the links between conservative eco-nomic and welfare policies and the "welfare mother" under a current of liberal concern, he hides the knowledge that "welfare mothers" are the inevitable product of the policies that have advantaged those from whose position he speaks, regardless of their party allegiance. The same social forces underlay the emergence of both Clarence Thomas and Emma Mae Martin, and to deny their influence, Thomas had to individualize the difference between him and his sister in order to make his "success" the consequence of his abilities, and her "failure" that of her inadequacies. We should not be surprised, then, to find Clarence Thomas using statistics in the same way as Dan Quayle and Bill Moyers to paint a simi-larly stereotypical picture: in a speech to students at historically Black Clark College in Atlanta, he pointed out that 48 percent of Black mothers were unmarried and that 40 per-cent of Black youths were on welfare, and concluded that massive federal involvement has still left African Americans at the bottom of the ladder and that more government inter-vention is not necessary, for "we control the values that our kids have."[61] Stereotypes, such as that of the "Black welfare mother," are neither reflections of social reality nor merely distortions of it: they are active in producing it. The power interests that control economic and welfare policies also control the discursive policies that produce stereotypes. The stereotype is an application of discursive power that is as material as the application of eco-nomic and political power, and the effectiveness of any one power axis is affected by its multiaxial relations to the others.

One multiaxial commonality is the need to recode racial power and thus to deny its operation while exerting it. Bill Moyers has to deny the racism that underlies his com-mentary and, inevitably, to echo Bush's denial that race played any role in his nomination of Clarence Thomas. Moyers, however, may have been less confident than Bush that his denial would work, for when the program was repeated, three months later, he included in its opening shots one of a Black welfare worker reassuring viewers that the problems of poverty have nothing to do with racism, and that their solution lay within the Black community itself.[62]

Moyers may be a liberal and Quayle a Republican, but that does not prevent the same discursive strategy being used by both of them: as whites, both can recode racism into "family values." *The Cosby Show*'s popularity during this period aided this recoding. As Jhally and Lewis point out, it tended to be seen by whites as the story of a Black *family;* for African Americans, however, its topic was a *Black* family. The shift in emphasis is subtle but important, for it carries a significant redirection of the racial politics of the show.

As I have argued, for both African and European Americans racial anxieties become intensified when sexuality enters the picture. Whether the family be Black or white, one of the key functions of its values is to contain sexuality, and when the family is a Black one that is highly visible to whites this containment increases in urgency. As Paula Giddings has pointed out, Black sexuality when seen and interpreted by whites has historically resulted in rapes and lynchings. Equally, for Bill Moyers and Dan Quayle it underlay the so-called collapse of the Black family and thus the disintegration of the Black neighborhood and of Black society. Incarnated in the figure of the unwed teenage mother, Black sexuality is used to put the blame for the public problems of African America upon its own private parts.

This frail figure of the pregnant teenaged African American has a lot to bear, and in this context it is not surprising that *The Cosby Show* handles Black sexuality with kid gloves (or, given Cliff's profession, rubber ones). In one episode, for example, Cliff rushes into the house, tells Vanessa to assemble the kids for a family conference, and goes into the kitchen, where Clair is, predictably, preparing supper. Instead of his usual designer sweater, he is wearing his white doctor's coat, a sign that he is bringing his professional persona home with him. The following exchange takes place:

CLIFF: Do you think our children tell us everything?

CLAIR: Who's in trouble?

CLIFF: No one's in trouble. I've just come back from the office: now a young girl comes in scared about what she might have. It turns out all she has is a mild bladder infection which can be cleared up in a couple of weeks . . . a lovely girl, intelligent, beautiful, could have been one of our children . . .

CLAIR: But what's the point?

CLIFF: The point is that she never told her parents and she let it go four weeks. Now the question is do we have the kind of children who never get into any kind of trouble whatsoever, or do we have children who get into trouble—and don't tell us?[63]

The family conference that follows is typical Huxtable domesticity. The kids tease their parents, the parents stumble around an embarrassing subject but finally succeed in exerting their parental authority in a noncoercive, good-humored way. The children turn the discussion away from their own "troubles" to their parents' propensity to get mad when "troubles" are raised. All the troubles are hypothetical ones, but even so, Cliff and Clair are provoked into anger. The pedagogical point, however, that good families can solve their problems by drawing upon their own resources, is strengthened, not weakened, by the comic difficulty of the Huxtables in following their own advice. The hypothetical trouble that Cliff finds hardest to cope with is that Theo may have driven his car with neither permission nor a license. Clair's difficulties are caused by Denise's pretending that, instead of sleeping over with a girlfriend, she had spent the night at her boyfriend's house when his parents were on vacation—although "nothing happened." The Theo-Cliff trouble is resolved through an all-boy pillow fight. The Denise-Clair one remains more open as Clair leaves to phone the mother of Denise's girlfriend to check that she really had slept there.

What is not spoken is at least as significant as what is. The almost repressed figure here, of course, is that of the Black unwed pregnant teenager who is so firmly centered in Bill Moyers's and Dan Quayle's discourse. The race of Cliff's patient is never given, though her being just like the Huxtable daughters hints she is African American. If so, the adjectives Cliff uses to describe her, "beautiful" and "intelligent," recode "Black," and "young" recodes "single." In addition, not only is none of the three Huxtable teenagers nor Cliff's patient pregnant, nor is the word ever spoken, but none of the Huxtables, at least, could have been, not because of practicing safe sex but because of practicing no sex. The historically pertinent figure of the Black single mother, so central to white strategy, is not countered here but marginalized, just as she was in *Murphy Brown*. Even if the traces are recovered, and the figure pulled back into visibility, her "problem" is restricted to the relationships among the young woman, her doctor, and her parents. Any viewer who wishes to articulate this Black young woman's nonpregnancy with the current social conditions of the African American family and the political uses made of them has to overcome a double dose of discursive repression. One wonders if many viewers would find the semiotic labor worthwhile. Indeed, it almost appears as though the topic were raised in order to repress its social context and thus to contain it safely within the family values shared by conservatives of all races.

It is also worth speculating here about what white viewers might make of the choice of gynecology for Cliff's profession. As Foucault has shown us, the medicalization of sexuality throughout the nineteenth century worked to contain it socially and to pathologize any forms that escaped their container. Orrin Hatch and his colleagues had to fight as hard as they did to deny the existence of any loose sexuality in Clarence Thomas because they knew the sanctions it would occasion: Clarence Thomas had to be sexually contained to be acceptable to white America. One wonders if making Cliff into a gynecologist is a way of rendering Black sexuality safe by medicalizing it and thus of defusing its threat to the white imagination. To carry this line of speculation to its extreme, one might also wonder whether Thomas's white wife, constantly glimpsed behind him on our screens, and Cliff Huxtable's possibly white patients, never spoken nor shown, might not serve as guarantors of their safeness, as living proof that Black male sexuality has, in these men at least, been tamed, and is thus containable within family values.

It is common white strategy to make sense of Black single motherhood, unemployment, welfare, and the disintegrating family by linking them, through family values, to morality rather than to economic and social policy. By this means the problem can be laid squarely upon the shoulders of its victims, and any white assistance in reaching its solution must at least begin, and in some cases end, with preaching.

Today's women are readily deployable in this strategy: Murphy Brown can figure single motherhood by choice, not by circumstance; Anita Hill can figure Black hypersexuality or immorality (another white reason for Black single motherhood and the disintegration of Black family values that need not be spoken to be put to work); and Clair Huxtable can be made to demonstrate that family values are both effective and available to all who choose to adopt them, regardless of their race. When Dan Quayle blamed the L.A. uprisings on Murphy's single motherhood and when Tom Bradley urged Los Angelenos to watch Bill Cosby instead of "rioting," they were both tapping into the same currents of meaning as had Bill Moyers some seven years previously.

Clair Huxtable may be the opposite of what white conservatives made Anita Hill into, but from other viewpoints the two could appear to be similar. Both are successful lawyers, and their privilege has caused class resentment among some less-privileged Black women. One audience member in Jhally and Lewis's study commented:

> I can't stand [Clair]. . . . Because she's not a typical black person. She walks around dressed up all the time, now come on. We don't walk around dressed up all the time. She's a lawyer and we understand that. She comes home from work . . . how come her hair's not in rollers? How come she can't walk around with her blue jeans on? You know what I'm saying? Now come on.[64]

This echoes Nellie McKay's account of why some lower-class Black women did not support Anita Hill: We can recall, too, that Zoë Baird's illegal alien child-care worker provoked anger among women who were excluded from her privileged solution to a problem that they shared. Social identities and thus social alliances always include elements of class, race, and gender, but the proportions of the mix cannot be predicted or generalized.

Other audience members, therefore, allied themselves strongly with Clair's Blackness and overlooked any economic differences. In particular, her way of speaking could be a signal of Black community:

> One reason is that we talk differently. I can close my eyes and tell it is a black show. They still use in the show street language, they are comfortable at home. . . . Clair is a lawyer, you never see her use legal jargon, or whatever; she talks just like a black woman. I was raised by a black man and woman and this is how they talked, so when I close my eyes I can totally tell the difference. Also we have a tone to our language and it comes from our history. It is a singing type, very melodic type of talk, or conversation that is just natural for our people. So if you are watching an all-white show, you will not hear that; you would hear the standard English. You will not hear the melodic sound of the voice as you can when the Huxtables speak.[65]

Significantly this offers a Black pleasure from which whites are excluded: "You can hear like Clair with a little accent to her voice: you know, like an accent that only black people would understand."[66] The way of talking is an embodied language, a way of making direct bodily connections between those who share it. It is therefore uncolonizable. However white the language, however white the television system, Blacks can still accent both to speak to each other.

Anita Hill allowed whites to see what Blacks would prefer them not to; Clair, however, is quite different:

> I like Clair's character per se. She's a strong, black woman, very independent. . . . I like her character per se because it depicts blacks in a different mold than what white America thinks.[67]

It is not easy to negotiate among Clair's Blackness, her privilege, and the positive image she presents to both Blacks and whites.

> You know, it's always that upper middle class, upper class mentality. . . . It's just not real for me. Again, I like the show per se because it does depict blacks in a more positive way than we usually—we're not killing each other. We're not raping people. You know, we're some ordinary people who like the nice things in life like everybody else.[68]

The figure of Willie Horton lurks just below the surface of this woman's discourse as the one commonly used by whites to distance or "other" Blacks: she counters it by emphasizing Blacks' similarity to "everybody else" without losing the awareness that "everybody else" is predominantly white.

Both Downing and Lewis argue that Clair Huxtable demonstrates gently progressive gender politics, insofar as when there is gender conflict between her and Cliff or Theo, she generally wins both the argument and the audience's sympathy.[69] (We must note here that not all feminists, particularly Black and "third" world ones, would agree with their sense of the word *progressive*.) But such progressiveness as there may be is traditionally framed. She plays all the conservative feminine roles in the economy of the household, and the kitchen is unequivocally her room: Cliff rarely cooks a family meal, and his occasional attempts to get himself a sandwich invariably end up with a comic display of feminine control over food consumption, as Clair monitors his attempted intake of unhealthy foods. But in the social economy of the household, that of ideas and influence, Clair often appears stronger than Cliff. Cliff's attempts to be masculine are typically subject to gentle mockery, almost never reach their objective, and frequently cause mild chaos. By contrast, Clair's femininity provides a calm core of common sense that works to solve each episode's family crisis. The gender progressiveness of the show *is* gentle, it *is* contained within a conservative value system, but it is demonstrated week after week and both female and male viewers comment favorably upon it. There were some women, however, who judged the containment to be stronger than the progress, but most found pleasure in the way they saw Clair advancing women's interests.[70] Indeed, many viewers of both sexes applauded the show's delicate balance in managing to promote feminine causes without alienating men and provoking their hostility.

But, having recognized that achievement, we must also note that Clair has a full-time profession, is raising five children, does all the cooking and household management, all without any hired help or child-care workers, and, to cap it all, she never has a hair out of place and rarely shows any signs of strain. Murphy Brown and Zoë Baird found incomplete and unsatisfactory ways of coping with "today's woman's" problems in negotiating the demands of career and motherhood: Clair offers no solution because she has no problems. Neither her Black sexuality nor her feminine gender pose a threat to white male security: Murphy Brown caused Dan Quayle far greater anxiety.

Equally, Clair Huxtable is not the Anita Hill who troubled Orrin Hatch so deeply, though the words that a Black fan used to describe Clair ("a strong Black woman, very independent"[71]) could well have been directed toward her. Both are Black women who speak in public. Clair's speech may not challenge the power structure as directly as Anita Hill's, but accommodating and unthreatening though her voice may be, it is still a Black woman's public voice, and, as we hear in Jhally and Lewis's book, Black women take pleasure in listening to one of their own, a pleasure that public discourse offers all too rarely.

Nancy Fraser has pointed out that much of the gender politics of the hearings was fought around the gendering of the public sphere, and the public-private dichotomy that accompanied it.[72] As a man, Clarence Thomas was able to control which aspects of his life and opinions were suitable for which sphere in a way that Anita Hill could not. Thomas, for instance, was able to assert, "I am not here . . . to put my private life on display for prurient interests or other reasons. I will not allow this committee or anyone else to probe into my private life" or "I will not get into any discussions that I might have had about my personal life or my sex life with any person outside of the work place."[73] The committee accepted his definitions of the private and the public, and his right to keep the private to himself.

That was not the case with Anita Hill. Despite her struggles to control and defend her privacy, her "private" characteristics were dragged into the public arena by men in order to disqualify her public speech. She was called, at various stages in their strategy "a lesbian, a heterosexual erotomaniac, a delusioned schizophrenic, a fantasist, a vengeful spurned woman, a perjurer and a malleable tool of liberal interest groups."[74] Fraser concludes:

> Given the gender differential in ability to define and protect one's privacy, we can understand some of the deeper issues at stake in Thomas's insistence on avoiding the "humiliation" of a "public probe" into his "privacy." This insistence can be understood in part as a defense of his masculinity: to be subject to having one's privacy publicly probed is to risk being feminized.[75]

Anita Hill's attempts to control her presence in public have a long history of masculine power to overcome. From at least the nineteenth century, a woman in public without a man was all too easily cast as a prostitute: Orrin Hatch had a deep history to help him hypersexualize Anita Hill. The woman walking (or talking) in public lays herself open to male abuse because of the masculine power to define and control the public domain as men's. Faced with this power and danger, women have seized on what limited public space they can define as theirs. Rachel Bowlby has argued, for instance, that the department store and, later, the shopping mall are public places where a woman alone could move without danger or masculine harassment. They constitute a feminine public space, albeit one that is physically and discursively contained. Similarly, one might argue that sitcoms, soap operas, and talk shows can serve as feminine discursive places, where women's discourse can circulate comparatively free of harassment within the containment of sitcoms, soap operas, and talk shows. Once Murphy Brown's single motherhood was brought out of this feminine space into the "masculine" one of "real" politics and the "real" public sphere, she, like Anita Hill, could be constructed as a social-sexual threat. Quayle's attempts to degrade her were less vicious than the Hatchet job on Anita Hill, probably because racial guilt could not be mobilized against her and also because the public arena into which Quayle pulled her, that of the news media, was less directly under masculine control than the Senate chamber in which Anita Hill had to speak. Murphy could return to her sitcom to answer the politician in her terms and on her terrain, and beat him. On television and in public, Anita Hill had more feminine power than in the Senate, and could turn her defeat in one arena into victories in the others. Clair Huxtable, however, remained safely within her sitcom and never provoked male, public hostility, but, nevertheless, she still managed to say what many Black women wished to hear.

The public domain is one where white masculinity guards its power most zealously. The Black women who cringed on hearing issues of Black sexuality raised in front of a white audience knew all too well that once out in public the meanings of Black sexuality would be out of their control and would be directed against them. On the television documentary that aired these fears, a Black woman student at Spelman College lamented that Black gender struggles had to be fought out on white media.[76] Her complaint that African Americans do not have a national broadcast medium where they can control and circulate their own discourse is well founded and not accidental; at the local level, however, radio stations such as WLIB in Harlem and Black Liberation Radio in Springfield, Illinois . . . , do fill the lack she identifies.

NOT *THE COSBY SHOW*

The Cosby Show, with its clearly conservative meanings of race and family, although contested, however murkily, by quite contradictory ones, came under attack from 1988 onward by the upstart Fox network and its two "antifamily values" sitcoms, *Married . . . with Children* and *The Simpsons.*

A brief look at these two shows will enable us to trace how the axes of class and age can be mobilized alongside those of gender and race within that contested terrain of "family values." It is not surprising that sitcoms should be so hotly political, for generically, most of them are about, and designed to be watched by, the family. And the family is the site where the internal politics of age, gender, class, and race are most immediately put into practice.

In the 1992 campaign, the family was important to the Republicans because it was the only domestic issue on which they could fight with any confidence—the Bush presidency had ignored the economy, the inner cities, the public school system, the public health system, and almost all the other domains of everyday life in which Washington's actions (or lack of them) become the mundanity of lived experience. Citing the restoration of the traditional family as the solution to all these social problems has long been Republicans' strategy to justify their refusal to address them directly. When Dan Quayle blamed the L.A. uprisings on the collapse of the Black family he was treading a well-worn path.

Ronald Reagan, too, had made family values as central in his election campaigns of 1980 and 1984 as had Bush in 1988 and 1992. The so-called collapse of the traditional nuclear family has been a fact of U.S. life for the past fifty years, so the conservative emphasis on the need to return to it was a reaction to social conditions that were moving in the opposite direction. The 1980s continued the development of nontraditional families so far that the ideological norm became one that only a minority could achieve. When most people live in conditions that differ from such a norm, social anxieties are bound to result. *The Cosby Show,* with its deeply nostalgic vision of a golden age of the family, was one consequence of these anxieties; *Married . . . with Children,* with its skeptical disbelief in that same utopian family, was another; and *The Simpsons* was a third.

Even fans of *The Cosby Show* commented on its lack of "realism," and found the Huxtables just too perfect in both economic and ethical values: the family demonstrated too precisely the glossy opposite of Quayle's "poverty of values." This "unrealisticness" could produce pleasure for the fans only as long as they could believe that the gap between the material conditions of most families and the utopian ones of the Huxtables was bridgeable. This belief became harder to sustain as the Reagan years passed. Murphy Brown's baby was one sign that Cosby's nostalgic utopianism had lost its broad-based credibility; *Married . . . with Children* and *The Simpsons* were earlier signs of the same loss.

The first televisual cracks in *The Cosby Show*'s hegemonic family values were opened around generational differences, though they quickly spread to include ones of class and gender. Since its origin in the 1950s, the category of "the teenager" has always been a source of anxiety for adult America, because within it traditional family values have been most keenly tested and contested. Rupert Murdoch, Fox's owner, decided in the mid-1980s that this highly charged controversial terrain was the best upon which to fight the dominance of the three national networks. He planned to develop his new Fox network by combining the existing networks' wide geographical reach with a new ability to deliver accurately segmented audiences, particularly ones that lay outside the massed middle America over whom the three other networks vied with one another. So he launched his new network on weekends with a schedule aimed at the teenage and young adult nonfamily audience. With programs such as *The Tracey Ullman Show* and *It's Garry Shandling's Show,* Fox quickly won a core audience in its targeted segment, but *Married . . . with Children* and *The Simpsons* were its first shows to achieve general ratings that challenged those of the big three.

But Fox's success was not solely the result of its ability to produce shows whose skepticism could be used to disrupt and interrogate traditional family values. Change in a nation's structure of feeling never occurs on one front alone. There were also significant technological changes during the 1980s. The dominance of network television in home-based entertainment was steadily eroded by new technologies, particularly cable, but also VCRs, video games, and home computers. During the 1980s, network audiences shrank from 91 percent to 67 percent.

New technologies cannot in themselves produce social change, though they can and do facilitate it. These new technologies met the marketing strategies of late capitalism, or post-Fordism, which can be summarized briefly as ones of product differentiation and market segmentation rather than mass production and mass marketing. The networks, however, were irredeemably Fordist—they had grown and prospered by attracting the largest and least differentiated audiences possible.

However dominant the market economy is, our society is not determined by it entirely. Post-Fordism's market segmentation was not just a result of industrial strategy, but was also an economic transformation of changes in the social order at large. Throughout the 1970s and 1980s people's sense of social differences began to challenge the homogenizing effect of consensual social norms. The women's movement was one key player as it asserted women's rights to control not only their economic and domestic relations, but also the sense of the feminine and thus the meaning of feminine identity. Similar demands were made by the Black power and gay liberation movements. As Reaganism and Reaganomics widened the gaps between rich and poor, men and women, whites and those of color, the sense of social differences sharpened and became conflictual. *The Cosby Show*'s appeal depended largely upon its ability to paint a consensual gloss over differences of race, class, and gender; and so, by the end of the Reagan/Bush administrations, it had lost touch with the nation's changing structure of feeling.

This conjuncture of forces, sociocultural, technological, and economic, was part of the changing structure of feeling within which *Married . . . with Children* gained, and *The Cosby Show* lost, popular appeal. This change may be characterized by interpreting *The Cosby Show*'s slide down the ratings as a sign that a dominant cultural current was changing to a residual one, and *Married . . . with Children*'s climb up them as an emergent current pushing its way into the mainstream. In 1989 Cosby still topped the ratings, but the Bundy family's loud and obnoxious voices were becoming widely heard. And many of those who heard them were deeply offended, mainly because the show was sending the "wrong" message to teenagers. By publicly inverting the norms of the "good" family, it offended those whose social interests were inscribed in them and appealed to those who identified themselves as outside-the-family.

The relationships among the family members conflict across both age and gender. The language in which they are conducted is scatological and often emphasizes their bodily and sexual attributes as markers of identity and of social relationships. Indeed, much of the comedy of the show falls in the disciplinary category of "the dirty joke" (see *Sidebar: Dirty Jokes and the Bundys*). Clarence Thomas used the dirty joke of claiming to find a pubic hair on his Coke can as an expression of masculine power. The Bundy males frequently make these traditional dirty jokes, but, in *Married . . . with Children,* unlike Thomas's EEOC office, they are quickly countered by the Bundy women, who, like the Designing Women, have developed a subversive genre of antimale dirty jokes. The politics of turned dirty jokes is contradictory and risks alienating some women who might applaud its ends but be offended by its means. And there were many liberal women who were offended by the show and saw nothing progressive in it.

But their offense was minor compared to that of conservative women. Terry Rakolta, for example, was a wealthy Michigan housewife who gained much publicity for her campaign to persuade advertisers to withdraw from the show on the grounds that the offensive bodies and jokes of the Bundys resembled soft-core pornography, and that the show contained "blatant exploitation of women and sex, and anti-family attitudes."[77] According to a front-page story in the *New York Times,* Procter & Gamble, McDonald's, Tambrands, and Kimberly-Clark all withdrew advertising support or promised to monitor the show's values more carefully in future.[78] Procter & Gamble cited the show's "negative portrayal of American family life"; the chairman of Coca-Cola wrote to Rakolta that he was "corporately, professionally and privately embarrassed" that ads for Coca-Cola had appeared on it; and Gary Lieberman, chairman of Columbia Pictures Television, which produced the show, offered Rakolta "our sincere apology."[79]

Rakolta's husband was president of a family-owned construction firm worth $400 million (which gives a particular inflection to the term *family values*), so the social positions of those forming this set of right-wing alliances were particularly close, in the upper reaches of corporate America. Although class was not explicitly cited as a feature of the offensiveness of the program, the class difference between the Bundys and their objectors inevitably framed the contestation. Rakolta attempted to broaden the allegiance, but not its intent, by enlisting the support of lobbying groups within conservative "middle America" and the religious right, specifically, Concerned Women of America and the American

DIRTY JOKES AND THE BUNDYS

The Bundys have just been ejected from a party at their respectable neighbors' house.

AL: But you've got to give me credit, I did try to liven things up.

PEG: You know, Al, I don't think a banker's party is the right place to stand on the buffet and yell, "Let's wet the wives' T-shirts and rate their hooters."

AL: You'd have won.

PEG: Oh, Al.

KELLY (as Buck, the family dog, takes a fur coat from next door's party upstairs): Mom, why can Buck have the coat upstairs and I can't have boys in my room?

PEG: Because the coat can't get pregnant.

BUD: Obviously neither can Kelly!

BUD (after having been caught stealing gas from the guests' cars): Kel, this is it, the last time I'm working for Dad. From now on, I go solo.

KELLY: Much like at Lover's Lane?

FORTUNE TELLER (from the party, as she sits on the couch): Sit down, I feel very strong vibrations here.

AL: Did you leave your toy running under the couch again?

PEG: No, it's in the shop. It's being turbo-charged.

Family Association (which had started life as the National Federation for Decency, an organization founded by a fundamentalist minister, the Reverend Donald Wildmon). Rakolta's rallying cry, around which this allegiance was forged, was "Free TV is the last bastion for the American family, or anybody who wants decent programming."

Initially, the press reaction to her campaign was favorable. The *Detroit News* (her local newspaper) was typical in applauding "Mrs. Rakolta's stand for decency."[80] (It is noteworthy how frequently the concept of "decency" is used to disguise class taste and power under the mask of universally agreed-upon standards.) But the press support for the alliance weakened as its narrow social base and repressive strategy became clearer: in the months that followed, the typical line became "If the show offends you, switch it off, don't try and censor it."[81] Ironically, the longer-term result of Rakolta's campaign was to increase the show's ratings and expose an alliance within the power structure to popular rejection.

Rakolta's campaign against the program did not originate in her own living room only; it was part of a sociocultural context in which "family values" were a crucial political battlefield. Many of my undergraduate students recognized that the difference between *The*

Cosby Show and *Married . . . with Children* reproduced the difference between "normal" family values and the material conditions of the majority of U.S. families. Consequently, they considered *Married . . . with Children* to be the most "realistic" show on television (an accolade that was later bestowed on *The Simpsons*) and used its carnivalesque elements as ways of expressing their sense of the differences between their experience of family life and that proposed for them by the dominant social norms.

A graduate student of mine spent a season watching the show with a typical audience of young people.[82] They were undergraduates, mainly freshmen and sophomores, of both sexes who attended a Catholic university and met every Sunday after evening Mass, which many attended, in one or another of their apartments. Some of the group had known each other through high school, others were more recent members, but this particular social formation was organized around the shared taste for *Married . . . with Children.*

The seven members who attended one particular Sunday met in Mick and John's apartment, the main room of which had once been the living room of the single-family house that was now converted into student apartments. The furniture was an eclectic mix of whatever they had been able to scrounge from their families. The couch, for instance, carried the scars of its history, during which it had moved from living room to family room to kids' basement, to student apartment. Its stains and tears spoke against the domestic order still faintly discernible in the traces of what it used to be. During the show, beer was spilled on it and nobody cared, a half-eaten hamburger on a thin piece of paper was set down on it with no thought of grease or ketchup stains seeping through, and, later on, John and Sarah lay on it in a body-hugging embrace that would have sent their parents into conniptions had the couch still been in the family living room.

The walls were decorated with posters of pop and film stars that may have been tolerated at home, though not in the living room, and with signs advertising beer, which would certainly have been prohibited, particularly as they had clearly been stolen from a bar, not purchased from a store. Nobody in the apartment had reached the legal drinking age, so the signs were doubly illicit.

The theme music of the show, "Love and Marriage," a Frank Sinatra number from their parents' generation, provoked the group into singing along in vacuous parody of both its "older" style and "older" sentiments. A similar parody of their parents' taste (as they saw it) hung on the wall—a somewhat moth-eaten painting of Elvis on black velvet. The "bad taste" of the picture was different from the "bad taste" of the program, for it was their view of teenage culture then as opposed to now. The picture was a site for experiencing the differences between their parents-as-teenagers and themselves, just as the program enabled them to mock the differences between their parents now and themselves.

Watching the program involved a series of interactive comments that took every opportunity offered to draw disrespectful parallels between the show and the families these viewers had so recently left. These comments ranged from delight in representations of a counterknowledge ("My Dad does that"—said of an action that a father would disown as typically his but that a teenager would know differently) to more engaged family politics ("I wish Mom had seen that").

The show enabled these viewers to engage in and reconfigure the age politics of their relations with their absent parents; equally, they used it to engage in gender politics with their present partners. The gender conflicts between the parents and the children consisted of verbal punches and counterpunches in which, generally, the females outpointed the males. This caused few problems for the men in this particular audience, and though both sexes would cheer the punches thrown by their own sides, they also gained great pleasure from the well-aimed riposte. When a girl nudged her boyfriend at a remark on the TV, she was bringing their own interpersonal history to the program just as significantly as the Fox network was bringing the program to them.

This particular audience, or rather group of people who came together to "audience" the show, did not appear to align themselves with the class identities of the blue-collar Bundys, but confined their observable alignments to ones of gender and age. The fact that no class alignments were observable does not necessarily mean that none were made, but it probably indicates that if made they were made with a fluid sense of class that enabled class disempowerment to stand in for age disempowerment, particularly when experienced as lack of money. Lack of money is a constant in the Bundy family. Al never earns enough, and consequently his wife and children are always bemoaning their inability to become real American consumers. Blue-collar sitcoms, such as *Married . . . with Children* and *Roseanne* provide some of the few televisual sites where the failure of Reaganomic wealth to trickle down is consistently represented. Class difference is often experienced as short-age of money, and thus, for most teenagers, it can be readily used as an expression of age difference. In this sense, age and class were axes of alignment along which to oppose official family values.

Three ways of valuing the family were at stake here: for Fox it was a market segment defined by its consumer preferences and buying power; for Rakolta, as for Dan Quayle, it was where values were inculcated; and for the students it was a site where they could develop their own sense of their social identities and social relations. Fox and Rakolta struggled over the concept of "the teenager." For Fox the teenager was a market segment to be differentiated from the adult; for Rakolta, a child to be kept under adult control within the family. This prefigured Quayle's argument with "the Hollywood elite," whose liberalism, in his eyes, pandered to the taste of the wrong market segment and so led the "real" America away from the great traditions that had shaped it, particularly the traditional family. Between Rakolta and this particular student audience was a struggle over the meanings of the family, over the age and gender politics within it, and thus over the social identities of those occupying different roles within its structure of relationships. And between Fox and the teenage audience was the struggle between incorporation and excorporation, in which the industry constantly seeks to incorporate the tastes and practices of subordinate social formations whose members, in their turn, scan the products of the culture industries looking for elements they can excorporate and use to promote their own sociocultural interests.

This particular student audience is better understood as a social formation than as a social category, though most of its members belonged to one—that of white middle-class youth. They formed themselves as a group around this particular program and a set of sociopolitical interests, but they did not experience all their social relations in this antifamily mode, nor did they necessarily spend much time together as a social formation with other interests in common. A social formation, then, unlike a category or class, is formed and dissolved according to the interests activated in its immediate context, and as such is better identified by what its members do than by who they are. And what this audience did was to engage in the practice of culture, to participate in the generation and circulation of meanings. They themselves were not necessarily a representative sample of the total accumulation of audiences of the show (though they did conform closely to the profile of its target audience): their "audiencing" of the program was, however, an instance of culture in practice, just as speaking a sentence is an instance of language in practice.

Even the most trivial objects of everyday life can be used as a cultural practice. When John places his half-eaten hamburger on a sofa that was once in a family living room while watching Peg Bundy "failing" to produce a family meal, he is making the hamburger part of the family values debate. On most Sundays he will have bought it from the nearby McDonald's, but if he feels particularly self-indulgent and wishes to reward himself he will have gone further afield to buy a "better" burger at a small one-off burger joint. Which burger he bought will be connected to whether or not he finished a class paper he had to write, or whether or not he and Sarah had had a minor tiff, or whatever. The couch is where hamburgers, beer, *Married . . . with Children,* and Sarah come together in John's Sunday night, and where he turns them into ways of living that weave antifamily values into the politics of his everyday life. Whether the hamburger was one-off or mass produced by McDonald's connects not only with John's sense of the week or day that has passed, but also with the fact that McDonald's advertises on the show despite Terry Rakolta's campaign to persuade it not to, and that its advertising promotes its restaurants as places for the family, particularly for parents to take children. In doing so, it is attempting to deny the contradictions between fast food and the family dinner table, and thus to defuse any suggestion that it might be implicated in the breakdown of the family. John, of course, is using his hamburger in precisely the antifamily way that McDonald's, though happy to sell it to him, wishes he wouldn't. A hamburger is much more than ground beef; and had he thought to do so, Dan Quayle might have as persuasively attributed L.A.'s problems to McDonald's as to Murphy Brown.

BLACK BART

Like his vice president, George Bush also took a swipe at a popular sitcom: "We need a nation closer to *The Waltons* than *The Simpsons,*" he said. Bart Simpson was too smart to miss the opportunity: on the night of Bush's acceptance speech at the Republican convention he fired back, "Hey, we're just like the Waltons. Both families spend a lot of time praying for the end of the Depression."[83]

Bush had picked the wrong opponent. *The Simpsons* had developed a large and devoted audience of young people and young-thinking leftish adults. The generational gap between the parties that the Democrats stressed and eventually rode to the White House was here invoked by the president, who, in one stroke of naïveté, associated himself and family values with the older generation, the 1930s, and the Great Depression. The media paid little attention to his remark, probably because, unlike Quayle's swipe at Murphy, it was not linked directly with a specific issue such as the L.A. "riots."

The Simpsons are a cartoon family of working-class characters who developed out of weekly segments on Fox's *Tracey Ullman Show* into their own program. They continued the subversion of traditional family values begun by *Married . . . with Children,* and by October 1990, Fox felt confident enough in its youngster's strength to schedule it against *The Cosby Show.* For seven years *The Cosby Show* had been invincible in its time slot, but on the first night of competition between them, *The Simpsons* held it to a tie; 29 percent of the audience watched each.[84] From that moment, *The Cosby Show* began the slide down the ratings that ended in its death as Los Angeles erupted. It may be going too far to claim that Bart sank Bush in the same way, but the change in the family values of *The Cosby Show* to those of *Married . . . with Children, The Simpsons,* and *Murphy Brown* is both a sign and an agent of the change in the structure of feeling that did.

Bart Simpson is the family's troublemaker. He is a cocky preteenager, a failure at school and misunderstood at home, who struggles not always successfully to keep his spirits up in a world that appears to have no place for him. He is street smart, not school smart: his smarts are those of an oral culture, not a literate one, and many of his sayings have been enthusiastically taken into the vernacular cultures of the United States, including those of African America. One of his sayings in particular attracted the anger of authority. Reproduced on a best-selling T-shirt, it proclaimed, "Bart Simpson, underachiever and proud of it." Other "Bartisms" (which in T-shirt form alone had sold more than 15 million by the spring of 1990)[85] included "I'm Bart Simpson, who the hell are you," "Eat my shorts," and "Don't have a cow, man." On *Murphy Brown,* Bart's voice echoed in the headline of one of the fictional papers as it proclaimed "Quayle has a cow."

One of many nonfictional authority figures who also had a cow was Principal Brown of the Cambridge Elementary School in Orange, California, who thundered, "For a child to wear a T-shirt with the word 'hell' on it—that's not exactly the type of behavior we hope elementary schools model. And I don't want kids even thinking that being an underachiever is cool."[86] William Bennett, then U.S. secretary of education, also condemned the show, and Bart T-shirts were banned from schools across the nation. Bart quickly became the mascot of America's disaffected youth, particularly Black youth. Unlicensed "Black Bart" T-shirts were widely sold, one of which depicted him mooning and saying, "Kiss the butt of this." Bart's defiance, his street smarts, his oral skills, together with his rejection, appeared to resonate closely with many African Americans. The Simpsons are a blue-collar family whose class difference from mainstream America is frequently emphasized, and as race is often recoded into class, so class difference can be decoded as racial. Bart's double disempowerment, by class and age, made him readily decodable as socially "Black." The fact that he was actually bright yellow made it easier to blacken him visually, which the illegal T-shirts did, thus appropriating his color along with his sayings. Bart could readily be made to speak, visually and orally, with a Black accent.

Bart was not only scheduled against Bill Cosby, he argued with him (as he did any authority figure). For Bill Cosby and his show, education was of supreme value. In the show's credits Cosby's name carried his Ed.D.; he stressed the value of education in interviews and filled the show with good educational advice. His son on the show, Theo, is a non-subversive Bart; as Downing points out, he is a muted echo of the alienation of the high school dropout.[87] His scholastic problems, however, unlike Bart's, provide the excuse for constant messages about the value of education. His math teacher is a Latina who in one episode tells Theo of her previous jobs as a waitress and cab driver and concludes, "I didn't mind. I was in America. I knew that if I worked hard I could be whatever I wanted. That's why I make you work so hard. I don't like it when I see children take education for granted."[88] The Huxtables would have agreed with her, despite Theo's problems. Their oldest daughter, Sondra, was at Princeton, the next, Denise, went to college later in the series, and indeed became the star of her own sitcom, *A Different World,* set in and around her dorm. At least three generations of Huxtables were college educated: none of the Simpsons was. Indeed, according to Budd and Steinman, "Cosby has acknowledged that for a time the show became a bit too educational."[89]

Downing sets Cosby's pedagogic earnestness in the context of the debate about Black scholastic underachievement and the arguments about whether the fault for it lies in the white education system or in the Black community. *The Cosby Show* and *The Simpsons* positioned themselves on opposite sides. As more African Americans came to believe that the white education system was the reason for, not the solution to, their "underachievement," so Black Bart voiced their concerns better than Bill Cosby.

Bart Simpson, a rejected ten-year-old with no apparent place in his society's educational or economic systems, who cockily refuses to submit and ingeniously turns to his advantage the few opportunities that come his way, was not surprisingly expropriated by Black youths to figure their own disaffection with the white social order. Equally unsurprisingly, Cliff Huxtable and Theo were not. The race-age-class disaffection that was worn on the Black Bart T-shirts in cities across the nation in 1990 and 1991 erupted violently on the streets of Los Angeles in 1992. Like Bart Simpson, Rodney King refused to submit.

NOTES

1. *U.S. News & World Report,* October 21, 1991, 35.
2. David Brock, "The Real Anita Hill," *American Spectator,* March 1992, 18–30.
3. *Frontline, Clarence Thomas and Anita Hill: Public Hearing, Private Pain,* directed and produced by Ofrah Bikel, Ofrah Bikel Production Corp., aired October 13, 1992.
4. bell hooks, *Ain't I a Woman: Black Women and Feminism* (Boston: South End, 1981); bell hooks, *Talking Back: Thinking Feminist, Thinking Black* (Boston: South End, 1989); bell hooks, *Black Looks, Race and Representation* (Boston: South End, 1992).
5. hooks, *Black Looks,* 85.
6. Trellie L. Jeffers, "We Have Heard, We Have Seen, Do We Believe? The Clarence Thomas-Anita Hill Hearing," *Black Scholar* 22, nos. 1/2 (1992): 56; also in *Court of Appeal: The Black Community Speaks Out on the Racial and Sexual Politics of Thomas vs Hill,* ed. Black Scholar (New York: Ballantine, 1992), 119.
7. Charles R. Lawrence III, "Cringing at Myths of Black Sexuality," *Black Scholar* 22, nos. 1/2 (1992): 65; also in *Court of Appeal: The Black Community Speaks Out on the Racial and Sexual Politics of Thomas vs Hill,* ed. Black Scholar (New York: Ballantine, 1992), 136.
8. *Chicago Defender,* October 19, 1991, 16.
9. The *New York Times* counted nineteen; the *Los Angeles Times,* twenty-three. *New York Times,* April 18, 1993; Staff of the Los Angeles Times, *Understanding the Riots* (Los Angeles: Los Angeles Times, 1992), 33.
10. I am grateful to Rose Byrd for this analogy.
11. David Lionel Smith, "The Thomas Spectacle: Power, Impotence and Melodrama," *Black Scholar* 22, nos. 1/2 (1992): 95; also in *Court of Appeal: The Black Community Speaks Out on the Racial and Sexual Politics of Thomas vs Hill,* ed. Black Scholar (New York: Ballantine, 1992), 193.
12. Marion Barry was the mayor of Washington, D.C., who was videotaped receiving drugs and sex from an ex-girlfriend in an FBI setup. He was imprisoned as a result.
13. Margaret A. Burnham, "The Supreme Court Appointment Process and the Politics of Race and Sex," in *Race-ing Justice, En-gendering Power,* ed. Toni Morrison (New York: Pantheon, 1992), 311.
14. Kimberle Crenshaw, "Whose Story Is It, Anyway: Feminist and Anti-racist Appropriations of Anita Hill," in *Race-ing Justice, En-gendering Power,* ed. Toni Morrison (New York: Pantheon, 1992), 415.
15. Barbara Smith, "Ain't Gonna Let Nobody Turn Me Around," *Black Scholar* 22, nos. 1/2 (1992): 91; also in *Court of Appeal: The Black Community Speaks Out on the Racial and Sexual Politics of Thomas vs Hill,* ed. Black Scholar (New York: Ballantine, 1992), 186.

16. Calvin Hernton, "Breaking Silences," *Black Scholar* 22, nos. 1/2 (1992): 42; also in *Court of Appeal: The Black Community Speaks Out on the Racial and Sexual Politics of Thomas vs Hill,* ed. Black Scholar (New York: Ballantine, 1992), 56–57.

17. Julianne Malveaux, "No Peace in a Sisterly Space," *Black Scholar* 22, nos. 1/2 (1992): 71; also in *Court of Appeal: The Black Community Speaks Out on the Racial and Sexual Politics of Thomas vs Hill,* ed. Black Scholar (New York: Ballantine, 1992), 147.

18. hooks, *Ain't I a Woman,* 7.

19. Crenshaw "Whose Story Is It, Anyway," 403.

20. *New York Times,* November 17, 1991; reprinted in Black Scholar, ed., *Court of Appeal: The Black Community Speaks Out on the Racial and Sexual Politics of Thomas vs Hill* (New York: Ballantine, 1992), 291–92.

21. Smith, "Ain't Gonna Let Nobody," 91.

22. hooks, *Black Looks,* 82–83.

23. "The Year of the Black Woman," *Ebony,* October 1992, 112.

24. Other achievements in the political sphere include the emergence from the L.A. uprisings of "a new political star, Rep. Maxine Waters, who has emerged as the central advocate for urban renewal" and numerous candidates for office at state and local levels. In the arts, three Black women had their novels simultaneously on the *New York Times* best-seller lists, and others won major awards in music, cinema, and television. In sport, Black women won thirty-two medals, including eight gold, in the Olympics, and, professionally they were "presiding in corporate boardrooms, leading national professional organizations and leading major colleges and universities more than ever before." Ibid., 118.

25. Ibid.

26. Jane Gross, "Suffering in Silence No More: Fighting Sexual Harassment," *New York Times,* July 13, 1992, A1, D10.

27. Elizabeth McLemore, University of Minnesota.

28. Rush Limbaugh, *The Way Things Ought to Be* (New York: Pocket Books, 1992), 126.

29. Ibid., 124.

30. Phyllis Schlafly, lecture at the University of Wisconsin–Madison, March 2, 1993.

31. Phyllis Schlafly, remarks made at a press conference preceding the lecture in Madison, Wisconsin; reported in the *Capitol Times,* March 3, 1993, 3A, 4A.

32. Quoted in *New York Times,* October 15, 1991, A15.

33. Cited in Nancy Fraser, "Sex, Lies and the Public Sphere: Some Reflections on the Confirmation of Clarence Thomas," *Cultural Inquiry* 18 (Spring 1992): 595–612.

34. Ibid., 609.

35. Cornel West, "Black Leadership and the Pitfalls of Racial Reasoning," in *Race-ing Justice, En-gendering Power,* ed. Toni Morrison (New York: Pantheon, 1992), 398; and Cornel West, *Race Matters* (Boston: Beacon, 1993), 21–32.

36. *New York Times,* October 17, 1992, 6L.

37. Sarah E. Wright, "The Anti-Black Agenda," *Black Scholar* 22, nos. 1/2 (1992): 109; also in *Court of Appeal: The Black Community Speaks Out on the Racial and Sexual Politics of Thomas vs Hill,* ed. Black Scholar (New York: Ballantine, 1992), 225.

38. Jill Nelson, "Anita Hill: No Regrets," interview with Anita Hill, *Essence,* March 1992, 116.

39. Robert Staples, "Hand Me the Rope—I Will Hang Myself: Observations on the Clarence Thomas Hearings," *Black Scholar* 22, nos. 1/2 (1992): 96; also in *Court of Appeal: The Black Community Speaks Out on the Racial and Sexual Politics of Thomas vs Hill,* ed. Black Scholar (New York: Ballantine, 1992), 196–97.

40. Nellie McKay, talk and reading given at Borders Bookstore, Madison, Wisconsin, December 1, 1992, to promote Toni Morrison, ed., *Race-ing Justice, En-gendering Power* (New York: Pantheon, 1992).

41. Henry Louis Gates, "TVs Black World Turns—But Stays Unreal," *New York Times,* November 12, 1989, sec. 2, p. 1.
42. Quoted in Herman Gray, "Television, Black Americans, and the American Dream," *Critical Studies in Mass Communication* 6 (1989): 376–86.
43. Sut Jhally and Justin Lewis, *Enlightened Racism: The Bill Cosby Show, Audiences, and the Myth of the American Dream* (Boulder, Colo.: Westview, 1992).
44. Quoted in Timothy Phelps and Helen Winternitz, *Capitol Games: The Inside Story of Clarence Thomas, Anita Hill and a Supreme Court Nomination* (New York: HarperCollins, 1993), 85.
45. *U.S. News & World Report,* September 1, 1986.
46. Quoted in Susan Faludi, *Backlash: The Undeclared War on American Women* (Garden City, N.Y.: Doubleday Anchor, 1991), 263.
47. Mike Budd and Clay Steinman, "White Racism and the Cosby Show," *JumpCut* 37 (July 1992): 5–14.
48. Jhally and Lewis, *Enlightened Racism,* 88.
49. Michael Eric Dyson, *Reflecting Black: African American Cultural Criticism* (Minneapolis: University of Minnesota Press, 1993), 188.
50. "Questions and Answers on the NAACP's Position on Judge Clarence Thomas," August 21, 1992; cited in Black Scholar, ed. *Court of Appeal,* 276.
51. A. Leon Higginbotham, Jr., "An Open Letter to Justice Clarence Thomas from a Federal Judicial Colleague," in *Race-ing Justice, En-gendering Power,* ed. Toni Morrison (New York: Pantheon, 1992), 3–28.
52. Nell Irvin Painter, "Hill, Thomas and the Use of Racial Stereotype," in *Race-ing Justice, En-gendering Power,* ed. Toni Morrison (New York: Pantheon, 1992), 201–2. The same point is made by West, "Black Leadership," 394–95.
53. Robert Entman, "Modern Racism and the Images of Blacks in Local TV News," *Critical Studies in Mass Communication* 7 (1990): 332–45.
54. Dyson, *Reflecting Black,* 82.
55. John Downing, "'The Cosby Show' and American Racial Discourse," in *Discourse and Discrimination,* ed. G. Smitherman-Donaldson and T. van Dijk (Detroit: Wayne State University Press, 1988), 46–73.
56. Cited in hooks, *Black Looks,* 83, 85.
57. *National Review,* June 8, 1992, 31.
58. Gray, "Television, Black Americans."
59. Quoted in ibid., 381.
60. Quoted in ibid., 380.
61. Quoted in Phelps and Winternitz, *Capitol Games,* 88.
62. See Downing, "'The Cosby Show,'" 50.
63. *The Cosby Show,* August 7, 1986.
64. Quoted in Jhally and Lewis, *Enlightened Racism,* 30.
65. Quoted in ibid., 55.
66. Quoted in ibid., 54.
67. Quoted in ibid., 123.
68. Quoted in ibid.
69. Downing, "'The Cosby Show'"; Justin Lewis, *The Ideological Octopus: An Exploration of Television and Its Audience* (New York: Routledge, 1991).
70. Lewis, *The Ideological Octopus.*
71. Quoted in Jhally and Lewis, *Enlightened Racism,* 123.
72. Fraser, "Sex, Lies and the Public Sphere."
73. Both cited in ibid., 599, 600.
74. Ibid., 601–2.

75. Ibid., 601.
76. *Frontline, Clarence Thomas and Anita Hill.*
77. Chad Dell, "Secondary Circulations" (paper presented at the annual meeting of the Popular Culture Association, Toronto, 1990).
78. *New York Times,* March 2, 1989, Al, D20.
79. *Los Angeles Times,* March 4, 1989, sec. V, pp. 1, 8.
80. *Detroit News,* March 3, 1989, 8A, 1B, 4B.
81. See, for example, the *Denver Post, Detroit News,* and *Wall Street Journal,* all cited in Dell, "Secondary Circulations."
82. David Brean, "Viewers and Viewing: An Ethnographic Study" (paper presented at the annual meeting of the Popular Culture Association, Toronto, 1990).
83. *Time,* September 21, 1992, 44.
84. Budd and Steinman, "White Racism."
85. *People Weekly,* May 21, 1990, 130; cited in Kevin Glynn, "'I'm Bart Simpson, Who the Hell Are You': Social Identity, Cultural Loser, and Critical Ethnography" (paper presented at the annual meeting of the International Communication Association, Miami, May 1992).
86. Ibid.
87. Downing, "'The Cosby Show,'" 52.
88. Quoted in ibid., 53.
89. Budd and Steinman, "White Racism," 8.

REFERENCES

Alley, Robert and Brown, Irby. *Murphy Brown: The Anatomy of a Sitcom.* New York: Delta, 1990.

Alvarado, Manuel, and Thompson, John (eds.). *The Media Reader.* London: British Film Institute, 1990.

Anger, Max. "From Gulf War to Class War: We All Hate the Cops." *Anarchy: A Journal of Desire Armed* 34 (1992): 44.

Baker, Houston. "Scene . . . not heard." In *Reading Rodney King Reading Urban Uprising,* ed. Robert Gooding-Williams, 38–48. New York: Routledge, 1993.

Barthes, Roland. "The Photographic Paradox." In *Image-Music-Text,* 15–32. London: Fontana, 1977.

Bell, Derrick. *Faces at the Bottom of the Well: The Permanence of Racism.* New York: Basic Books, 1992.

Black Scholar (ed.). *Court of Appeal: The Black Community Speaks Out on the Racial and Sexual Politics of Thomas vs Hill.* New York: Ballantine, 1992.

Bray, Rosemary. "Taking Sides against Ourselves." In *Court of Appeal: The Black Community Speaks Out on the Racial and Sexual Politics of Thomas vs Hill,* ed. Black Scholar, 47–55. New York: Ballantine, 1992.

Brean, David. "Viewers and Viewing: An Ethnographic Study." Paper presented at the annual meeting of the Popular Culture Association, Toronto, 1990.

Budd, Mike, and Steinman, Clay. "White Racism and the Cosby Show." *JumpCut* 37 (July 1992): 5–14.

Burnham, Margaret. "The Supreme Court Appointment Process and the Politics of Race and Sex." In *Race-ing Justice, En-gendering Power,* ed. Toni Morrison, 290–322. New York: Pantheon, 1992.

Cantwell, Alan. *AIDS and the Doctors of Death: An Inquiry into the Origin of the AIDS Epidemic.* San Francisco: Aries Rising, 1988.

_____. *Queer Blood: The Secret AIDS Genocide Plot.* San Francisco: Aries Rising, 1993.

Carswell, J. W., et al. "How Long Has the AIDS Virus Been in Uganda?" *Lancet* (May 24, 1986).

Cho, Sumi. "Korean Americans vs African Americans: Conflict and Construction." In *Reading Rodney King Reading Urban Uprising,* ed. Robert Gooding-Williams, 196–211. New York: Routledge, 1993.

Classen, Steven. "Standing on Unstable Grounds: A Re-examination of the WLBT-TV Case, Consumerism and Legal Standing." *Critical Studies in Mass Communication* 11, no. 1 (1994): 5–6.

Cohen, Lizbeth. "Consumption and Civil Rights." Paper presented at the annual meeting of the American Studies Association, Costa Mesa, Calif., November 8, 1992.

Crenshaw, Kimberle. "Whose Story Is It, Anyway: Feminist and Anti-racist Appropriations of Anita Hill." In *Race-ing Justice, En-gendering Power,* ed. Toni Morrison, 402–40. New York: Pantheon, 1992.

Crenshaw, Kimberle, and Peller, Gary. "Reel Time/Real Justice." In *Reading Rodney King Reading Urban Uprising,* ed. Robert Gooding-Williams, 56–70. New York: Routledge, 1993.

D'Acci, Julie. *Defining Women: Television and the Case of Cagney and Lacey.* Chapel Hill: University of North Carolina Press, 1994.

Davis, Mike. *City of Quartz: Excavating the Future in Los Angeles.* London: Verso, 1990.

_____. *Beyond Blade Runner: Urban Control, the Ecology of Fear.* Westfield, N.J.: Open Magazine Pamphlet Series, 1992.

_____. "Burning All Illusions in LA." In *Inside the LA Riots,* ed. Institute for Alternative Journalism, 96–100. New York: Institute for Alternative Journalism, 1992.

_____. *LA Was Just the Beginning.* Westfield, N.J.: Open Magazine Pamphlet Series, 1992.

_____. "Uprising and Repression in LA." In *Reading Rodney King Reading Urban Uprising,* ed. Robert Gooding-Williams, 142–54. New York: Routledge, 1993.

de Certeau, Michel. *The Practice of Everyday Life.* Berkeley: University of California Press, 1984.

Dell, Chad. "Secondary Circulations." Paper presented at the annual meeting of the Popular Culture Association, Toronto, 1990.

Dower, John. *War without Mercy: Race and Power in the Pacific War.* New York: Pantheon, 1986.

Downing, John. "'The Cosby Show' and American Racial Discourse." In *Discourse and Discrimination,* ed. Geneva Smitherman-Donaldson and Teun van Dijk, 46–73. Detroit: Wayne State University Press, 1988.

Dunn, Thomas. "The New Enclosures: Racism in the Normalized Community." In *Reading Rodney King Reading Urban Uprising,* ed. Robert Gooding-Williams, 178–95. New York: Routledge, 1993.

Dyson, Michael Eric. *Reflecting Black: African American Cultural Criticism.* Minneapolis: University of Minnesota Press, 1993.

Entman, Robert. "Modern Racism and the Images of Blacks in Local TV News." *Critical Studies in Mass Communication* 7 (1990): 332–45.

Faludi, Susan. *Backlash: The Undeclared War on American Women.* Garden City, N.Y.: Doubleday Anchor, 1991.

Fiske, John. *Power Plays Power Works.* London: Verso, 1993.

Foucault, Michel. *Discipline and Punish: The Birth of the Prison.* New York: Vintage, 1979.

Frankenberg, Ruth. *White Women, Race Matters: The Social Construction of Whiteness.* Minneapolis: University of Minnesota Press, 1993.

Frankenberg, Ruth, and Mani, Lata. "Cross Currents, Cross Talk: Race, 'Postcoloniality' and the Politics of Location." *Cultural Studies,* 7 no. 2 (1993): 292–310.

Fraser, Nancy. "Sex, Lies and the Public Sphere: Some Reflections on the Confirmation of Clarence Thomas." *Cultural Inquiry* 18 (Spring 1992): 595–612.

Giddens, Anthony. *The Nation-State and Violence.* Cambridge: Polity, 1987.

Girard, Bruce (ed.). *A Passion for Radio.* Montreal: Black Rose, 1992.

Glynn, Kevin. "'I'm Bart Simpson, Who the Hell are You?': Social Identity, Cultural Loser, and Critical Ethnography." Paper presented at the annual meeting of the International Communication Association, Miami, May 1992.

Goodfield, June. *Quest for the Killers.* Cambridge, Mass.: Birkhauser Boston, 1985.

Gooding-Williams, Robert (ed.). *Reading Rodney King Reading Urban Uprising.* New York: Routledge, 1993.

Granholm, Jennifer. "Video Surveillance on Public Streets: The Constitutionality of Invisible Citizen Searches." *University of Detroit Law Review* 64 (1987): 687–713.

Gray, Herman. "Television, Black Americans, and the American Dream." *Critical Studies in Mass Communication* 6 (1989): 376–86.

————. "The Endless Slide of Difference: Critical Television Studies, Television and the Question of Race." *Critical Studies in Mass Communication,* 10 (1993): 190–197.

Grossberg, Lawrence, Nelson, Cary, and Treichler, Paula (eds.). *Cultural Studies.* New York: Routledge, 1991.

Guilshan, Christine. "A Picture Is Worth a Thousand Lies: Electronic Imaging and the Future of the Admissability of Photographs into Evidence." *Rutgers Computer and Technology Law Journal* 18, no. 1 (1992).

Hacker, Andrew. *Two Nations: Black and White, Separate, Hostile, Unequal.* New York: Charles Scribner's Sons, 1992.

Hall, Stuart. "The Whites of Their Eyes: Racist Ideologies and the Media." In *The Media Reader,* ed. Manuel Alvarado and John Thompson, 8–23. London: British Film Institute, 1990.

Hernton, Calvin. "Breaking Silences." *Black Scholar,* 22, nos. 1–2, (1992): 42–45. (Reprinted in *Court of Appeal: The Black Community Speaks Out on the Racial and Sexual Politics of Thomas vs Hill,* ed. Black Scholar, 86–91. New York: Ballantine, 1992.)

Higginbotham, A. Leon, Jr. "An Open Letter to Justice Clarence Thomas from a Federal Judicial Colleague." In *Race-ing Justice, En-gendering Power,* ed. Toni Morrison, 3–28. New York: Pantheon, 1992.

hooks, bell. *Ain't I a Woman: Black Women and Feminism.* Boston: South End, 1981.

————. *Feminist Theory from Margin to Center.* Boston: South End, 1984.

————. *Talking Back: Thinking Feminist, Thinking Black.* Boston: South End, 1989.

————. "Representing Whiteness." In *Cultural Studies,* ed. Lawrence Grossberg, Cary Nelson, and Paula Treichler, 338–46. New York: Routledge, 1991. (Reprinted in hooks, bell, *Black Looks, Race and Representation,* 165–78. Boston: South End, 1992.)

————. *Black Looks, Race and Representation.* Boston: South End, 1992.

Institute for Alternative Journalism (ed.). *Inside the LA Riots.* New York: Institute for Alternative Journalism, 1992.

Jeffers, Trellie L. "We Have Heard, We Have Seen, Do We Believe? The Clarence Thomas-Anita Hill Hearing." *Black Scholar* 22, no. 1–2 (1992): 54–56. (Reprinted in *Court of Appeal: The Black Community Speaks Out on the Racial and Sexual Politics of Thomas vs Hill,* ed. Black Scholar, 116–19. New York: Ballantine, 1992.)

Jhally, Sut, and Lewis, Justin. *Enlightened Racism: The Bill Cosby Show, Audiences, and the Myth of the American Dream.* Boulder, Colo.: Westview, 1992.

Jones, John. *Bad Blood: The Tuskegee Syphilis Experiment—A Tragedy of Race and Medicine.* New York: Free Press, 1984.

King, Martin Luther. *Stride Towards Freedom: The Montgomery Story.* New York: Harper & Row, 1958.

Kochman, Thomas. *Black and White Styles in Conflict.* Chicago: University of Chicago Press, 1981.

Lawrence, Charles, R., III. "Cringing at Myths of Black Sexuality." *Black Scholar* 22, nos. 1–2 (1992): 65–66. (Reprinted in *Court of Appeal: The Black Community Speaks Out on the Racial and Sexual Politics of Thomas vs Hill,* ed. Black Scholar, 136–38. New York: Ballantine, 1992.)

Lerner, Gerda. *Black Women in White America.* New York: Vintage, 1973.

Lewis, Justin. *The Ideological Octopus: An Exploration of Television and Its Audience.* New York: Routledge, 1991.

Limbaugh, Rush. *The Way Things Ought to Be.* New York: Pocket Books, 1992.

Lipsitz, George. "The Possessive Investment in Whiteness: Racialized Social Democracy in America" (paper presented at the annual meeting of the American Studies Association, Boston, November 1993).

Mackey, Heather. "I Told You So." In *Inside the LA Riots,* ed. Institute for Alternative Journalism. New York: Institute for Alternative Journalism, 1992.

Malveaux, Julianne. "No Peace in a Sisterly Space." *Black Scholar* 22 nos. 1–2 (1992): 68–71. (Reprinted in *Court of Appeal: The Black Community Speaks Out on the Racial and Sexual Politics of Thomas vs Hill,* ed. Black Scholar, 143–47. New York: Ballantine, 1992.)

Morrison, Toni. "The Pain of Being Black." *Time,* May 22, 1989, 120.

———. (ed.). *Race-ing Justice, En-gendering Power.* New York: Pantheon, 1992.

———. *Playing in the Dark: Whiteness and the Literary Imagination.* New York: Vintage, 1993.

Oliver, Melvin, Johnson, James, and Farrell, Walter. "Anatomy of a Rebellion: A Political-Economic Analysis." In *Reading Rodney King Reading Urban Uprising,* ed. Robert Gooding-Williams, 117–41. New York: Routledge, 1993.

Omi, Michael, and Winant, Howard. "The LA Race Riot and US Politics." In *Reading Rodney King Reading Urban Uprising,* ed. Robert Gooding-Williams, 97–114. New York: Routledge, 1993.

Painter, Nell Irvin. "Hill, Thomas and the Use of Racial Stereotype." In *Rac-ing Justice, Engendering Power,* ed. Toni Morrison, 200–214. New York: Pantheon, 1992.

Phelps, Timothy, and Winternitz, Helen. *Capitol Games: The Inside Story of Clarence Thomas, Anita Hill and a Supreme Court Nomination.* New York: HarperCollins, 1993.

Rocco, Raymond. "The Theoretical Construction of the 'Other' in Postmodernist Thought: Latinos in the New Urban Political Economy." *Cultural Studies* 4, no. 3 (1990): 321–30.

Said, Edward. *Orientalism.* New York: Vintage, 1979.

Sakolsky, Ron. "Zoom Black Magic Liberation Radio: The Birth of the Micro-Radio Movement in the USA." In *A Passion for Radio,* ed. Bruce Girard, 106–13. Montreal: Black Rose, 1992.

Sharp, Saundra. *Black Women for Beginners.* New York: Writers and Readers, 1993.

Smith, Barbara. "Ain't Gonna Let Nobody Turn Me Around." *Black Scholar,* 22, nos. 1–2 (1992): 90–93. (Reprinted in *Court of Appeal: The Black Community Speaks Out on the Racial and Sexual Politics of Thomas vs Hill,* ed. Black Scholar, 185–89. New York: Ballantine, 1992.)

Smith, David Lionel. "The Thomas Spectacle: Power, Impotence and Melodrama." *Black Scholar* 22, nos. 1–2 (1992): 93–95. (Reprinted in *Court of Appeal: The Black Community Speaks Out on the Racial and Sexual Politics of Thomas vs Hill,* ed. Black Scholar, 190–93. New York: Ballantine, 1992.)

Smitherman-Donaldson, Geneva, and van Dijk, Teun (eds.). *Discourse and Discrimination.* Detroit: Wayne State University Press, 1988.

Staff of the Los Angeles Times. *Understanding the Riots.* Los Angeles: Los Angeles Times, 1992.

Staples, Robert. "Hand Me the Rope—I Will Hang Myself: Observations on the Clarence Thomas Hearings." *Black Scholar* 22, nos. 1–2 (1992): 95–99. (Reprinted in *Court of Appeal: The Black Community Speaks Out on the Racial and Sexual Politics of Thomas vs Hill,* ed. Black Scholar, 194–200. New York: Ballantine, 1992.)

Terkel, Studs. *Race: How Blacks and Whites Think and Feel about the American Obsession.* New York: New Press, 1992.

Thomas, Stephen, and Quinn, Sandra. "The Tuskegee Syphilis Study, 1932 to 1972: Implications for HIV Education and AIDS Risk Education Programs in the Black Community." *American Journal of Public Health* 81, (November 1991): 1498–1505.

Turner, Patricia. *I Heard It through the Grapevine: Rumor in African-American Culture.* Berkeley: University of California Press, 1993.

Uhrich, Kevin. "Policeville: Why People Who Know West Ventura County Weren't Surprised by the Verdict." In *Inside the LA Riots,* ed. Institute for Alternative Journalism, 57–58. New York: Institute for Alternative Journalism, 1992.

Welsing, Frances Cress. *The Isis Papers.* Chicago: Third World, 1991.

West, Cornel. "Black Leadership and the Pitfalls of Racial Reasoning." In *Race-ing Justice, Engendering Power,* ed. Toni Morrison, 390–402. (Reprinted in West, Cornell, *Race Matters,* 21–32. Boston: Beacon, 1993.)

———. *Race Matters.* Boston: Beacon, 1993.

White, Mimi. "What's the Difference? *Frank's Place* in television." *Wide Angle* 13, nos. 3–4 (1991): 82–96.

Wilhelm, Sidney. *Who Needs the Negro?* Cambridge, Mass.: Schenkman, 1970.

Williams, Patricia. *The Alchemy of Race and Rights.* Cambridge: Harvard University Press, 1991.

———. "The Rules of the Game." In *Reading Rodney King Reading Urban Uprising,* ed. Robert Gooding-Williams, 51–55. New York: Routledge, 1993.

Williams, Raymond. *Marxism and Literature.* Oxford: Oxford University Press, 1977.

Wright, Sarah E. "The Anti-Black Agenda." *Black Scholar* 22, nos. 1–2 (1992): 109–11. (Reprinted in *Court of Appeal: The Black Community Speaks Out on the Racial and Sexual Politics of Thomas vs Hill,* ed. Black Scholar, 225–28. New York: Ballantine, 1992.)

8

A MYTH OF ASSIMILATION
"Enlightened" Racism and the News

Christopher P. Campbell

In the world of television, [America's] open and multiracial society operates within a carefully defined social, cultural and economic assumption that keeps alive the assimilationist assumptions of racial interaction.

—Herman Gray (1986, p. 232)

In the apparently enlightened welcome that white viewers extend to the Huxtables, [we end up with] a new, sophisticated form of racism. The Huxtables' success implies the failure of a majority of black people . . . who have not achieved similar professional or material success. Television, which tells us nothing about the structures behind success or failure, leaves white viewers to assume that black people who do not measure up to their television counterparts have only themselves to blame.

—Sut Jhally & Justin Lewis (1992, pp. 137–138)

The newsman actively squeezes events into categories suitable for the smooth running of the media bureaucracy as well as ideologically significant in upholding a particular world view.

—Stanley Cohen & Jock Young (1973, p. 20)

Most Americans are quite familiar with Cliff Huxtable and his family, the characters whose lives were featured on NBC's *The Cosby Show*. Comedian Bill Cosby's hugely successful situation comedy led the television ratings wars week after week during the second half of the 1980s. That America's most popular show featured an African American cast would seem to indicate a liberal acceptance of black life and culture among the white viewers who made up a majority of the show's audience. But some critiques of the show question the positive effects the show had on race relations in the United States. Jhally and Lewis (1992), for example, think the show contributed to an "enlightened" form of racism—a contemporary attitude among whites who look at the success of a limited number of African Americans as an indication of a progressive America in which racial discrimination no longer exists. As Jhally and Lewis explain,

> The Huxtables and other black TV characters like them are exceptions to the class-bound rules of a generally racially divided society. The rules, which patently disadvantage most African Americans, suddenly are made to appear equitable and just. We are, as a nation, lulled into a false sense of equality and equal opportunity. (p. 86)

Reprinted from Christopher P. Campbell, *Race, Myth and the News* (Thousand Oaks, CA: Sage, 1995).

Similarly, West (1993) argues that the "conservative behaviorist" understanding of race ignores the realities of political and economic structures, choosing to "highlight the few instances in which blacks ascend to the top, as if such success is available to all blacks, regardless of circumstances" (p. 13). He writes:

> Such a vulgar rendition of Horatio Alger in blackface may serve as a source of inspiration to some—a kind of model for those already on the right track. But it cannot serve as a substitute for serious historical and social analysis of the predicaments of and prospects for all black people, especially the grossly disadvantaged ones. (p. 13)

The politically conservative attitude West describes seems to be dictating the kinds of programs seen nightly in American homes, raising questions about the effects that prime-time network TV shows may be having on America's racial attitudes. Gray (1986) argues that network situation comedies misrepresent African American life and contribute to racial misunderstandings:

> [Sitcoms] emphasize black Americans who have achieved middle-class success, confirming in the process the belief that in the context of the current political, economic and cultural arrangements, individuals, regardless of color, can achieve the American dream. However, these images also exist in the absence of significant change in the overall position of black Americans as a social group. (p. 224)

Gray contends that the programs feed "the general and dominant assimilationist view of American race relations" (p. 227); that is, the depiction of black sitcom characters in middle- and upper-class situations and exhibiting values and behavior associated with those classes creates a false reality about race in America. Gray contends that the assimilationist view defines racial interaction in the simplistic terms of prosocial values and attitudes espoused by the white members of the middle and upper classes while dismissing the more complex and problematic notions of racial conflict. Writes Gray,

> Also missing are black situations and viewpoints that provide different and competing alternatives to the dominant assimilation model. Where alternative viewpoints appear, they are fragmented, momentary and eventually absorbed into the conventional code of problem and solutions characteristic of the genre. (p. 227)

Gray (1991) has also argued that portrayals of privileged African Americans on prime-time fictional television can contrast with underclass life portrayed in TV's nonfictional programming. (He contrasts images from *The Cosby Show* with those from the 1985 PBS documentary *The Vanishing Family: Crisis in Black America.*) Nonfictional images of African Americans as poverty-stricken welfare recipients, drug-users or criminals contribute to an understanding of underclass African Americans as inferior to middle- and upper-class blacks—like those on prime-time television. Gray argues that members of the underclass may well possess the same qualities of the sitcom characters—hard work, sacrifice, intelligence—but in reality they "lack the options and opportunities to realize them" (p. 303). He concludes,

> Against fictional television representations of gifted and successful individuals, members of the urban under class are deficient. They are unemployed, unskilled, menacing, unmotivated, ruthless, and irresponsible. . . . At television's preferred level of meaning, these

assumptions—like the images they organize and legitimate—occupy our common sense understandings of American racial inequality. (p. 303)

Those "commonsense understandings" serve to augment the notions of enlightened racism. White Americans can smugly argue that racial prejudice and discrimination are things of the past and point to prominent and successful African Americans as proof. But this is mythological thinking—the myth of The American Dream, of America as a melting pot, of racial assimilation. Minority Americans are economically, educationally, socially and politically disadvantaged, despite the images we see on prime-time television.

Does the imagery of local television news feed similar mythological understandings of African American life? The purpose of this chapter is to examine the news in terms of its contribution to the assimilationist mythology that sustains enlightened racism. First, I will examine Entman's (1990) notion of how "modern" racism surfaces in the news; that discussion will include considerations of American views about *class* and how those views may affect thinking about *race*. Second, I will examine the newscasts recorded for this study for evidence of contemporary notions about race that advance an understanding of minority members of the underclass as inherently inferior to the privileged African Americans who have attained social status and financial success. Specifically, I will inter- pret local television news coverage of the January 18, 1993, Martin Luther King, Jr. holi- day in terms of a journalistic common sense that is rooted in and maintains the notions of enlightened racism.

"MODERN" RACISM, CLASS AND THE NEWS

Entman (1990) argues that local television news coverage can contribute to a sophisticat- ed form of contemporary racism described as "modern" (by McConahay, 1986) or "sym- bolic" (by Sears, 1988) racism. This form of racism has three basic characteristics: first, a general animosity among whites toward African Americans; second, a resistance to black political demands—for instance, affirmative action or hiring quotas; and third, a belief that racial discrimination is a thing of the past. Entman found the portrayal of crime on local television news to contribute to the first characteristic; that is, the menacing images of African American criminals . . . contribute to a modern racist hostility toward African Americans. He also found that local television coverage "exaggerated the degree to which black politicians (as compared with white ones) practice special interest politics" (p. 342), contributing to the second characteristic of modern racism—resistance to black political demands. Finally, Entman argues that the presence of black anchors and authority figures on the news contributes to the third characteristic of modern racism, the belief that racial discrimination no longer exists.

Entman's arguments are quite reasonable. The stereotypical portrayals of people of color described in this study and elsewhere support his contention that the news media sus- tain menacing images of African American criminals. Entman's findings on the coverage of black politicians is supported by Martindale's (1990) study in which she identifies the black politician as a contemporary news stereotype; that is, she found an overabundance of coverage of black politicians at the expense of "a more varied and accurate picture of black Americans" (p. 49), although she found the stereotype to be a generally positive one.[1] And Entman's argument about the "meaning" of African American anchors appears to parallel the thinking of Jhally and Lewis (1992), who contend that the presence of black middle- and upper-class television characters "implies the failure of a majority of black people . . . who have not achieved similar professional or material success" (p. 137).

Entman's interpretation of the significance of black anchors also seems tenable when considering the presence of African American journalists in stories that feed traditional racist stereotypes. Two of the stories interpreted in the last chapter to contribute to those stereotypes included contributions from a black anchor and a black reporter. Coverage of Charles Barkley's tirade, for instance, was introduced by Emery King, African American anchor on Detroit's WDIV 11 p.m. newscast, who contrasted Barkley's behavior with that day's King holiday and its emphasis on peace and nonviolence. The anchor's comments inadvertently contribute to the news media stereotype of the "savage" African American. Similarly, African American reporter Phil Harris's coverage of Milwaukee's midnight basketball league also advanced stereotypical notions about African American men from the inner city.

Entman argues that the mere presence of African American anchors—economically and socially successful representatives of middle- and upper-class black America—contributes to the modern racist conception of racism as a thing of the past. But perhaps more important is their apparent acceptance of majority culture common sense, which lends credence to the news media's racial mythology. That minority journalists might adopt the hegemonic news values of overwhelmingly white, middle-class newsrooms is not surprising. Research has indicated that journalists tend to conform to the values of their news organizations as a means of socialization (Breed, 1960; Dimmick, 1974). For minority journalists, that socialization can be a perplexing matter. As journalist/author Jill Nelson (1993) argues,

> For most African American journalists, working in mainstream media entails a daily struggle with [the white, male] notion of objectivity. Each day we are required to justify ourselves, our community, and our story ideas. The more successful of us refashion ourselves in the image of white men. We go to Ivy League colleges and socialize primarily with white folks. . . .
>
> We must be emotional and professional self-censors, constantly aware that when dealing with white editors, our enthusiasm, passion, and commitment are often perceived as intimidation, anger, and lack of objectivity. Human characteristics and personality traits—such as being outspoken, stubborn, proud—are viewed as "racial," and therefore negative. (pp. 86–88)

As Gans (1979) observed, "News supports the social order of public, business, and professional, upper-middle-class, middle-aged, and white male sectors of society" (p. 61). And as Breed noted, "The cultural patterns of the newsroom produce results insufficient for wider democratic needs" (p. 194).

The "social order" Gans describes is as much about class as it is about race; America's view of its ethnic minorities is directly linked to its view of economic and social class. Jhally and Lewis (1992) think that prime-time television—with its emphasis on middle- and upper-class situations and characters—has created an understanding of members of those privileged classes as superior to members of the working and underclass; on network television's evening programming, life among the nonprivileged is generally ignored.

Because most African Americans live their lives outside of the walls of the economic and social success defined by television, their stories are simply not included during prime time. With the nonprivileged out of the picture, the life of the privileged becomes TV's norm and contributes to an American perception of poor and working-class Americans as marginal, abnormal, inferior. With a majority of Americans of color living outside of the standards defined by television, they too become marginal, abnormal, inferior. Write Jhally and Lewis, "[Fictional] television, having confused people about class, becomes incomprehensible about race" (p. 135).

The news media may be contributing to similar confusion about class and race. Simmons (1993) contends that American journalists "appear unable to distinguish between race and class issues" (p. 146). He points out that many whites suffer from inadequate housing, health care and education and that the largest portion of Americans living in poverty are white. But, he writes, "The media consistently neglect to report these facts of American life" (p. 146). Mainstream journalism's commonsense notion of issues related to race and class resembles that of prime-time television programming. It marginalizes and stereotypes the lives of people who fall outside of its narrow definition of respectability. Often, this means people of color. But not always. When we see that Bill Cosby and other minority prime-time characters—as well as prominent minority TV journalists—fit nicely into the media norms, we are left with the mythical understanding that the life of privilege is equally accessible to all. As Jhally and Lewis (1992) sardonically ask, "After all, if the world is like it is on *The Cosby Show,* what is the problem?" (p. 128)

The possibility that nonwhite television journalists might be contributing to contemporary racist attitudes is certainly a perplexing matter, especially when considering the alternative of whites-only news broadcasts. But considering the arguments of prime-time television researchers and notions like enlightened racism, it seems that minority journalists may indeed be inadvertently playing a role in advancing the sophisticated attitudes of contemporary racism. Stories by journalists of all colors reflect the "preferred" meanings that Hall (1980) describes; that is, dominant newsroom values will dictate similar understandings of events by minority and nonminority newspeople.

This is especially significant when considering that the battle against racism in the news media has largely been fought in terms of minority employment. The American Society of Newspaper Editors, for instance, publishes yearly reports on minority hiring. One goal of that organization is to see that the minority population of America's newsrooms matches the general minority population of the United States. By increasing the number of minority journalists, so the thinking goes, news organizations would more fairly and accurately cover minority life. But that might not be the case, especially considering the possibility that the presence of journalists of color might not dramatically affect news coverage and could contribute to contemporary racist attitudes. But whether or not an increase in the numbers of minority journalists changes the way news gets covered, the alternatives— fewer or no minority journalists—are unacceptable. As Philadelphia columnist Linda Wright Moore (1990) argues,

> While it is likely that African Americans involved in decision making roles will adopt the news values of the white institutions for which they work, it is self-evident that, if they are *not* involved, the mix of options to be considered in making such decisions on a day-to-day basis will be unnecessarily and perhaps irresponsibly restricted. (p. 23)

It is with this paradox in mind—that minority journalists may actually contribute to contemporary racist myths, but that that is preferred to their absence—that this chapter shall proceed. Jhally and Lewis (1992) argue that *The Cosby Show* contributed more to enlightened racist attitudes than it did to truly pluralistic understandings of race. I would contend, however, that although the presence of minority journalists may be contributing to the subtle attitudes of contemporary racism, their absence would be unacceptable and would contribute to the overtly discriminatory attitudes of the traditional racism of the past. I will, however, continue examining stories in the "negotiated/oppositional" approach described by Hall (1980); these readings are necessary in order to interpret the subtleties and nuances of contemporary racism that may be surfacing in journalistic interpretations of events. . . . In this chapter, I will consider the implications of contemporary notions of racism, keeping in mind the intricacy and sophistication of these notions.

"ENLIGHTENED" RACISM AND COVERAGE OF THE MARTIN LUTHER KING, JR. HOLIDAY

Minority journalists and researchers point out that news coverage of ethnic holidays is often a less-than-serious attempt to cover minority communities; rather, it can be a cynical gesture to placate those communities. Wilson and Gutiérrez (1985), for example, argue that such coverage is often a matter of a predetermined journalistic routine:

> Stories about ethnic minorities focusing on special occasions—such as Cinco de Mayo, Chinese New Year, or Dr. Martin Luther King, Jr.'s birthday—to the exclusion of more substantive reporting is . . . indicative of policy. (p. 144)

And Greg Freeman (1991), a columnist and editor at the *St. Louis Post-Dispatch,* contends that the news media

> must begin to provide more than superficial coverage—the occasional crime story, the Martin Luther King Day events, the annual Cinco de Mayo parade, the Native American Day that comes once a year—and reach out to understand these various cultures, to cover the stories that are truly relevant to these peoples. (p. 4)

Much of the local television news coverage of the January 18, 1993, Martin Luther King, Jr. holiday may have been a superficial—even self-conscious—attempt to highlight African American communities that are generally neglected. The holiday was granted coverage on all 28 stations whose programs were recorded for this study on that date. The stories ranged from short "readers" about the various communities' events to "packages" that included contributions from several reporters and camera crews. Most of the stories reflected a sense that King's dream—of an America that does not discriminate on the basis of race—had been attained, and that the day's events represented America's triumph over its racist past. Occasionally, coverage would hint at the failure of that dream to come to fruition and acknowledge the persistence of racism in America.

The stories that would seem to fuel the notions of enlightened racism most directly were those that emphasized America's success at combatting racism. That theme was prevalent in a variety of ways. Syracuse's WTVH, for instance, acknowledged the holiday by concluding its 5:30 p.m. broadcast with a 3½ minute feature on an African American family and its members' views on King. (WTVH-TV declined a request for permission to reproduce a complete transcript of the story.)

On a denotative level, the story is a "package" covered as part of the station's recurring "Our Kids" feature. It is introduced by anchor Ron Curtis as a look "into how two generations within the same family see the man and his message." Reporter Pat Nilsen explains that many parents were alive during the civil rights era, but that "children are left to read about it in history books." She first introduces us to William Pollard, dean of the Syracuse University School of Social Work, who grew up in the pre–civil rights era South. He recalls working at a restaurant that refused service to African Americans. That recollection is followed by black and white footage of King's "I Have a Dream" speech, in which King pleads for a nation in which "my four little children will not be judged by the color of their skin but by the content of their character."

Nilsen asks, "Have things changed since [the civil rights movement]?" Pollard then relates a story in which his son Frederick's white classmate assumes that Pollard's son stole the expensive jacket that the son was wearing. The son says that "sometimes ignorance can't be helped." Nilsen next says that the recently released, Spike Lee–directed film *Malcolm X* may have made Malcolm a more popular figure than King among young African Americans. Pollard's son, William II, explains that "because of the violent ways of today's youth, they see that actions speak louder than words." But he argues that King's life demonstrates "that you can accomplish a lot of things without using your fists."

We see more of the film of King speaking as Nilsen asks, "What legacy do father and mother hope their sons will remember from Martin Luther King, Jr.?" Pollard's wife Meriette says she wants her children to "remember that they can solve conflicts peacefully." Pollard says he wants his children to have "the capacity to understand the difference between right and wrong and the courage to act to make sure the right comes to the forefront." Nilsen concludes the piece from the news desk, explaining that "the point he was making, too, Dean Pollard, with that statement, was that applies to the courage to stand up for it, with drugs, with racism, so many of our problems, and that's what we *all* want for our kids." Anchor Curtis agrees and calls the family "wonderful."

Although the story briefly acknowledges the persistence of racism, in its entirety it feeds the mythology of enlightened racism. The Pollard family is a financially and socially successful one, the father the dean of a college at a major university. American racism is largely depicted in images of the past. The nation "honors the memory" of King, and children "read about [him] in history books." His battle against racism is relegated to the black and white film-clips of another time—the white men who taunt the civil rights marchers and wave a Confederate flag represent the bigotry of an era gone-by. William Pollard recalls the injustice of the segregated South of his youth, but his present status as an esteemed academic speaks to America's triumph over that injustice.

Reporter Nilsen asks if things have changed since the days of Pollard's youth. Pollard and his son tell the story of a white boy who presumes that the son's new jacket was stolen. We are to understand that stereotypes still exist, that perhaps things haven't changed. But the anecdote fails to contradict the story's more dominant imagery of a well-adjusted and highly principled upper-middle-class African American family. As Gray (1986) argues about situation comedies that "absorb" nonassimilationist ideas "into the conventional code of problem and solutions" (p. 227), here the news coverage simultaneously admits to the persistence of racism but "absorbs" it into assimilationist ideology that contradicts it.

The Pollard family—like the fictional Huxtable family—attests to the attainability of The American Dream. Their strong sense of values is stressed and becomes the common-sense explanation of why they are different from those who are less fortunate. Pollard's older son separates himself from "the violent ways of today's youth" by identifying with King and not Malcolm X; his peers, he says, "refer more back to Malcolm" and see that "actions speak louder than words," but William Pollard II prefers King's nonviolent approach and says, "You can accomplish a lot of things without using your fists." Nilsen asks, "What legacy do father and mother hope their sons will remember from Martin Luther King, Jr.?" The mother espouses her philosophy of nonviolence; the father extols knowing the "difference between right and wrong" and having "the courage to act to make sure that the right comes to the forefront."

The family's successful assimilation into the financial and moral high ground of middle-American society is lauded by the white journalists who cover the story. Nilsen says that what the Pollards want for their kids "is what we *all* want for our kids"—the stressed "all" apparently meant to mean whites as well as African Americans. Curtis agrees, and adds, "Quite a family isn't it?" Their awe continues. Nilsen says, "Very, very impressive," and Curtis adds, "They're wonderful." The doting of the white journalists contributes to an understanding of the Pollards as special, as different. Their treatment of the family reinforces what Essed (1991) has described as "underestimation"; that is, their success stands out because of the apparent failure of other African American families to succeed. As she explains,

> One black who succeeds becomes salient because the invisibility of the oppressed major-ity is not questioned. In a social system where it is explicitly claimed that "accomplish-ment" is the result of "individual merit," *underestimation* is a crucial legitimization of the continuing exclusion of blacks from fair access to and use of resources. Historically the idea of white intellectual superiority has been one of the most persistent features of Euro-American ideologies on race. (p. 232)

The Pollards mythologically represent an open American society in which dreams can be fulfilled for those with the right values. They stand in stark contrast to the impoverished and criminal images of African Americans that are far more common in the news. . . . The Pollards are real-life Huxtables. Their success carries similar connotations to that of Bill Cosby's fictional family, which Jhally and Lewis (1992) argue implies "the failure of a majority of black people . . . who have not achieved similar professional or material success" (p. 137).

Coverage of the King holiday by New Orleans's WWL was more typical of the kind of stories local news audiences nationwide saw January 18, 1993. That station led off its 6 p.m. newscast with a 4-minute "package" that included contributions from two anchors and two reporters. . . . After an introduction by the coanchors, reporter Susan Roberts covered that day's downtown parade and interviewed a number of participants. We see several of shots of the marchers and hear from three unidentified men who participated. One tells us that King was "a man who was very dedicated to some very serious principles that we need to live by in order to get along." Roberts says the day "is a time for a celebration in that we can take pride in the progress, but look forward to even more unity." A second marcher says King "made contributions to society for all people, not just for black people but people of all races." A third says he is pleased with the parade's yearly growth and says he likes "the different variety of people that came out." Finally we see a segment of a speech given at a rally that concluded the march. Roberts ends the story by saying, "Organizers say it is up to people of all races to keep Dr. King's message alive, not just on this day but all year long."

Next, reporter Elizabeth Renshaw covers some of the march participants who were colleagues of King. She interviews The Reverend Simmie Harvie, who helped found the Southern Christian Leadership Conference with King in a New Orleans church. Harvie says King "had what is called a magnet. You meet him, you walk with him, he had drawing power." Renshaw then interviews another civil rights leader, Morris Jeff, Sr., who recalls King's soft-spoken manner, adding, "but what he said had meaning." We then see black and white film coverage of King's "I Have a Dream" speech and footage of white protestors at a civil rights march. (It is the same footage used in the Pollard family story.) Mr. Harvie recalls the risk of participating in the civil rights struggle. He says white opponents "were rough on us" and would attack participants as they left meeting places. We then see footage of a King speech in which he seems to sense his own martyrdom. "Longevity has its place," he says, "but I'm not concerned about that now." We see film of the balcony where he was assassinated followed by a shot of King's corpse on display. Renshaw concludes, "An assassin's bullet silenced his speech, but followers say it did not silence his message." We return to the anchors, where John Snell describes the evening's King holiday events.

Like the story on the Pollard family by Syracuse's WTVH, the New Orleans King Day coverage mythically relegates American racism to the past. In the story's second report, in fact, we see the same archival footage of angry whites jeering King and other civil rights marchers. That report, introduced with a graphic that reads "Carrying the Message," focuses on two marchers who were colleagues of King. Their memories of King and of the dangers they faced place the battle against racism in a purely historical context. The images that evoke King's assassination—including an excerpt from the speech in which he seemed to prophesy his death—are from the distant past. Reporter Elizabeth Renshaw's commonsense conclusion to the story—"an assassin's bullet silenced his speech, but followers say it did not silence his message"—speaks to the triumph of King's dream. The New Orleans's coverage feeds the same assimilationist notions as the Syracuse coverage of the Pollards: America has put its racist past behind it; we have plenty to celebrate.

The first report in the New Orleans coverage, titled "Celebrating a Dream," feeds similar notions of contemporary American race relations. One marcher tell us that King's dream "lives on and on." Although another says that "a lot of people are not getting along the way they're supposed to," his comments are contradicted by the story's assimilationist theme. Reporter Susan Roberts tells us that "King's day is a time for a celebration in part in that we can take pride in the progress, but look forward to even more unity." One marcher says King made "contributions for all people, not just for black people but for people of all races." Another says the march is "a real positive expression of people remembering Martin Luther King," and he points to "the variety of people that came out." (That "variety" seems to be contradicted by the video coverage of the march, which shows few—if any—nonblack participants.) Roberts concludes her segment by saying, "The celebration is now over but the work is not. Organizers say it is up to people of all races to keep Dr. King's message alive, not just on this day but all year long." Again, there is a hint at the persistence of America's racial intolerance, but it has been contradicted by the celebratory spirit of the coverage.

Like most of the coverage of the King holiday that was recorded for this study, the New Orleans's stories repeatedly refer to King's "dream" and "message." Stations in many cities carried footage of his "I Have a Dream" speech to articulate that message: "I have a dream that my four little children will one day live in a nation where they will not be judged by the color of their skin but by the content of their character." The theme of many of the stories was one of festivity, indicating the journalists' apparent belief in America's successful attainment of that dream. As Roberts tells us, we can "take pride in the progress." Certainly, King Day is a day for Americans to celebrate the life of one of its greatest leaders. But the stations' commonsense views of harmonious race relations fail to explain the economic and social distress that exist among so much of America's minority populations. That view seems particularly preposterous coming from a Louisiana station. Only 14 months before, white supremacist David Duke won more than 665,000 votes in his run for the state's governorship.

As in the Syracuse story, all of the journalists who contributed to the New Orleans King Day coverage were white—coanchors Snell and Angela Hill and reporters Roberts and Renshaw. But in several other cities, coverage that also contributed to assimilationist notions about race included reporting by African American journalists. WSYX in Columbus, OH, for example, sent two black reporters to cover the King holiday in that city. (WSYX declined a request for permission to reproduce a complete transcript of the story.)

The Columbus coverage, on a denotative level, was handled as a 4½ minute "package" and included a "live" report from two field reporters as well as their pretaped stories. The station's coanchors introduce the coverage, that evening's "top story." In a split-screen shot, coanchor Deborah Countiss introduces reporter Charlene Brown, who begins the coverage with a short look at the "live" entertainment at a post-march program. She explains that the boys' choir concert that we have just seen is one of a number of events planned for the evening. We then see footage of the day's march, and Brown tells us, "There are usually at least a couple of thousand people, frequently more, who join in that march, young, old, black, white, people from many different religions."

Brown says, "One thing that is significant in everything that has been happening around town is the number of kids who have participated." She then introduces reporter Tanya Hutchins, who is with her at the King Day program. Hutchins then reports on the participation of children at two of the day's events. First, we see services at a Catholic church where, according to Hutchins, "people of all races and denominations came to worship." We see city councilman Michael Coleman at the podium, saying, "When Dr. King was assassinated in 1968, he passed the torch of his dream to a new generation." Hutchins says, "And that generation was listening more intently than most would think." We hear the comments of several children about the church service and about King. Says one 10-year-old of Coleman's address, "I learned more in that speech than I did at school." Says another of King, "He is very special to me because he fought for our rights so we could sit at a lunch counter and eat."

Hutchins then reports on the performances at a different event held that day, and we see some of the rappers and dancers who appeared earlier at a performing arts complex named for King. Hutchins is then rejoined "live" by Brown, and she tells her, "It was a great example, Charlene, of kids not on the streets but actually performing and participating in activities all throughout the city." Brown agrees, also touting the participation of young people at the day's events—"the kind of thing you don't expect young people to do given so much of what we cover every day and so many of the problems that we have with our young people." The story ends with a return to a split screen showing Brown and anchor Countiss. Countiss says, "The thing that always comes to me on Martin Luther King Day is the fact that the death of Dr. King really is one of the very sad chapters in our nation's history, and yet it has been turned into a celebration of his life and everything that he stood for, and that's such a positive thing." Brown agrees, adding, "It is a celebration of his life, and not just a memorial to his slaying, and that gives it a much more upbeat and—for a lot of people—much more meaningful message."

On a connotative level, the Columbus coverage—like that in Syracuse and New Orleans—assigns American racism to the past. Brown describes the day's march as "very symbolic" in that it commemorated "the marches that Dr. Martin Luther King, Jr. himself led." The marchers "braved the cold weather to come out and join in [honoring] . . . a peace-maker and a man that worked for equality for all." The children who are interviewed contribute to the story's commonsense understanding of the struggle for racial equality as a part of American history. In introducing the kids' remarks, reporter Hutchins says "their generation" listened to church service speakers "more intently than most would think," and that they "understand what Martin Luther King was all about." One says he is "very special to me because he fought for our rights so we could sit at a lunch counter and eat." Another says, "He helped blacks and whites make friends." The children's innocent failure to fully grasp the true nature of race relations in America is understandable. But their simplistic explanations of King's apparent triumph over racism is little different from the mythological theme espoused by the station's journalists. As coanchor Countiss remarks at the story's conclusion, "One of the very sad chapters in our nation's history . . . has been turned into a celebration."

Like the Syracuse and New Orleans stories, the Columbus coverage contains allusions to the persistence of racism, but they are overshadowed by the story's more prevalent assimilationist ideology. For instance, city councilman Michael Coleman, in his speech at the Catholic church, echoes King in saying, "We are not free until all of us are free." And in the reporters' "live" discussion of the day's events, Brown tells Hutchins that the participation of young people is "the kind of thing that you don't expect . . . given so much of what we cover every day and so many of the problems that we have with our young people." Hutchins agrees. These hints at the persistence of a society plagued with racial problems fail to contradict the story's assimilationist narrative.

Although Coleman suggests "we are not free," his status as a successful African American politician speaks to an America of equal access for all of its citizens. His polished attire may also carry a different meaning than the clothing of the black political leaders of the 1960s. As West (1993) writes,

> The black dress suits and white shirts worn by Malcolm X and Martin Luther King, Jr. signified the seriousness of their deep commitment to black freedom, whereas today the expensive tailored suits of black politicians symbolize their personal success and individual achievement. Malcolm and Martin called for the realization that black people are somebodies with which America has to reckon, whereas black politicians tend to turn our attention to *their* somebodiness owing to *their* "making it" in America. (pp. 37–38)

Similarly, the images of the African American reporters who admit to "the problems we have with our young people" confute the notion that those problems may be linked to racism. The black civic leader and journalists contribute to the mythology of enlightened racism. As Jhally and Lewis (1992) observe,

> Among white people, the admission of black characters to television's upwardly mobile world gives credence to the idea that racial divisions, whether perpetuated by class barriers or racism, do not exist. Most white people are extremely receptive to such a message. (p. 135)

The story's focus on the celebratory nature of the day's events is compounded by the journalists' frequent references to the diversity of the participants. After showing us the predominantly black boys' choir, Brown says their concert is "just one of the things that's on the program." She adds,

> We'll be hearing from various speakers. There will also be entertainment by a jazz group, a rock groups—there's going to be a little bit of everything on the program this year.

We see two shots of the day's march. The first one, a long shot from above the marchers, does seem to show a number of white participants in the crowd. The second is a full shot of five marchers, one of whom is white. Brown describes the participants as "young, old, black, white, people from many different religions." In introducing coverage of the church service, Hutchins says, "People of all races and denominations came to worship at St. John the Evangelist Church in East Columbus." The shots of the ceremony indicate the crowd does appear to be well integrated. The assimilationist ideology continues in the children's responses to the reporter's questions. A 10-year-old African American boy says King symbolized "justice, well, for black people, standing up for black and white." A white boy says, "He helped blacks and whites make friends."

The approach of the WSYX journalists to the story suggests that the children's interpretation of race relations is an accurate one. Brown concludes the story by agreeing with Countiss's assessment of the celebratory nature of the events as "a positive thing." Says Brown,

> I think that's one of the most important things to keep in mind about this celebration. It is a celebration of [King's] life, and not just a memorial to his slaying, and that gives it a much more upbeat and—for a lot of people—much more meaningful message.

Among that "lot of people" are clearly the station's journalists. Although a celebration of the life of Dr. Martin Luther King, Jr. is appropriate, the tone of the coverage smugly denies America's failure to attain his dream. In its words and images, it presents a contrived understanding of racial harmony. Both the white and black journalists contribute to the mythical existence of the American melting pot. Perhaps most significant are the remarks made by the African American reporters who contribute to . . . negative stereotypes. . . . Hutchins says the participation of young people—and almost all of those we have seen are black—in the days events "was a great example . . . of kids not on the streets but actually performing and participating in activities all throughout the city." And Brown adds that that participation is "the kind of thing that you don't expect young people to do given so much of what we cover every day and so many of the problems that we have with our young people." Although the coverage of the events could serve to counter the stereotypes, the emphasis on their uniqueness simply compounds the standard notions of negative behavior.

Brown's use of collective pronouns raises other questions. Her use of the phrase "given what *we* cover every day" seems to link her to WSYX, or perhaps to the news media in general. And that connection seems particularly appropriate; for audience members who rely on the news media's stereotypical images of African Americans to interpret their world, the young people's King Day behavior is certainly not "the kind of thing that you'd expect young people to do." But what group is Brown aligning herself with when commenting about "the problems that we have with our young people"? She seems now to be aligning herself not with her fellow journalists but with the audience. As an African American, is she commenting about a problem in the black community? If so, she would seem to be putting the responsibility for the problems she is referring to solely in the hands of that community, contributing to the enlightened racist view that white racism has nothing to do with the economic and social injustice that pervades black America. But her use of "we" and "us" could be aligning her simply with Americans of all colors; in that case, she becomes a representative of television's notion of middle-America, her blackness a symbol of equal opportunity, her comments about the problematic nature of young people reinforcing television's mythological interpretation of race and class. Because of the station's interpretation of King Day as a celebration of America's triumph over racism, Brown's comments—however she may have intended them to be understood—directly reinforce the beliefs of enlightened racism: Prejudice and discrimination no longer exist; Americans of color who fail to achieve financial and social success have only themselves to blame.

Coverage in several other cities acknowledged the failure of King's dream to be fully realized, yet remained focused on the progress made by King and the civil rights movement. In Phoenix, for instance, where the holiday was being officially celebrated by the state of Arizona for the first time, coverage by KTVK focused on the state's delayed recognition of King Day, suggesting both the advancement of racial tolerance and the persistence of racism. . . .

Denotatively, that coverage was handled as a 1-minute "reader" in which coanchor Patti Kirkpatrick narrates videotape of the day's events. We see several long shots of the march as Kirkpatrick tells us that an estimated 10,000 people attended. She says, "This was truly a victory march since voters approved the statewide holiday just last November." Next we see a medium shot of Rabbi Robert Kravitz, a march participant. He says that Arizona's holiday is a "landmark" for the state and a "benchmark for the rest of the country. We voted for the holiday, and we passed it." We then see a second marcher, The Reverend Warren Stewart, who says, "It's something they should have done years ago. So it's mixed emotions: Yes, there's joy, but—hey—it's about time." Next we see several long shots of a parade in Mesa, AZ. Kirkpatrick says that it is "not a paid city holiday parade in Mesa, but many residents celebrated by holding a march for unity." She concludes, "Participants say they want people to know that King Day is not only a holiday for minorities."

KTVK's coverage hints at assimilationist mythology, but that mythology is not left entirely without contradiction. We are told that the 10,000 marchers were there "to commemorate the birthday" of King, although the marchers' chants indicate their frustration with the state's earlier votes against recognition of the day as a state holiday. Members of the crowd—seen in several long shots that indicate it is almost entirely made up of African

Americans—seem to be there as much to vent their feelings of frustration as to commemorate King's birthday. "We finally got it," chants a leader. "King Day," chant members of the crowd. "Was it worth it?" he asks. "Yes," they respond. Kirkpatrick's telling of the story ignores the marchers' sense of frustration. She says the event "was truly a victory march since voters approved the statewide holiday just last November."

The assimilationist angle is supported in the use of Rabbi Kravitz—one of what is apparently only a few nonblack participants—as the story's first source. He says, "What was a landmark of the state of Arizona is now a benchmark for the rest of the country. We voted for the holiday, and we passed it." Kravitz implies that Arizona's vote to approve the holiday sets a standard for states whose legislatures approved the holiday without a popular vote. His comments indicate that Arizona's vote is a symbol of its racial tolerance, a model for the rest of the country. Those comments are clearly contradicted, however, by those that follow from Mr. Stewart, an African American. He says, "It's something they should have done years ago. So it's mixed emotions: Yes, there's joy, but—hey—it's about time." In his view, the day's events hardly represent the racially tolerant America that the story attempts to portray. But the coverage ends with a look at a parade in nearby Mesa, reasserting the assimilationist angle. The long shots of the crowd indicate a racially mixed group of marchers. Kirkpatrick tells us that the theme of that march "is a celebration of diversity," and that "participants say they want people to know that King Day is not only a holiday for minorities." That Arizona finally celebrated King Day was a story worth telling, but featuring the state as a paragon of racial harmony raises serious questions about the credibility of the coverage.

The station's coverage of the Phoenix march came nearly 10 minutes into the newscast, following a series of stories on storms and flooding that had hit the area. The weather coverage likely preempted what might have been lengthier coverage of King Day events; several stations in other parts of the country, in fact, covered the Phoenix march in more detail than did KTVK. The station's approach to the coverage—in both its brevity and its assimilationist theme—plays down the racist image of an Arizona that had refused to enact a King holiday. As in many cities, the station included some evidence of lingering racism in its coverage, but that angle was played down.

Neither the racial makeup of the stations' on-camera journalists nor of their viewing audiences seemed to affect their approaches to coverage of King Day. For instance, several stations that covered the holiday in assimilationist fashion were in areas with substantial African American populations and utilized African American reporters. The audience for WSYX, for example, is primarily made up of Columbus's 633,000 citizens, 23% of whom are African American (U.S. Department of Commerce, 1990). And the largest portions of the New Orleans's television audience live in Orleans and Jefferson Parishes, where the population is approximately 40% black. But in Billings, MT—a city where only 7% of its population of 81,000 is nonwhite—coverage by KTVQ directly acknowledged the persistence of societal racism.

KTVQ's 4 minutes of King holiday coverage included a "live" report from reporter Jennifer Elliot as well as excerpts from an interview with a Native American representative of the Intertribal Resource Center. . . . The story is introduced by anchor Gus Koernig, who says, "For the first time, Americans all across the country are celebrating Martin Luther King Day." He introduces Elliot, who stands in front of a local church and tells us about the flashlight procession that will wind through Billings that evening. She then introduces Greg Krueger of the Billings Ecumenical Council. Krueger gives us more information on the march—we find out that it will pass by several churches of different denominations—and the Christian unity service that will follow.

Elliot points out that this is the 9th year of the march, but that this is the first time that it is being held in celebration of King's birthday. She asks, "Why is that different this year?" Krueger responds:

> We decided that with the rise of some different hate groups—not only worldwide but here in Billings, too—that we would join Wayman Chapel and show our support for Martin Luther King's holiday and his message of social justice and peace and tolerance.

Elliot asks if racism and "the growth of hate groups and all that here in Billings" is a bigger problem this year, and if that is "why the service is being celebrated the way it is?" Krueger says racism is "a big problem anywhere. Even if there are just a few people involved, it makes it a big problem because it is such a divisive type of thing." He points out that King's widow, Coretta Scott King, had also recently described "a resurgence of hate in our society as well as the world society." We find out that the sermon at the unity service that evening will be delivered by a Kentucky theologian who will speak on racism within religious denominations.

The coverage ends with comments by Native American leader Alda Small. Anchor Koernig introduces this segment by pointing out that "Martin Luther King's dream included *all* Americans, and the campaign for equal rights for Native Americans had its beginnings around the time King was assassinated." He says that Native American leaders in the Billings area say "change has been slow in coming, and there is still a lot of progress to be made." Next, we see Small, who says,

> If we can build just a basic understanding of one another's culture—traditions, lifestyles, family systems—I definitely believe that some of these problems with racism can be alleviated.

Koernig ends the coverage by saying that Small "hopes the new administrations in Helena and Washington will pay more attention to needs of all ethnic and racial minorities."

Although coverage in most of the cities viewed for this study—including Syracuse, New Orleans, Columbus and Phoenix—reflected a mythological understanding of King Day as a celebration of American racial tolerance, the Billings coverage directly contradicts that myth, focusing on the persistence of American racism. That Billings would employ such an approach is remarkable. Its African American population is less than 0.5%. Two white journalists steer the coverage, and a white source—Greg Krueger—expounds on the enduring racism in Billings, America and the world. The coverage also incorporates the perspective of a larger Billing's ethnic minority—Native Americans make up about 3% of its population—by interviewing a Native American leader who also points to America's failure to overcome racism.

Koernig's introduction to the story hints at that failure. By pointing out that "for the first time, Americans all across the country are celebrating Martin Luther King Day," he alludes to the fact that the state of Arizona had finally approved the day as a state holiday after highly publicized and controversial debates and votes on the issue. Reporter Elliot's questions also lead to a direct discussion of contemporary racism. She asks why the Billings Ecumenical Council had decided to celebrate the King holiday for the first time this year. Krueger, the council's representative, acknowledges that the "rise of some different hate groups" in Billings and elsewhere had motivated the group to "show our support of [King's] message of social justice and peace and tolerance."

Elliot repeats the question, asking if racism is "a bigger problem—seeing the growth of hate groups and all that here in Billings" and if that is the reason for the new approach to the service. Krueger says that racism is a "big problem anywhere. Even if there just a few people involved, it makes it a big problem because it is such a divisive type of thing." The interview is far different from what audiences saw in most other cities. Here, a white reporter and white source acknowledge and confront the persistence of racism. The two do not feed the mythology of enlightened racists who look elsewhere for reasons for the plight of American minorities.

Elliot asks about the sermon for that evening's service, and Krueger tells us that The Reverend Michael Kinnamon, a theologian and scholar from the Lexington, Kentucky Theological Seminary, will speak on racism in churches, a topic on which he is an authority. Compared to the Columbus coverage—which portrayed church life as a bastion of integration and tolerance—the Billings coverage includes religion as part of America's racist legacy.

Of the King Day stories on the 28 stations viewed for this study, the Billings coverage was the only to use a white man as its primary source. Certainly a black source was available somewhere—even in a city with so few African Americans. But KTVQ's choice to use Krueger as a spokesman against racial intolerance is an interesting one. It is possible that white audience members—particularly those who hold the subtle attitudes of contemporary racism—would find a white source who condemns racism more credible than an African American source. For the "modern" racist who believes that African Americans are overly demanding in their push for equal rights, a white man who acknowledges the persistence of racism is more difficult to refute. For the viewers of *The Cosby Show* who smugly defend their racial attitudes on the grounds that a few successful minorities prove that prejudice and discrimination do not exist, the presence of a white source who contradicts their argument may well have more impact.

But the coverage is not entirely white. Anchor Koernig's transition to the view of Native Americans includes their sense that "change has been slow in coming, and there is still a lot of progress to be made." Spokesperson Small says, "If we can build just a basic understanding of one another's culture—traditions, lifestyles, family systems—I definitely believe that some of these problems with racism can be alleviated." Koernig concludes the story with Small's view that "one way to build that understanding is providing greater ethnic representation in local and national government." The common sense of this coverage is far different from that in the many cities that chose to focus on America racial harmony. Here, the journalists and the sources they interview all seem determined to emphasize America's failure to overcome its racist legacy.

SUMMARY

In this chapter, I have attempted to apply the findings of researchers who have examined fictional television to the nonfictional images of local television journalism. It appears that prime-time TV's messages about race and class are reinforced in coverage by local television news organizations. The interpretations of news coverage of the Dr. Martin Luther King, Jr. holiday also support Entman's (1990) findings on the existence of "modern" racism in local TV news, including the likelihood that the appearance of minority journalists may contribute to the attitudes of contemporary racists who cite the success of a limited number of African Americans in arguing that racism no longer exists in this country. This chapter further suggests that African American journalists whose reporting reflects the common sense of racial assimilation also reinforce the mythological thinking of "enlightened" racists.

The ultimate message of nearly all of the coverage of the King holiday viewed for this study was that American racism was a thing of the past. The occasional contradiction of that notion was overshadowed by the dominant theme of storytelling and imagery that testified to America as a melting pot. In its coverage of King Day, local television journalism constructed a world in which The American Dream lives, a parallel world to that of nightly network sitcoms, the world of the Huxtable family. Considering the more typical coverage of people of color on local television news—coverage that tends to marginalize and stereotype members of ethnic minorities—the existence of this other world becomes more profound. If our society is the just and fair one that was portrayed on King Day, the constant barrage of menacing images of minorities that more commonly appear on local TV news will undoubtedly fuel racist attitudes. As Jhally and Lewis (1992) write,

> Although television portrays a world of equal opportunity, most white people know that in the world at large, black people achieve less material success, on the whole, than white people. They know that black people are disproportionately likely to live in poor neighborhoods and drop out of school. How can this knowledge be reconciled with the smiling faces of the Huxtables? If we are blind to the roots of racial inequality embedded in our society's class structure, then there *is* only one way to reconcile this paradoxical state of affairs. If white people are disproportionately successful, then they must be disproportionately smarter or more willing to work hard. (p. 136)

That King Day was covered the way it was is not surprising. The social and professional processes that dictate how news is covered are based on an implicit common sense, a common sense that may have more to do with stereotyped notions about the world than with a true understanding of it. Most Americans would like to believe that their country is a tolerant and fair one, that discrimination does not exist, that equal opportunity is there for all. But what we would like to believe and what actually exists are clearly at odds. Certainly America has made strides toward King's dream, but those strides have fallen well short of the kind of racial justice that was signified in so much of the King Day reporting. The stations' superficial attempts to project racial harmony serve instead to reinforce contemporary racist notions.

That a station in Billings, MT—among the whitest places in the United States—would adopt such a different thematic approach to its coverage of the King holiday is surprising. Perhaps it was simply a matter of a small-market news organization that had not been affected by the trappings of American journalism's predetermined understanding of its world. By avoiding the standard newsroom common sense of King Day as a tribute to American racial tolerance, Billings's KTVQ contributed to a much less optimistic understanding of race relations in America. Although that understanding might be resisted by its audience, it fails to contribute to the assimilationist ideology that is at the root of enlightened racism. By avoiding commonsense, predetermined notions about race in covering the news, a news organization is more effectively playing its role as a provider of the kind of information needed for a democratically just society. As Martindale (1986) argues,

Since the media are, by the very nature of their work, thrust into a central role in race relations, it seems only logical that they would strive to perform their jobs in such a way as to contribute toward the development of a healthier and more democratic society, rather than produce coverage that creates even more divisiveness and interracial hostility. (p. 182)

NOTE

1. The appearance of African American politicians in the newscasts recorded for this study was primarily limited to their appearances at Martin Luther King, Jr. holiday celebrations. It is possible that these appearances might contribute to the modern racist notion that African American politicians practice special interest politics; however, there were only a few such appearances, and it seems their more significant meaning may be in the fact that they are successful social figures whose prominence might lend credence to the belief of contemporary racists that racial discrimination no longer exists. That is an issue that will be discussed later in this chapter.

REFERENCES

Breed, W. (1960). Social control in the newsroom: A functional analysis. In W. Schramm (Ed.), *Mass communications* (pp. 178–197). Urbana: University of Illinois Press.

Dimmick, J. (1974). The gatekeeper: An uncertain theory. *Journalism Monographs, 37.*

Entman, R. M. (1990). Modern racism and the images of blacks in local television news. *Critical Studies in Mass Communication, 7*(4), 332–345.

Essed, P. (1991). *Understanding everyday racism.* Newbury Park, CA: Sage.

Gans, H. (1979). *Deciding what's news.* New York: Pantheon.

Gray, H. (1986). Television and the new black man: Black male images in prime-time situation comedy. *Media, Culture and Society, 8*, 223–242.

Gray, H. (1991). Television, black Americans, and the American dream. In R. K. Avery & D. Eason (Eds.), *Critical perspectives on media and society* (pp. 294–305). New York: Guilford.

Hall, S. (1980). Encoding/decoding. In S. Hall, D. Hobson, A. Lowe, & P. Wills (Eds.), *Culture, media, language* (pp. 128–138). London: Hutchinson.

Jhally, S., & Lewis, J. (1992). *Enlightened racism: The Cosby Show, audiences, and the myth of the American dream.* Boulder: Westview.

Martindale, C. (1986). *The white press in black America.* Westport, CT: Greenwood Press.

Martindale, C. (1990a). Changes in newspaper images of black Americans. *Newspaper Research Journal, 11*(1), 40–50.

Martindale, C. (1990b). Coverage of black Americans in four major newspapers, 1950–1989. *Newspaper Research Journal, 11*(3), 96–112.

McConahay, J. B. (1986). Modern racism, ambivalence, and the modern racism scale. In S. L. Gaertner & J. F. Dovidio (Eds.), *Prejudice, discrimination, and racism* (pp. 91–125). Orlando: Academic Press.

Moore, L. W. (1990). How your news looks to us. *Columbia Journalism Review, 28*(4), 21–24.

Nelson, J. (1993). *Volunteer slavery: My authentic Negro experience.* Chicago: Noble Press.

Sears, D. O. (1988). Symbolic racism. In P. A. Katz & D. A. Taylor (Eds.), *Eliminating racism* (pp. 53–84). New York: Plenum.

Simmons, C. E. (1993). The Los Angeles rebellion: Class, race and misinformation. In H. R. Madhubuti (Ed.), *Why LA happened* (pp. 141–155). Chicago: Third World Press.

West, C. (1993). *Race matters.* Boston: Beacon.

Wilson, C. C., II, & Gutiérrez, F. (1985). *Minorities and media: Diversity and the end of mass communication.* Beverly Hills, CA: Sage.

9

THE POLITICS
OF REPRESENTATION
IN NETWORK TELEVISION

Herman Gray

Along with the structural shifts, cultural discourses, and institutional transformations of the television industry, contemporary television representations of blackness are linked to the presence and admittedly limited influence of a small number of highly visible black producers, writers, directors, and on-screen talent in the entertainment industry. Within the institutional constraints and cultural traditions of a collaborative and producer-driven medium such as television, the successes of Bill Cosby, Oprah Winfrey, Stan Lathan, Arsenio Hall, Marla Gibbs, Keenen Ivory Wayans, Stanley Robertson, Kellie Goode, Dolores Morris, Suzanne de Passe, Topper Carew, Frank Dawson, Sherman Hemsley, Quincy Jones, Thomas Carter, Carl Franklin, Michael Warren, Debbie Allen, and Tim Reid increased their individual abilities at studios and the networks to shape the creation, direction, and tone of television representations of African Americans (Gunther 1990; Horowitz 1989; O'Connor 1990; Zook 1994).[1]

Of course, there is nothing particularly remarkable about the presence of black producers, writers, and directors in network television. Indeed, directors and producers Michael Moye, Thomas Carter, Suzanne de Passe, and others have been central to the production of such critically acclaimed programming as *Equal Justice* and *Lonesome Dove* (Gunther 1990).[2] What is remarkable, however, is that these critically and commercially successful shows have not necessarily been organized around black themes and black cultural sensibilities. Television clearly needs more of this kind of black presence.

At the other extreme are television shows that traffic heavily in themes and representations about blacks, but that, by and large, operate under the creative control and direction of white studio and network executives. Successful comedies such as *Sanford & Son,* Norman Lear/Bud Yorkin staples *The Jeffersons* and *Good Times,* and more recent shows such as *Amen* and *227* come immediately to mind. To be sure, these shows employed black writers and actors, and they drew their creative direction, look, and sensibility from African American culture. But ultimately, the overall creative responsibility for these shows rested with white executive producers—Bud Yorkin, Norman Lear, the Carsey-Werner Company, Irma Kalish, Ed Weinberger, and Miller-Boyett Productions (Newcomb and Alley 1983).

Reprinted from Herman Gray, "The Politics of Representation in Network Television," in *Television: The Critical View,* 6th ed., ed. Horace Newcomb (New York: Oxford University Press, 2000).

In the final analysis, the creative vision of the white producers predominated even if situations and themes they explored were drawn from African American culture (Newcomb and Alley 1983; interviews with black writers from *227,* 1990). Although the programs were shows about blacks (rather than black shows), there were clearly boundaries concerning cultural representations, social themes, and professional conventions that they dared not transgress. As some of the black television writers from *227* explained to me, the nuances and sensibilities of African American culture that many of them found funny and attempted to bring to particular scripts or scenes became points of professional contention or were eliminated because white head writers and producers thought otherwise.[3] Black writers seldom had the same veto power over white characters, situations, and themes (interview with writers from *227,* 1990).

For many of the shows based on the situations and experiences of blacks, the conventions of television production (especially collaborative writing) serve to discipline, contain, and ultimately construct a point of view. Not surprisingly, this point of view constructs and privileges white middle-class audiences as the ideal viewers and subjects of television stories. In the producer-driven medium of television, a paucity of producers of color continues to be the rule. In a 1989 report issued by the National Commission on Working Women, researcher Sally Steenland (1989) notes that "minority producers constitute only 7% of all producers working on shows with minority characters. Minority female producers comprise only 2% of the total. Of 162 producers working on 30 shows containing minority characters, only 12 are people of color, while 150 (93%) are white. Of the 12 minority producers, 8 are male and 4 are female" (p. 11).

African American writers, directors, and producers in the television industry must still negotiate the rough seas of an institutional and cultural system tightly but subtly structured by race and gender (Dates 1990).[4] It is all the more remarkable, then, that a small number of visible and influential black executive producers, directors, and writers forced open creative spaces within the productive apparatus of television. And within this discursive and industrial space—between black invisibility and white-authorized representations of blackness—black producers such as Cosby, Wayans, Hall, and Jones have had some impact. Rather than simply placing blackness and black themes in the service of the creative visions of white producers or inserting blackness within existing aesthetic visions, these producers have helped to challenge and transform conventional television treatments of blackness by introducing black viewpoints and perspectives (Hampton 1989). In short, they have introduced different approaches and placed existing aesthetic and production conventions in the service of blackness and African American cultural perspectives (Gunther 1990; O'Connor 1990; Ressner 1990). By trying to construct and represent the experiences, nuances, and explicit concerns of African Americans, these producers offer not only different stories, but alternative ways of negotiating and realizing them. Indeed, Kristal Brent Zook (1994) argues quite convincingly that in the 1980s and 1990s television has been an especially important discursive and institutional space because it serves as a vehicle for intertextual and autobiographical dialogue for blacks.

In a business long criticized for the absence of people of color in decision-making positions and authority, efforts on the part of black executives to hire and train African Americans are, to say the least, hard to sustain.[5] In terms of hiring, training, and placement of black talent in all phases of the industry, Bill Cosby, Quincy Jones, and Keenen Ivory Wayans have been singled out. For example, Susan Fales, former executive producer of the

The Cosby Show spinoff, *A Different World,* began her career in television as an intern with *The Cosby Show* (interview with Susan Fales, 1990).

The impact of this small cohort of influential black producers occasionally, but all too rarely, reaches beyond the generic and thematic boundaries of situation comedy and the thematic dominance of streetwise masculinity that pervades so much of contemporary television representations of blacks. *The Women of Brewster Place, Lonesome Dove,* and *Motown 25: Yesterday, Today, Forever, Polly,* and *The Mary Thomas Story* were all projects created, engineered, or produced by black women: Oprah Winfrey (Harpo Productions), Suzanne de Passe (Motown), and Dolores Morris (Disney Television). As core members of *A Different World*'s production team, black women such as executive producer Susan Fales, director and writer Debbie Allen, and writers Neema Barnette and Yvette Lee were all responsible for the creative look, feel, and direction of the program. As Jacqueline Bobo (1991) points out, these and other black women tell stories about black women that are different from those told by others, and they tell those stories differently. Thus, these black women contribute to the more general project of "fleshing out their female characters to become more multi-dimensional and like actual women and . . . experimenting with important issues and themes" (Steenland 1987:24).

Like their counterparts in cinema and literature, this recent cohort of black television producers has experienced growing visibility and success that has heightened the expectations of black audiences and critics. These heightened expectations have, in turn, produced conflict among and criticism from African Americans. For instance, heated public criticism has been directed toward Keenen Ivory Wayans, creator and former producer of *In Living Color,* for staging his irreverent humor at the expense of blacks; toward Arsenio Hall for his failure to place more blacks on the staff and technical crew of his late-night talk show; and toward Bill Cosby because his series often failed to address social issues facing black Americans (Braxton 1991; Christon 1989; Collins 1990; Dyson 1989; Fuller 1992; Gray 1989; Jhally and Lewis 1992).

The mere presence of a critical group of successful black producers, directors, and writers has, nevertheless, helped to bring different, often more complex, stories, themes, characters, and representations of blackness to commercial network television. Questions about the continuing presence of racism and sexism in the television industry as well as the social impact and cultural meaning of these stories are ongoing subjects of heated debate and study. The fact remains, however, that the variety and sheer number of stories about blacks proliferated in the 1980s to a degree perhaps unparalleled in the history of television (Siegel 1989a; Waters and Huck 1988).

THE HISTORICAL AND DISCURSIVE FORMATION OF TELEVISION TREATMENTS OF BLACKNESS

Alone, the argument that television representation of blackness is primarily shaped by changing industrial and market conditions that enabled a small number of black producers, directors, and writers to tell stories about black life from the perspective of blacks is reductionist. To avoid such reductionism, I want to argue also for a reading of the social meaning and cultural significance of television's representations of blackness in terms of their political, historical, and aesthetic relationship to earlier generations of shows about blacks. I contend that contemporary television representations of blacks depend heavily on shows about families, the genre of (black) situation comedy, entertainment/variety programming, and the social issue traditions of Norman Lear (Allen 1987; Dates 1990; MacDonald 1983; Spigel 1992; Taylor 1989).

Ultimately, then, I argue that our contemporary moment continues to be shaped discursively by representations of race and ethnicity that began in the formative years of television (Lipsitz 1990b; Riggs 1991a; Spigel 1992; Winston 1982). The formative period of television and its representation of race and ethnicity in general and blacks in particular is central to my argument in two crucial ways: first, together with dominant representations of blacks in film, radio, the press, and vaudeville, this inaugural moment helped to shape the cultural and social terms in which representations of blacks appeared in mass media and popular culture (Dates 1990); second, as illustrated by Marlon Riggs's (1991a) documentary film, *Color Adjustment,* this formative period is a defining discursive and aesthetic moment that enabled and shaped the adjustments that black representations continue to make. It remains the moment against which all other television representations of blackness have reacted. And it is the defining moment with which subsequent representations, including those in the 1980s and beyond, remain in dialogue (Dates 1990; Riggs 1991b; Taylor 1991; Winston 1982).

In the early 1950s, programs such as *Amos 'n' Andy, Beulah, The Jack Benny Show,* and *Life with Father* presented blacks in stereotypical and subservient roles whose origins lay in eighteenth- and nineteenth-century popular forms (Cripps 1983; Dates 1990; Ely 1991; Winston 1982). Blacks appeared primarily as maids, cooks, "mammies," and other servants, or as con artists and deadbeats. These stereotypes were necessary for the representation and legitimation of a racial order built on racism and white supremacy. Media scholars and historians have clearly established the formative role of radio in the institutional and aesthetic organization of early television (Czitrom 1982). As Winston (1982), Barlow and Dates (1990), and Ely (1991) suggest, the networks, first with radio and later with television shows such as *Beulah, Amos 'n' Andy,* and *The Jack Benny Show,* played an active and crucial role in the construction and representation of blacks in American mass media.[6] In the televisual world of the early 1950s, the social and cultural rules of race relations between blacks and whites were explicit: black otherness was required for white subjectivity; blacks and whites occupied separate and unequal worlds; black labor was always in the service of white domesticity (*The Jack Benny Show, Life with Father, Beulah*); black humor was necessary for the amusement of whites.[7]

Culturally, because blackness served whiteness in this way, the reigning perspective of this world was always staged from a white subject position; when television did venture inside the separate and unfamiliar world of blacks—in, say, *Amos 'n' Andy*—viewers found comforting reminders of whiteness and the ideology of white supremacy that it served: here was the responsible, even sympathetic, black domestic in *Beulah;* there were the responsible but naive members of the world of *Amos 'n' Andy.* But seldom were there representations of the social competence and civic responsibilities that would place any of the black characters from these shows on equal footing with whites (Dates 1990:204). Black characters who populated the television world of the early 1950s were happy-go-lucky social incompetents who knew their place and whose antics served to amuse and comfort culturally sanctioned notions of whiteness, especially white superiority and paternalism. These black folk could be trusted to manage white households, nurture white children, and "restore balance and normalcy to the [white] household" (Dates 1990:262), but they could not be trusted with the social and civic responsibilities of full citizenship as equals with whites.

In the racially stratified and segregated social order of the 1950s United States, there was enough about these representations to both comfort and offend. So pervasive and secure was the discourse of whiteness that in their amusement whites were incapable of seeing these shows and the representations they presented as offensive. At the same time, of course, many middle-class blacks were so outraged by these shows, particularly *Amos 'n' Andy,* that the NAACP successfully organized and engineered a campaign in 1953 to remove the show from the air (Cripps 1983; Dates 1990; Ely 1991; Montgomery 1989). As racist and stereotypical as these representations were, the cultural and racial politics they activated were far from simple; many poor, working-class, and even middle-class blacks still managed to read against the dominant discourse of whiteness and find humor in the show. However, because of the charged racial politics between blacks and whites, as well as the class and cultural politics within black America, the tastes, pleasures, and voices in support of the show were drowned out by the moral outrage of middle-class blacks.[8] To be sure, although blacks and whites alike may have found the show entertaining and funny, these pleasures meant different things. They were situated in very different material and discursive worlds. The social issues, political positions, and cultural alliances that shows such as *Amos 'n' Andy* organized and crystallized, then, were powerful and far-reaching in their impact, so much so that I believe that contemporary representations remain in dialogue with and only now have begun to transcend this formative period.[9]

By the late 1950s and throughout the 1960s, the few representations of blacks that did appear on network television offered more benign and less explicitly stereotypical images of African Americans. Shows such as *The Nat "King" Cole Show* (1956–57), *I Spy* (1965–68), and *Julia* (1968–71) attempted to make blacks acceptable to whites by containing them or rendering them, if not culturally white, invisible.[10] In these shows the social and cultural "fact of blackness" was treated as a minor if not coincidental theme— present but contained. In the racially tense and stratified United States of the middle 1960s, Diahann Carroll and Bill Cosby lived and worked in mostly white worlds where whites dare not notice and blacks dare not acknowledge their blackness. Where the cultural and social "fact of blackness" was irrepressible, indeed, central to the aesthetics of a show, it had to be contained. (Whiteness also operated as the dominant and normative place of subjectivity both on and off the screen. In this racialized world of television common sense neither whites nor blacks had any need to acknowledge whiteness explicitly.)

This strategy of containment was used with Nat Cole, the elegant and sophisticated star of *The Nat "King" Cole Show.*[11] An accomplished jazz—read black—pianist, Cole was packaged and presented by NBC to foreground his qualities as a universally appealing entertainer. Cole was the host of a television variety show that emphasized his easy manner and polished vocal style, and the containment of his blackness was clearly aimed to quell white fears and appeal to liberal white middle-class notions of responsibility and good taste. In the social and cultural climate of the times, NBC thought it necessary to separate Cole from any association with the black jazz life (an association made larger than life with the sensational press coverage of Billie Holiday, Charlie Parker, Charles Mingus, and Miles Davis), equating black jazz artists with drugs, sex, rebellion, and social deviance. Despite this cautious strategy, the network's failure to secure national sponsors for the show, especially in the South, resulted in cancellation of *The Nat "King" Cole Show* after only one season. Sanitized and contained representations of blacks in the late 1950s and the 1960s developed in response to the stereotypical images that appeared in the early days of television. They constitute signal moments in discursive adjustment and readjustment of black representations in commercial television (MacDonald 1983; Montgomery 1989; Winston 1982).

Against this discursive backdrop as well as the social rebellions of the 1960s, the representations of black Americans that appeared throughout the 1970s were a direct response to social protest and petitions by blacks against American society in general and the media in particular for the general absence of black representations (MacDonald 1983; Montgomery 1989; Winston 1982). Beginning in 1972, television program makers and the networks produced shows that reached for "authentic" representations of black life within poor urban communities.[12] These programs were created as responses to angry calls by different sectors of the black community for "relevant" and "authentic" images of black people.

It is easy to see now that both the demand for relevant shows and the networks' responses were themselves profoundly influenced by the racial and cultural politics of the period. The new shows offered were designed to contain the anger and impatience of communities on the move politically; program makers, the networks, and "the community" never paused to examine critically the notions of relevance or authenticity. As a visible and polemical site of cultural debate, television moved away from its treatment of blacks in the previous decade. The television programs involving blacks in the 1970s were largely representations of what white liberal middle-class television program makers assumed (or projected) were "authentic" accounts of poor black urban ghetto experiences. *Good Times* (1974–79), *Sanford & Son* (1972–77), and *What's Happening!!* (1976–79), for example, were all set in poor urban communities and populated by blacks who were often unemployed or underemployed. But more important, for the times, these black folk were good-humored and united in racial solidarity regardless (or perhaps because) of their condition. Ironically, despite the humor and social circumstances of the characters, these shows continued to idealize and quietly reinforce a normative white middle-class construction of family, love, and happiness. These shows implicitly reaffirmed the commonsense belief that such ideals and the values they promote are the rewards of individual sacrifice and hard work.

These themes appeared in yet another signal moment in commercial television representations of African Americans—in the hugely successful miniseries *Roots*. Inhabiting the televisual space explored three years earlier in the miniseries *The Autobiography of Miss Jane Pittman*, *Roots* distinguished itself commercially and thematically as one of the most-watched television shows in history. Based on Alex Haley's book of the same name, *Roots* presented the epic story of the black American odyssey from Africa through slavery to the twentieth century. It brought to millions of Americans, for the first time, the story of the horrors of slavery and the noble struggles of black Americans. This television representation of blacks remained anchored by familiar commitments to economic mobility, family cohesion, private property, and the notion of America as a land of immigrants held together by shared struggles of hardships and ultimate triumph.

There is little doubt that the success of *Roots* helped to recover and reposition television constructions and representations of African Americans and blackness from their historic labors in behalf of white racism and myths of white superiority. But the miniseries also contributed quite significantly to the transformation, in the popular imaginary, of the discourse of slavery and American race relations between blacks and whites. That is to say, with *Roots* the popular media discourse about slavery moved from one of almost complete invisibility (never mind structured racial subordination, human degradation, and economic exploitation) to one of ethnicity, immigration, and human triumph. This powerful television epic effectively constructed the story of American slavery from the stage of emotional identifications and attachments to individual characters, family struggles, and the realization of the American dream. Consequently, the social organization of racial subordination, the cultural reliance on human degradation, and the economic exploitation of black labor receded almost completely from the story. And, of course, this quality is precisely what made the television series such a huge success.

From the distance of some seventeen years, I also want to suggest another less obvious but powerful effect of *Roots,* especially for African American cultural struggles over the sign of blackness. My criticisms of the dominant labors of the series notwithstanding, I want to propose that for an entire generation of young blacks, *Roots* also opened—enabled, really—a discursive space in mass media and popular culture within which contemporary discourses of blackness developed and circulated. I think that it is possible to locate within the media discourse of blackness articulated by *Roots* some of the enabling conditions necessary for the rearticulation of the discourse of Afrocentric nationalism. In other words, I would place *Roots* in dialogue with the reactivation and renewed interest in black studies and the development of African-centered rap and black urban style, especially their contemporary articulation and expression in popular culture and mass media. It seems to me that *Roots* enabled and facilitated the circulation and saturation of the popular imaginary with television representation of Africa and blackness. Finally, relative to the televisual construction of African Americans and blackness in the 1950s and 1960s, *Roots* helped to alter slightly, even momentarily interrupt, the gaze of television's idealized white middle-class viewers and subjects. However minimal, with its cultural acknowledgment of black viewers and subjects, the miniseries enabled a temporary but no less powerful transitional space within which to refigure and reconstruct black television representations.[13]

In black-oriented situation comedies of the late 1970s and early 1980s, especially the long-running *The Jeffersons,* as well as *Benson, Webster, Diff'rent Strokes,* and *Gimme a Break,* black upward social mobility and middle-class affluence replaced black urban poverty as both setting and theme (Gray 1986).[14] Predictably, however, the humor remained. Even though these situation comedies were set in different kinds of "families"—single-parent households, homes with cross-racial adoptions—that were supposed to represent an enlightened approach to racial difference, in the end they too were anchored by and in dialogue with familiar themes and emblems of familial stability, individualism, and middle-class affluence (Gray 1986). Although blackness was explicitly marked in these shows, it was whiteness and its privileged status that remained unmarked and therefore hegemonic within television's discursive field of racial construction and representation (Kelley 1992). As with their predecessors from the 1950s and 1960s, blacks in the shows from the 1970s and early 1980s continued to serve as surrogate managers, nurturers, and objects of white middle-class fascination (Dates 1990; Steenland 1989). Furthermore, as conventional staples of the genre, they required unusual and unfamiliar situations (e.g., black children in white middle-class homes) for thematic structure and comedic payoff. In appearance, this generation of shows seems more explicit, if not about the subject of race, at least about cultural difference. However, because they continued to construct and privilege white middle-class viewers and subject positions, in the end they were often as benign and contained as shows about blacks from earlier decades.

THE COSBY MOMENT

Discursively, in terms of television constructions of blackness, *The Cosby Show* is culturally significant because of the productive space it cleared and the aesthetic constructions of black cultural style it enabled. Pivotal to understanding the social position and cultural significance of contemporary television representations of blackness is what I shall call the Cosby moment. Like the miniseries *Roots, The Cosby Show* reconfigured the aesthetic and industrial spaces within which modern television representations of blacks are constructed.

Indeed, under Bill Cosby's careful guidance the show quite intentionally presented itself as a corrective to previous generations of television representations of black life. In countless press interviews, Cosby voiced his frustrations with television's representation of blacks. Here is just one:

> Run down what you saw of black people on TV before the Huxtables. You had "Amos 'n' Andy," one of the funniest shows ever, people say. But who ever went to college? Who tried for better things? In "Good Times," J. J. Walker played a definite underachiever. In "Sanford & Son," you have a junk dealer living a few thousand dollars above the welfare level. "The Jeffersons" move uptown. He owns a dry-cleaning store, lives in an integrated neighborhood. Where are the sociological writings about this? (quoted in Christon 1989:45)

Positioning *The Cosby Show* in relation to the previous history of programs about blacks helps explain its upper-middle-class focus. More significantly, the show's discursive relationship to television's historical treatment of African Americans and contemporary social and cultural debates (about the black underclass, the black family, and black moral character) helps to explain its insistent recuperation of African American social equality (and competence), especially through the trope of the stable and unified black middle-class family (Dates 1990; Downing 1988; Dyson 1989; Fuller 1992; Jhally and Lewis 1992).

In *The Cosby Show,* blackness, although an element of the show's theme, character, and sensibility, was mediated and explicitly figured through home life, family, and middle-classness. Cosby explained the show's treatment of race: "It may seem I'm an authority because my skin color gives me a mark of a victim. But that's not a true label. I won't deal with the *foolishness* of racial overtones on the show. I base an awful lot of what I've done simply on what people will enjoy. I want to show a family that has a *good* life, not people to be jealous of" (quoted in Christon 1989:7; emphasis added).[15] The Huxtable family is universally appealing, then, largely because it is a middle-class family that happens to be black (Dates 1990; Dyson 1989; Fuller 1992; Gray 1989; Greely 1987; Jhally and Lewis 1992).

In an enactment of what Stuart Hall (1981b) calls the "politics of reversals" in black-oriented shows from the 1970s, the merger of race (blackness) and class (poverty) often provided little discursive and textual space for whites and many middle-class blacks to construct meaning for the shows that was not troubling and derisive. *The Cosby Show* strategically used the Huxtables' upper-middle-class status to invite audience identifications across race, gender, and class lines. For poor, working-, and middle-class African

Americans, Asian Americans, latinos, and whites it was impossible simply to laugh at these characters and make their blackness an object of derision and fascination. Rather, blackness coexisted in the show on the same discursive plane as their upper-middle-class success (Dyson 1989; Jhally and Lewis 1992).

In this respect, *The Cosby Show* is critical to the development of contemporary television representations of blacks. The show opened to some whites and affirmed for many (though by no means all) blacks a vast and previously unexplored territory of diversity within blackness—that is, upper-middle-class life.[16] On the question of *The Cosby Show*'s importance to the representation of differences within blackness, Michael Dyson (1989) perceptively notes:

> *The Cosby Show* reflects the increasing diversity of African American life, including continuous upward social mobility by blacks, which provides access to new employment opportunities and expands the black middle class. Such mobility and expansion insures the development of new styles for blacks that radically alter and impact African American culture. *The Cosby Show* is a legitimate expression of one aspect of that diversity. Another aspect is the intra-racial class divisions and differentiation introduced as a result of this diversification of African American life. (p. 29)

Discursively, the show appropriated the genre of situation comedy and used it to offer a more complex representation of African American life than had been seen previously.

This ability to organize and articulate different audiences together successfully through televisual representations of upper-middle-class African Americans accounts for *The Cosby Show*'s popularity as well as the criticisms and suspicions it generated (Dyson 1989; Gray 1989; Jhally and Lewis 1992). If, to its credit, the program did not construct a monolithic and one-dimensional view of blackness, then, as Dyson points out, its major drawback was its unwillingness to build on the very diversity and complexity of black life that it brought to television. That is to say, the show seemed unwilling to critique and engage various aspects of black diversity that it visually represented. In particular, *The Cosby Show* often failed even to comment on the economic and social disparities and constraints facing millions of African Americans outside of the middle class.

The show seemed unable, or unwilling, to negotiate its universal appeals to family, the middle class, mobility, and individualism on the one hand and the particularities of black social, cultural, political, and economic realities on the other. While effectively representing middle-class blackness as one expression of black diversity, the show in turn submerged other sites, tensions, and points of difference by consistently celebrating mobility, unlimited consumerism, and the patriarchal nuclear family (Dyson 1989; Gray 1989). Notwithstanding its political and cultural desires, *The Cosby Show* seemed nevertheless underwritten by the racial politics of "unity," which comes at the cost of subordinating key differences within that unity. In the social climate of the Reagan and Bush years and amid debates about affirmative action and the urban underclass, the show as Dyson (1989) puts it,

> presented a black universe as the norm, feeling no need to announce the imposition of African American perspectives since they are assumed. Cosby has shown us that we need not construct the whole house of our life experience from the raw material of our racial identity. And that black folk are interested in issues which transcend race. *However, such coming of age progress should not lead to zero-sum social concerns so that to be aware of*

race-transcending issues replaces or cancels out concerns about the black poor or issues which generate interracial conflict. (p. 30; emphasis added)

As Dyson suggests, *The Cosby Show*'s strategic stance on the "foolishness of racial overtones" has its limits. This was made painfully obvious in April 1992 with the entirely coincidental, but no less poignant, juxtaposition of the show's final episode with news coverage of the Los Angeles riots. The televisual landscape that evening dramatically illustrated that no matter how much television tries to manage and smooth them over, conflict, rage, and suspicion based on race and class are central elements of contemporary America. Next to the rage that produced pictures or Los Angeles burning, the representations and expressions of African American life and experience on *The Cosby Show* (and so much of contemporary television) seemed little more than soothing symbolic props required to affirm America's latest illusion of feel-good multiculturalism and racial cooperation.

Many of the same contradictions and labors of blackness found in the representations of African Americans on *The Cosby Show* were also present in other black-oriented shows that appeared in the aftermath of the show's success. *Amen, Homeroom, 227, Snoops, Family Matters,* and *True Colors* all provided familiar (and comfortable) renderings of black middle-class family life in the United States. The cultural traditions and social experiences and concerns of many African Americans, although much more explicit, nevertheless functioned in these programs as comedic devices, to stage the action or signal minor differences. Although often staged from a black normative universe, these shows seldom presented black subjectivities and cultural traditions as alternative perspectives on everyday life.[17] That is to say, as a cultural and experiential referent, blackness was seldom privileged or framed as a vantage point for critical insights, guides to action, or explanations for what happens to African American people in modern American society.

By contrast, *Frank's Place,* some of the programming on the Black Entertainment Television cable network, *A Man Called Hawk,* early programs on *The Arsenio Hall Show, Yo! MTV Raps, Pump It Up, Rap Street, A Different World,* and *In Living Color* often deployed race and class in different ways.[18] These shows present visions and perspectives in which African American social locations and experiences are more central to the programs' structure and viewpoint. Of course, all of these shows operate squarely within the conventional and aesthetic boundaries of their particular genres—situation comedy, variety, talk, or whatever. But, as I suggest below, in significant respects these shows are different from the others, including *The Cosby Show.* At the same time, however, they are dependent on *Cosby* and the shows that preceded it for representations of black experiences in America. That is, how they construct black subjects can be read only against previous shows. In this respect, I regard *The Cosby Show* as a critically important moment, a transitional point, if you will, in the development of television representations of blacks. *The Cosby Show* and some of the innovative shows that followed it (e.g., *Frank's Place, Roc, A Man Called Hawk*) form part of a continuing discourse of adjustment and dialogue with the history of television representations of blacks.

The Cosby Show's most significant contribution to television's representations of blacks and the ongoing discursive adjustments that are central to such a project has been the way that it repositioned and recoded blackness and black (middle-class) subjectivity within television's own discursive and institutional practices. To be sure, the limitations and criticisms of the show, especially the cultural labors it performed in the rearticulation of a new, more "enlightened" racism, as well as the consolidation of Reaganism on the question of race and morality, must be registered (Gray 1993a; Jhally and Lewis 1992; Miller 1988). However, coming as it did in the midst of neoconservative assaults, African American cultural debates, and the transformation of the television industry, the show has also had an enabling effect within television. Indeed, *The Cosby Show* itself became the subject of parody and imitation. In its last few seasons the show turned its thematic gaze away from its narrow preoccupation with familial domesticity to pressing social issues, including education and employment, affecting urban black youth.[19]

For most of its run I remained ambivalent about *The Cosby Show.* As a regular viewer, on many occasions I found pleasures in the predictable humor and identified with the idealizations of family, mobility, and material security represented on the show. I took particular delight in the program's constant attempt to showcase black music and such musicians as John Birks (Dizzy) Gillespie, B. B. King, Mongo Santamaria, and Betty Carter. On the other hand, in my classes, at conferences, and in print I have criticized the show for its idealization of the middle class and its failure to address issues that confront a large number of African Americans. I have often regarded this ambivalence as my unwillingness to stake out a position on the show, to make up my mind. But this unwillingness, I am increasingly convinced, is part of the show's appeal, its complexity in an age of racial and cultural politics where the sign of blackness labors in the service of many different interests at once. As I have been arguing, *The Cosby Show* constructed and enabled new ways of representing African Americans' lives. But within black cultural politics of difference the strategy of staging black diversity within the limited sphere of domesticity and upper-middle-class affluence has its costs.

DISCURSIVE PRACTICES AND CONTEMPORARY TELEVISION REPRESENTATIONS OF BLACKNESS

Having mapped the institutional and discursive history of commercial network television representations of blackness, I now want to suggest that contemporary images of African Americans are anchored by three kinds of discursive practices. I shall refer to these as assimilationist (invisibility), pluralist (separate but equal), and multiculturalist (diversity). In each of these discursive practices, I am interested in how the strategies of signification employed in representative television programs construct, frame, stage, and narrate general issues of race and, more specifically, black subjectivity and presence in contemporary U.S. society.

These practices are historically and discursively related to one another and to contemporary social discourses about race. Thus, the dominance and primacy of a particular set of images and representations from each of these television constructions and representations of blackness are contingent on the social, technological, and institutional conditions in which they are situated. Through reruns, cable networks, syndication, and independent stations, viewers have virtually unlimited access to the complete body of television representations of blacks. Thus, these programs constitute a vital part of the contemporary television landscape and should be examined by media and television scholars in terms of the shifting meanings and pleasures they offer in our present moment (see Butsch 1990).

ASSIMILATION AND THE DISCOURSE
OF INVISIBILITY

Assimilationist television discourses treat the social and political issues of black presence in particular and racism in general as individual problems. As complex social and political issues, questions of race, gender, class, and power are addressed through the treatment of racism and racial inequality as the results of prejudice (attitudes), and through the foregrounding of the individual ego as the site of social change and transformation. I consider shows assimilationist to the extent that the worlds they construct are distinguished by the complete elimination or, at best, marginalization of social and cultural difference in the interest of shared and universal similarity. These are noble aspirations, to be sure, but such programs consistently erase the histories of conquest, slavery, isolation, and power inequalities, conflicts, and struggles for justice and equality that are central features of U.S. society (see Lipsitz 1990b). Programs organized by such assumptions are framed almost entirely through codes and signifying practices that celebrate racial invisibility and color blindness (see Gray 1986). Beginning with *I Spy* and continuing with *Julia, Mission: Impossible,* and *Room 222,* these early shows integrated individual black characters into hegemonic white worlds void of any hint of African American traditions, social struggle, racial conflicts, and cultural difference.

Contemporary variations on this theme remain with us today. In the 1980s, assimilationist television representations of African Americans could be found in daytime soaps, advertising, and local and network news programs as well as in such prime-time shows as *Family Ties, The Golden Girls, Designing Women, L.A. Law,* and *Night Court.* Without a doubt, some of these shows, including *L.A. Law, The Golden Girls,* and *Designing Women,* featured episodes that explicitly addressed issues of contemporary racial politics, but I nonetheless maintain that where such themes were explicitly addressed they were underwritten and framed by assumptions that privilege individual cooperation and color blindness. In other words, at their best these shows acknowledged but nevertheless framed cultural distinctions and conflicts based on race in ways that ultimately appealed to visions of color blindness, similarity, and universal harmony. In terms of black participation (and inclusion), black characters' acceptance seemed to be inversely related to the degree of separation from black social life and culture. Unique individual black characters (such as Anthony in *Designing Women*) seemed to demonstrate the principle of racial exceptionalism. That is, they seemed to be appealing because of their uniqueness and their neatness of fit into a normative television universe.

Assimilationist programs construct a United States where the historic and contemporary consequences of structured social inequality and a culture deeply inflected and defined by racism are invisible and inconsequential to the lives of its citizens. Seldom on these shows is there ever any sustained engagement with the messiness, confusion, and tension caused by racism and inequality that punctuate the daily experience of so many members of our society. In these televisual worlds American racial progress is measured by the extent to which individual citizens, regardless of color, class, or gender, are the same and are treated equally within the existing social, economic, and cultural (and televisual) order. When they exist, race, class, and gender inequalities seem quite extraordinary, and they always seem to operate at the level of individual experience. Put differently, to the extent that these tensions and conflicts are addressed at all, they figure primarily through individual characters (white and black) with prejudiced attitudes, who then become the focus of the symbolic transformation required to restore narrative balance.

In keeping with television's conventional emphasis on character and dramatic action, assimilationist television discourses locate the origins and operation of prejudiced attitudes at the level of the individual, where they stem from deeply held fears, insecurities, and misunderstandings by individual whites who lack sufficient contact with blacks and other peoples of color. For blacks, on the other hand, they are expressed as the hurts and pains of exclusion that have inevitably hardened into victimization, anger, and irrationality. Typical examples from episodes of *Family Ties* and *The Golden Girls* used the presence of black neighbors and a potential romantic interest, respectively, to identify and draw out white prejudices and suspicions about blacks. In the end, misunderstandings and mistrust were revealed as the source of fear and suspicion. With television's conventional reliance on narrative resolution, once identified, such troubling issues as racial prejudice are easily resolved (or contained) in the space of thirty minutes.

One other characteristic defines shows embedded in an assimilationist discourse: the privileged subject position is necessarily that of the white middle class. That is to say, whiteness is the privileged yet unnamed place from which to see and make sense of the world. This very transparency contributes to the hegemonic status of this televisual construction of whiteness, placing it beyond critical interrogation. Indeed, relative to the hegemonic status that whiteness occupies in this discourse, blackness simply works to reaffirm, shore up, and police the cultural and moral boundaries of the existing racial order. From the privileged angle of their normative race and class positions, whites are portrayed as sympathetic advocates for the elimination of prejudice.

PLURALIST OR SEPARATE-BUT-EQUAL DISCOURSES

Separate-but-equal discourses situate black characters in domestically centered black worlds and circumstances that essentially parallel those of whites. Like their white counterparts, these shows are anchored by the normative ideals of individual equality and social inclusion. In other words, they maintain a commitment to universal acceptance into the transparent "normative" middle class. However, it is a separate-but-equal inclusion. In this television world, blacks and whites are just alike save for minor differences of habit and perspective developed from African American experiences in a homogeneous and monolithic black world. In this televisual black world, African Americans face the same experiences, situations, and conflicts as whites except for the fact that they remain separate but equal.

I have in mind such programs as *Family Matters, 227, Amen,* and *Fresh Prince of Bel Air;* earlier shows with predominantly black casts that currently run in syndication from previous seasons, such as *The Jeffersons, What's Happening!!, Sanford & Son,* and *That's My Mama;* as well as some of the programming featured on Black Entertainment Television.[20] What makes these shows pluralist and therefore different from the assimilationist shows is their explicit recognition of race (blackness) as the basis of cultural difference (expressed as separation) as a feature of U.S. society.[21] As in so much of television, the social and historical contexts in which these acknowledged differences are expressed, sustained, and meaningful are absent. The particularity of black cultural difference is therefore articulated with(in) the dominant historical, cultural, and social discourses about American society. It is possible, then, to recognize, indeed celebrate, the presence of African Americans, latinos, Asians, Native Americans, and women and the particularly distinct tradition, experiences, and positions they represent without disrupting and challenging the dominant narratives about American society. In other words, race as the basis of inequality, conquest, slavery, subordination, exploitation, even social location is eliminated, as are the oppositions, struggles, survival strategies, and distinctive lifeways that result from these experiences. In this manner cultural difference and diversity can be represented, even celebrated, but in ways that confirm and authorize dominant social, political, cultural, and economic positions and relationships. From the separate-but-equal televisual world inaugurated by *Amos 'n' Andy*, a large number of black representations remain separate, even if they have gained, symbolically at least, a measure of equality.

Contemporary black-oriented shows and the representations they offer occupy a discursive space still marked by their relationship to an unnamed but nevertheless hegemonic order. Like assimilationist representations, pluralist representations are constructed from an angle of vision defined by that normative order. The assumptions organizing pluralist representations of black life offer variations and modifications of the representations in the assimilationist paradigm. These shows are also tethered to this hegemonic white middle-class universe in yet another way—through the conventional formulas, genres, codes, and practices that structure their representations. Hence, on the face of it, shows from *227* to *Family Matters* present themes, experiences, and concerns that seem, and in some instances are, "uniquely African American"—for example, the black church (*Amen*) and black women's friendships (*227* and, more recently, *Living Single*). Of course, the images of black life in these shows do represent one mode of black participation in American society. However, representations of blackness in these separate-but-equal worlds depend on an essential and universal black subject for their distinction from and similarity to the normative center. On programs such as *Amen, 227,* and *Family Matters,* black people live out simple and largely one-dimensional lives in segregated universes where they encounter the usual televisual challenges in the domestic sphere—social relations, child rearing, awkward situations, personal embarrassment, and romance.

Culturally, these shows construct a view of American race relations in which conflict, tension, and struggles over power, especially claims on blackness, depend on the logic of a cultural pluralism that requires a homogeneous, totalizing blackness, a blackness incapable of addressing the differences, tensions, and diversities among African Americans (and other communities of color).[22] Shows organized by such pluralist logic seldom, if ever, critique or engage the hegemonic character of (middle-class constructions of) whiteness or, for that matter, totalizing constructions of blackness.

Discursively, the problem of racial inequality is displaced by the incorporation of blacks into that great American stew where such cultural distinctions are minor issues that enrich the American cultural universe without noticeably disturbing the delicate balance of power, which remains unnamed, hidden, and invisible. Obscured are representations of diversity within and among African Americans, as well as the intraracial/ethnic alliances and tensions that also characterize post–civil rights race relations in the United States. Together with assimilationist discourses, these television programs effectively work for some viewers to produce pleasures and identifications precisely because their presence on commercial network television symbolically confirms the legitimacy and effectiveness of the very cultural pluralism on which America's official construction and representation of itself depend. Obscured in the process is the impact (and responses to it) of structured social inequality and the social hierarchies that are structured by it.

MULTICULTURALISM/DIVERSITY

I argued earlier in this chapter that *The Cosby Show* reconfigured representations of African Americans in commercial network television. Although this program marked an aesthetic and discursive turn away from assimilationist and pluralist practices, key elements of both continued to structure and organize aspects of *The Cosby Show,* which remained rooted in both sets of discourses. In style and form, the show operated from the normative space of a largely black, often multicultural world that paralleled that of whites. It appealed to the universal themes of mobility and individualism, and it privileged the upper-middle-class black family as the site of social life.

At the same time, the show moved some distance away from these elements through its attempt to explore the interiors of black lives and subjectivities from the angle of African Americans. *The Cosby Show* constructed black Americans as the authors of and participants in their own notion of America and what it means to be American. This transitional moment was most evident in the show's use of blackness and African American culture as a kind of emblematic code of difference.

More central to the transition from assimilationist and pluralist discourses to an engagement with the cultural politics of difference, however, are *Frank's Place* and, more recently, *Roc* and *South Central.* The short-lived *Frank's Place* was coproduced by Tim Reid and Hugh Wilson and aired on the CBS television network during the 1987–88 season. The show was distinguished by its explicit construction and positioning of African American culture at the very center of its social and cultural universe. From this position the show examined everyday life from the perspective of working-class as well as middle-class blacks. It seldom, if ever, adjusted its perspective and its representation of African American cultural experiences to the gaze of an idealized white middle-class audience. The discursive practices that structured *Frank's Place* (and *Roc*) are also distinguished by an innovative approach to television as a form—the program's explicit attention to African American themes, the use of original popular music from the African American musical tradition (i.e., blues), the blurring of genres (comedy/drama), the lack of closure and resolution, the setting and location, and the use of different visual and narrative strategies (e.g., a cinematic look and feel, lighting, and production style). (In the case of *Roc,* I would add to these the use of live/real-time production.)

In addition to *Frank's Place* I would count some of the very early seasons of *The Arsenio Hall Show, A Different World,* and *In Living Color* as representative programs that have explicitly engaged the cultural politics of diversity and multiculturalism within the sign of blackness. Television programs operating within this discursive space position viewers, regardless of race, class, or gender locations, to participate in black experiences from multiple subject positions. In these shows viewers encounter complex, even contradictory, perspectives and representations of black life in America. The guiding sensibility is neither integrationist nor pluralist, though elements of both may turn up. Unlike in assimilationist discourses, there are Black Subjects (as opposed to black Subjects), and unlike in pluralist discourses, these Black Subjects are not so total and monolithic that they become THE BLACK SUBJECT.

The issue of cultural difference and the problem of African American diversity and inclusion form the social ground from which these shows operate. As illustrated by *The Cosby Show,* the discourse of multiculturalism/diversity offers a view of what it means to be American from the vantage point of African Americans. But, unlike *The Cosby Show,* this is not a zero-sum game. The social and cultural terms in which it is possible to be black and American and to participate in the American experience are more open. Although these terms often continue to support a "normative" conception of the American universe (especially in its class and mobility aspirations), in other respects shows such as *Frank's Place* and *Roc* stretch this conception by interrogating and engaging African American cultural traditions, perspectives, and experiences.[23]

In shows that engage cultural politics of difference within the sign of blackness, black life and culture are constantly made, remade, modified, and extended. They are made rather than discovered, and they are dynamic rather than frozen (Hall 1989). Such programs create a discursive space in which subject positions are transgressive and contradictory, troubling, and pleasurable, as are the representations used to construct identity (see Lipsitz 1990b), a space that is neither integrationist nor pluralist—indeed, it is often both at the same time. Not surprisingly, black middle-class cultural perspectives and viewpoints continue to shape and define these shows; however, they are driven less by the hegemonic gaze of whiteness. (This gaze is detectable in the assimilationist attempt to silence cultural difference and in the pluralist attempt to claim that African American cultural experiences are parallel to white immigrant experiences.)

It is not that the representations that appear within this set of discursive practices and strategies simply offer a more culturally satisfying and politically progressive alternative to assimilationist and pluralist discourses. Indeed, they often do not. They do, however, represent questions of diversity within blackness more directly, explicitly, and frequently, and as central features of the programs. *A Different World, Frank's Place, Roc,* and *In Living Color* have consistently and explicitly examined issues of racism, apartheid, discrimination, nationalism, masculinity, color coding, desegregation, and poverty from multiple and complex perspectives within blackness.

In these shows, differences that originate from within African American social and cultural experiences have been not just acknowledged, but interrogated, even parodied as subjects of television. *In Living Color* and *A Different World,* for instance, have used drama, humor, parody, and satire to examine subjects as diverse as Caribbean immigrants, black fraternities, beauty contests, black gay men, the Nation of Islam, Louis Farrakhan, Jesse Jackson, Marion Barry, racial attitudes, hip-hop culture, and white guilt. The richness of African American cultural and social life as well as the experience of otherness that derives from subordinate status and social inequality are recognized, critiqued, and commented on. The racial politics that helps to structure and define U.S. society is never far from the surface.

WATCHING TELEVISION, SEEING BLACK

In many of the programs located in both pluralist and multiculturalist discourses, African American culture is central to the construction of black subjects as well as program content, aesthetic organization, setting, and narrative. These discourses, especially those that I regard as multiculturalist, operate at multiple levels of class, gender, region, color, and culture, and though fractured and selective, their dominant angle of vision, social location, and cultural context are African American (Fiske 1987; Hall 1980, 1989; Newcomb 1984). In all of the television representations of cultural difference there remains a contradictory character, one where the leaks, fractures, tensions, and contradictions in a stratified multi-cultural society continue to find expression.

Although contained within the larger hegemonic terms of the dominant American discourse on race and race relations driven by the narrative of inclusion, many of the shows circulating within these various discursive practices provide different representations of African Americans on commercial network television (Hall 1981b). Within commercial television representations of African American culture, the most compelling and powerful representations mark, displace, and disarticulate hegemonic and normative cultural assumptions and representations about America's racial order. At their best, such representations fully engage all aspects of African American life and, in the process, move cultural struggles within television and media beyond limited and narrow questions of positive/negative images, role models, and simple reversals to the politics of representation (Fregoso 1990a; Hall 1989).

Contemporary television representations of blackness require a sharper, more engaged analytic focus on the multilayered, dialogic, intertextual, and contradictory character of racial representations in commercial network television. I do not claim, of course, that these representations are inherently resistant or oppositional. The hegemonic terms and effects of racial representation are no longer hidden, silenced, and beyond analytic and political interrogation. To make sense of television representations of blackness politically, we must theorize and understand them in relation to other television representations and to discourses beyond the television screen.

NOTES

1. One of the very specific ways in which the presence of these limited spheres of individual influence has been expressed in the organization and production of television programs about blacks is through the use of black professionals as consultants and advisers in the development of programs featuring blacks. For an interesting discussion of this phenomenon in the cases of women, Mexican Americans, and blacks in television, see Kathryn Montgomery's *Target Prime Time* (1989).
2. See Horowitz (1989) for a detailed discussion of the role of black film executives in the production of several commercially successful films in the 1980s.
3. In some instances, black actors and actresses exert some influence on the creative vision and direction of black representations. These actors and actresses, however, do not or may not choose to receive production and writing titles (interview with Marla Gibbs, 1990; see also Zook 1994).
4. My interview data confirm observations made by Gitlin (1983), Horowitz (1989), and Steenland (1987, 1989).
5. Black studio and network executives with whom I spoke reported that black executives are concentrated at the middle levels of the management structure, where they often have the power to stop a project, but few are positioned at the very top, where they can "green-light" a project (interviews with Stanley Robertson, Dolores Morris, and Frank Dawson, 1990). See also Horowitz (1989).
6. See *Black Film Review* (1993) for a discussion of the crucial role of black filmmakers such as Oscar Micheaux in generating counterrepresentations of blacks.
7. Also, black women were big, loud, and dark, and fulfilled the role of the nurturing caretaker of the white home (e.g., *Beulah*).
8. In 1952, *Amos 'n' Andy* received an Emmy Award nomination (Ely 1991).

9. Many of the criticisms leveled at rap music and programs such as *In Living Color* have their roots in the black cultural politics of this period. Concerns about racial embarrassment, black perpetuation of stereotypes, and so on were as urgent, especially for the black middle class, then as they are now.

10. Another show from the period that followed this pattern for the social construction and representation of blackness was *Room 222*.

11. Other variety shows of the period featuring black hosts included *The Leslie Uggams Show* (1969), *The Flip Wilson Show* (1970–74), and *The New Bill Cosby Show* (1972–73).

12. In the early 1970s, *The Flip Wilson Show,* a comedy-variety show starring comedian Flip Wilson, enjoyed a four-year run. The show has been characterized as a breakthrough in commercial television because it was the first black-led variety show to rate consistently among the top-rated shows in television. This show included, among other things, the kind of black-based parody and humor that would reappear in the late 1980s with the explosion of black comedy and variety (see Kolbert 1993).

13. See Dates (1990:257) for an inventory of black-oriented miniseries that aired following the commercial success of *Roots*.

14. *The Jeffersons* originally aired in 1975 and enjoyed a ten-year run. I place the series in relationship to these other programs because of the centrality of the mobility narrative in the show. Discursively, the series is important to the shows set in poverty because it serves to reinforce (rather than simply realize) the mobility myth.

15. African American writers from *227* told me that in the culture of the industry, black-oriented programs that explicitly attempt to address issues of inequality and racism or that seem to have a didactic function are regarded as "message shows." They also suggested that from the perspective of studios and the networks, such shows are perceived as risky and difficult to bring to the screen without stirring up trouble or offending some primary constituent (e.g., producers, networks, advertisers) in the production process (interviews with writers, 1990).

16. *The Arsenio Hall Show* is similar in this respect. The chatty format is really about the class and mobility aspirations of a new generation of young blacks and whites.

17. One of the executive producers at *227* described the show as a "reality-based show about a nice middle-class black family," therefore not a show with "messages or anything of that nature." She also conceded that the primary interest of the show is comedy (interview with Irma Kalish, 1990).

18. During the 1992–93 season, shows such as *Roc* and *Where I Live* continued this approach to programs about blacks.

19. Although designed to showcase the individual stars of the show, aesthetically *The Cosby Show's* style also moved through subtle but noticeable changes, the most remarkable being the slow evolution of the show's opening strip over successive seasons. The background setting and theme music for the show's opening moved steadily from an empty blue screen (accompanied by jazz) background to a tropical island setting (accompanied by steel pans and Caribbean music) to a grafitti-filled wall on an urban street corner (accompanied by urban-based funk).

20. The continued circulation and availability of many of these older programs through reruns and cable are central to my claim that these programs are structured by pluralist discourses.

21. See Dates and Barlow (1990) for discussion of the formation, operation, and impact of black media organizations and black participation in mass media in the United States.

22. See Fregoso (1990a:264). The special issue of *Cultural Studies* published in October 1990 represents an important intervention by Chicana/o scholars on the issue of identity, racial politics, and cultural representation (Chabram and Fregoso 1990). See also Hall (1988).

23. Paul Gilroy (1991b) has written rather persuasively about the cultural impress of blacks in England on the normative notions of what it means to be British, especially black and British. George Lipsitz (1990a) makes a similar argument.

REFERENCES

Allen, Robert, ed. (1987) *Channels of Discourse: Television and Contemporary Criticism.* Chapel Hill: University of North Carolina Press.

Bobo, Jacqueline. (1991) "Black Women in Fiction and Non-Fiction: Images of Power and Powerlessness." *Wide Angle* 13, nos. 3–4: 72–81.

Braxton, Greg. (1991) "To Him Rap's No Laughing Matter." *Los Angeles Times* July 14, Calender, 4, 82, 84.

Butsch, Richard. (1990) "Home Video and Corporate Plans: Capital's Limited Power to Manipulate Leisure." In Richard Butsch (ed.) *For Fun and Profit: The Transformation of Leisure into Consumption,* 215–35. Philadelphia: Temple University Press.

Chabram, Angie C. and Rosa Linda Fregoso (eds.) (1990) *Chicana/o Representations: Reframing Alternative Critical Discourses.* Special Issue, *Cultural Studies* 4 (October):

Christian, Barbara. (1988) "The Race for Theory." *Feminist Studies* 14, no. 1:69–79.

Christon, Lawrence. (1989) "The World According to the Cos." *Los Angeles Times,* December 10, Calender, 6, 45–47.

Collins, Patricia Hill. (1990) *Black Feminist Thought: Knowledge, Consciousness and the Politics of Empowerment.* New York: Routledge.

Cripps, Thomas. (1983) "Amos 'n' Andy and the Debate over American Racial Integration." In John E. O'Connor (ed.) *American History, American Television: Interpreting the Video Past,* pp. 33–54. New York: Frederick Ungar.

Czitron, Daniel. (1982) *Media and the American Mind: From Morse to McLuhan.* Chapel Hill: University of North Carolina Press.

Dates, Jannette. (1990) "Commercial Television." In Jannette Dates and William Barlow (eds.) *Split Image: African Americans in the Mass Media.* Washington, D.C.: Howard University Press.

Dates, Jannette and William Barlow (eds.) (1990) *Split Image: African Americans in the Mass Media.* Washington, D.C.: Howard University Press.

Downing, John. (1988) "The Cosby Show and American Racial Discourse." In G. Smitherman-Donaldson and T. A. Van Dijk (eds.), *Discourse and Discrimination,* pp. 46–74. Detroit: Wayne State University Press.

Dyson, Michael. (1989) "Bill Cosby and the Politics of Race." *Z Magazine,* September, 26–30.

Ely, Melvin Patrick. (1991) *The Adventures of Amos 'n' Andy: A Social History of an American Phenomenon.* New York: Free Press.

Fiske, John. (1987) *Television Culture.* London: Methuen.

Fregoso, Rosa Linda. (1990a) "Born in East L.A.: Chicano Cinema and the Politics of Representation." In Angie C. Chabram and Rosa Linda Fregoso (eds.), *Chicana/o Representations: Reframing Alternative Critical Discourses* (special issue). *Cultural Studies* 4 (October): 264–81.

Fuller, Linda K. (1992) *The Cosby Show: Audiences, Impact, and Implications.* Westport, Connecticut: Greenwood.

Gilroy, Paul. (1991b) *There Ain't No Black in the Union Jack: The Cultural Politics of Race and Nation.* Chicago: University of Chicago Press.

Gitlin, Todd. (1983) *Inside Prime Time.* New York: Pantheon.

Gray, Herman. (1993a) "African American Political Desire and the Seductions of Contemporary Cultural Politics." *Cultural Studies* 7: 364–74.

_____. (1989) "Television, Black Americans, and the American Dream." *Critical Studies in Mass Communication* 6: 376–87.

_____. (1986) "Television and the New Black Man: Black Male Images in Prime Time Situation Comedy." *Media, Culture and Society* 8: 223–43.

Greely, Andrew. (1987) "Today's Morality Play: The Sitcom." *New York Times,* May 17, Arts and Leisure, 1, 40.

Gunther, Marc. (1990) "Black Producers Add a Fresh Nuance." *New York Times,* August 26, Arts and Leisure, 25, 31.

Hall, Stuart. (1989) "Cultural Identity and Cinematic Representation." *Framework* 36: 68–92.

———. (1981b) "Whites of Their Eyes: Racist Ideology and the Media." In George Bridges and Rosalind Brunt (eds.) *Silver Linings.* London: Lawrence & Wishart.

———. (1980) "Encoding/Decoding." In S. Hall et al. (eds.) *Culture, Media, Language.* London: Hutchinson.

Hampton, Henry. (1989) "The Camera Lens as a Two-Edged Sword." *New York Times,* January 15, H29, H37.

Horowitz, Jay. (1989) "Hollywood's Dirty Little Secret." *Premiere,* March, 56–59–64.

Jhally, Sut, and Justin Lewis. (1992) *Enlightened Racism: The Cosby Show, Audiences, and the Myth of the American Dream.* Boulder, Colorado: Westview.

Kelley, Robin D. G. (1992) "Notes on Deconstructing 'the Folk.'" *American Historical Review* 97: 1400–1406.

Kolbert, Elizabeth. (1993) "From 'Beulah' to Oprah: The Evolution of Black Images on TV." *New York Times,* January 15, B4.

Lipsitz, George. (1990b) *Time Passages: Collective Memory and American Popular Culture.* Minneapolis: University of Minnesota Press.

MacDonald, J. Fred. (1983) *Blacks and White TV: Afro-Americans in Television Since 1948.* Chicago: Nelson-Hall.

Miller, Mark Crispin. (1988) "Cosby Knows Best." In Mark Crispin Miller (ed.) *Boxed In: The Culture of TV.* Evanston, Illinois: Northwestern University Press.

Montgomery, Kathryn. (1989) *Target Prime Time.* New York: Oxford University Press.

Newcomb, Horace. (1984) "On the Dialogic Aspects of Mass Communication." *Critical Studies in Mass Communication* 1: 34–50.

Newcomb, Horace and Robert S. Alley. (1983) *The Producer's Medium: Conversations with Creators of American TV.* New York: Oxford University Press.

O'Connor, John J. (1990) "On TV Less Separate, More Equal." *New York Times,* April 29, sec. 2: 1, 35.

Ressner, Jeffrey. (1990) "Off Color TV." *Rolling Stone,* August 23, 50.

Riggs, Marlon. (1991a) *Color Adjustment* (film). San Francisco: California Newsreel.

———. (1991b) "Confessions of a Snap Queen." In Valery Smity, C. Billops, and A. Griffin (eds.) Special Issue: *Black American Literature Forum* 25, no. 2.

Siegel, Ed. (1989a) "The Networks Go Ethnic." *Boston Globe,* September 16, Living/Arts, 7, 14.

Spigel, Lynn. (1992) *Make Room for TV: Television and the Family Ideal in Postwar America.* Chicago: University of Chicago Press.

Steenland, Sally. (1989) *Unequal Picture: Black, Hispanic, Asian, and Native American Characters on Television.* Washington, D.C.: National Commission on Working Women.

———. (1987) *Prime Time Power: Women Producers, Writers, and Directors in TV.* Washington, D.C.: National Commission on Working Women.

Taylor, Ella. (1989) *Prime-Time Families: Television Culture in Postwar America.* Berkeley: University of California Press.

Waters, Harry F. and Janet Huck. (1988) "TV's New Racial Hue." *Newsweek,* January 25, 52–54.

Winston, Michael R. (1982) "Racial Consciousness and the Evolution of Mass Communication in the United States." *Daedalus* 111: 171–82.

Zook, Kristal Brent. (1994) "How I Became the Prince of a Town Called Bel Air: Nationalist Desire in Black Television." Doctoral Dissertation, University of California, Santa Cruz.

10

RALPH FARQUHAR'S *SOUTH CENTRAL* AND *PEARL'S PLACE TO PLAY*
Why They Failed Before *Moesha* Hit

Kristal Brent Zook

In this chapter, I use the work of television writer-producer Ralph Farquhar to . . . illustrate caste and class dynamics in black television. Like *The Fresh Prince* and *Sinbad,* shows produced by Farquhar engaged in head-on ideological battles around economic mobility and color. It should be noted that this chapter is somewhat unique in its discussion of black authorship, given that Farquhar's most controversial show, *South Central,* was actually created by a white man, Michael Weithorn. Although Farquhar shared co-producer and co-creator credits with Weithorn, it was the latter who initially pitched the idea for the show.

"I met with Michael at the suggestion of Rose Catherine Pinkney [a television executive who worked on both *In Living Color* and *New York Undercover*]," recalled Farquhar. "He created the show, so I knew he had the sensibility to do it. Also, he was committed to learning. We did a lot of focus groups with [black] single mothers so we would have accurate and current information. We didn't want the show to look like it came out of a white Hollywood imagination." The dynamics of black authorship become even more intricate when we consider that Weithorn was at that time married to an African American woman.

Having said all this, I refer to *South Central* as a black production for two reasons: one, because it was inextricably wedded to black lives, memories, and experiences; and two, because Farquhar himself was at least half of its creative force. It was his autobiographical history—that is, his memory of color, class, and gender, not Weithorn's—that was clearly engaged in these narratives. I want to make it clear that it is not my intention to dismiss Weithorn's presence in these texts in any way. Rather, I focus on Farquhar because this book is dedicated to exploring the concept of "black" authorship, however mythical that may be.

In fact, Farquhar's insistence (conscious or otherwise) on collective black autobiography was even more dogged than that of Benny Medina, Quincy Jones, or Sinbad. Whereas the latter group of producers sought to reference "blackness" within largely mainstream contexts, Farquhar's texts remained wholly inside their own racial constructs, only rarely allowing entry to crossover audiences.

Reprinted from Kristal Brent Zook, *Color by Fox: The Fox Network and the Revolution in Black Television* (New York: Oxford University Press, 1999).

Before looking at the texts themselves then, I should offer a bit of background on Ralph Farquhar. In the early 1980s the young writer launched his television career as an apprentice on the hit series *Happy Days.* When that stint ended, Farquhar went on to explore the world of feature films, eventually penning the screenplay for *Krush Groove,* a 1985 cult classic. In 1987 Farquhar was hired as a supervising producer on Fox's *Married . . . with Children,* an opportunity that would soon become one of his great career coups.

As Farquhar notes, there was no such thing as an African American executive producer in the 1980s. Although he was only at the start of a long upward climb with *Married,* his supervising producer credit was a fortuitous beginning. We should recall that Fox's offbeat tastes had provided a black writer, Michael Moye, with the opportunity to co-create *Married . . . with Children.* It was only fitting that the network would give Farquhar a chance to produce it.

To his advantage, the series went on to become the longest-running sitcom ever produced. This was important in that its growing success gave Farquhar the leverage he needed to pursue his own agenda. With the *Married* credit under his belt, the producer was able to set about crafting culturally specific shows. In 1988 Farquhar created two pilots for ABC: *Living Large* and *New Attitude.*

Living Large was a dramedy about an aspiring New York artist/hairdresser struggling to make ends meet for his young wife and baby. Produced by Stephen Cannell and Quincy Jones (before Jones had *Fresh Prince* weight to throw around), the show had several serious moments. Needless to say, *Living Large* was rejected by the network for lack of a "companion" show to schedule alongside it.

New Attitude was slightly more successful. In 1990 ABC aired eighteen episodes of this snappy comedy from feature film producers George Jackson and Doug McHenry. Based on the chitlin-circuit stage play *Beauty Shop* the show featured young hairdressers cuttin' up in a black environment. "Maybe we're just three unhip white guys," Farquhar was later told by ABC's heads of programming, "but we don't understand it." The series, they eventually determined, was "too black." "It *was* a raucous black show," agreed Farquhar years later. "And it was one of the earliest shows written and produced by blacks. The network didn't know what to do with it."

Although neither pilot met with long-term success, by 1992, when he left *Married,* Farquhar had achieved a level of respectability all too rare among black producers. That same year he partnered with Michael Weithorn to create his most prized project to date: *South Central.* A dramatic depiction of a working-class mother and her three children, the series was virtually stripped of laugh tracks. Not only did it reject the standard joke-per-page format, the dramedy absolutely refused polite resolutions to issues such as unemployment, poverty, teen sex, homicide, and drug addiction.

Predictably, the show languished on network shelves for years. Although CBS had initially committed to buying it, the Tiffany network" dropped the ball after viewing the pilot. "You've got to make a decision on whether you're doing a comedy or a drama," said Peter Tortorici, then vice president of entertainment at the network. "We can do an 'important' show or we can do one that gets watched."[1] After calling the series "brilliant," CBS passed, with regrets.

In the meantime, the newly launched *Sinbad Show* was having problems of its own. To help salvage the floundering series, Fox called on now veteran producers, Farquhar and

Weithorn, who agreed to come onboard only after signing an historic deal with the network. In exchange for their expertise on *Sinbad,* Farquhar and Weithorn were promised an order for thirteen episodes of *South Central* as a midseason replacement.

This was a crucial moment in the annals of black television. Although unknown to the general viewing public, a unique window of opportunity was being presented to select African Americans during the early 1990s. Because Fox was in desperate need of "urban" viewers to build its name brand, producers such as Farquhar and Weithorn were able not only to create dramatic, collective autobiography, but to actually get such shows on the air. It wasn't that *South Central* was better than *Living Large* or *New Attitude* (although I think it was that, too). What was important here was Fox's short-lived marketing strategy that required African American and Latino audiences.

The premise of *South Central* revolves around Joan Mosley (Tina Lifford), a single mother raising three children in Los Angeles's inner city. Joan's seventeen-year-old son, Andre (Larenz Tate), is a kindhearted teen confronting the terrors and temptations of street life in a way that Will Smith never did. Meanwhile, Tasha (Tasha Scott), age fourteen, faces challenges of her own: acne, boys, identity crises, and the heartbreak of an absent father. Joan's firstborn son, Marcus, was a homicide victim before the season even began. And five-year-old Deion (Keith Mbulo), who refuses to speak, is a troubled foster child—a "crack baby"—adopted by Joan after Marcus's death.

Described by one television critic as "gritty, urban, and down with the streets," *South Central* was deeply unsettling to some viewers. Cinema-verité shots of neighborhood streets were nothing like the bright, staged interiors of typical sitcoms. Disjointed camera angles and ambiguous conclusions were particularly disconcerting for viewers accustomed to cardboard smiles and happy endings. In contrast, the camera offered off-center and unexplained snapshots of black life: a Muslim selling bean pies; "round-the-way" girls skipping rope; a dreadlocked brothah on a park bench; neighbors fanning themselves from a porch.

The series met with immediate controversy following its 1994 debut. While some (mainly African American) viewers lambasted its "negative" representations of drugs and gangs, other (mainly white) fans praised the show's unflinching "realism." Mainstream television critics, generally speaking, raved. Tom Shales of the *Washington Post* called the series the "bravest" since *NYPD Blue,* while the *Los Angeles Times* said it was the very best of Fox's "conveyor belt" of black comedies.[2] From a cultural studies perspective, of course, such mixed reactions held great promise, as they indicated, at the very least, the presence of a richly complicated production.

In the premiere episode of *South Central* we learn that Joan Mosley, a public-school administrator, has been fired due to budget cuts and is entering her fourth week without a paycheck. While shopping for groceries in the black-owned Ujamaa co-op (one of the seven principles of Kwanzaa, meaning "cooperative economics"), Joan is informed that her last check bounced and that she's now on the cash-only list. When Joan protests, Lucille, a sharp-tongued Latina cashier (played by Jennifer Lopez), spits back: *"Mira, no empiezas conmigo, porque no juego!"* ("Look, don't start with me, because *I don't play!*") One is reminded here of Sinbad's critique that Latinos and African Americans are always seen as fighting on television. In this case however the fight is used as a setup to explore, in later episodes, black-Latino solidarity.

We also see how Ujamaa's aesthetics are central to the underlying ideology of the text. On one wall, a Martin Luther King Jr. quote warns: "We shall learn together as brothers or perish together as fools." Another sign promises "Jobs for Guns." For in-group viewers aware of African American history, the co-op is highly reminiscent of 1970s black nationalism. Ujamaa sponsors community services such as free blood-pressure testing and literacy programs, much as the Black Panthers once did. There are other nods to "the movement" and racial solidarity as well: homeless men are hired to work there, and when store manager Bobby Deavers (Clifton Powell) appears, his dashiki and skullcap are in keeping with the store's Afrocentrism.

In mediating the dispute between Joan and Lucille, Deavers soon realizes that Joan is unemployed, and he offers her a job as assistant manager at Ujamaa. Although she is clearly overqualified, Joan eventually accepts the position in order to put food on her family's table. This is a key move, as it grounds the series (and its viewers) in a distinctly black context. Whereas the premiere episode began with Joan begging a white man for a corporate position across town, the Ujamaa job returned her (and us) "home," by providing an opportunity to contribute to the economic and spiritual empowerment of black people.

"Welcome to Ujamaa," says Joan, greeting customers with the store's mantra. "When you support the co-op, you support the community." Before long, Joan has even learned to greet Latino customers in Spanish: *"Cuando sostiene el co-op, sostiene la comunidad."* Soon she and Lucille have become comrades in the struggle. A good example of this tentative black-Latino alliance is seen in an episode that celebrates "Black Dollar Day" at Ujamaa.

After showing up late for her shift and rolling her eyes repeatedly, Lucille finally tells Bobby Deavers what's on her mind. "I'm sorry. You know, I wasn't sure I should work on Black Dollar Day. I thought it might be Black Cashier Day too. And why is it always 'black' this and 'black' that? What about the brown dollars? . . . Thank you for shopping at Ujamaa," she adds sarcastically, addressing the next customer. "When you support the co-op, you ignore the Latinos in the community."

Such scenes invite Latinos and African Americans to co-create culturally insular dialogues by taking seriously the possibilities of political allegiance, *familia,* and solidarity. "You're right, Lucille," concedes Bobby Deavers. "Latinos should be included too. Next year we'll have a Black Dollar Day and a Brown Dollar Day." Like Sinbad's efforts to incorporate Gloria into the Bryan family, the producers of *South Central* made conscious attempts to redefine what is meant by the "black" community by including Latinos.

I focus next on a two-part episode of *South Central* that, as we shall see below, is thematically linked—although not intentionally—with Farquhar's later creation, *Pearl's Place to Play.* While the surface narrative of this two-part story was both praised and criticized for its daring treatment of gang violence, I propose that most critics and viewers failed to consider the complexities of gender, color, and caste that were also at work in the text.

The first episode begins with Andre riding the bus to Inglewood to see his mentor, Dr. Ray McHenry (Ken Page). Once there, Andre meets Nicole (Maia Campbell), McHenry's young intern. Although they are instantly attracted to each other, there are also caste and class barriers between the teenagers. Nicole is from the wealthy community of Ladera Heights. Andre is from South Central. The only way for him to see her is to ride the bus through gang territory—a practice his mother strictly forbids.

One Sunday, however, Andre convinces Joan to make an exception and allow him to meet Ray, Nicole, and her parents at church. "Come on, Ma," urges Andre. "Gangbangers been drinking forties all night. They too hung over to mess with anybody." But he's wrong. Hours later Nicole's parents are seen waiting impatiently for Andre, who has yet to arrive.

Clearly Nicole's parents are members of the black elite; if they had appeared on *The Sinbad Show,* they would most certainly have belonged to the Dick and Jane club. Nicole's mother is seen wearing a classically tailored pink outfit and matching hat, while her husband is elegantly suited. When Nicole suggests that they go ahead to church while she waits for Andre, her mother looks down her nose as if her daughter had belched aloud: "Young lady, *please.*"

Eventually Andre stumbles in—bruised, bloodied, and without shoes. "I got jacked by a trick-ass punk who stole my gym shoes," he explains to Nicole's dismayed parents, who are as shocked by his language as by the crime. Nicole's mother refuses even to shake Andre's hand, and quickly instructs her husband to gather up their daughter. "I'll see you later, Andre," suggests Nicole hopefully. "Oh, no, you won't," interjects her mother. But Andre doesn't give up so easily. After arranging to meet his "honey dip" again, the seventeen-year-old slinks into his mother's closet and unearths a gun. Then, after concealing the "gat" in the front of his pants, he heads north to Inglewood for the third time.

It is interesting that Nicole's mother is adamantly opposed to Andre, while her father remains relatively silent on the subject. Like Beverly Winter on *The Sinbad Show,* she represents a certain materialism and an estrangement from working-class black people that is constructed as oddly female. To wit, Nicole's mother promises her a Jeep if she stays away from Andre. Nicole agrees. Her father says nothing.

In fact, as Farquhar informed me, his own mother, unlike his father, was also quite "bourgie." "She grew up in Evanston, Chicago," he explained. "There were very few black people there at the time. She went to Evanston Township, which was one of the best high schools in the country, and she spoke real proper. . . . My mother's father played golf, and his wife had very strong Indian features. My father, on the other hand, was as dark as a chunk of coal. My parents had to elope because my mother's parents *hated* the fact that she married my father. My grandmother, who was senile, would talk to the walls at night and say, 'Those Farquhars, those dark people.' That's how she referred to my father."

We see here how color and class overlap into a uniquely African American phenomenon that I refer to here as "caste." "Most shows ignore the dynamics of black families," continued Farquhar. "It's just more acceptable to present us in a white environment, like *Cosby.*" But *South Central* was not *Cosby.* Just as Farquhar's parents eloped to escape family disapproval, so too does Andre creep onto Nicole's roof in order to see her. When he discovers that his buppie girlfriend has been avoiding him for a new Jeep, however, Andre lashes out.

"Rashad is right," he tells Nicole. "You just another bourgie sell-out, thinking you better than everybody else. . . . And you know that [straight] hair ain't nothin' but a ultra perm!" As if the point were not yet clear for viewers, at least four additional scenes refer to Nicole as "bourgie." In one, Nicole asks her best friend, Candy, "Why do you have to act so bourgie?" "Because I am," replies Candy. "And so are you."[3]

A series of events in this two-part episode eventually leads to the end of Andre and Nicole's relationship. In another confrontation on the bus, Andre is shaken by having to show his gun. But he also begins to enjoy the protection it seems to offer, and soon he's in the habit of carrying it—that is, until Bobby Deavers steps in to confront him. "I heard you had an incident on the bus the other day," says Deavers. "Look, I know how it is out there. A little beef escalates into something big, and everybody is carrying guns these days. I wouldn't want [you] to get into that. . . . We gotta keep the black man strong in our community. We're becoming an endangered species."

There is closure to this episode—true to sitcom format. In the end, Andre reassures his mother (who has no idea that he has been "strapped" with her gun) that he's going to do "the right thing." What sets this episode apart from happy-ending sitcoms, however, is actor Larenz Tate's presentational speech, which comes at the show's conclusion. "Guns don't protect you," he warns, facing the camera directly. "They only raise the stakes." As we pull back from this close-up, viewers see that Tate stands in the midst of several dozen equally serious African American faces, also facing the camera. This tag scene further confirms the non-comedic nature of *South Central.*

And yet discussion about the series among viewers, critics, and producers was misleading in that it presented these dramatic episodes as if they were *solely* about guns and gang violence. My point here is that caste differences were also clearly raised. In fact, color and class tensions between Nicole and Andre were more directly autobiographical for Farquhar than were the show's allusions to gangs. Indeed, the series's overt focus on street life, masculinity, and violence was yet another indication of the narrow manner in which "blackness" is marketed, sold, and received.

In the next section of this chapter, we see how Farquhar's subsequent creation, *Pearl's Place to Play,* made color conflicts central to the text's story line. *Pearl's* was a pilot brought into being by four black men: Ralph Farquhar and Calvin Brown Jr. wrote the pilot; rap mogul Russell Simmons was a producer; and Stan Lathan directed. (Michael Weithorn pursued other projects following the cancellation of *South Central.*)

In *Pearl's,* comic Bernie Mac plays Bernie, the owner of a down-home southern diner. His wife Lillian (Angela Means), is an extremely light-skinned woman whose "bourgeois wanna-be" family disapproves of Bernie. Also central to the narrative are Bernie's ex-wife, Jocelyn (Adele Givens), and their daughter, Selina (Countess Vaughn, who later appears on *Moesha*).

What's striking about *Pearl's,* in addition to its color dynamics, is the fact that all of the women and girls surrounding Bernie are schemers, in the habit of manipulating, threatening, coddling and/or seducing Bernie for his money. In the pilot, Bernie is seen serving coffee, grits, and fried chicken to his clientele. Enter Lillian, who's come for his approval to invite her sister and brother-in-law to dinner. But Bernie doesn't care for his color-prejudiced sister-in-law, Vivian (Khandi Alexander). "When we were dating," he reminds his wife, "she told everybody in the neighborhood you had 'jungle fever.'"

An odd bit of business follows. As the couple discusses dinner Lillian offhandedly opens Bernie's cash register. Without a word, Bernie closes the drawer and moves her away—never missing a beat of the conversation. Lillian eventually gets her way by whispering promises of sex in her husband's ear. And later that evening Bernie discovers the real reason for Vivian's visit. "Vivian," he notes, "you ain't never thought nobody as black as me was cute. Now, what in the hell do you want?"

As it happens, Vivian and her husband want ten thousand dollars for a summer home on Martha's Vineyard (that ever-present symbol of the black elite). "That's the irony," explained Farquhar, who in real life summers at the Vineyard. "They think they're better than he is [because of color] and yet he's got more money!" At the same time that Bernie is being set up by his in-laws, his ex-wife, Jocelyn, is also milking him for cash, demanding alimony payments for first-class trips to Las Vegas.

I want to emphasize that the central ideological tensions of this show lie within the intersections of color, class, and gender. This is again made clear in a street brawl between Marcus (Lillian's proper-speaking, light-skinned son by a previous marriage played by Theodore Borders) and Selina (Bernie's daughter with Jocelyn). "Marcus said my mama is a loud, no-class, low-life," yells Selina. "Selina said my mother was a stuck-up, bourgie wannabe," responds Marcus.

"See, Bernie Mac," explained Farquhar in an interview with me, "is the same complexion as my father. Whereas the woman who played his wife is like your [the author's] complexion—the same as my mother's.[4] Now, black people don't talk about color prejudice a lot, but there are holdover attitudes. We know that."

Some of these holdover attitudes, about skin color, are consciously engaged in Farquhar's work, while others are not. For example, the notion that women require material goods and are willing to lie and scheme to get them is never challenged. The closing tag scene of *Pearl's,* in fact, reproduces such a myth. Bernie owes his daughter $20 but tries to get away with paying her $10. "Uh-uh!" shouts Selina, imitating Rosie Perez in *Do the Right Thing.* "Gimme my money, Mookie!" "All right," agrees Bernie. "You sound just like your mama."

Whereas *South Central* began the fascinating work of exploring intraracial caste differences, *Pearl's Place to Play* went even further by making such dynamics central to the text. In the end, however, both shows were far too in-house for mainstream audiences and timid executives. In fact, *Pearl's* (taped just one month before Fox's cancellations of *South Central, Roc, Sinbad,* and *In Living Color)* was never picked up at all.

"There was a wall between black and white audiences," explained Farquhar. "Black response was very good, but white viewers didn't get it."[5] A critic for *Black Film Review,* however, saw a different reaction at a Los Angeles screening. "Some audience members were upset," he noted. "[Bernie] Mac's ex-wife is a dark-skinned woman who bore him a very dark and boisterous daughter. But his new wife, played by the very funny Angela Means, a tall, light-skinned, long-haired socialite and their very nice, intelligent, fairer-skinned son are just peachey."

On the surface, then, Farquhar's productions appeared to be straightforward critiques of economic mobility among blacks. In actuality, his narratives were knotty struggles with class and racial identity. Indeed, black America's strained relationship with the American dream was made evident in these shows' various references to *Cosby.* "Look, everybody don't live all perfect like you and the damn Huxtables," Andre tells Nicole in *South Central.* "Girl, don't make me take my belt off. I ain't no Bill Cosby," says a character from *Pearl's.*

In 1996 *South Central* had been off the air for over two years. I interviewed Ralph Farquhar in his office at Sunset Studios, where his latest creation, *Moesha,* was being taped for the United Paramount Network (UPN). There was art by Ernie Barnes on the walls, and a desk plaque that read: "Life is more important than show business." Farquhar, who wore a stunningly bright yellow shirt over tailored black slacks, settled into a couch opposite me and proceeded to explain the difference between *South Central* and *Moesha.*

This time Farquhar shared co-creator and co-executive producer credits with two black women: Sara V. Finney and Vida Spears. Of all the shows Farquhar pitched and created, this was his first real commercial success. Charting the evolution of his work, as well as the space it eventually occupied at UPN, reveals much about the politics of black television in the 1990s. For although *Moesha* was highly similar to *South Central* in style and content, there were key differences between the two shows.

"Fox kept calling *South Central* a sitcom," recalled Farquhar. "But it never was. *Moesha* is a sitcom." Put another way, *Moesha* focused on the trials and tribulations of teen life; *South Central* focused on the trials and tribulations of teen life in a low-income, single-parent household in a high-crime black community.

Even when *Moesha* ventured into dramatic story lines involving race, these were produced and marketed in a very different manner than for *South Central*. In one episode, for example, Moesha's friends accuse her of thinking she's "too good for the 'hood" when she dates a white boy. Although the episode was allowed to air (unlike *The Sinbad Show*'s rejected script about interracial dating), its potentially serious premise was buried by UPN's promotional department. "They showed wacky, nonsensical clips," recalled Farquhar, "that were totally unrelated to the story line." What's more, Farquhar was later told that the episode was "over the top" and that UPN was "not interested in issues."

But we should wonder what is lost when television refuses black drama. "*South Central* was the most startling and uncompromising of my shows," noted Farquhar. "*Moesha* is still honest, but it's different tonally . . . in terms of style and production. Like, there's no single-camera stuff in conjunction with the multi-camera, all of which makes [the story] seem more immediate. . . . [And] we button the seams of *Moesha* with jokes, whereas we didn't make that concession on *South Central*."[6] "If you were expecting a laugh a minute," agreed Rose Catherine Pinkney, "that's not what you were going to get. *South Central* had a different cadence and style."

The key difference lies in *South Central*'s autobiographical content and dramatic approach versus *Moesha*'s traditional sitcom format and mainstream story lines. "*Moesha* is different from a woman losing her job and her son going out and getting money from a dope dealer," acknowledged Farquhar. "It's not to say that middle-class kids don't have problems. Just that . . . *South Central* had an air of gloom. With *Moesha*, we've chosen not to go for the grittier side."

Reflecting on his long career in television, Farquhar arrived at this observation: "The biggest fights with networks were not about money or ratings. They were about different ways of seeing the world." In fact, Farquhar's productions occupy an important space at the far end of black television. As bold as Fox claimed to be in the early 1990s, even it was unwilling to stand by such a controversial series as *South Central*. By the time UPN came along, Farquhar had, of course, changed his approach and had consciously crafted a more lighthearted, uncomplicated comedy in *Moesha*.

In 1997, a year after that interview, I found the producer housed at Universal Television with a three-year development deal. Hard at work on several new sitcoms, Farquhar described his latest project as "multicultural" rather than "black." "It takes place in a church which was traditionally white," he explained, "but with integration has become a community of the working class, the underclass, immigrants, Asians, and Latinos." Another concept recently developed by Farquhar was the ABC pilot *Blendin'*, about a black upper-class family and the young white female companion they hire to care for their aged patriarch.

Clearly there has been a progression away from strictly black conversations and settings for Farquhar—which raises interesting questions. Is this trend the result of purely market-driven considerations, the changing positionality of Farquhar himself, or the shifting autobiographies of viewers? Insofar as real-life African Americans confront increasingly integrated settings, our texts begin to wrestle with these memories as well as racially insular ones. As we move toward the end of the 90s, the question "What is black?" becomes even more enigmatic. Our stories, it seems, must work harder to keep up.

NOTES

1. In something of a non sequitur, Tortorici then added: "and I don't think the two are mutually exclusive." See Du Brow 1994.
2. See Shales and DuBrow 1994, respectively.
3. Nicole's materialism is later reincarnated on NBC's *In the House* (a Winifred Hervey/Quincy Jones production), where the same actress, Maia Campbell, again plays a snooty, upper-income teen. Women are not always presented monolithically on *South Central,* though. When Joan's best friend asks why she doesn't just marry Dr. McHenry ("Isn't $100,000 a year good enough?"), Joan protests that he simply "doesn't turn her on."
4. Another ironic case of intertextuality: In the feature film *House Party 3* Angela Means again plays a rich girl engaged to marry a man her family doesn't approve of, while her fiancé's uncle is played by Bernie Mac!
5. Another possibility is that white executives "got it" but didn't like it. Some particularly bold dialogue has a customer noting that white NBA owners don't like to see black men with "their" women. "Man, what you talking about?" responds Bernie. "Every [white] brother in sports got a white woman. . . . That's how the white man get his money back."
6. There are also similarities between the two shows that viewers may not be aware of. Aesthetically, for example, both utilize the same Ujamaa set. Although it was revamped as a black-owned café for *Moesha,* residual signs of Africanesqueness remain. Moreover, both series were committed to hiring a majority of African American writers and staff members. In 1998, *Moesha*'s staff was listed by the Writer's Guild of America as having the highest percentage of black writers on any show—with a total of eight African Americans and one Latina.

REFERENCES

Du Brow, Rick. "South Central: The Right Time, the Right Stuff." *Los Angeles Times,* Calendar section, January 11, 1994: F1.
Shales, Tom. "Superior 'South Central.'" *Washington Post,* April 5, 1994: E1, E6.

PERSONAL INTERVIEWS

Ralph Farquhar, January 1994 and June 1996.
Rose Catherine Pinkney, June 1998.

TELEVISION PROGRAMS

The Bill Cosby Show, NBC, 1969–71.
Blendin', unaired pilot, 1998.
The Cosby Show, NBC, 1984–92.

The Fresh Prince of Bel Air, NBC, 1990–96.
Happy Days, ABC, 1974–84.
In Living Color, Fox, 1990–94.
Living Large, unaired pilot, 1988.
Married . . . with Children, Fox, 1987–97.
Moesha, UPN, 1996–present.
New Attitude, ABC, 1990.
New York Undercover, Fox, 1994–98.
NYPD Blue, ABC, 1993–present.
Pearl's Place to Play, unaired pilot, 1994.
Roc, Fox, 1991–94, and BET, 1994–95.
The Sinbad Show, Fox, 1993–94.
South Central, Fox, 1994.

FILMS

House Party 3, Eric Meza, 1994.
Krush Groove, Michael Schultz, 1985.

11

BODY AND SOUL
Physicality, Disciplinarity, and the Overdetermination of Blackness

C. Richard King
Charles Fruehling Springwood

In common with many Americans, David Duke, a self-declared Nazi, a one-time grand dragon of the Ku Klux Klan (KKK), a former Louisiana state representative, and a presidential candidate, seems captivated by sports. And while he is not an average sports fan, his ideological platform, as extreme as it is, gives voice to many mainstream preoccupations with race and sports. In fact, his recently published memoirs, *My Awakening: A Path to Racial Understanding* (1999), with Glayde Whitney, which is less a personal narrative than a treatise on race in America, continually return to athletics, underscoring the supposed inferiority of African Americans while advancing the imperiled superiority of Euro-Americans. His attention to race and sport unfolds in the context of a broader effort to promote what he terms "white civil rights" (see Bridges, 1994; Hill, 1992; Moore, 1992). It punctuates, illustrates, and supplements his discussions of standard neoconservative and neo-Nazi concerns, intelligence, affirmative action, moral decline, integration, and welfare. Throughout, he reminds readers that African Americans are simultaneously dumber and largely at fault for America's financial and social ills, and that Euro-Americans who negligently support the equality of the races retard the achievement of a more perfect society. Others, occasionally even scholars, have expressed similar points of view (see Levin, 1997, pp. 114–115). Although we do not assert that Duke's views are representative of white America, his repeated engagements with sports and race in his nearly 800-page fascist text not only mirror many of the themes of great concern to a broader public, but his take on these "problems" frequently echoes more mainstream voices as well. His central preoccupation is with foregrounding, indeed explaining, the predominance of the African-American male athlete through a bizarre mix of folk genetics and intelligence theories.

The following are sample commentaries from Duke's analyses of sport, each of which was selected from the David Duke Web site because his cyber-commentary seems even less restrained than that found in the book (Duke, 2000):

> The truth is that many of the colleges sporting mostly black football and basketball teams have had some sort of scandal which included the assault or rape of white women by black players. Even the enemies of our heritage must shake their heads in amazement as seeing

Reprinted from C. Richard King and Charles Fruehling Springwood, *Beyond the Cheers: Race as Spectacle in College Sport* (New York: State University of New York Press, 2001).

many whites who would angrily call for the maximum legal penalties against blacks who assaulted white women, cheering the same such scum on the football and basketball arenas of America.

Some whites have wrongly suggested that blacks do not have the mental ability for certain sports and positions. Intelligence may be a factor at the quarterback position, but one must still understand that such play is still based on repetition and experience and fundamental skills. The quarterback does not have to design the plays or even call them, he simply has to have the physical skills necessary to execute them. Although there are some times when a quick-thinking quarterback will have an advantage over a slower-thinking one, and that probably is the reason for the preponderance of white quarterbacks in an 80% black sport.[1]

During my race for the governorship of Louisiana, our sports crazy fans were told that our universities' sports programs would have trouble recruiting if I were elected. It pains me to acknowledge that I probably lost some votes because some members of our race were more worried about their school's football team than the safety of our own kind from black crime or the racial discrimination practiced against thousands of whites with affirmative action.

The goal here is not to work through a careful critique of Duke's racist claims, nor do we attempt to (dis)prove in a scientific manner claims about the genetic bases of athletic superiority.[2] We do, however, suggest that Duke's inability to avoid the topic of sport, in offering readers his philosophy of race, politics, and power in the United States, does indeed reflect a national preoccupation with racial difference—in particular, *blackness*—in the context of American sport (see Davis, 1993; Entine, 2000; Hoberman, 1997). As extreme as Duke's thinking on race and sport appears to be, it exposes the centrality of white supremacy to mainstream representations, helping us think critically about the imprint of racist ideologies on sports spectacles.

In what follows, we examine the predominance of African-American athletes on the fields and courts where so many Indian and other collegiate mascots prevail. We analyze the inflated political economy of racial signs associated with intercollegiate sports spectacles through which particular formulations of blackness become meaningful and powerful. That is, whereas in previous chapters we have directed our attention to the means and meanings of "playing Indian at halftime," the use of stereotypical images of Native Americans as mascots, in this chapter we seek to understand how gazing at black bodies at play mobilizes important Euro-American *desires*. We read the norms and forms of blackness emergent in collegiate athletics while pondering the location of the black athlete within this system as well. Identifying the various ways in which the black athlete has been constructed as a *site* of pleasure, dominance, fantasy, and surveillance, we argue that in a post–civil rights America, African Americans have been essentially invented, policed, and literally (re)colonized through Euro-American idioms such as discipline, deviance, and desire. White America has created certain spaces and opportunities for African-American athletes, and these openings have emerged in the context of a legacy of denied access and forbidden spaces.

Images and accounts of African-American athletes challenge, reproduce, transcend, and even deploy contemporary domains of blackness. At the same time, they continually (re)create an ambivalent conceptual space for European Americans to know, enjoy, and fashion themselves. Throughout American history, blackness has been mobilized variously in terms of at least three predominant tropes, each of which informed the other. First, the bodies of African Americans have been seen as grotesque, in a manner that contrasted the black body with the Native American body. Second, the black body has been rendered, aesthetically, as a superior body, in terms of strength, speed, and resilience, and this discourse articulates with prior conceptualizations of the black body as animalistic and hypersexual. Third, blackness has long signified deviance—sexuality, style and presentation of self, and criminality—and presently it animates the contemporary space of the black athlete in complex, pervasive ways. Each of these tropes have served as colonizing technologies, or ways that allow Euro-Americans to engage the presence of the African American—a mixture of fear, longing, and ambivalence that has long characterized the sensibility of European-American whiteness in relation to the nonwhite, transgressive Other.

CONDITIONS OF (IM)POSSIBILITY

Euro-Americans do not only "play Indian," they mimic African Americans as well. Repeating a pattern common throughout the twentieth century, Euro-American youth and popular cultures borrow, modify, recycle, and reinvent the style and stylings of urban African-American subcultures. Increasingly, they poach the language, dress, music, and bodily praxis associated with rap and hip-hop to fashion meaningful identities and imagined communities (Midol, 1998). These selective, romantic readings of marginalized people and practices have not facilitated the use of African Americans as club emblems, team spirits, or school mascots as they did a century ago, when Euro-Americans began adopting Native American iconography in association with athletic spectacles. Such an action, no matter how well intentioned, surely is absurd, literally unthinkable. What would such a symbol look like? What would the team be named? What would it convey? Would the rhetoric of honor and respect, often advanced to defend Native American mascots, suffice as a rationale? How would players, alumni, and students respond? As thought provoking as such questions may be, they are ridiculous. Undoubtedly, in the wake of the civil rights movement, prevailing social and political circumstances would render any effort to fashion an athletic team in the imagined likeness of African Americans impossible. Importantly, save for the instance discussed in the opening chapter, such a context never really existed in the United States. In Euro-American public culture, both before and after emancipation, racist ideologies devalued and denigrated African Americans. Formerly enslaved, they did not embody the spirited resistance, aggressive defiance, or noble wildness ascribed to Native Americans but rather were thought to be shiftless, undisciplined, primal, childish, and dependent.

Although it would be unthinkable to invent a sports mascot that embodied such African-American stereotypes as "Sambo," the ubiquitous black athlete is celebrated in ways both more subtle and more obvious than halftime show spectacles. African-American athletes have emerged at the center of a multibillion-dollar collegiate and professional sports industry, and the black athlete has been transformed into an aesthetic commodity, controlled by the gaze of a largely white but also an African-American consumer (D. Andrews, 1996; V. Andrews, 1996; Cole & Andrews, 1996; Davis & Harris, 1998; Kellner, 1996). As the increasing presence of African-American students on many campuses in post-segregation America was often defined largely by the presence of the black student athlete, a new political economy of sport was already maturing. This economy deeply linked NCAA Division I revenue sports, such as football and basketball, to the professional leagues. It is difficult, if not inappropriate, to critique big-time college sports without also taking full account of this relationship to professional sports. By the time universities were commonly recruiting black student athletes, certainly by the 1970s, a moment had emerged in which the premier athletes of any race were invited to campus primarily as performers and players. Schools whose student bodies remained largely white often had athletic teams that were increasingly black. Significantly, these racialized social fields literally structured social relations and informed the production of social knowledge. It is essential to appreciate, for example, that white students are indeed relating to black students in particular ways when they cheer African-American celebrity athletes who also are fellow students. Likewise, the experiences of black student athletes recruited to play sports at a largely white university confront daily the consequences and stereotypes embodied in these social relations.

While imperialist nostalgia for Native Americans centered on courage, a sexualized wildness, bellicosity, and warring aggression, a particular nostalgia also emerged surrounding African Americans. Although these white discourses of racialized longing overlapped in some ways, as both the black and Indian body were hypersexualized, for example, in the white imagination, blackness arguably was evermore "grotesque," polluting, and transgressive than Indianness. Historically, a contradictory set of meanings has been ascribed to blackness. At once a lack (undisciplined, lazy, dumb) and an excess (strength, endurance, libido) (see Chideya, 1995; Cole, 1996; Cole & Andrews, 1996; Cole & Denny, 1995; Davis & Harris, 1998; Lipsitz, 1998; Lott, 1999; Pieterse, 1992; Wonseck, 1992), it has symbolized "the multiple, bulging, over- or under-sized, dirty, protuberant and incomplete" (Mellinger & Beaulieu, 1997). Popular, political, legal, academic, and religious discourses fashioned African Americans as infantile, animalistic, primal, base, servile, subhuman, unintelligent, and carnal.

Nineteenth-century postcards and advertisements exemplified this pattern. These media depicted African Americans with a series of exaggerated features, such as thick lips, bulging eyes, huge ears, and gaping mouths. In still other cases, black people were featured with opposable toes. A predominant theme that organized these imaginary images of black people was hygienic practice and toilet use: black figures are seen sitting on toilets, sweating and straining, and on others are seen farting and blowing their noses. Such excessive images of black bodies and lifestyles as dirty and "undisciplined" served to define a white bourgeois society in terms of a projected opposite. Black people were imagined ultimately to be what white people were not.

At the same moment Euro-Americans were using blackness to cement a playfully refined, civil version of whiteness, they began mimicking, actually mocking, African Americans within the increasingly popular tradition of black-face minstrel performances. To the amusement of paying audiences, particularly in urban centers, white men staged theatrical, caricatured portrayals of blacks. The minstrel show obscured the explicit and implicit terror that characterized the social institution of slavery by animating the slave as a silly, generally happy buffoon (Lott, 1993). Further, these exhibitions embodied various black expressive traditions, such as song and dance, into passive, complacent, childlike figures who would then signify a sentimentality for the "good ole days" of plantation life

(Hale, 1998). Indeed, icons emerging from this tradition linger into the present, from such subservient grocery emblems as Uncle Ben and Aunt Jemima to the folk narrations of Uncle Remus and Little Black Sambo (Manring, 1998).

The Harlem Globetrotters of recent decades appear in many ways to embody this discursive tradition. This all-black basketball team travels from arena to arena staging exhibition games against, most recently, the Washington Generals (their eternal opponent, whom they always beat). The performances turn on the humorous, comedic antics of the Globetrotters, who frequently interrupt the game to tease opponents, referees, and audience members. They display flashy basketball skills such as spinning the ball on their fingers, bouncing passes off of their knees and elbows, and rolling passes down their backs. These frolicking, happy Globetrotters have created such celebrity figures as Meadowlark Lemon, Goose, and Curly. Although conspicuously black, the Harlem Globetrotters have successfully effected a thorough erasure of race as a complicating factor of their existence. They play now before largely suburban white audiences, and they project accommodating and charming personas. They did not, however, as they do now, function almost exclusively as a traveling comedy troupe. This shtick emerged only after the NBA and collegiate basketball began to sign black players. Prior to that, the Globetrotters were a much more serious team, with black players who were among the most talented in the nation.

Abe Saperstein, a first-generation Jewish American of Polish descent who grew up in Chicago's North Side neighborhood, Ravenswood, founded the Harlem Globetrotters (see Vescey, 1970). They were actually situated in Chicago during their early years, but Saperstein wanted to include Harlem as part of the team's name to advertise that the players were black. Although the Globetrotters first official game was in 1927, they actually got their start a few years earlier. Saperstein organized the "Savoy Big Five," which played its games at the Savoy Ballroom on Chicago's South Side. Since the ballroom was an African-American establishment, the players, too, were all black. Soon, after it became clear that dancing and basketball would not mix, the team was without a job. They decided to stay together, however, and became the Globetotters, a team of traveling basketball performers. Saperstein was a savvy promoter, and the team soon became well known. It seemed to enjoy access to the best black players in the country since, until the 1950s, the NBA and most large universities refused to accept an African-American presence.

The Harlem Globetrotters scheduled a special tour for the spring of 1950. An all-white team of college all-stars agreed to play the Globetrotters in a twenty-game series, to take place on twenty consecutive nights in twenty different cities. Using an impressive combination of skill, pizzazz, and showmanship, led by Marques Haynes, the Globetrotters won thirteen of the eighteen contests (Vescey, 1970, pp. 42–43). Finally, that same year, professional basketball began to integrate, as the Boston Celtics drafted Chuck Cooper of Duquesne University, and the New York Knickerbockers paid Saperstein $25,000 for the contract of Globetrotter Nathaniel (Sweetwater) Clifton, the latter of whom became the NBA's first black player. Saperstein's response to the Celtic's drafting of Cooper belied the perception that he was committed to African-American progress. He was angered, thinking that he had earned the exclusive domain of black players, and he indeed boycotted the Boston Garden for years after the Cooper selection (Fitzpatrick, 1999, p. 61).

From nineteenth-century minstrel shows to twentieth-century sports spectacles, the tropes of the grinning, banjo-strumming, tap-dancing comic or of a happy, maternal (or avuncular) servant have characterized white longings for blackness (Early, 1994, pp. 155–162; Hale, 1998; Lott, 1993; Mellinger & Beaulieu, 1997; Turner, 1993). Read against this backdrop, contemporary sport becomes a troubling racial drama. Increasingly in the wake of integration, mass-mediated spectacles return the white gaze to the black body. As with imagined Indians, performance paces the significance of blackness—physicality, play, and control of the body.

It is nearly impossible for many white people to think about sports without also pondering the predominance and success of African-American athletes. African-American Bill Russell, a Hall of Fame basketball player, wryly underscored this preoccupation when he claimed that, "A smart college basketball coach plays three blacks at home, four on the road, and five when he is behind" (Funk, 1991, p. 101). Russell's musing foregrounds also the ambivalence behind white *knowledge* of athletic blackness. This preoccupation of the African American as jock, with natural prowess, is one of several key white stereotypes of blackness, along with the African American as criminal, the African American as buffoon, and the African American as hypersexual.

If it is impossible for many white Americans to consider sport without thinking, at one level or another, about blackness, in 1966 it was impossible for Adolph Rupp to imagine his basketball team in terms of anything but whiteness. This is not to suggest, however, that Rupp did not have particular understandings of black America; by most accounts, he loathed and feared it. When on March 25 of that year, Rupp's all-white Kentucky Wildcats lost to the all-black Texas Western Miners in the national championship game, the nation was intrigued with the conspicuous racial mapping of the two teams. Rupp had long been a vocal opponent of integration, and he had steadfastly refused to recruit black players for his seemingly invincible Kentucky team (Fitzpatrick, 1999). Frank Deford, well-known *Sports Illustrated* writer, reported that Rupp referred to the Texas Western players as "coons" while speaking to his team before the game (ibid., p. 214). After the 1966 loss, he ridiculed Texas Western, accusing their coach of using players "out of the penitentiary and off the streets of New York" ("The Final Four," 1989; see also Funk, 1991, p. 102). Some Kentucky fans seemed oddly impressed by the "blackness" of Western Texas. Current Maryland coach Gary Williams, who observed the historic game in person, recalls, ". . . after the game, I remember hearing the Kentucky people saying, 'We gotta get us some of them'" (quoted in Feinstein, 1998, p. 128).

The game served, perhaps for the first time, as a national stage for what is often referred to as stylistically "black" basketball. The Miners' players, partly in response to the encouragement of their white coach, Don Haskins, had effected a style of play characterized by a certain flashiness, highlighted in particular by the "slam dunk." To perform a slam dunk, a player jumps up to the basket, usually with great force, and directly forces the ball through the hoop with both hands. Although he forbid his players from behind-the-back dribbling and passing, Haskins encouraged dunking because he recognized its potential to intimidate opponents. Frank Fitzpatrick (1999, p. 162) speculated, "That image of mean, muscular manliness was essential in Haskins' physical system. When he wanted to wound his players, he would challenge their manhood, calling them 'girls' or 'sissies.' They in turn took it out on their opponents in the same fashion."

Before the championship game, some supporters of Texas Western apparently heard Rupp claim on a radio broadcast that five black players could never beat his Wildcat team (Fitzpatrick, 1999, p. 205). Hoping to inspire his team, Haskins included this comment in a pre-game motivational speech. As the players were heading out of the locker room,

Haskins grasped the arm of David Lattin, his large, flamboyant center, and demanded, "First chance you get, flush it. Flush it as hard as you can" [Haskins usually referred to the dunk as a "flush"] (quoted in Fitzpatrick, 1999, p. 205). During Texas Western's second possession, Lattin took a quick pass from the guard and "jammed the ball through [Pat] Riley's outstretched arms and down into the basket" (ibid., p. 210). Lattin then turned to Riley and shouted, "Take that, you white honky." Many, including Wildcat player Tommy Kron, sensed that Kentucky was intimidated. Kron commented on Lattin's dunk: "We were all just kind of standing there and he soared up and it seemed to be a real exclamation point. It really picked their team up, and I think we were intimidated by their quickness and power" (ibid., p. 211). Texas Western won, 72–65.

When Rupp relented in 1969 by finally recruiting and signing Tom Payne, Kentucky's first black player, he may have purposely set up the "integration experiment" for failure by selecting someone with both less scholastic and social preparation than many other available black recruits (see Fitzpatrick, 1999). Payne was a 7-foot center who sat out his freshman year with academic problems. After his sophomore year, he declared hardship status and entered the NBA. His brief career was unremarkable, and he ended up serving time in prison on a rape conviction.

By 1991, black players had become prevalent within the landscape of big-time collegiate basketball, as 19 out of the 20 players who comprised the starters of the Final Four teams were African American. The Nike shoe corporation had by then become inextricably woven into the political economy, uniting collegiate and professional sport. While their professional clients, such as Michael Jordan, were critical of the global rise of its trademark Swoosh, Nike was never technically able to highlight specific collegiate stars in its ads due to NCAA restrictions. Nevertheless, the company has regularly sponsored collegiate events, has held high school player recruitment camps, has pursued college coaches and universities to sign them to contracts obligating their athletes to sport Nike footwear, and has utilized nondescript college players in its advertisements. Acclaimed black filmmaker Spike Lee has been central to the success of Nike, ever since he teamed with Michael Jordan in a series of commercials that portrayed Jordan interacting with a youthful, urban black teenager known as "Mars Blackmon" (played by Lee). Viewers watch several scenes of Jordan's famous, elegant flight to the basket and then hear Blackmon, clumsily sporting large eyeglasses and a loose ball cap, exclaim, "It must be da shoes!" as if to explain the greatness of Jordan. David Andrews (1996, p. 140) has argued that, "Nike's promotional strategy systematically downplayed Jordan's blackness by contrasting him with Spike Lee's somewhat troubling caricature . . . Jordan was Jordan, he wasn't really black. Mars was a 'nigger'." Spike Lee, perhaps more than any other non-sports celebrity, is associated with a fanaticism of professional and collegiate sport. A fixture at New York Knicks games, he is commonly the focus of television cameras capturing his playful bantering of Knick opponents Jordan and Indiana Pacer star Reggie Miller.

One of the more significant spaces where the political economy uniting professional and collegiate sport is mobilized unfolds at the annual Nike summer basketball camps. One such Nike camp was featured in *Hoop Dreams,* as one of the documentary's stars, William Gates, was invited to attend as one of the best 100 high school players in the nation. Nike flies these students in, houses and feeds them for four days, and provides coaching and medical care, so that they can perform on the court before the eyes of college basketball's top coaches. Indeed, Bobby Knight, P. J. Carlisimo, and Rick Pitino are among those coaches seen in *Hoop Dreams*. In addition to playing basketball, students are required to attend a series of lectures, covering everything from study skills to financial advice. In one of the film's more significant scenes, Spike Lee appears before a large group of these high school basketball players, nearly all of them black.

The bespectacled Lee's advice to the players is cautionary as he urges them not to mistake the motivations of the system into which they are being recruited:

> You have to realize, that nobody cares about you. You're black! You're a young male! All you're supposed to do is deal drugs and mug young women. The only reason why you're here [is] you can make their team win. If their team wins, these schools get a whole lot of money. This whole thing is revolving around money.

Although Lee's comments do not run counter to the claims that we are making in this book, the context of his cautionary tale seems rife with contradictions. That a black celebrity of Lee's stature would be brought in by Nike to speak to high school students to warn them about their fateful purpose within an exploitative system is surprising since, in our view, for years Nike has been at the very center, valorizing the very spaces and narratives of this exploitation. Further, Lee's participation as an outspoken, youthful, liberal director and producer of films, which so often have eloquently critiqued America's relationship to African-American citizens, seems doomed from the outset. He does not appear to recognize that his very platform, the recruitment camps provided by Nike, is a significant commercial pillar of the system. Further, he has earned a great deal of money in partnership with Nike, himself valorizing the popular marriage of sport and blackness.

BODY POLITICS

In intercollegiate athletics, the body fosters the racialization of African Americans. It is an excessive, if ambivalent, semiotic nexus, (de)composed of historic sediments and emergent sentiments. Ultimately a social artifact, it naturalizes distinction, physically inscribing racial difference and materially legitimating social asymmetries. The body of the African-American athlete, as a site and source of (exceptional) ability, (criminal) deviance, and (spectatorial, if not sexual) pleasure, simultaneously facilitates imagination and exploitation. And as it entertains, inspires, troubles, and revolts, it legitimates, if not encourages, discipline, regulation, and control. In this section, we deconstruct the fabricated body of African-American athletes and the body politics inscribed upon it.

To return to the Nike camp and *Hoop Dreams,* shortly after William Gates and his fellow Nike campers are cautioned by Lee that their value within the system was predicated on their bodily talents as players, viewers witness a conversation among three college coaches, all coaches of color. As several campers stroll by, Bo Ellis, then assistant coach at Marquette, remarks, "Look at some of these young boys' bodies! They got NBA bodies already." In the next camp scene, Bob Gibbon, a white independent scout, innocently informs viewers that, "It's already become a meat market, but I try to do my job, you know, and serve up professional meat." While sport has commodified the bodies of all young student athletes, American sporting culture increasingly has turned on and has become decidedly "turned on" by the bodies of African Americans. Just as those Kentucky fans, amazed at upstart Western Texas's victory in 1966, began to embrace the idea of going out to "get some" black bodies, after Southern California soundly defeated powerhouse Alabama in football in 1970, due largely to the three-touchdown effort of a black running back named Sam Cunningham, legendary Alabama coach Bear Bryant muttered as he left the field, "He did more for integration in the South in sixty minutes than Martin Luther King did in twenty years." That very night, reportedly, he began to arrange to recruit his very first black players (see Lapchick, 1991, p. 227).

The longing for and appropriation of black bodies in intercollegiate sporting spectacles reveal an encrusted racial ideology that explains the presence and success of African-American athletes through accounts of their (supposed) natural physicality. Indeed, this (Euro-)American fascination, even obsession, pivots on the *perceived* excessive athletic agility, speed, and strength of the black body (Davis, 1990; Hawkins, 1995/1996; Hoberman, 1997; Sandell, 1995). The intense interests and investments in the athletic "essence" of the African American animate sports and popular culture more generally, particularly films such as *White Men Can't Jump, Blue Chips, He Got Game,* and *Hoop Dreams.* Even as the rhetoric of integration and racial harmony prevails in intercollegiate sporting contexts, the national media, administrators, coaches, analysts, fans, and players continually reinscribe this ideology. Two infamous comments exemplify the logic of this ideology. Jimmy "the Greek" Snyder explained the superiority of black athletes as a result of breeding during slavery. Later, Al Campanis, then vice president of the Los Angeles Dodgers, told ABCs Ted Koppel that blacks "are gifted with great musculature and various other things. They're fleet of foot. And this is why there are a lot of black major league ballplayers" (quoted in Davis, 1990).

Sentiments about African-American athletic superiority are both advanced and contested within the black community. For example, a few years ago, ESPN televised a program focusing on race and sport. The opening segment featured African-American NBA player Charles Barkley's visit to a sixth-grade school class to discuss the topic. Soon after Barkley introduced himself, the following dialogue unfolded in response to a question from a black child, who asked "Do you think the movie *White Men Can't Jump* is very racist?" Barkely answered politely:

> No, I don't, and I answered that question when that movie came out. Every time somebody speaks, they're not trying to be racist. If you want to say the movie *White Men Can't Jump* is racist, yeah, you can say that, but it's not true. But if you want to be a real jerk or you want to start some racial b.s. as I call it, you know, you can say, well that movie's racist. You know but that's not true. It was just a movie, they came up with a name. Now like when I said, like I'll give an example: Black guys can jump higher than white guys—most of them—you think that's racist?

A different student, an African-American boy, (bravely) responded, "Yes." Surprised, Barkley asked, "Do you think so? Why do you think that's racist?"

The boy who first asked about the movie then admitted, "Well actually I do too."

Barkley said, "I'm asking, well, I'm just asking why."

"Well, first of all, you didn't go out like, for a survey to see which, like you didn't have like ten people—five white guys and five black guys—and see who could jump higher. So if you didn't do that, then you are racist," reasoned the boy.

Barkley explained:

> Well, I feel like, considering what I've done for the last 20 years, 25 years, I've had plenty of surveys. And my recommendation if I was asked a question, I said, can black guys

jump higher than white guys, I would say yeah, I think they can, and I don't consider that statement racist at all. I mean if you want to make it racist you could, you could. But I don't see it as racist cause my, I guess my proper definition of racism would be with intent, if you wanted to debate whether what, what somebody says is racist or what they say is not racist, is the intent to harm or to belittle another group. I don't belittle white guys if I say I think black guys can jump higher. Like if I want to say um, I think um, basketball players, black basketball players are better than white basketball players, would you, would you consider that racist?

The boy said, "I have, like, a little problem with that because . . . there are like, there are . . . most white kids at this school could beat me at basketball, and they can jump higher than I can, and they're in the same grade. And like most of them are about, like at my old school, most of them were like the same height as me, and they could still jump higher than me and play basketball better than I could."

Barkley attempted to offer closure about the debate with the persistent youth. "Well, I guess I can't speak for you. I can only speak for my, my perception of the last twenty-five years. My opinion for the last twenty-five years, most of the black guys who I've been around can out-jump white guys. And they're better players at basketball."

These remarks revealed what scholars such as Kobena Mercer (1994) and David Andrews (1996) have argued is a historically significant racial epistemology based on a mind-body dualism in which brains and brawn are opposed in popular discourse. Indeed, Mercer (1994, p. 138) notes that, "Classical racism involved a logic of dehumanization, in which African peoples were defined as having bodies but not minds: in this way the super-exploitation of the black body as a muscle-machine could be justified," and warns, "Vestiges of this are active today." Importantly, scholars have linked this preoccupation with natural strength and speed to the easy projection of criminality and intellectual inferiority onto the black body (D. Andrews, 1996, forthcoming; V. Andrews, 1991, 1996; Cole, 1996; Cole & Andrews, 1996; Cole & Denny, 1995; Davis, 1990; Hoberman, 1997).

While graduate students at the University of Illinois in 1994, the authors encountered clearly more than a mere vestige of this racial discourse. The Undergraduate Anthropology Student Association (UGASA) had posted a number of meeting notices in and around Davenport Hall, where the anthropology and geology departments are located. To attract attention, the students who designed the flyers advertised the meeting through an announcement for a new course, "Experimental Primatology 304 (same as Kinesiology 009)." The fictitious class promised to address subjects such as "Tree Climbing, Brachiating, and Termite Fishing," and "includes mandatory all expense paid field trips to Ecuador, Kenya, and Sumatra." Two images at the center of the flyer (over)determined its message. On the right, a photograph captures a gibbon hanging by its right hand from a tree branch; on the left is a photograph of the well-known bronze statue of Michael Jordan—in mid-flight, with right arm outstretched, preparing to dunk a basketball—which stands outside of the United Center in Chicago. The juxtaposition of the celebrated Jordan and the anonymous gibbon, the black athlete and the arboreal primate, dunking and brachiating—not to mention kinesiology and primatology—gives material expression to racial ideologies grounded in the black body, ideologies so commonsensical and invisible that students of anthropology perpetuate them without pause. In part, the flyer suggests that African Americans are base, natural, and animalistic; that they are better studied along with, if not as, lower-order primates; that their skills and talents, in turn, should be understood as natural, if not evolutionary, effects—that blacks dunk and gibbons brachiate.

European-American racial ideologies, as this example clarifies, have frequently terrorized their African and African-American objects by advancing hierarchies of humankind that directly question the humanity of nonwhite others. Specifically, for centuries the black body has been (mis)cast as a more primitive manifestation of humanness, often and without much subtlety, linked to apes and monkeys (Gould, 1996/1981; T. Lott, 1999; Pieterse, 1992; Smedley, 1993; Takaki, 1993). Tommy Lott (1999, p. 7) identifies this preoccupation as the mobilization of "Negro-ape metaphor," and claims, "The association of apes with black people in Western discourse was facilitated by the European discovery of apes and the continent of Africa at about the same time." Lott examines how the Negro-ape mythology informed ostensibly scientific discourse as well as the writings of colonial travelers and naturalists. Sir Thomas Herbert even contended that similarities between Hottentots (a black, southern African population) and apes implied that the black race might have been a by-product of sexual intercourse between humans and apes. Others believed that oversexed, libidinous apes would occasionally kidnap and "enslave" black women and children, and thus Lott (1999, p. 9) suggests that such beliefs allowed Europeans to rationalize the enslavement of Africans as a manifestation of the natural order of things.

Mediated by this discourse that locates the African American as animalistic, white America has imagined, exploited, regulated, desired, and feared the physicality of blackness throughout its history. Even today, such knowledge terrorizes humane sensibilities. For example, in the wake of the beating of Rodney King by members of the Los Angeles Police Department, the nation learned that one of the officers, Stacey Coon, harbored racist tendencies when, among other things, an audiotape was introduced during the King trial that featured Coon describing his intervention during a domestic abuse call in an African-American neighborhood as "Something out of *Gorillas in the Mist*" (Feldman, 1994). The history of attempts to position the black body, in particular, the black male body, as animalistic and bestial has fostered the cultivation of two overlapping, articulating discourses of blackness: the black body as naturally athletic and the black body as criminal.

In fact, these two discourses of blackness form a dialectic that illustrates well the ambivalence animating the white imaginary. This ambivalence turns on the tension between a fear of and a fascination with the black body (D. Andrews, 1996, p. 132). Consider, for example, the comments of Daryl Gates, who was the chief of the Los Angeles Police Department during the Rodney King beating and subsequent trial. Responding defensively to criticisms of his department for the high number of deaths of African-American men while in police custody, he reasoned, "We may be finding that in some blacks when [the carotid chokehold] is applied, the veins or arteries do not open as fast as they do on normal [*sic*] people" (quoted in Davis, 1992, p. 272). This (mis)application of folk biology underscores the deep investment of white America in racial difference. Fascination with the superior athletic black body too easily transmutes into the fear of the pathological black body.

This association has profound implications for African-American collegiate athletes. Indeed, increasingly in the wake of the Reagan revolution, Len Bias' death, the war on drugs, the Rodney King beating, and the subsequent trial and insurrection, the O. J. Simpson trial, and Latrell Sprewell, criminality indelibly marks the African-American athlete. Public perceptions and media representations transform minor infractions into moral dramas and major transgressions into scandals, often of national import. To be sure, popular attitudes toward and coverage of the illicit activities and wrongdoings of athletes, regardless of race, have attained unprecedented importance; however, the particular history of blackness and the peculiar return of race in sociopolitical discourse imprint all African Americans as deviant, not simply those who break the law. Comparing the reception of two University of Nebraska football players accused of criminal activity exemplifies this pattern. In 1994, Christian Peter, an outstanding (Euro-American) defensive end for Big Red was convicted of assaulting a former Miss Nebraska; a year later, Lawrence Phillips, the Cornhuskers' star (African-American) running back, was charged with beating his white ex-girlfriend. Although both athletes have extensive records and had committed offenses certain to evoke public contempt—violence against women—the scrutiny they were subjected to differed immensely. Whereas Peter's actions received little attention beyond Lincoln, Nebraska, Phillips' action ignited a firestorm of controversy, heightened when Nebraska coach Tom Osborne opted to let Phillips continue playing after a brief suspension. Phillips' story circulated far beyond campus, receiving intense national recognition, including a segment on *60 Minutes*. Given the similarity of their social standing and transgression, the (over)determining feature undoubtedly was race and the interracial relationship. For Phillips, and countless other African-American collegiate athletes, who more often than not do not break the law, the inscriptions of animalistic qualities, deviant capacities, and extraordinary abilities onto their bodies prefigure public understanding of their moral character, no less than their physical talents.

The excesses of the black body and the ambivalences of white public culture do not desist with either the athletic superiority or deviance inscribed upon it. Indeed, Euro-American fears and desires in post–desegregation sports support and rehabilitate another corporeal cliche, the myth of the hypersexual African American. Over the past several decades, precisely as they have desegregated, one of the greatest concerns of white universities and their communities—after integrating their sports teams—has been interracial dating. More specifically, there is evidence that once the black athlete arrives on the largely white campus, a fear—at times subtle, at times overstated—of the "primally driven" black sexual appetite emerges. At the University of Texas at El Paso, formerly Texas Western University, in the late 1960s, for instance, Coach Don Haskins commonly scrutinized the women his black players were dating, discouraging them from seeing white women. This policing was not limited to a single individual but was pervasive. Willie Cager outlined the shape of this context: "I used to talk to a white girl . . . but one day she said that she couldn't talk to me anymore, because some of the professors had been cornering her and telling her she would get a bad name" (quoted in Olson, 1968). Teammate Fred Carr highlighted the implications. "When you date a white girl, you get in trouble and she gets bad-mouthed all over campus" (ibid.).

Similarly, a report detailing the various forms of racial prejudice faced by black athletes at the University of Illinois in the 1960s suggests that "the most severely sanctioned social activity [of black athletes] was interracial dating" (Spivey & Jones, 1983, p. 946). A number of players were actually approached by a member of the Athletic Association in 1963, who warned them "to stop dating or being seen with white girls" (ibid.). In the early 1960s, at the University of Washington, football star Junior Coffey—the nation's third leading rusher at the time—was warned not to date white women. He refused to comply with the ultimatum and thus was never allowed to start another game (Lapchick, 1991,

p. 245). This preoccupation with the imagined sexual appetite of the black male athlete is not merely an artifact of years-gone-by racism. Howie Evans, a one-time black assistant coach at Fordham University, once told sports-studies scholar Richard Lapchick that during his years of work at a black community center in New York in the 1990s, recruiters from white Southern schools would arrive seeking to sign black women to attend their schools. The reasoning, according to Evans, was that these women would be able to provide the black athletes at these Southern schools with *appropriate* female companionship (see Lapchick, 1991, pp. 244–248, 1996, p. 13). Lapchick, who suggests that a white paranoia prevails that views black athletes as potential rapists, reports that from 1988 through 1990, a total of thirty news accounts of female sexual assault by athletes was produced. Of these thirty assaults, twenty-one were by white athletes. He insists further that when an African-American athlete is the focus of such a report, it is indeed his blackness that is foregrounded, through text and image. On the other hand, reports of white athletic sexual crimes remain racially unmarked, even though they represent the majority of cases (Lapchick, 1991, p. 248).

As the foregoing discussions of the black body indicate, the set of beliefs and apprehensions about the blackness that has been constructed within the European-American imagination derives its meaning from the competing emotions of fascination and fear. On the one hand, the African-American athlete is engaged by collegiate institutions, as well as by the professional sports industry, as a highly desired corporeal commodity. On the other hand, the male African-American athlete, as well as the African-American male, generally, is the object of white paranoia. Increasingly, the ambivalent (physically) overdetermined black body has become the site of discipline, regulation, and management.

THE RULES OF THE GAME

Euro-American understandings of African Americans being excessive and transgressive have always fostered, if not demanded, disciplinarity, the application of regimes of control, regulation, and management; the bondage, beatings, surveillance, and dehumanization of slavery; and later, the lynchings, terror, spatial constraints, and segregation of Jim Crow. Although much kinder and gentler, veiled as it is in the rhetoric of opportunity, equality, and education, intercollegiate athletic spectacles construe African Americans as deviants in need of refinement, correction, training, and supervision. Informed by the taken-for-granted and largely white norms of etiquette, bodily practice, the life cycle and the good life, a succession of public panics has erupted in which fans, administrators, coaches, and media commentators have voiced grave concerns, if not blatant condemnations, of the choices, behaviors, language, and self-presentation of African Americans in paternalistic tones. The place of race in two recent public panics clarifies the articulations of paternalism, disciplinarity, and cultural difference in the domain of college sports—the increasing frequency with which African-American athletes opt out of college and African-American expressiveness on the field of play.

In the spring of 1997, Peyton Manning, the Euro-American quarterback of the University of Tennessee, decided to stay in school rather than to turn professional. Against the backdrop of talented athletes, most of whom were African American, skipping college or leaving college to pursue lucrative professional careers, his decision was widely celebrated for its (apparent) endorsement of amateurism, higher education, and (embattled) traditional values. Manning was hailed as an exemplary student athlete, balancing scholastic and sports to become a more complete citizen. Often latent, these comments were assessments of the characters and choices of those who had turned pro prematurely—immature, materialistic, disinterested in education, lacking discipline, and taking the easy way out—or they were rationalizations of their decisions—the athlete feels responsible for his family in the projects, so this is a way for him to give something back. Neither media commentators nor fans evaluated Manning so cynically. The authors do not recall hearing, "He is doing it to win the Heisman," or "He wants to win the national championship." Although we do not know why Manning opted to remain in college for his senior season, what is important about this, especially public reception of it, is that it points to a deeper racialized structure.

In the mid-1990s, two young superstar athletes, Drew Henson and Kobe Bryant, faced an exciting decision: to go to college or to go pro. Whereas Henson opted to attend the University of Michigan and play minor league baseball during the summer, Bryant decided to play professional basketball and hoped to take college courses on-line. Through their compromises and strategies, Henson and Bryant plotted very similar trajectories. In the media, their choices were starkly different, presented in black-and-white terms as polar opposites: Henson was applauded for his decision, and Bryant, in contrast, was challenged, if not condemned, for his. Beyond incidental elements—hometown, sport, and grade-point average—two key differences distinguished Henson from Bryant: first, their priorities, particularly the emphasis placed on college, and second, race—Henson is white, and Bryant is black. And racial difference is the difference that makes a difference.

Although they ultimately elected divergent paths, Bryant and Henson were strikingly similar. Both were phenomenal athletes. Bryant, 6′6″, excelled at basketball, averaging 31 points, 12 rebounds, 7 assists, 4 blocks, and 4 steals a game; Henson, 6′5″, distinguished himself in football, throwing over 50 touchdown passes during his senior season, and in baseball, a 0.70 earned run average and a .650 batting average augmented his 95 mph fast ball. Both were from middle-class families involved in sports. While Bryant's father was a former professional basketball player in the United States and Italy, Henson's father coached high school sports in Michigan. And before either had played a single college game, professional teams expressed interest in the young superstars. Whereas Bryant's announced intention to go pro secured him a top slot in the NBA's draft and a $10 million contract, the New York Yankees openly courted Henson, offering him a $2 million signing bonus to play minor league baseball during the off-season. Importantly, the media attached great expectations to the untested pair as well, labeling Bryant "the next Michael Jordan" (Bamberger, 1996) and Henson "the next Michael Jordan" of professional sports (Montville, 1998).

Despite the fact that their experiences and possibilities nearly mirrored one another, media coverage, colored by popular racist stereotypes, painted a very different image. This difference begins with the titles of articles in *Sports Illustrated* about Bryant and Henson. The former is profiled in a piece called "School's Out" (Bamberger, 1996); the latter is heralded in a story entitled "Golden Boy: Michigan-Bound Quarterback and Yankee Bonus Bay Drew Henson—Who Also Averaged 22 Points in Basketball and 4.0 in the Classroom Is Almost Too Good to Be True" (Montville, 1998). From this beginning, the differences multiply in disturbing ways. Immediately after Bryant announced his intention to enter the NBA draft and to forgo his college eligibility, a public outcry questioned his decision. His physical and emotional maturity was debated in the media—was he ready to go pro? Did he have the necessary experience or strength to make it? Could he handle the pressure? Could he play with the likes of Shaquille O'Neal, Charles Barkley, and Michael Jordan? College, it was argued, would refine Bryant, granting him the opportunity to earn a diploma and to improve his game. It not only would make him a better player but a better person as well. In contrast, Henson's choices were celebrated by commentators. Their support persisted, even as the Yankees actively sought to lure him into a professional career. In the words of General Manager Brian Cashman, "We're selling, man. Selling the major-league experience and our tradition. We'd love for him to play only baseball, but if that's unrealistic, we'll try to help him decide to do both." This action and Henson's decision to take $2 million to play minor baseball went unremarked in the national media. There were no arguments about maturity, no assumptions about mobility, and no mention of the value of a college degree. The underlying assumptions in these feature stories and commentaries appear to be first that Bryant is lacking and second that he is breaking the rules of the game. In turn, commentators suggest that the African-American athlete needs training, regulation, and discipline, but that his Euro-American counterpart does not. He needs the refinement and upward mobility secured by college, in spite of his background, that Henson does not. In college sports, the linkage of race and deviance imposes discipline—control and improvement—on the black body.

The racialized contours of this public concern over the amateur and scholastic fates of high school and college athletes become clearer when considering the absence of such discourse in other instances. For example, as Russel Curtis Jr. (1998, p. 886) notes, when "blackness" was much less an issue, no one seemed disturbed that Ted Williams or Mickey Mantle entered major league baseball at age eighteen, bypassing college altogether. Additionally, neither the predominance of tennis stars in their middle teens or the decision of Jimmy Connors to forgo his eligibility at the University of California at Los Angeles to "turn pro" disturbed an American public. Perhaps such public concerns and panics are best understood as a form of racial paternalism, in which white America struggles to come to terms with its (exploitative) enjoyment of the African athlete by advancing a linkage between the ostensibly moral and disciplinary space of the university and big-time sports.

Even when they stay in school and play the game, African-American athletes unsettle as they entertain. Indeed, in addition to the (often contradictory) meanings associated with the black body, the means of using and practicing it often transgress the norms of civility, the hegemonic forms of whiteness governing intercollegiate athletics. In response, unspoken etiquette, team codes, and the rules of the game combine to police African-American expressiveness and style.

The emergence of end zone celebrations in college and professional football in the 1980s and 1990s offers a stunning illustration of the disciplinary impulse central to racialized sports spectacles. One of the author's acquaintances exclaimed, "Look at those jungle-bunnies jumping around, slapping each other silly!" while watching a televised football game in the late 1980s. The blatantly racist remark was a reaction to several of the players—all African Americans—performing what is known as an end zone celebration. To celebrate a touchdown, several players gather in the end zone to enact an obviously choreographed "dance" of sorts. Such orchestrated and extended expressions of victory and triumph became increasingly common by the mid-1980s. Vernon Andrews concluded that, generally, African-American players performed the longest, most elaborate end zone dances, and further, that African-American players were more likely to enact their athletic roles with conspicuous individuality, defiance, trash talk, and taunting (V. Andrews, 1991). Researchers have argued that black expressiveness—characteristically more colorful, improvisational, expansive, deliberate, and self-conscious—is a prevailing African-American cultural mode of communication and style (Fiske, 1993; Gay & Baber, 1987; Jones, 1986; White & White, 1998).

The National Football League (NFL), partly in concert with spectator opinion, attempted to control and indeed erase such colorful expressions of triumph by asserting that these were unsportsmanlike displays. It amended its rules in 1984 and 1991 in order to temper "any prolonged, excessive, or premeditated celebration by individual players or groups of players" (quoted in Fiske, 1993, p. 60). College football followed with its own attempts to limit on-field celebrations (see V. Andrews, 1998). John Fiske (1993, p. 62) claims that such struggles to control these embodied displays of success are, in essence, a struggle over racial power:

> The argument is not *what* constitutes sportsmanlike conduct, but over *who* controls its constitution. . . . Because the issue is not one of behavior but one of control. In different social conditions, the same expressive behavior can be viewed by the power-bloc quite differently. In its TV commercials for the World Football League (which is the NFL's attempt to spread U.S. football to Europe), the NFL relies largely on images of black expressiveness that it attempts to repress back home. [For European audiences presumably] the expressive black body signals not a challenge to white control but an American exuberance, vitality, and stylishness which European sport lacks.

Once again, the Euro-American reaction to both the expressive and spontaneous bodies of the nonwhite Other is decidedly ambivalent, characterized by adulation on the one hand and discomfort on the other hand.

Although not all black players have highly individualistic expressive repertoires and a number of white players do, black players are more likely to be identified and indeed penalized in these terms. Clearly, the scoring movement known as the "slam dunk" epitomizes the stylistic impact of black players since their presence became common in college and professional basketball by the late 1960s. Frequently, after making the basket, a player hangs, and then swings from the rim after the ball has dropped through. Such behavior has been considered by officials at both the collegiate and professional levels an unsportsmanlike way of "showing up" the other team, and indeed, referees were given the right to whistle players for technical fouls for hanging on the rims, unless a player was doing so clearly in an effort to avoid landing on another player. Interestingly, a year after the 1966 championship between Kentucky and Texas Western, in which David Lattin's dunks highlighted his all-black team's victory, the NCAA Rules Committee banned the slam dunk shot. The all-white committee, over which Rupp continued to enjoy a significant influence, explained that the ban would prevent injuries and equipment damage. This ban would remain until the 1976–77 season.

Perhaps the most famous singular group of college athletes that embodied what has been perceived as a flashy, showboating, in-your-face style of play was the University of Michigan's "Fab Five." The Fab Five was a group of five black, highly touted high school basketball players who signed with Michigan in 1991. Recognized as the best basketball recruiting class in the country, the Fab Five led Michigan to the championship in their freshman year, and in 1993, during their sophomore year, they returned to the championship finals again. Led by Chris Webber, the team had forged a flashy style of play and presence, characterized by shaved heads, long trunks, and glossy black shoes. They often would utilize extra passes, even bouncing the ball off of the backboard to set teammates up for slam dunks.

In the waning seconds of that championship game in 1993, Chris Webber had the ball with his team down by two when he called for a time-out. Unfortunately, since his team had no additional time-outs, he was whistled for a technical foul. Vernon Andrews noted the remarks by ESPN announcer Keith Olberman during the post–game coverage, who said:

> Webber failed to remember his team had no time-outs remaining and was thus penalized with a technical foul, thus losing the ball and the game by four points. Michigan played all this year with that in-your-face style and they got caught on a little fundamental. *It's a kind of morality play,* if you believe in that sort of thing. [emphasis added] (see V. Andrews, 1996, p. 53)

Olberman, in effect, claimed that Michigan was punished for its flashy, loud, if not black, style of play.

For years, then, such styles have been confronted by disapproving league eyes, which viewed these actions as rude, undisciplined, and transgressive modes of expression. Such concern, we suggest, is a tool of social control, in which the power bloc(s) within a state society localizes its power through an attempt to control and advance a surveillance of particular bodies in particular spaces (Fiske, 1993). Disciplinary mechanisms such as these limits on celebration and nineteenth-century prohibitions of Native American dance[3] are informed by a fear that these racial others have natural impulses that demand a civilizing force in order to rein them in. Michel Foucault would understand these league sanctions against victorious expression as disciplinary power, which allows the hegemonic forces within a society to manipulate the bodies of its citizens and to exact from them greater degrees of social control, so that imperial *discipline* might supersede *punishment* (Foucault, 1979).

CONCLUSIONS

Clearly, the racial spectacles of (intercollegiate) athletics overdetermine blackness, as they incorporate and exploit and discipline and display African-American athletes. Encrusted ideologies and well-worn stereotypes imprint the means and meanings of participating in, performing, and consuming the stagings of racial difference, both on and beyond the playing field. Indeed, as we have argued here, entrenched, often invisible, popular notions of blackness center on the black body and its purported excesses—extraordinary ability, criminal deviance, and libidinal pleasure. The excessive and transgressive physicality of African-American athletes, as we have further demonstrated, does not merely shape public perceptions—panics no less than pleasures—but structure the regimes of control, management, and even care applied to the black body as well. To close this chapter, we return to white supremacy, not as formulated by people such as David Duke but as a sociocultural field animated by the articulations race, corporeality, and disciplinarity.

In March 1992, during what has arguably become the nation's most conspicuous collegiate sporting spectacle—the NCAA Division I basketball championship, known fondly as March Madness—Indiana University's head coach Bobby Knight became embroiled in yet another controversy. During a press conference in Albuquerque, New Mexico, a photograph was taken of Knight, a large, white figure, brandishing a bullwhip and towering over Calbert Cheaney, one of his black players (Hurd, 1992; Wieberg, 1992). Cheaney apparently was following Knight's "playful" lead in this most incredulous form of theater, as he kneeled down under the coach with his practice shorts pulled down and faced the camera with a wide-toothed grin as Knight, softly struck his backside. The stunt by Knight, whose nickname is, tellingly, the "General," was an attempt to inject humor into public speculation about his abuse of players.

Naturally, the national publication of this photograph set off a firestorm of protest. The leader of Indiana's General Assembly's Black Caucus, Representative Hurley Goodall, wrote to Indiana University President Ehrlich urging that the popular basketball coach be fired. Meanwhile, the Albuquerque chapter of the National Association for the Advancement of Colored People (NAACP) condemned the stunt. Among many, the sentiment was that this caricatured performance was an insult to African Americans, for whom the image of a white man taking a whip to a black man might be expected to invoke a painful social memory. Of course, neither Knight, his players, or local supporters were willing to view the incident in racial terms.

We are not prepared to accuse Bobby Knight of being a racist based on this moment; neither, however, are we prepared to assert that he is enlightened when it comes to racial injustice and inequality. Our concern is not really with Knight at all but rather with the social and political milieu that made it possible (in the minds of Knight and others) to mock this deadly image of white authority and black subservience in a context already highly charged by contours of African-American exploitation, acknowledged even by other NCAA Division I coaches such as Joe Paterno and Dean Smith.

Black players on the University of California at Los Angeles team, which lost to Indiana just prior to the photo incident, were not amused. "That just shows," claimed Tyus Edney, "even though it's a joke, what some people may think about black players." Gerald Madkins confessed, "Fear is what comes to my mind when I see a whip, not motivation" (quoted in Hurd, 1992). It is Knight's position at Indiana University, however, that raises the greatest concern. He is the highest paid, most visible employee of the state institution, and while technically not faculty, symbolically he shares responsibility with faculty members for guiding the educational and ethical development of students. We cannot imagine a context in which Knight, having dreamed up this performance, approached Cheaney to ask for his participation; more difficult, however, is to imagine how a player on his team could muster up the energy to refuse to play his games, without being punished—either in the short or long run.

This spectacular moment exaggerates the racial contours of contemporary intercollegiate athletics, inscribing a hyberbolic instance of blackness, especially in relation to whiteness. That is, as Knight, the white coach, with bullwhip in hand, stands over and playfully strikes Cheaney, his smiling and stooped black player, this evocative exchange (rendered through the icons of American slavery) not only reduces the African-American athlete to a set of corporeal fragments requiring discipline but also affirms white supremacy. Indeed, it highlights the central ironies of post–civil rights college sports.

African-American athletes have become central to college sports, yet institutional structures and ideological practices continue to control, marginalize, and disempower them, albeit in novel and unanticipated forms. Euro-American coaches, commentators, and spectators in turn remain dominant, retaining authority to define and discipline, interpret and enjoy, and exploit and appropriate African-American athletes. Pamela Wonsek's (1992, p. 454) interpretation of television coverage of the NCAA tournament nicely summarizes the significance of this reconfiguration.

> Although the sporting event itself is dominated by black players, these images are undercut by the overwhelming predominance of white images. . . . Not only does this place the black players in a secondary and entertainment role, but it may also serve to reassure the white majority that its dominance is not really being threatened.

Whites reign supreme, even as African Americans eclipse them on the courts. We have outlined in this chapter the constellation of signifying practices producing, problematizing, and policing blacks, while securing, at least for the moment, white supremacy.

NOTES

1. In contrast with Duke's assertion, in actuality, African Americans comprise much closer to 50 percent of all football players.
2. We view attempts to demonstrate or prove the inherent superiority of the black athlete, or the disproportionate athletic success of any "racial" group, to be misguided. Such scholarship often is based on a misunderstanding of the complexity of human biophysical variation (see Marks, 1995) as well as an oversimplified understanding of relative success in athletics. We direct readers to an overview of studies of sports, race, and genetics: Davis (1990), Harpalani (1998), Hoberman (1998), and Hunter (1998).
3. Elsewhere (King & Springwood, 2000; Springwood & King, 2000), we have discussed nineteenth-century efforts by the U.S. government to control, suppress, and even eliminate various forms of Native American expression, such as the Sun Dance, war dances, the Ghost Dance, and potlatch celebrations. We claimed that such efforts were driven, in part, by a colonial worldview in which the colonists feared non-Christian forms of bodily performance as dangerously sexual and transgressive.

REFERENCES

Andrews, David. (1996). The fact(s) of Michael Jordan's blackness: Excavating a floating racial signifier. *Sociology of Sport Journal, 13* (2), 125–158.

Andrews, David. (forthcoming). Just what is it that makes today's lives so different, so appealing? Commodity-sign culture, Michael Jordan, and the cybernetic postmodern body. In C. Cole, J. Loy, & M. Messner (Eds.), *Exercising power: The making and remaking of the body.* Albany: State University of New York Press.

Andrews, Vernon. (1991). *Race, culture, situation and the touchdown dance.* Master's thesis, University of Wisconsin, Madison.

Andrews, Vernon. (1996). Black bodies—White control: The contested terrain of sportsmanlike conduct. *Journal of African American Men, 2* (1), 33–59.

Andrews, Vernon. (1998). African American player codes on celebration, taunting, and sportsmanlike conduct. In G. Sailes (Ed.), *African Americans in sport* (pp. 145–180). New Brunswick: Transaction Press.

Bamberger, Michael. (1996, May 6). School's out. *Sports Illustrated, 50–57.*

Bridges, Tyler. (1994). *The rise of David Duke.* Jackson: University Press of Mississippi.

Chideya, Farari. (1995). *Don't believe the hype: Fighting cultural misinformation about African Americans.* New York: Plume.

Cole, Cheryl L. (1996). American Jordan: P.L.A.Y., consensus, & punishment. *Sociology of Sport Journal, 13,* 366–397.

Cole, Cheryl L., & Andrews, David. (1996). Look—It's NBA show time!: Visions of race in the popular imaginary. *Cultural Studies: A Research Annual, 1,* 141–181.

Cole, Cheryl L., & Denny, H. (1995). Visualizing deviance in the post–Reagan America: Magic Johnson, AIDS, and the promiscuous world of professional sport. *Critical Sociology, 20* (3), 123–147.

Curtis, Russel L. Jr. (1998). Racism and rationales: A frame analysis of John Hoberman's *Darwin's athletes. Social Science Quarterly, 79* (4), 885–891.

Davis, Laurel. (1990). The articulation of difference: White preoccupation with questions of racially linked genetic differences among athletes. *Sociology of Sport Journal, 7,* 179–187.

Davis, Laurel. (1993). Protest against the use of Native American mascots: A challenge to traditional, American identity. *Journal of Sport and Social Issues, 17* (1), 9–22.

Davis, Laurel, & Harris, Othello. (1998). Race and ethnicity in U.S. sports media. In Lawrence A. Wenner (Ed.), *MediaSport* (pp. 154–169). London: Routledge.

Davis, Mike. (1992). *City of quartz: Excavating the future of Los Angeles.* New York: Random House.

Duke, David. (2000). Tiger Woods, race, and professional sports. [essay posted on Web site, 2/14/00]: <http://www.Duke.org/writings/tigerwoods.html>

Duke, David, with Whitney, Glayde. (1998). *My awakening: A path to racial understanding.* Louisiana: Free Speech Books.

Early, Gerald. (1994). Collecting the artificial nigger: Race and American material culture. In *The culture of bruising* (pp. 155–162). Hopewell, NJ: Ecco Press.

Entine, Jon. (2000). *Taboo: Why black athletes dominate sports and why we're afraid to talk about it.* New York: PublicAffairs.

Feinstein, John. (1998). *A march to madness: The view from the floor in the Atlantic Coast conference.* New York: Little Brown and Company.

Feldman, Allen. (1994). On cultural anesthesia: From Desert Storm to Rodney King. *American Ethnologist, 21* (2), 404–418.

The final four. (1989, March 20). [Special advertising section]. *Sports Illustrated.*

Fiske, John. (1993). *Power plays, power works.* London: Verso.

Fitzpatrick, Frank. (1999). *And the walls came tumbling down: Kentucky, Texas Western, and the game that changed American sports.* New York: Simon & Schuster.

Foucault, Michel. (1979). *Discipline and punish: The birth of the prison.* New York: Vintage.

Funk, Gary D. (1991). *Major violation: The unbalanced priorities in athletics and academics.* Champaign, IL: Leisure Press.

Gay, Geneva, & Baber, Williw L. (Eds.). (1987). *Expressively black: The cultural basis of ethnic identity.* New York: Praeger.

Gould, Stephen Jay. (1996/1981). *The mismeasure of man* (2nd ed.). New York: W. W. Norton and Company.

Hale, Grace Elizabeth. (1998). *Making whiteness: The culture of segregation in the South, 1890–1940.* New York: Pantheon.

Harpalani, Vinay. (1998). The athletic dominance of African Americans—Is there a genetic basis? In G. Sailes (Ed.), *African Americans in sport* (pp. 103–120). New Brunswick, NJ: Transaction Press.

Hawkins, Billy. (1995/1996). The black student athlete: The colonized black body. *Journal of African American Men, 1* (3), 23–35.

Hill, Lance. (1992). Nazi race doctrine in the political thought of David Duke. In Douglas D. Rose (Ed.), *The emergence of David Duke and the politics of race* (pp. 94–111). Chapel Hill: University of North Carolina Press.

Hoberman, John. (1997). *Darwin's athletes: How sport has damaged black America and preserved the myth of race.* Boston: Houghton Mifflin Co.

Hunter, David W. (1998). Race and athletic performance: A physiological review. In G. Sailes (Ed.), *African Americans in sport* (pp. 103–120). New Brunswick, NJ: Transaction Press.

Hurd, Michael. (1992, March 31). Knight needs to apologize. *USA Today,* 6C.

Jones, James M. (1986). Racism: A cultural analysis of the problem. In John Dovidio & Samuel Gaertner (Eds.), *Prejudice, discrimination, and racism.* San Diego: Academic Press.

Kellner, Douglas. (1996). Sports, media culture, and race—Some reflections on Michael Jordan. *Sociology of Sport Journal, 13,* 458–467.

King, C. Richard, & Springwood, Charles Fruehling. (2000). Choreographing colonialism: Athletic mascots, (dis)embodied Indians, and Euro-American subjectivities. *Cultural studies: A research annual.* Stamford, CT: JAI Press.

Lapchick, Richard. (1991). *Five minutes to midnight: Race and sport in the 1990s.* Lanham, MD: Madison Books.

Levin, Michael. (1997). *Why race matters.* Westport, CT: Praeger.

Lipsitz, George. (1998). *The possessive investment in whiteness: How white people profit from identity politics.* Philadelphia: Temple University Press.

Lott, Eric. (1993). *Love and theft: Blackface minstrelsy and the American working class.* New York: Oxford University Press.

Lott, Tommy. (1999). *The invention of race: Black culture and the politics of representation.* Malden, MA: Blackwell Publishers.

Manring, M. M. (1998). *Slave in a box: The strange career of Aunt Jemima.* Charlottesville: University Press of Virginia.

Marks, Jonathan. (1995). *Human biodiversity: Genes, racism and history.* New York: Aldine de Gruyter.

Mellinger, Wayne, & Beaulieu, Rodney. (1997). White fantasies, black bodies: Racial power, disgust and desire in American popular culture. *Visual Anthropology, 9,* 117–147.

Mercer, Kobena. (1994). *Welcome to the jungle: New positions in black cultural studies.* London: Routledge.

Midol, Nancy. (1998). Rap and dialectical relations: Culture, subculture, power, and counter-power. In Genevieve Rail (Ed.), *Sport and postmodern times* (pp. 333–343). Albany: State University of New York Press.

Montville, Leigh. (1998, August 3). Golden boy. *Sports Illustrated.*

Moore, William V. (1992). David Duke: The white knight. In Douglas D. Rose (Ed.), *The emergence of David Duke and the politics of race* (pp. 41–58). Chapel Hill: University of North Carolina Press.

Olsen, Jack. (1968, July 15). In an alien world. *Sports Illustrated,* 28–37.

Pieterse, Jan Nederveen. (1992). *White on black: Images of Africa and blacks in western popular culture.* New Haven, CT: Yale University Press.

Sandell, Jillian. (1995). Out of the ghetto and into the marketplace: *Hoop Dreams* and the commodification of marginality. *Socialist Review, 25* (2), 57–82.

Smedley, Audrey. (1993). *Race in North America: Origin and evolution of a worldview.* Boulder: Westview.

Spivey, Donald, & Jones, Thomas A. (1983). Intercollegiate athletic servitude: A case study of the black Illini student athletes, 1931–1967. *Social Science Quarterly, 55,* 939–947.

Springwood, Charles Fruehling, & King, C. Richard. (2000). Race, power, and representation in contemporary American sport. In P. Kivisto & G. Rundblad (Eds.), *The color line at the dawn of the 21st century.* Thousand Oaks, CA: Pine Valley Press.

Takaki, Ronald. (1993). *A different mirror: A history of multicultural America.* Boston: Little, Brown and Company.

Turner, Patricia. (1993). *I heard it through the grapevine: Rumor in African-American culture.* Berkeley: University of California Press.

Vescey, George. (1970). *Harlem Globetrotters.* New York: Scholastic Book Services.

White, Shane, & White, Graham. (1998). *Stylin': African American expressive culture from its beginnings to the zoot suit.* Ithaca, NY: Cornell University Press.

Wieberg, Steve. (1992, April 2). Stage set for knight's act in final four. *USA Today,* 10C.

Wonsek, Pamela L. (1992). College basketball on television: A study of racism in the media. *Media, Culture, and Society, 14,* 449–461.

12

"WHERE MY GIRLS AT?"
Negotiating Black Womanhood in Music Videos

Rana A. Emerson

The literature on Black youth culture, especially hip-hop culture, has focused primarily on the experiences of young men, with the experiences of Black girls being all but ignored. However, the recent appearance of Black women performers, songwriters, and producers in Black popular culture has called attention to the ways in which young Black women use popular culture to negotiate social existence and attempt to express independence, self-reliance, and agency. This article is an exploration of the representations of Black womanhood as expressed in the music videos of Black women performers. The author first identifies themes that reflect controlling images of Black womanhood, then those that exemplify an expression of agency, and finally those appearing ambivalent and contradictory. Overall, the music videos express how young Black women must negotiate sexuality and womanhood in their everyday lives.

Today's American youths of all racial and ethnic heritages are living in a cultural environment dominated by the idioms of Black youth and working-class culture that have been articulated since the late 1970s and early 1980s by hip-hop culture. Since its emergence in the mass media mainstream in the early 1990s, hip-hop culture has affected the arenas of film, fashion, television, art, literature, and journalism (Watkins 1998). In the mid- to late 1990s, African American youth emerged as an important segment of this teenage audience and consumer population (Watkins 1998). Recent ethnographic studies of Black youth in the 1990s have demonstrated the importance and impact that popular culture in general and hip-hop culture in particular have on the ways in which young African Americans make sense of their lives, social surroundings, and the world around them (Arnett Ferguson 2000; Patillo-McCoy 1999). Therefore, it is important for those who wish to better understand the lives of young African Americans to investigate the attributes of the popular cultural products that inform their everyday lives and attempt to make sense of their participation with and within popular culture. Paying attention to the role of popular culture in the lives of these youths also contributes to sociological theory by further elucidating the significance of the mass media as a social institution and how ideologies of race, class, and gender are represented and reproduced within it.

Reprinted from Rana A. Emerson, "'Where My Girls At?' Negotiating Black Womanhood in Music Videos," *Gender & Society* 16, no. 1 (February 2002): 115–135.

While much has been written about the significance and impact of hip-hop culture on the lives of Black youth, young Black women, until very recently, have failed to be located as substantial producers, creators, and consumers of hip-hop and Black youth culture (George 1998; Perkins 1996; Rose 1994; Watkins 1998). Most of the contemporary research and criticism has focused on the experience of young men of African descent and, with rare exceptions, has implicitly and often explicitly identified Black popular culture, specifically hip-hop culture, with masculinity (George 1998; Perkins 1996; Rose 1991, 1994).

Yet, African American women have a significant presence in hip-hop and Black popular culture, and in music videos, where they appear as dancers; models; and, most significantly, as performers. At the same time, the hip-hop genre and the music videos that are used to promote records and performers have been harshly critiqued for the antiwoman (specifically anti-Black woman) messages and images contained within them. Critics have pointed out that many discourses in hip-hop culture reproduce dominant and distorted ideologies of Black women's sexuality (hooks 1992; Morgan 1999; Perkins 1996).

Nevertheless, despite the misogynistic representations of Black womanhood that pervade music videos, the 1990s witnessed the emergence of Black women performers, producers, writers, and musicians who have also made the music video into a site for promotion, creativity, and self-expression. Black women performers, songwriters, and producers, including Erykah Badu, Missy "Misdemeanor" Elliott, and Lauryn Hill, have profoundly affected hip-hop culture as well as the wider sphere of popular culture. While most music videos, including those of some Black women performers, exacerbate the exploitation of the Black woman's body and perpetuate stereotypes of Black womanhood, Badu, Elliott, and Hill depict themselves as independent, strong, and self-reliant agents of their own desire, the masters of their own destiny.

The medium of the music video, the primary promotional vehicle for the recording industry today, is an especially rich space to explore the ways in which race, gender, class, and sexuality intersect in the construction and proliferation of ideologies of Black womanhood in the mass media and popular culture. This study explores Black women's representation in music video through the analysis of a sample of videos by African American women singers, rappers, and musicians produced and distributed at the end of the 1990s.

Most of the previous studies of Black women's representation in music videos have, on one hand, either focused on the hegemonic and stereotypical imagery and discourses of Black femininity or, on the other hand, exaggerated the degree of agency that Black female performers in music video have by emphasizing the resistant and counterhegemonic elements of the music video representations. Instead, this study demonstrates that in the cultural productions of Black women, music videos in this case, hegemonic and counterhegemonic themes often occur simultaneously and are interconnected, resulting in a complex, often contradictory and multifaceted representation of Black womanhood.

LITERATURE REVIEW

The vast majority of representations of Black women in popular culture are firmly grounded in the dominant ideologies surrounding Black womanhood in American society. Patricia Hill Collins (1991a) described these ideologies as controlling images that are rooted in the maintenance of hegemonic power and serve to justify and legitimize the continued marginalization of Black women. The media and popular culture are primary sites for the dissemination and the construction of commonsense notions of Black womanhood. Music videos, which have been criticized for their objectifying and exploitative depictions of women of all races and ethnicities (Aufderheide 1986; Dines and Humez 1995; Frith, Goodwin, and Grossberg 1993; Hurley 1994; Kaplan 1987; Stockbridge 1987; Vincent 1989; Vincent, Davis, and Boruszkowski 1987), often represent Black women according to the controlling images discussed by Hill Collins. The images that are seen most often are the hypersexualized "hot momma" or "Jezebel," the asexual "mammy," the emasculating "matriarch," and the "welfare recipient" or "baby-momma" (a colloquial term for young, unwed mothers).

Although Black female representation generally draws directly from the controlling images of Black womanhood, Black women's performances in popular culture often generate representations that counter the dominant ideological notions of Black womanhood. Consequently, the possibility that popular and expressive culture may exist as a site for resistance and revision of these stereotypical representations emerges. Hazel Carby (1986) and Angela Davis (1998) have shown that such phenomena occurred in the early part of this century. At the time, performers such as "Ma" Rainey, Bessie Smith, and Ethel Waters offered, in their music and on-stage performances, a portrait of Black womanhood in which they asserted empowerment and sexual subjectivity. In both Carby's and Davis's views, this female blues culture was grounded in a Black feminist consciousness. Although some authors (Delano Brown and Campbell 1986; Kaplan 1987; Lewis 1990; Peterson-Lewis and Chennault 1986) have looked at race and gender representations in music videos, there have been few systematic studies of Black female representation within the medium (Goodall 1994; Roberts 1991, 1994; Rose 1991, 1994). Even fewer studies have looked at the music videos by Black women performers themselves. Notable exceptions are Tricia Rose's discussion of Black women rappers in her social history of hip-hop culture, *Black Noise* (Rose 1994), as well as the works of Nataki Goodall (1994) and Robin Roberts (1991, 1994).

Rose (1991, 1994) has connected Carby's (1986) work on the blues with the images and lyrics of female rappers and has proposed that rap music and hip-hop culture, instead of being entirely oppressive to women, may actually enable Black women to assert independence, agency, and control of their sexuality. She argues,

> Salt-N-Pepa are carving out a female-dominated space in which Black women's sexuality is openly expressed. Black women rappers sport hip hop clothing and jewelry as well as distinctively Black hairstyles. They affirm a Black, female, working-class cultural aesthetic that is rarely depicted in American popular culture. Black women rappers resist patterns of sexual objectification and cultural invisibility, and they also resist academic reification and mainstream, hegemonic, white feminist discourse. (Rose 1991, 126)

However, Rose's historical work is not based on a systematic content analysis of the music videos themselves, and Goodall's (1994) and Roberts's (1991, 1994) textual analyses are limited even further by focusing only on a few groups. Roberts (1991, 1994) attempted to demonstrate that Black women rappers articulate a feminist sensibility through their music videos. She cites Queen Latifah, MC Lyte, and other Black women rappers' and singers' assertive rhetoric, aggressive sexuality, and defiant stance as evidence of a firmly and markedly feminist consciousness. Goodall (1994) also attempted to locate feminism in Black female performance by chronicling the development of antisexism in the songs and videos of the R&B/hip-hop group TLC. Goodall underscores the ways in which TLC's music displays a growing sense of sexual freedom and contestation of sexism and racial discrimination.

While Goodall (1994) emphasizes how the lyrics of this single group directly comment on sexism and the exploitation of Black women, she fails to consider how the group's image still caters to a male audience. Similarly, Roberts commits the error of assigning Queen Latifah a feminist label without noting that the identity she projects is not unequivocally feminist. I argue that both Goodall and Roberts (1991, 1994), in their efforts to discover patterns of resistance and transgression, overemphasize the degree of agency that Black woman performers possess. Despite their valuable conclusions about Black women's participation in Black popular culture, these works nevertheless fail to problematize the notion of resistance itself.

By conducting a close analysis of a much larger sample of music videos, my study provides an empirical basis for identifying the ways in which Black women use the realm of culture and performance for social commentary and to respond to the controlling images of Black womanhood that were identified and discussed by Hill Collins, Carby, Davis, Rose, and other Black feminist theorists and critics. This study improves on the previous research on Black female music video performance because it problematizes the often-unexamined notion of resistance. Overall, this study furthers the inclusion of Black female youth in the conversation surrounding hip-hop culture by recognizing the active participation of Black female performers and audiences within it (McRobbie 1991, 1993, 1997; McRobbie and Nava 1984). In this way, it serves to question the identification of hip-hop culture with Black masculinity and Black male youth by demonstrating that music videos also serve as sites for expressing the lived experiences of Black female youth.

In this article, I will first identify how music videos exhibit and reproduce the stereotypical notions of Black womanhood faced by young African American women. Next, I discuss the ways that Black woman performers use music videos for contesting hegemonic racist and sexist notions of Black femininity and asserting agency. Third, I demonstrate how contradictory themes in the music videos reflect a sense of ambivalence on the part of Black girls regarding the relationships between Blackness, womanhood, and sexuality.

METHOD

I collected a purposive sample of 56 music videos that featured Black women performers using the method of "theoretical sampling" (Lindlof 1995; Strauss 1987). The videos were tape-recorded from the daily broadcast programming of cable networks BET, MTV, and VH1 and were collected during the week of 7 January 1998. The majority of the Black women's videos collected in the sample (38) were taped from BET. Fewer videos by Black women artists were collected from MTV (13) and VH1 (5). According to *Billboard* magazine, for the week ending 11 January 1998, 11 videos featuring Black women artists were in heavy rotation on BET, while MTV featured 5 and VH1 included 2. The sample included those videos in heavy rotation on all three channels, plus all other videos played during the time period that met the criteria.

I assumed that music video programming is strategically targeted by the broadcast outlets and recording companies toward a youth market and that the scheduling of music videos would reflect the viewing patterns of adolescents and young adults in the target age range. Therefore, I taped videos at times of the day when teenagers and young adults would most likely view them: in the morning before school, between 7:00 A.M. and 8:00 A.M.; late afternoon after school, between 2:00 P.M. and 6:00 P.M.; prime time, from 7:00 P.M. to 10:00 P.M.; and late nights on Fridays and Saturdays, between 11:00 P.M. and 2:00 A.M. Recording took place on all channels during these time periods. Videos were purposively sampled and chosen on the basis of the following characteristics: They featured Black female performers (defined as singers, rappers, or other musicians), who were either lead performers or appeared as guests in the videos of other performers (excluding background dancers and singers) regardless of race and gender. An additional criterion for selection was that the performers whose videos I included self-identified as having African or African American heritage. I judged this by observing the signifiers of race in the marketing of the artist, the signs and indicators of Black culture apparent in their work, and my knowledge of this self-identification obtained from outside sources such as interviews and other journalistic accounts.

The videos included in this analysis mirror *Billboard* magazine's rotation playlists for MTV, VH1, and BET. The rotation, or frequency at which a video is shown, is determined by a number of factors including the promotional efforts of the record company, the anticipation of the release, and ongoing sales of the single or album. For example, the playlists show that Janet Jackson, Missy "Misdemeanor" Elliott, Erykah Badu, Allure, and Mariah Carey were all in heavy rotation on the video outlets during late December 1997 and early January 1998, and they appear in this sample.

My analysis of the music videos was conducted in two stages. First, I coded the entire sample of videos, and second, I performed a close textual analysis of a subsample of the videos. Coding categories were developed to identify emergent themes and patterns within and among the videos and to facilitate an interpretive analysis of those compelling and important themes. All aspects of the 56 videos in the sample, including both the visual narratives and the musical tracks of the songs, were analyzed using these codes.

The coded variables were as follows: the camera's gaze or point of view; the mode of address or the gender of those being "spoken to" in the video; presentation and performance of gender roles; physicality and the body; relationships between women; relationships with men; the presence and degree of female anger, rage, or aggression; the presence of violence; expression of female sexual desire; what sexual behavior, if any, is present; images of motherhood; the number and gender composition of group members; the presence of dance in the video; sound; the type of narrative (if any) in the video; the type of image the artist is projecting: inter-textuality or references to other videos, songs, or other media; apparent signifiers of Blackness; class or occupational markers; geographic setting; and age.

Those coding categories that occurred most frequently across the sample of videos or appeared to have the most impact and significance within a critical subgroup of videos were identified as the key themes and issues. To assess the relative importance of these factors, I selected 20 music videos in the sample (indicated by bold italics in Table 12.1), which exhibited the most salient emergent themes. I conducted a close reading and textual analysis of the visual images, the narrative and representations, and the accompanying musical tracks and lyrics of each of these 20 videos to confirm, contextualize, and further clarify the observations made during the first stage of the analysis.

TABLE 12.1 List of Videos Selected

Title	Artist	Year
All Cried Out	Allure featuring 112	1997
Everyday	Angie Stone and Devox	1997
A Rose Is Still a Rose	Aretha Franklin featuring Lauryn Hill	1997
I've Got This Feelin'	***Bobby Brown, with Whitney Houston***	***1997***
Morning	Bridgette Mc Williams	1997
Retrospective for Life	***Common and Lauryn Hill***	***1997***
Give It to You	***Da Brat***	***1995***
No, No, No	***Destiny's Child featuring Wyclef Jean***	***1997***
Reality	Elusion	1997
Too Gone Too Long	***En Vogue***	***1997***
MyLovin' (You're Never Going to Get It)	En Vogue	1992
Don't Let Go	En Vogue	1996
Givin' Him Something He Can Feel	***En Vogue***	***1993***
Tyrone	***Erykah Badu***	***1997***
On and On	***Erykah Badu***	***1997***
Killing Me Softly	Fugees	1996
Anytime Anyplace	Janet Jackson	1994
Together Again	Janet Jackson	1997
Got Till It's Gone	Janet Jackson	1997
Together Again (Deeper Remix)	Janet Jackson	1997
Love Will Never Do Without You	Janet Jackson	1990
The Party Continues	Jermaine Dupri featuring DaBrat	1997
Ghetto Superstar	***Joi***	***1997***
Swing My Way	***KP and Envyi***	***1997***
Young Sad and Blue	Lysette	1997
Honey	***Mariah Carey featuring Puff Daddy and Mase***	***1997***
Butterfly	Mariah Carey	1997
Breakdown	Mariah Carey featuring Bone Thugs and Redman	1997
The Roof	Mariah Carey featuring Mobb Deep	1997
Seven Days	Mary J. Blige featuring George Benson	1997
I'm Not Gonna Cry	***Mary J. Blige***	***1997***
I Can Love You	Mary J. Blige featuring Li'l Kim	1997
All I Need	***Method Man and Mary J. Blige***	***1995***
Beep Me 911	***Missy Elliot featuring 702***	***1997***
Sock It to Me	***Missy Elliot featuring Da Brat & Lil' Kim***	***1997***
Am I Dreaming	Ol' Skool featuring Xscape & Keith Sweat	1997
So Long	Phaija	1997
Don't Stop the Music	Playa featuring Missy Elliot	1997
All about the Benjamins	Puff Daddy featuring The Lox, Lil' Kim and B.I.G.	1997
It's All about the Benjamins	***Puff Daddy featuring The Lox, Lil' Kim, Dave Grohl, and Fuzzbubble***	***1997***

TABLE 12.1 (*Continued*)

Title	Artist	Year
I'll Be Missing You	Puff Daddy, Faith Evans, and 112	1997
Man Behind the Music	***Queen Pen featuring Teddy Riley***	***1997***
All My Love	Queen Pen featuring Eric Williams of Blackstreet	1997
We Getz Down	Rampage featuring 702 and Billie Lawrence	1997
R U Ready	***Salt n' Pepa***	***1997***
Wannabe	Spice Girls	1997
Say You'll Be There	Spice Girls	1997
Rain	SWV	1997
Silly	Taral Hicks	1998
Firm Biz	The Firm (Nas, AZ, and Foxy Brown)	1997
Luv 2 Luv Ya	Timbaland and Magoo featuring Shaunte	1997
Red Light Special	***TLC***	***1994***
You're Making Me High	Toni Braxton	1997
Unbreak My Heart	Toni Braxton	1996
What about Us	Total featuring Missy Elliot	1997
DJ Keep Playing	***Yvette Michelle***	***1997***

Note: Titles in bold italics indicate videos that were used in both content and textual analysis.

STEREOTYPES AND CONTROLLING IMAGES

The videos reflect how race, class, and gender continue to constrain and limit the autonomy and agency of Black women. Music videos contain imagery that reflects and reproduces the institutional context in which they are produced, and they are permeated by stereotypical controlling images of Black womanhood. Several stereotypes emerge in the ways Black women's videos are programmed, as well in the content of the videos themselves. First, the videos emphasize Black women's bodies. Second, they construct a one-dimensional Black womanhood. Finally, the presence of male sponsors in the videos and a focus on themes of conspicuous consumption and romance further exhibit the types of social constraints faced by young Black women.

The Body

The first way that patterns of social constraint emerge is in the emphasis on the body. It is clear that female rap and rhythm and blues (R&B) performers are required to live up to dominant notions of physical attractiveness and measure up to fairly rigid standards of beauty. The most striking example of this is the lack of variety in body size and weight. This was surprising, considering the conventional wisdom that the Black community possesses alternative beauty standards that allow for larger body types. Many authors have concluded that these standards contribute to a more positive body image among Black women (Cash and Henry 1995; Flynn and Fitzgibbon 1996; Harris 1994; Molloy and Hertzberger 1998). However, the majority of the videos I coded (30) featured artists who would be considered thin by most standards, while only 9 featured performers who would be considered overweight. The only women who are larger than the ideal are Missy "Misdemeanor" Elliott, Angie Stone, and a member of the group Xscape.

In those 30 videos, the thin, physically attractive performers are clearly constructed as objects of male desire. In Bobby Brown's video, *I've Got This Feelin'*, featuring his real-life wife Whitney Houston, Whitney is broken up fetishistically into her body parts. The viewer is only allowed glimpses of her mouth and legs, her arms caressing Bobby's shoulder, and her hair. The implication is that the audience is not supposed to know who she is (although we do have our suspicions), until the shot widens to reveal her in her entirety, laughing knowingly and almost conspiringly with her husband. Cutting Whitney up into visual pieces undercuts her power.

In another example of the camera's focus on the Black female body, many women appear scantily clad. Like Whitney Houston, Mariah Carey's body parts are also fetishized as she changes into a wet suit and bikini in *Honey*. Her extremities are centered in the camera's gaze. In *Breakdown,* where Carey performs as a Las Vegas Casino showgirl, she is even less clothed than her background dancers. Melanie Brown of the Spice Girls is also scantily clad, performing decked out in a tiger print bustier, which additionally suggests the savage, uncontrollable woman of color who is inherently defined by her body, a notion supported by her nickname, "Scary Spice."

One-Dimensional Womanhood

For the most part, the portrait of Black womanhood that emerges from the video analysis is flat and one-dimensional. Black women are not represented in their full range of being. They are not multifaceted but are reduced to decorative eye candy. Black women performers are not allowed to be artists in their own right but must serve as objects of male desire. In the videos, only three of the featured artists were older than 30 (Janet Jackson, Whitney Houston, and Aretha Franklin). Indubitably, this reflects the youth-oriented nature of popular culture.

Pregnant women and mothers, as well as women older than 30, are not desirable as objects of the music video camera's gaze, reinforcing the sense that only women who are viewed as sexually available are acceptable in music videos. Only two of the videos depicted motherhood: Erykah Badu is visibly pregnant in *Tyrone,* and Joi is shown with her infant daughter in her video, *Ghetto Superstar.*

Sexual diversity is another element of Black womanhood that is conspicuously absent and also reflects the desirability of perceived sexual availability for men. None of the videos featured performers who were lesbian or bisexual, nor did they show even implicit homosexual or bisexual themes. This was interesting in light of the emergence of critically acclaimed and commercially popular bisexual and lesbian artists, most notably, Me'Shell Ndgeocello (whose most controversial video *Leviticus: Faggot* was censored by BET). As can be gleaned from the frequently homophobic rhetoric in hip-hop and R&B songs, sexual difference and nonconformity are still not legitimized in Black popular culture. As a result, it is not particularly surprising that bisexual and lesbian themes do not emerge in a sample of popular Black women's music videos.

"Man Behind the Music": The Male Sponsor

The one-dimensional depiction of Black women as objects of male pleasure undermines their legitimacy and agency as artists. Because their role is primarily sexual, they are not taken seriously. Add to that mix the notion that legitimacy in hip-hop culture is identified with masculinity, and the result is that many Black women artists are presented to the public under the guidance of a male sponsor.

Although male sponsorship, defined as the prominence of a male producer, songwriter, or fellow artist, was only coded in four of the videos, when it does occur, it is fairly significant. In such videos, not only is the male sponsor (who is most often one of the so-called megaproducers such as Sean "Puffy" Combs or Jermaine "J. D." Dupri) prominent visually and narratively in the video, but he literally takes precedence over the artist herself, essentially becoming the true star of the video. The most interesting example of male sponsorship occurs in Queen Pen's *Man behind the Music,* featuring producer, songwriter, and member of the group Blackstreet, Teddy Riley. Many R&B and hip-hop videos feature the producer of the song, reflecting the increased role of the producer in the production of Black music (George 1998). However, in this video, the producer role has been taken to an extreme. Teddy is the "Man," and the song and video are basically all about him. As Queen Pen drives around New York City through the boroughs and Times Square, Teddy reclines and swivels in the studio as the refrain "I . . . am the magnificent" repeats in the background track. He is assigned as much or more screen time as Pen. The song and video imply that Queen Pen is not the author of her rhymes and she is not the creator of her own success. Teddy's writing and producing give Pen her legitimacy, her entrée into the business. The viewer gets the distinct impression that if it were not for Teddy, we would not be watching Pen.

Although Combs, Riley, and Dupri also appear in the videos for male artists that they produce, the impact that they have on the image of women artists appears to be greater. They occupy a primary position within the camera's gaze and on the musical track. As demonstrated in the Queen Pen video example, they also receive a great deal of credit for the creativity and success of the women artists' musical output.

Since Black women have little or no clout in the music industry and Black men dominate the hip-hop world, the presence of a male impresario undermines any sense of creative autonomy for woman artists. In fact, the producer in today's record industry wields an unprecedented amount of control over the musical product, often to the point of overriding an artist's creative decisions and input over the content of a song, and occasionally the video as well (George 1998). The producer and record company executives often choose the video director and contribute to the construction of the artist's image and presentation. These videos give the impression that women are unable to be successful without the assistance and creative genius of a male impresario.

BLACK WOMEN'S AGENCY: COUNTERING CONTROLLING IMAGES

Despite the continuing objectification and exploitation of Black women in music videos, I found evidence of contestation, resistance, and the assertion of Black women's agency in many others ($n = 25$) as well. This agency emerged through the identification with signifiers of Blackness; an assertion of autonomy, vocality, and independence; and expressions of partnership, collaboration, and sisterhood with other Black women and Black men.

Signifiers of Blackness: Black Aesthetic, Black Context

In these videos, Blackness does not carry a negative connotation. Instead, it is the basis for strength, power, and a positive self-identity. Darker skin is privileged among Black women artists, actresses, models, and dancers in the videos. Thirty of the videos featured women with darker complexions or a combination of lighter and darker skinned women. This was an especially interesting finding after the controversies of the 1980s and 1990s about the frequent use of light-skinned women in music videos, which was criticized for valuing a white standard of beauty (Morgan 1999). In contrast, the videos examined in this study evinced a Black aesthetic in which standards of beauty, while problematic in themselves, were nevertheless based on a more African aesthetic.

The prevalence of a clear hip-hop sensibility supports the valuation of Black culture. Twenty of the videos were coded as being evocative of an urban hip-hop style. What emerges from these observations is the construction of a clear Black aesthetic. In fact, it becomes obvious that these videos exhibit an essentially Black universe. Although this was not specifically coded, white people appeared rarely if ever in the videos. When they do appear, they tend to be minor characters such as the gangsters in *Firm Biz* and Mariah's kidnappers in *Honey.*

Erykah Badu's *On and On* is an excellent example of the construction of a Black context and a Black world. It highlights the specificity, difference, and particularity of the Black experience. *On and On* is a "Color Purple"-style version of the Cinderella fairy tale. It is set on a farm in the rural south during an unspecified time period that appears to be the 1940s. Badu, as the protagonist of the narrative, is left to clean, to tend the farm animals, and to watch the children who are running around the house with their hair undone. We then follow Badu as she performs her chores while singing. After tripping and falling into the mud of a pig sty, and as shots are interspersed of well-dressed Black people going to some unspecified destination, Badu realizes that she has nothing to wear. As she glances at the green tablecloth, she looks into the camera with a "why not" expression. "Cinderella" triumphs as we then see her performing in a "juke joint" to an enthusiastic crowd, wearing the tablecloth. At the end of the video, Badu jumps into the crowd, and as they lift her up, her beat-up work boots are revealed. We, the viewers, are left with the impression that we have emerged from an emphatically southern Black context that affirms the validity of the Black experience.

This construction of a Black universe leads to questioning the notion of Blackness as male or Black youth culture's association with masculinity. Instead, I found Black women firmly contextualized among signifiers and codes of Blackness. They explore themes of womanhood that directly associate them with Blackness and Black life, and they construct a significant and solid space (albeit limited by the fact that male artists continue to receive more representation than women in heavy video rotations) for girls and women in Black youth and hip-hop culture. By appropriating signs of Blackness, Black women artists are able to assert the particularity and forcefulness of Black femininity and agency through the music video.

Autonomy, Vocality, and Independence

Despite the predominance of traditional gender roles in the music videos, Black women performers are frequently depicted as active, vocal, and independent. This vocality is most frequent within the context of traditional relationships, where the performers express discontent with, and contest, the conditions faced by Black women in interpersonal relationships.

Instead of exhibiting representations of physical violence and aggression, sometimes found in men's videos, this sample of videos demonstrates the significance of verbal assertiveness. Speaking out and speaking one's mind are a constant theme. Through the songs and videos, Black women are able to achieve voice and a space for spoken expression of social and interpersonal commentary.

A video by Erykah Badu, *Tyrone,* is the most conspicuous example of this theme. The lyrics, in which Badu dismisses a neglectful lover who prefers the company of his shiftless, unemployed friends, demonstrate her ability to get out of a bad relationship in which her sexual, emotional, and financial needs are not being met. Her words are underscored by her performance style. Badu is at center stage wearing African attire, including her signature headdress, and standing next to an ankh, an ancient Egyptian symbol of life. As she sings, her gestures, inflections, and facial expressions underscore the meaning of the song and increase her rapport with the very enthusiastic women in the audience. The "Tyrones" of the world know who they are, and the women they are involved with have an example of the most expedient and effective way of dealing with them. Badu clearly speaks her mind and asserts her own interests forcefully.

Although they are not clearly and unequivocally rejecting the desirability and basic dynamics of heterosexual relationships, Black women in these videos assert their own interests and express dissatisfaction with the unequal state of Black men-women interpersonal relations. Black women also express their own agency and self-determination through direct action. What emerges is the ability of a Black woman to define her own identity and life outcomes.

Sisterhood, Partnership, and Collaboration

Although Black women assert independence, they do not accomplish their goals alone. In these videos, Black women look to each other for support, partnership, and sisterhood. Collaborations between women artists are a constant and recurring theme throughout the videos and suggest a sense of community and collectivity. This shows that women need each other for guidance and support to succeed and survive in the recording industry and the world at large. Within these collaborations, unlike the male sponsorships discussed above, the spotlight is shared, and the guest star does not overshadow the featured artist.

The most interesting video in which this occurs is *Sock It to Me,* in which Missy Elliott collaborates with the rappers Lil' Kim and Da Brat. It has an outer-space, fantasy theme, and in the visual narrative, Missy and rapper Lil' Kim appear in red and white bubble space suits as explorers on a mission. As soon as they land on an uncharted planet, they are pursued by an army of monstrous robots under the control of the evil "mad scientist," portrayed by Missy's collaborator and producing partner Timbaland. They are chased throughout the rest of the video through space and on various barren planets. The chase scenes are interspersed with scenes of Missy, as she dances in the forefront of a troupe of dancers wearing futuristic attire. Missy also appears solo, seemingly suspended in space as she sings the track of the song. Just as Missy and Kim appear to be in danger of succumbing to Timbaland's goons, fellow rapper, Da Brat, during her rap sequence on the music track, comes to the rescue on a jet ski–type spacecraft. They speed off through space, fighting off the mad scientist's crew, and arrive safely at Missy's mothership, prominently marked with the letter *M.*

Throughout the chase sequences, the viewer's identification remains squarely with Missy and Kim, solidified by the close-up shots of their frightened facial expressions as they flee the goons and the (albeit short-lived) satisfaction apparent on their faces when they mistakenly believe that they have escaped their pursuers.

The extended chase scene signifies the continued quest to escape the threat of male dominance. It symbolizes the agency of women who refuse to be subsumed or annihilated by male dominance, as represented by the monstrous troops of the male mad scientist. The sisterhood that is implied by the camaraderie between Missy and Lil' Kim, their ability to escape Timbaland's evil troops, and the fact that they are rescued by another woman, Da Brat, further demonstrates the collective power of Black women to help each other be self-sufficient and not dependent on men.

Overall, what emerges from this combination of agency, voice, partnership, and Black context is a sense of the construction of Black woman–centered video narratives. Within these narratives, the interests, desires, and goals of women are predominant and gain importance in contrast to those in which they are exploited and subsumed. Black women are quite firmly the subjects of these narratives and are able to clearly and unequivocally express their points of view.

AMBIVALENCE AND CONTRADICTION: NEGOTIATING BLACK WOMANHOOD

In this section, I discuss the ambivalent and contradictory relationship that young Black women appear to have with Black popular culture and how those contradictions are reflected in the music videos in this sample. In this regard, music videos exemplify a tension between the structural constraints of race and gender on one hand and women's resistance and self-affirmation on the other.

Every day, young Black women face conflicting messages about their sexuality and femininity, as well as their status both in the Black community and society at large. They must figure out how they should construct and assert their identity as Black women. Therefore, it is not surprising that within the cultural productions of young Black women, themes of contradiction and ambivalence would emerge.

While it sometimes appears that these artists are directly reflecting and capitulating to oppressive social forces, this seeming compromise can be interpreted more accurately as ambivalence regarding contradictory messages about Black female sexuality, namely, the coexistence of hypersexual images and the denigration and denial of the beauty of the Black female body. In response to these contradictory notions of Black womanhood, Black women performers frequently reappropriate often explicit images of Black female sexuality. This strategy of self-representation as sexual may, on one hand, be interpreted as a sort of false consciousness that reflects an acceptance of the controlling images of Black womanhood. However, I argue that instead, these sometimes explicit representations of Black women's sexuality actually exemplify a process of negotiating those contradictory and often conflicting notions and, more significantly, represent an attempt to use the space of the music video to achieve control over their own sexuality. The four themes that I located that indicate this process include collaboration between Black men and women, representation of a multidimensional sexuality, returning the gaze, and the indeterminate gaze.

"Together Again": Black Male-Female Collaboration

Black men and women are frequently seen in these videos as coworkers and collaborators. They are fellow group members, found in duets, and they appear as nonmusical guest stars in each other's videos. Fourteen of the videos portray Black men as fellow group members or platonic friends. This theme occurs nearly as often as when men appear as romantic interests (18 videos). Collaboration emerges as an important aspect of Black women's performance. Despite the fact that strides have been made in recent years, it remains difficult for young women to enter the music industry on their own. As suggested in the discussion of sponsorship above, entrée into the business can be easier if they are associated with a man who is already established.

As opposed to the sponsorship and/or impresario videos, Black men and women collaborated frequently in apparently equal working relationships. In this context of partnership, Black women performers wield a great deal of creative control as songwriters, producers, and video directors. What this suggests is that Black men and women can work together and provide each other with mutual support to achieve success in a competitive cultural field. This phenomenon also is embedded in the tradition of collectivity and collaboration as a theme in African and African American culture (Hill Collins 1991a, 1991b).

In these collaborative relationships, Black women performers gain an equal footing with their fellow male artists. For example, Missy "Misdemeanor" Elliott collaborates with her partner in crime, Timbaland, and Magoo in *Sock It to Me* and *Beep Me 911*. She also makes an appearance in the video for the male group Playa's party anthem, *Can't Stop the Music*. Lauryn Hill collaborates with Pras and Wyclef in the Fugees and is the director and costar in rapper Common Senses' reflection on fatherhood, *Retrospective for Life*. Not only do these women have the same level of creative control and autonomy as the men, they also are able to execute many actions previously assigned only to male performers. Most significantly, the Black women artists within these videos are able to construct themselves as textual subjects and wield their gaze in a similar manner to men. Woman performers are provided with space and opportunity to wield creative and artistic control and to construct their own narratives of Black womanhood that express their lived experience. In effect, these collaborative working relationships counter and overshadow the marginalizing and silencing that result from the sponsorship relationship. In fact, one could argue that Missy Elliott and Lauryn Hill have had more impact on American popular culture (and hip-hop culture) than their collaborators.

Multidimensional Sexuality: Reappropriating the Black Female Body

Most of the artists portray themselves with a highly stylized and glamorous image. Wearing designer gear, these women singers present themselves as sexy and provocative. In 21 of the videos, the artist was depicting a glamorous image, while in 17 they were coded as having a sexual image. This emphasis on appearance and physical attraction confirms the notion of the excessive sexuality of the Black woman. It supports the ideological controlling image of the hypersexual "sapphire" or "jezebel," effectively undermining Black womanhood and humanity.

However, in the videos analyzed, glamour and style are not the only salient attributes possessed by Black women artists. Instead, a sexualized image often occurs simultaneously with themes of independence, strength, a streetwise nature, toughness, and agency. Most of the time, the same artists express themselves in a single video as sexy and savvy, glamorous and autonomous. Fifteen of the videos depict artists having an independent image, and 13 are streetwise and tough. Many of these videos were also coded as glamorous and sexual.

What seems to emerge is a contradiction between the complex and often unconventional representations of Black women artists and the appearance of objectified and clearly one-dimensionally sexualized Black women dancers. Fifteen of the videos were coded as featuring female background dancers. For the most part, when these dancers appear on screen, they are scantily clad and move in a highly suggestive manner. Male dancers, in contrast, only appear in 8 of the 56 videos and are rarely explicitly sexualized. In Da Brat's *Give It to You,* which takes place at what appears to be a hip-hop industry party, Da Brat's tough and streetwise, even boyish, image contrasts sharply with the appearance of scantily clad female "groupies" who are mingling and dancing in the crowd. Missy Elliott's *Beep Me 911* is set in what seems to be a pornographic peep show. Missy and 702 dance among go-go dancers who appear to be life-sized marionettes, as Timbaland and Magoo observe through a glass barrier. Missy is demanding that her lover tells her what's up by beeping her, to tell her why "you're playing on me." She asserts her own interests, the fulfillment of her own physical and emotional desires, which is ironic considering that her demands are being articulated in a context of male sexual pleasure and satisfaction.

The fact remains that sex sells. In the entertainment industry, there is a call for bodies, namely, female bodies, to be on display to stimulate record sales. If it is not the artist herself, then models and dancers serve this purpose. Women remain the object of sexual desire, the selling point, and the bodies on display.

On the other hand, the juxtaposition and combination of sexuality, assertiveness, and independence in these videos can also be read as the reappropriation of the Black woman's body in response to its sexual regulation and exploitation. What emerges is an effort on the part of the Black female artist to assert her own sexuality, to gain her own sexual pleasure.

Whether this indicates compromise or capitulation to objectification and exploitation is not definitively clear. It is difficult to reach a conclusion on this solely from the data gathered from textual analysis. One would need to investigate the creative production decision-making process. However, the results of this analysis and interpretation indicate that trade-offs are made in the construction of an artist's image. Black womanhood, as expressed through Da Brat and Missy's performances, is the result of a process of negotiation in which objectification of the female body must be present in order for the performer to gain a level of autonomy, to gain exposure. While this seems on the surface like "selling out" to the dictates of patriarchy and the marketplace, I would argue that instead, it affirms the multidimensional nature of Black womanhood. A woman does not need to alienate her sexuality to be assertive, nor must she be a one-dimensional sex object. She can be allowed to express her sexuality, her body, and her own life simultaneously. In these texts, the Black woman is constructed, through this seeming contradiction, as being able to assert the pursuit of pleasure without sacrificing her humanity.

Returning the Gaze: Sexuality on a Woman's Terms

An interesting manifestation of the phenomenon of contradiction and ambivalence is the pattern of a reversal and returning of the gaze. A critical mass of videos feature men as objects of women's desire, where men's bodies are the center of the camera's gaze. What also occurs in these videos is a reversing of traditional gender roles in which men are objectified. Simultaneously, women remain the object of the camera's gaze as well. In *Swing My Way,* KP and Envyi pursue a male love interest in a club. In *You're Making Me High,* Toni Braxton and actresses Erika Alexander, Vivica Fox, and Tisha Campbell rate male visitors on a numerical scale as they appear in an elevator, while Toni's *Unbreak My Heart* features Black male supermodel Tyson Beckford. TLC (group members T-Boz, Left Eye, and Chilli) are the only women players (and the only fully clothed individuals) in a sexy game of strip poker in *Red Light Special,* and Janet Jackson's *Love Will Never Do Without You* centers the well-chiseled Black body of Djamon Hounsou and the buffed white body of actor Antonio Sabato Jr. alongside her own washboard abs. What all of these videos have in common is the construction of the male body, and particularly the Black male body, as the object of Black female pleasure. The male body is not merely looked at; rather, it is actively pursued. These women clearly and unequivocally express what they want, how and when they want it, and that they frequently get it.

What results is a space where the erotic can become articulated on a woman's terms. When videos featuring themes of sexual desire and fulfillment were coded, signifiers of mutual sexual fulfillment predominated, and women's sexual fulfillment was more often portrayed than for men. Although women were usually visually constructed as the source of male pleasure, when issues of sexual pleasure were articulated either in the lyrical or visual text, or both, the importance of female sexual desire became key. This construction of a sphere of erotic agency does not simply symbolize the subjectivity of the individual Black woman but also results in the construction of agency at the social and cultural level. It results in a space for an articulation of themes of freedom and liberty.

A long-standing theme in Black popular culture and the African American performance tradition has been the connection and interrelatedness of themes of sexuality to those of freedom (Davis 1998; Gilroy 1993). Angela Davis (1998) cites Audre Lorde's theory of "The Erotic as Power" in describing the ways in which the lyrics and performances of Black women artists included associations of sexuality as freedom and social commentary. In describing Billie Holliday's performance of "Some Other Spring," Davis elucidates how Holliday reappropriated the concept of love and sexual desire to symbolize liberty and autonomy:

> In a more complex racial and cultural context, she was able to carry on a tradition established by the blues women and blues men who were her predecessors: the tradition of representing love and sexuality as both concrete daily experience and as coded yearning for social liberation. (1998, 173)

Within the context of racial and sexual oppression and marginalization, love and sexuality have come to signify not only interpersonal relationships but also Black women's struggles for liberation and freedom at a broader level.

The Indeterminate Gaze

The address and gaze in these videos were frequently indeterminate. It was difficult to ascertain where the camera's gaze was intended to originate and to whom the video images and narrative were addressed. While clearly not ungendered, the gaze and address were frequently also neither male nor female. Both the male and female audience member or viewer appears to be constructed within these texts. The camera objectifies the Black female body in a traditional manner, while the lyrics of the song are addressed to a male subject. However, it becomes apparent that men are not the only intended audience. There appears to be a space constructed within the text that allows for Black women viewers to place themselves as subjects of the text, of the narrative.

A mélange of visual and aural strategies contribute to the construction of this indeterminate gaze. In these videos, the camera positioning, artist performance, and narrative structure are combined with visual omniscience. In addition, an indeterminate point of view and frequently non-gender-specific song lyrics contribute to the possibility of a multigendered and even ungendered gaze within music video texts. The Black female performers are not just looking at and talking to men but looking at and speaking with women as well. The unspecified and omniscient point of view constructed by camera positioning supports this by allowing both men and women to see themselves as subjects of the song and video.

The most compelling examples of this phenomenon occur in videos by the group En Vogue. In *Giving Him Something,* a remake of the Aretha Franklin R&B classic, En Vogue performs in a club for an all-male audience. They move seductively, gyrate their hips, and sing provocatively of "giving him something he can feel so he knows my love is real." The men in the audience are responding viscerally, biting their knuckles, and swooning. This scenario is interesting because while the group members are clearly objectified on stage and are explicitly sexualized, it is clear that they are gaining pleasure reciprocally along with a certain level of power over these men who are virtually losing control of their faculties as a result of their performance. Second, the men in the audience are extremely attractive themselves and are the objects of the camera's gaze. What is important here is that not only are men gaining pleasure from viewing the video, but women, as the viewers, are as well. This is not a mere role reversal but an example of an articulation of mutual pleasure and enjoyment. The Black woman is the agent of her own pleasure as well as the vehicle for the fulfillment of the man's desire. She is not just the object but also becomes the subject. As in the gaze reversal videos discussed above, not only does she give sexual pleasure, she also pursues, receives, and accepts it.

Informed by the context of the gender politics of Black male and female relationships, this construction of the unfixed, multiple gaze serves to level the sexual playing field. En Vogue, Toni Braxton, and TLC are not simply on display for men (although they surely are); their videos also place men on display for them and their fellow women viewers. In addition, and significantly, the simultaneous existence of their sexuality and independence contests inequality in man-woman relationships. As a result, instead of being the object of exploitation, the Black woman performer is able to construct a subject position for herself and her women viewers. While this is not articulated as a complete role reversal, which would ostensibly alienate male audiences, it is instead expressed as a mutual pursuit of sexual pleasure and satisfaction.

CONCLUSION

Despite the potentially limiting aspects of the frequently contradictory and stereotypical themes in music videos, I demonstrated that a more nuanced and complex depiction of Black womanhood emerges in the representations of Black woman performers.

My findings support and enhance the current literature in Black feminist theory. Whereas in *Black Feminist Thought* Hill Collins (1991a) demonstrated how the controlling images of Black womanhood are disseminated and legitimized through social institutions, my study extends her notion by showing how popular entertainment serves as a space for the proliferation of these controlling images. Hill Collins (1991a, 1991b) described the ways that Black women have countered these hegemonic notions of Black femininity through their culture, focusing on literature and performance in the Blues tradition. I show how Black women also are able to articulate other key themes of self-valuation, self-determination, and a critique of the interlocking nature of oppression. The themes of returning the erotic gaze and reappropriating the Black female body add an additional dimension to Black feminist theory by showing how Black women may use the sphere of culture to reclaim and revise the controlling images, specifically "the Jezebel," to express sexual subjectivity.

Of course, the conclusions drawn as a result of a textual content analysis of music videos are necessarily limited by the absence of inquiry into the production and reception of music videos and by the lack of a more comprehensive survey of the cultural landscape in which they exist. As a result, this study is not a complete analysis of the social context of Black female representation in music videos, and further investigation into Black women's reception and interpretation of music videos, as well as their role as cultural producers in the entertainment industry, is recommended.

REFERENCES

Arnett Ferguson, Ann. 2000. *Bad boys: Public schools in the making of masculinity.* Ann Arbor: University of Michigan Press.

Aufderheide, Pat. 1986. Music videos: The look of the sound. *Journal of Communication* 36:58–77.

Carby, Hazel V. 1986. It jus be's dat way sometime: The sexual politics of women's blues. *Radical America* 20:9–22.

Cash, Thomas F., and Patricia E. Henry. 1995. Women's body images: The results of a national survey in the U.S.A. *Sex Roles* 33:19–28.

Davis, Angela Yvonne. 1998. *Blues legacies and Black feminism: Gertrude "Ma" Rainey, Bessie Smith, and Billie Holiday.* New York: Pantheon Books.

Delano Brown, Jane, and Kenneth Campbell. 1986. Race and gender in music videos: The same beat but a different drummer. *Journal of Communication* 36:93–106.

Dines, Gail, and Jean Humez. 1995. *Gender, race and class in media.* Thousand Oaks, CA: Sage.

Flynn, Kristin, and Marian Fitzgibbon. 1996. Body image ideals of low-income African American mothers and their preadolescent daughters. *Journal of Youth and Adolescence* 25:615–30.

Frith, Simon, Andrew Goodwin, and Lawrence Grossberg. 1993. *Sound and vision: The music video reader.* New York: Routledge.

George, Nelson. 1998. *Hip hop America.* New York: Viking.

Gilroy, Paul. 1993. *The Black atlantic: Modernity and double consciousness.* Cambridge, MA: Harvard University Press.

Goodall, Nataki. 1994. Depend on myself: T.L.C. and the evolution of Black female rap. *Journal of Negro History* 79:85–94.

Harris, Shanette M. 1994. Racial differences in predictors of college women's body image attitudes. *Women & Health* 21:89–104.

Hill Collins, Patricia. 1991a. *Black feminist thought: Knowledge, consciousness and the politics of empowerment.* New York: Routledge.

———. 1991b. Learning from the outsider within: The sociological significance of Black feminist thought. In *Beyond methodology: Feminist scholarship as lived research,* edited by Mary Margaret Fonow and Judith A. Cook. Bloomington and Indianapolis: Indiana University Press.

hooks, bell. 1992. *Black looks: Race and representation.* Boston: South End.

Hurley, Jennifer M. 1994. Music video and the construction of gendered subjectivity (or how being a music video junkie turned me into a feminist). *Popular Music* 13:326–38.

Kaplan, E. Ann. 1987. *Rocking around the clock: Music television, postmodernism and consumer culture.* New York: Methuen.

Lewis, Lisa. 1990. *Gender politics and MTV.* Philadelphia: Temple University Press.

Lindlof, Thomas R. 1995. *Qualitative communication research methods.* Thousand Oaks, CA: Sage.

McRobbie, Angela. 1991. *Feminism and youth culture: From "Jackie" to "just seventeen."* Boston: Unwin Hyman.

———. 1993. Shut up and dance: Youth culture and changing modes of femininity. *Cultural Studies* 7 (3): 46.

———. 1997. *Back to reality? Social experience and cultural studies.* Manchester, UK, and New York: Manchester University Press.

McRobbie, Angela, and Mica Nava. 1984. *Gender and generation.* London: Macmillan.

Molloy, Beth L., and Sharon D. Hertzberger. 1998. Body image and self-esteem: A comparison of African-American and Caucasian women. *Sex Roles* 38:631–43.

Morgan. 1999. *When chickenheads come home to roost: My life as a hip-hop feminist.* New York: Simon & Schuster.

Patillo-McCoy, Mary. 1999. *Black picket fences: Privilege and peril among the Black middle class.* Chicago: University of Chicago Press.

Perkins, William Eric. 1996. *Droppin' science: Critical essays on rap music and hip hop culture.* Philadelphia: Temple University Press.

Peterson-Lewis, Sonja, and Shirley A. Chennault. 1986. Black artist's music videos: Three success strategies. *Journal of Communication* 1:107–14.

Roberts, Robin. 1991. Music videos, performance and resistance: Feminist rappers. *Journal of Popular Culture* 25:141–42.

———. 1994. Ladies first: Queen Latifah's Afrocentric feminist music video. *African American Review* 28:245–67.

Rose, Tricia. 1991. Never trust a big butt and a smile. *Camera Obscura* 23:9.

———. 1994. *Black noise: Rap music and Black culture in contemporary America.* Hanover, NH: Wesleyan University Press, University Press of New England.

Stockbridge, Sally. 1987. Music video: Questions of performance, pleasure and address. *Continuum: The Australian Journal of Media and Culture* 1(2). [cited 2 April 1997]. Available from www.mcc.murdoch.edu.au/readingroom/1.2/stockbridge.html.

Strauss, Anselm. 1987. *Qualitative analysis for social scientists.* Cambridge, UK, and New York: Cambridge University Press.

Vincent, Richard C. 1989. Clio's consciousness raised? Portrayal of women in rock videos re-examined. *Journalism Quarterly* 66:155–60.

Vincent, Richard, Dennis K. Davis, and Lilly Ann Boruszkowski. 1987. Sexism on MTV: The portrayal of women in rock videos. *Journalism Quarterly* 64:750–55, 941.

Watkins, S. Craig. 1998. *Representing: Hip hop culture and the production of Black cinema.* Chicago: University of Chicago Press.

13

THE SPECTACULAR CONSUMPTION OF "TRUE" AFRICAN AMERICAN CULTURE

"Whassup" with the Budweiser Guys?

Eric King Watts
Mark P. Orbe

Spectacular consumption is a process through which the relations among cultural forms, the culture industry, and the lived experiences of persons are shaped by public consumption. This essay examines how the spectacular consumption of "Whassup?!" Budweiser advertising is constitutive of white American ambivalence toward "authentic" blackness. The essay argues that Budweiser's hottest ad campaign benefits from a tension between the depiction of "universal" values and the simultaneous representation of distinctive culture. The illustration of blackness as sameness and blackness as otherness arises out of conflicted attitudes toward black culture. Thus, Budweiser's strategic attempts to regulate and administer "authentic" blackness as a market value also reproduce this ambivalence. Furthermore, as an object of spectacular consumption, the meaning of "authentic" black life and culture is partly generative of mediated and mass marketed images.

Charles Stone, III, must have felt as though he had gone to sleep and awoken in Oz. It was three short years ago that he captured on film candid moments among three of his friends, edited them into an engrossing and visually stunning short film called "True," and used it as a video resumé. Stone was "floored" when Anheuser-Busch asked him to translate his film into a 60-second commercial spot for Budweiser beer (McCarthy, 2000, p. 8B). Stone was equally surprised when, out of respect for "realism," he was allowed to cast those same friends from the short film for the commercial. It must have seemed even more surreal to be in Cannes during the summer of 2000 to accept the advertising world's version of the "Oscar," the Grand Prix and Golden Lion, and to hear his friends' greeting, now the world's most famous catchphrase, bouncing off café walls and rippling along the beaches— "Whassup?!" It must have been bizarre to witness the usually stodgy Cannes judges joyfully exchanging the greeting in international accents—especially since the advertising

Reprinted from Eric King Watts and Mark P. Orbe, "The Spectacular Consumption of 'True' African American Culture: 'Whassup' with the Budweiser Guys?" *Critical Studies in Media Communication* 19, no. 1 (March 2002): 1–20.

elite admits to a cultivated distaste for the popular (McCarthy, 2000). This admission, however, didn't hurt the market value of the Budweiser "True" commercials one bit. To understand why this is so, one must explore the nature of spectacular consumption.

Let us begin our journey by considering this odd commentary offered up by *Advertising Age*'s ad review staff after Stone's commercial aired during the 2000 Superbowl: "A bunch of friends, all black, greet each other with exaggerated 'Wuzuppppppppp?' salutations that sound like retching. [Our] staff, the single whitest enclave outside of Latvia, doesn't quite get it but suspects it is very funny . . . " (Garfield, 2000b, p. 4). But, what's so mysterious? These guys simply greet each other—over and over—with what has been described as a "verbal high-five" (Farhi, 2000, p. C1). Also of interest is the fact that *USA Today*'s Admeter rated the commercial as the Superbowl's most popular; and so let us turn the question on its axis: if *Advertising Age* is correct and the humor is baffling, why is it so popular? After all, the ad is about four friends sitting around doing "nothin'[but] watching the game, having a Bud"? How is it that a series of commercials about four African American friends can be simultaneously "pretty out there," incomprehensible, and yet enjoy such massive appeal so as to become Budweiser's hottest ad campaign ever? (Adande, 2000, p. D1).

The pop culture craze associated with the "Whassup?!" guys leaves some observers dumbfounded and amazed. But others chalk up the frenzy to either the universality of male bonding or to white America's continued fascination with black expression. On the one hand, the commercials' appeal is associated with these ads' depiction of a classic and commonly inarticulate male-bonding ritual. From this perspective, the secret to their popularity lies in their utter *familiarity.* On the other hand, their appeal is linked to the notion that the ads are "weird," "oddball," "strange," "funky," and "True": that is, "authentically" black. In other words, their appeal is also predicated upon their *unfamiliarity.*

Due to its parsimony, this dichotomy between the universal and the distinctive is misleading. If we perceive the ads as "universal" expressions of masculine communal norms, they speak in a single, unproblematic voice. They say, in essence, "I love you, man!" This time, the men just *happen* to be black. Thus, through a projection of "positive realism" (Cassidy & Katula, 1995), the "Whassup?!" ads testify to increased diversity in television commercials and to African American male affection. Understood in this manner, the American ideal of human universalism is affirmed through a display of black fraternal care made familiar. Indeed, according to David English, an Anheuser-Busch vice-president, the "universal" appeal of the short film allowed him to look "past the color of the guys to the situation of guys being guys, and the communication between friends" (Heller, 2000, p. 11). Hence, in attempts to explain the soaring market value of these ads, Anheuser-Busch spokespersons often reference their "universality"—that is, their colorlessness. But, since the ads are also described as "cool" and "edgy," and the "Whassup?!" guys are widely perceived as the hippest group of friends on TV, they signify a pleasure principle orienting white consumption of blackness (hooks, 1992). And so, it has occurred to us that this dichotomy between the universal and the distinctive conceals a strategy. That is, references to the ads' "universal" qualities obscure the way in which blackness can be made to behave in accordance with the American ideology of universalism. By encouraging viewers to "celebrate" blackness conceived in terms of *sameness,* the ad campaign deflects attention away from the ways in which blackness as *otherness* is annexed and appropriated as commodity and hides from view the fact that

American culture exhibits a profound *ambivalence* toward "authentic" blackness (Entman & Rojecki, 2000).

This essay seeks to explore this ambivalence as it is reproduced and displayed through Budweiser's "Whassup?!" ad campaign. We argue that the ad campaign constitutes and administers cultural "authenticity" as a market value. From the perspective of spectacular consumption, the intensity of the pleasure of consuming the other is directly (and para-doxically) related to the replication and magnification of "authentic" difference. Moreover, the logic of spectacular consumption compels us to pay attention to how the act of con-sumption transforms the relation between the consumer and the consumed. We contend that as the market economy seeks to regulate and integrate "authentic" difference, white American ambivalence toward blackness is paradoxically both assuaged by its "universal-ity" and heightened by its distinctiveness. This conflicted set of impulses and feelings can be witnessed in the commercials, disclosed in corporate strategy, and observed in focus group interviews. Hence, this essay proceeds in three stages: first, we explicate what we mean by spectacular consumption, relating it to the commodification of the "Whassup?!" guys. Second, we provide an interpretation of the original commercial so as to show how white American ambivalence concerning race is inscribed in the ad. Third, we discuss the results of focus group interviews that were used to gain insight into "consumer" percep-tions of the ads. We conclude with some observations about the on-going development of the "Whassup" line of commercials and the racial ambivalence they promote.

SPECTACULAR CONSUMPTION AND THE REPRODUCTION OF THE "AUTHENTIC"

Treating the spectacle as a rhetorical construction, David E. Procter focuses his critical attention on how a spectacle as an "event" can be called forth by rhetors seeking to build community (1990, p. 118). Drawing from the work of Murray Edelman, Thomas B. Farrell and others, Procter posits the concept of a "dynamic spectacle" as requiring "a fusion of material event with the symbolic construction of that event and with audience needs" (1990, p. 119). From this perspective, the spectacle is a choreographed happening like a celebra-tion or memorial that brings together the interpretive materials for rhetorical *praxis*. As Procter's analysis demonstrates, the critic is charged with the task of determining how rhetoric transformed the material event into a spectacle and how the spectacle builds com-munity. Our understanding of spectacle both converges with and diverges from this account. We share Procter's concern with the constructed nature of spectacle and the capacity of interested persons to shape it. In particular, we find useful Procter's understanding of spec-tacle as a mediated phenomenon that transforms persons' lived reality. However, we do not conceive of spectacle as an event or as a happening, with a clearly defined beginning, mid-dle, and an end; here, the spectacle is a *condition*—a characteristic of our collective being. It must, therefore, be understood ontologically as well as rhetorically.

Guy Debord (1983), in *Society of the Spectacle,* explains that as social systems shift from industrial to post-industrial economies they also undergo ontological change. Rather than being organized around the exchange of goods based upon actual use values, the spec-tacle establishes mass consumption as a way of life. When sign value replaces use value as the foundation of being in this fashion, human beings need no longer be concerned with discovering the essence of *Dasein,* for the "true" nature of one's being is up for grabs; it can be fabricated through *appearances* (Best & Kellner, 1997; Ewen, 1988). In the society of the spectacle, even facets of one's very body can be manufactured in keeping with the latest trend. Importantly, as Jean Baudrillard (1984) has forewarned, a society's capacity to replicate and manipulate forms of public culture forces upon all of us a virtual supersedure of the life world by the signifiers that previously represented it. By destabilizing the ways through which we ascribe meaning and value to our experiences, the spectacle mediates our understanding of the world through a distribution of commercialized signs. Although this process may not be conspiratorial (Hall, 1995), it is hardly random; the economics of the spectacle lead to the orchestration of meaning and value so as to realize the "moment when the commodity has attained the total occupation of social life" (Debord, 1983, p. 13). As the spectacle structures both work and play, diverse aspects of life are made significant inasmuch as they can be made marketable. Thus, these processes magnify—that is, make spectacular—previously private worlds and the persons who inhabit them.

Spectacular consumption is, thus, structured in a fashion different from traditional spectacle; its rhetorics respond to cultural variables in diverse patterns oriented by the logic of sign value. A key rhetorical resource in the economy of spectacular consumption, then, is the paradoxical tension between the "different" and the widely available. On the one hand, the pleasure of consuming otherness is advanced by the Other's uniqueness. On the other hand, in a mass consumer culture, commodity value rises to a sufficient level only when the Other undergoes massive replication: "In a hyperreal culture, things are conceived from the point of view of *reproducibility,* as we come to think something is *real* only insofar as it exists as a serialized commodity, as able to be bought and sold, as able to be made into a novel or a movie" (Best & Kellner, 1997, p. 102, emphasis added). The consuming rhetoric of the spectacle thus promotes a contradiction as it seeks strategically to reproduce on a massive scale the singularity associated with the "authentic." And yet these attempts persist because the market value of such reproductions escalates as long as the "aura" of "authenticity" can be maintained (Benjamin, 1984).

Clearly, cultural difference provides a particularly valuable resource for spectacular consumption. The differences found among cultures provide a resource of the new and the unfamiliar that is particularly valuable because those differences can be projected as "authentic" even as they are commercially manufactured. In the case of the Budweiser ads, public consumption of the ads triggers an overvaluation and fabrication of black bodies in living spaces represented as "real life." Spectacular consumption, then, describes the process by which the material and symbolic relations among the culture industry, the life worlds of persons, and the ontological status of cultural forms are transformed in terms generated by public consumption (Watts, 1997).

The successful masking of the fact that the "Whassup?!" guys are "ontologically eroded" as cultural forms (Best & Kellner, 1997, p. 102), thus, extends beyond the texts of the ads themselves to a series of related texts that together constitute the on-going production of spectacle. The "aura" of the "True" ads is itself replicated through corporate strategy linking public opinion, corporate discourse, and testimony from the "Whassup?!" guys themselves. Our understanding of "reality" is mediated through a matrix of imagery in the spectacle.

One key dimension of these appeals is the way the "universal" dimensions of the commercials enhance the "aura" of "authenticity" by making explicit claims to "real life." "Whassup?!" is called a "common guy greeting," (Farhi, 2000, p. C1) and "Whassup?!"

enthusiasts identify how the ads are said to reflect "the essence of what [men] do on Sunday afternoons" (Adande, 2000, p. D1). According to Bob Scarpelli, the creative director of the advertising agency responsible for the campaign, this doing nothing is labeled a "common experience" that "resonate[s]" because men can say, "'That's me and my buddies.'" Although there is a gender gap with the ads, and men like them more, many women nonetheless chime in by remarking "'That's my husband, my boyfriend or my brother'" (McCarthy, 2000a, p. 3B). Anheuser-Busch frequently cites marketing research that explains the ads' "crossover appeal" in terms of "universal" friendship and "about being with your buddies" (McCarthy, 2000d, p. 6B).

Discussing the fact that the target audience for this campaign was originally composed of "Everymen" (Garfield, 2000a, p. 2), meaning mostly white men, "Whassup?!" ad promoters like Anheuser-Busch V.P. Bob Lachky refer to focus group reviews where "predominately Anglo" crowds report that each of the ads "'is a colorless thing. . . . '" (Adande, 2000, p. D1). Similarly, after the first of the ads garnered the Cannes top prize, *Advertising Age* explained the accolade by saying that "America saw [the ad] not as an inside-black-culture joke but [as] a universal expression of eloquent male inarticulateness" (Garfield, 2000a, p. 2). The point that we are making here is that these statements posit as prima facie evidence for the existence of a color-blind society the fact that white folks *claim* identification with black (mediated) experiences. This claim seems reasonable and perhaps even promising when one understands that it is premised upon the captivating depiction of black male affection and camaraderie among real life friends. Commenting in the *Washington Post,* one observer writes that the ads "provide a glimpse into a private world of four men at leisure. The joy each man expresses in greeting and being greeted by his longtime friends is infectious, universal and, it seems, genuine" (Farhi, 2000, p. C2). This display is important given the fact that television advertising rarely shows black affection (Entman & Rojecki, 2000; hooks, 1992).

In spectacular consumption the linkages among the spheres of social life, the culture industry, and public consumption allow dynamic discursive and pragmatic interplays of influence; corporate appeals to universalism thus encourage backing from the "Whassup?!" guys as they recount their real life affections for an insatiable media. For example, Charles Stone has repeatedly testified to the ads' "universal message of male bonding" (McCarthy, 2000b, p. 2B) by describing how the whole thing got started: "'That's really how we talk to each other. We used to call each other on the phone 15 years ago, during our college years, and that was our greeting. People say it seems real to them. It *is* real'" (Farhi, 2000, p. C2, emphasis added). "'It really wasn't acting,'" remarks Paul Williams, the "Whassup?!" guy with the big hair. "'It was us being us'" (Adande, 2000, p. 2). Scott Brooks, who plays and is "Dookie" in the ads, agrees: "You can't fake that kind of chemistry,'" he remarked during a promotional tour in St. Louis. "We're really friends'" (McCarthy, 2000d, p. 7B). It is important to acknowledge that these messages arise out of bona fide and caring relationships among the men.

This appeal to a putatively universal experience of male bonding is a conflicted one, however, because it is made through black men in a white dominated culture, wherein the "universal" has long been portrayed in terms of whiteness. Thus, it is the very assertion of the "Whassup?!" crew inhabiting an "authentic" (black) life world that helps warrant the ads' presumed transcendence of blackness for white viewers. We do not want nor need to become involved in a debate over whether Western humanism actually allows for such transcendence. We mean only to demonstrate that there exists a discursive tension between appeals to colorlessness and appeals to black cultural distinctiveness. This discursive stress becomes most acute as we explore the contours and shapes of cultural "authenticity." Anheuser-Busch now boasts that the ads enjoy mass appeal by virtue of their essential colorlessness; it did not, however, begin conceiving of the ads with this virtue in mind. Originally, Anheuser-Busch wanted a "multicultural cast" (Farhi, 2000, p. C1). This sort of marketing strategy has rightly been understood as *color-conscious* because it arises out of a concern that an all-black cast would alienate predominately white audiences (Entman & Rojecki, 2000; Jhally, 1995). Additionally, Stone's argument about casting his friends was assented to by Anheuser-Busch because its ad agency, DDB World Wide, was equally concerned with keeping it "real." Similarly, early in the campaign's genesis, Stone thought that the conservative tendencies of the DDB would be placated if he altered the tagline, "True," to read "Right." A vice president of Anheuser-Busch asked that he change it back to the more desirable "slang" term saying that " 'True is cool' " (McCarthy, 2000c, p. 9B).

Hence we can see that despite the "universality" of the "Whassup?!" guys life world, Anheuser-Busch and its ad agency paid close attention to how black culture should be shaped for consumption. The many media references to how "Whassup?!" is now the "coolest way to say hello" (McCarthy, 2000d, p. 6B) and the "hip greeting of choice" (McCarthy, 2000c, p. 8B) testify to the fact that African American cultural forms are still the standard bearer of pop cultural fashion. Elijah Anderson argues that the commercials represent something "very specific to black people" (in Farhi, 2000, p. C3). Similarly, Michael Dyson believes that they convey the notion that "black vernacular" can be mass marketed without being white washed (in Heller, 2000, p. 11). Indeed, "authentic" blackness is *more* valuable to spectacular consumption than representations of blackness as sameness precisely *because* it is more anxiety producing.

The energy created within the interstices of spectacular consumption arises in part out of the desire for white folk to reconstitute their identities through acts of black consumption (hooks, 1992). To this end, the 1990s seemed to have normalized the market appropriation of black styles. " 'When they write the history of popular culture in the 20th century,' " comments MTV's Chris Connelly, " 'they can sum it up in one sentence which is, white kids wanting to be as cool as black kids' " (in Graham, 2000, p. D9.) This desire is undeniable, but as hooks so perceptively points out, white folk do not want to *become* black (1992). The discursive spaces of white privilege must be maintained even as the consumption of blackness intensifies. Spectacular consumption as a critical lens brings into focus how the energy from this dialectic is harnessed by the replication of specific features of the "authentic."

Budweiser ad executives want the funkiness and edginess of the "Whassup?!" campaign to become characteristics associated with Budweiser. The strategy is premised on the logic that Bud is a "colloquial beer" and fits in with the signs of the Other (Farhi, 2000, p. C2). There are corporate and legal means to enable such identification. For example, Anheuser-Busch has trademarked the term "Whassup?!" for its exclusive market use (McGuire, 2000). Moreover, unlike the African American life world out of which it comes, where its intonation and its spelling vary among its particular usages, Budweiser has suggested a proper pronunciation for "Whassup?!" and has copyrighted an "official spelling . . . w-h-a-s-s-u-p, although there's an optional p on the end" (Adande, 2000, p. 2). These technical measures are significant, but they cannot overcome a fundamental problem with consumption. That is, the "image-system of the marketplace reflects our desire and dreams, yet we have only the pleasure of the images to sustain us in our actual experience with goods" (Jhally, 1995, p. 80). This is so if we conceive of Budweiser beer as the good being consumed. This is not the case in spectacular consumption, however, where the "Whassup?!" guys themselves constitute the product. "And no one is better at making a complete, integrated promotional effort than Anheuser-Busch; they've gotten every ounce of publicity out of this that can be gotten" (McGuire, 2000, p. El).

During a 10-day promotional tour during the summer of 2000, Scott Brooks, Paul Williams, and Fred Thomas completed their transformations from product spokespersons to products—the "Whassup?!" guys. Bouncing from one Budweiser-sponsored media event to another, one reporter noted a pattern in the form of a question: "how many times do they estimate that they stick their tongues out in a given promotional day?" (McGuire, 2000, p. El). This question can be modified and multiplied to illuminate the operations of hyperreality. How often does one have to repeat one's background and display on cue one's genuine affection for the other guys to maintain the "aura"? How can such an "aura" even be cultivated through scripted "spontaneity"? How will the "Whassup?!" guys stay "True" to black expression given the contention made by Russell Rickford of Drexel University that "once a phrase has become mainstream, black folks stop using it and go on to something else"? (McGuire, 2000, p. El). Although the ad campaign may have already reached its saturation point, spectacular consumption compels the continued replication of value and handsomely rewards its replicants. Charles Stone, III, is now a hot directing commodity who has a movie deal, a contract with Anheuser-Busch for more commercials, and who gets meetings with actors like Dustin Hoffman. There is also a lot of talk about a possible sitcom or movie deal for the friends. At any rate, their "Q-rating," a TV recognizability quotient, is so high that Brooks, once a bouncer in Philadelphia, was forced to quit his job. Also, Williams, a typically out-of-work actor, has been able to sift through scripts and pay his rent for an entire year (McGuire, 2000, p. E2).

This media buzz translates into the sort of "talk value" (McCarthy, 2000b, p. 2B) that is partly responsible for convincing the Cannes officials to put aside their misgivings concerning the ads' popularity in the face of the "Whassup?!" guys' spectacularity (Garfield, 2000a). In other words, the public consumption of the ads and the actors is constitutive of a commitment to replicating image value. This commitment compels industry brokers like the Cannes folks to shift their values away from rewarding artistic accomplishment in advertising and toward recognizing ads "that work," ads that sustain spectacular consumption (McCarthy, 2000b, p. 2B). It also helps generate conflicted discursive performances that, through a critical reading of the first "True" ad, further reveal how white ambivalence helps mold public displays of "authentic" blackness.

"WATCHING THE GAME, HAVING A BUD": AN EXPLORATION OF COMPETING STRATEGIES AND VISIONS OF "TRUE" CONSUMPTION

The Budweiser "True" commercial offers a setting in which gender and cultural performances are conditioned by sports and spectatorship; "masculinity" and "blackness" emerge as key themes in this world where men lounge in front of televisions and make seemingly inconsequential conversation. Although the repose of these men is casual, even languid, there is quite a bit of action going on. This is so despite the fact that Stone is "laid back" on the couch transfixed by the game on TV; he and his friends appear in this ad as both observers and players of a spectacular "game." As actors in a commercial the fact that they are being watched cannot be denied, but their performances display a heightened sense of awareness of the politics and character of the white (consumptive) gaze. And so, the ad testifies to competing visions; the "True" commercial demonstrates a form of self-reflexivity that focuses our attention on how the "Whassup?!" guys play a game in which they recognize (that is, see) the ways that their "play" is overvalued as "authentic" cultural performance. The significance of these competing visions comes into view as we integrate a textual analysis with a critical lens that takes into consideration how spectacular consumption is constitutive of images that mediate "real life" social relations. The "True" ad emerges as a conflicted statement on how cultural commodities in the spectacle are made self-conscious—that is, made aware of how their appearance can maximize their market potential. In order to keep track of all of this seeing and being seen, let's begin with the opening scene.

Charles Stone sets the mood and tone for the first act of this three-part drama. Clutching a beer bottle and stretching out on a sofa he stares vacantly into the lights of a TV; we faintly hear the color commentary of a game. Unlike advertisements where the sports fanatic is caught up in the ecstasy and agony of the sporting event, Stone is nearly catatonic, not invested in the sporting event, but tuned in nevertheless to the ritualistic character of masculine spectatorship. Put simply, Stone seems nearly perfect as the Sunday afternoon "couch potato."

The telephone rings. Stone, without diverting his gaze, answers the phone: "Hello."

The camera cuts to Paul Williams who signals for us both a departure from how TV advertising depicts conventional male-bonding rituals oriented around sports spectatorship and an *intensification* of the mood and tone established by Stone. As we have already noted, Williams was not initially considered for his own part in the ad because Stone was told to find actors to make up an ethnic rainbow. Since such a cast would have been "diverse," the cast would not only collectively signify the ideal of American integration but it would also allow white viewers to "identify with fellow whites, and resonate to their on-screen relationships with each other" (Entman & Rojecki, 2000, p. 167). Williams is, therefore, a violation of this ad strategy precisely because his speech and his look mark him as other in a world of mainstream marketing. Compared to Stone's conservative style, Williams's Afro signifies "exoticism." On the other hand, Williams wholly identifies with Stone's tone and mood, endorsing a performance that testifies both to the timelessness of the ritual and the character of their relationship. Williams and Stone are watching the same game and having the same beer; their shared interest in the game does not testify to its importance, but rather it reinforces the significance of *being there for one another* during the game. Male bonding transmutes into black male affection as Williams and Stone demonstrate their interpersonal comfort and communal linguistic styles.

> **WILLIAMS:** "Ay, who, whassup?"
> **STONE:** "Nothin', B, watchin' the game, havin' a Bud. Whassup wit'chu?"
> **WILLIAMS:** "Nothin', watchin' the game, havin' a Bud."
> **STONE:** "True, true."

This dialogue punctuates the episode, signaling its end, and announces the following act. Fred Thomas enters the scene and greets Stone exuberantly. "Whassup?!" With flaring nostrils and wagging tongue, Stone mirrors Thomas's performance. Williams asks Stone, "yo, who's that" and Stone directs Thomas to "yo, pick up the phone." Williams, Thomas, and Stone share a joyful and comical verbal hug that ripples outward and embraces Scott "Dookie" Brooks. Stone's editing creates a visual montage of gleeful faces and a kind of musical tribute to the group expression as each man's voice contributes to a shrilling chorus. As a display of black masculine affection, the scene represents brotherly responsibility. As Williams asks about Thomas and as Thomas wonders "where's Dookie?," viewers bear witness to black men acknowledging their need and care for the well-being of other black men.

This mutual affection is nonetheless potentially troubling to white audience members. Ever since the importation of African slaves, black solidarity has been constituted as a threat to white power. Rather than being a detriment to white readings of the commercial, however, this well-spring of angst provides a potent commercial resource, specifically a resource for humor. At the heart of humor is the release of repression, the release of repressed hostility in particular (Gruner, 1997). As a corporate sign of control and regulation, "Whassup?!" thus signifies the comic relief of white angst.

It is precisely the affective display that is historically troubling to white consumption and most subject to being made pleasurable and docile by the operations of spectacular consumption (hooks, 1992; Madhubuti, 1990; West, 1994). During this second act, the greeting balloons into a full-blown caricature of itself and, thus, seems to fit within a tradition of clowning and buffoonery (Franklin, 2000). The "Whassup?!" guys play a role that is, in part, constitutive of white ambivalence toward "true" blackness. Entman and Rojecki (2000) argue that 21st century white attitudes find comfort in imagining racial comity because it affirms American ideals regarding our capacity to all get along. But racial comity can easily be turned into racial hostility if whites are confronted with portrayals of race that challenge the presumption of white privilege or articulate the presence of wide spread racism (Entman & Rojecki, 2000). Since the presumption of white privilege is tacitly maintained through the promotion of black fragmentation (Lusane, 1994; Allen, 1990), black community functions as a menace to white supremacy. And so, illustrations of black communalism are shaped at the outset so that the anxiety and fear aroused in white viewers can supercharge the consumption of black humor or black sex. Thus, the "aura" of "authenticity" that envelops the familial relations among the men functions like lightning in a bottle—a brilliant danger. White spectators have their fears initially triggered by "authentic" blackness, only to have them strategically vented by this self-parody of black community. Attuned in this way, we can now hear the nervous laughter of the *Advertising Age* staff that "doesn't quite get it but suspects [that is, *hopes*] it is very funny . . ." (Garfield, 2000, p. 4).

This comic display is, therefore, paradoxical. As a "play" in the game, it points to the impossibility of replicating black cultural "authenticity" even as it relies on its presumed aura. It gives the lie to claims of authenticity as the "Whassup?!" guys distort their real life expression—making it "untrue"—for the benefit of the white gaze. Rather than be "real" for a white audience, the "Whassup?!" guys are asked to play a game that is predicated on hyperreality and hyperbolic black acting. Moreover, since Scott Brooks has described the performance as "exaggerated," this play is understood as such by the "Whassup?!" guys themselves (Heller, 2000, p. 11). But this observation brings up another related insight. If the second act is a self-conscious play during the game of spectacular consumption, the other two acts (the third mirrors the first) can be understood as the "Whassup?!" guys attempt to remain "True." That is, they are representative of how the friends see themselves and a dramatization of their collective understanding of how one makes the "game" work for you. Indeed, Stone's script tells us as much.

In the first and third acts, Stone and Williams are concerned with their collective participation in a spectator ritual. The scenes are centered on the black masculine gaze and cool pose (Majors & Billson, 1992). Stone and Williams testify to the fact that they are not just objects under surveillance here, but rather they are engaged in subjective (subversive?) acts of observation and consumption. Specifically, they are *"watching* the game, *having* a Bud."* In the opening and closing acts of this commercial, the tagline "true" signifies the shared understanding of how to self-promote and shape-shift for the purposes of "having a Bud," of taking advantage of Budweiser's desire for (and fear of) their blackness and in the process, maximizing their own market value. The second act is a festive and troubling demonstration of just such a shared strategy, framed not by individualism, but communalism. The colorful exchange among the friends displays a joy that can still be seen and heard despite the deformations, contortions, and amplifications.

It is true that spectacular consumption *precedes* even the first act and therefore always already makes demands on the "Whassup?!" guys. From this perspective we can appreciate how previously private enclaves and persons can be colonized and transformed into sources for spectacular consumption. We should not be surprised that these operations convert and multiply "Whassup?!" into a series of commercialized signs that perhaps no longer say anything important concerning black culture but are nearly self-referential, standing for little more than their own market value. But the spectacular consumption of the "Whassup?!" guys brings up yet another concern. White imitation of black life alters the character of social relations among real folks. Not only is the appropriation of black styles profitable, the potential for racial hostility—a function of white ambivalence—is preserved and cultivated by stylish diversions (Kennedy, 2000).

Spectacular consumption functions as a capacitor for such ambivalence, seizing its energies and releasing them in planned microbursts directed at stimulating more consumption. White ambivalence toward blackness is, thus, replicated alongside consumable "blackness." And although this operation nears the character of *simulacra,* we can feel its effects in our everyday real world as black folk are told to "lighten up," or when one's refusal to "play the fool" provokes racial enmity. It may also be the case that "authentic" black affection emerges, however fleetingly, as an expression that is potentially redistributed among a wider circle of friends and communities as "True." But this is a question best left in abeyance until we explore how "real" folks consume these images.

FOCUS GROUP INSIGHTS:
DIVERSE PERSPECTIVES ON SIMILAR THEMES

Thus far, we have explicated how spectacular consumption provides insight into the commodification of the "Whassup?!" guys and have provided a textual analysis of the original commercial. Throughout these discussions, we have made reference to the various ways that the marketing potential of the commercials seems to be a function of the perceived "authenticity" of the "Whassup?!" guys. Consequently, we facilitated a number of focus group discussions to gain insight into one general research question: How are "Whassup?!" ads consumed by different viewers? As can be seen in the following section, accessing divergent perspectives in this manner proved invaluable in strengthening our current critical analysis. In order to gain insight into the various ways that television consumers interacted with the "Whassup?!" commercials, we conducted a series of discussions with undergraduate students at a large, Midwestern university.

Specifically, we drew from one 300-level communication class whose content focused on issues related to race and culture. A total of thirty-seven people were involved in this aspect of our analysis. These persons were diverse in terms of their race-ethnicity (17 African Americans, 11 European Americans, 3 Asian Americans, 3 Hispanic/Latino Americans, and 3 individuals who identify as biracial) and gender (24 women and 13 men). Thirty-six of the participants were 18 to 24 years of age.

Our focus group discussions included several steps. First, all thirty-seven participants were shown four of the "Whassup?!" commercials featuring the "Whassup?!" guys in different settings. Participants were then asked to write down their responses to a number of questions, including: what was your initial reaction to these commercials (either now or at an earlier time)?; is the reaction the same for all of the commercials, or do they vary from commercial to commercial?; and who do you think the target audience is for these commercials? Then, two spoofs of the "Whassup?!" commercials featuring "Superheroes" and "Grandmas" were shown. These spoofs were not produced by DDBO or Anheuser-Busch, but we thought they might help give depth to our understanding of audience responses to the advertisements. Again, participants were asked to record how, if at all, their perceptions of these commercials were different than the previous ones viewed. In addition, each person was asked to express their opinions about the apparent marketing strategy behind the series of "Whassup?!" ads.

During a subsequent session, the thirty-seven participants were randomly divided into seven small (5–6 person) groups to discuss their reactions to the commercials. Following these brief 10-minute discussions, a larger 30-minute discussion of all participants was facilitated in order to clarify and extend those insights that were included in the written responses. This larger discussion was unstructured in that participants were simply asked to share some of their perceptions of the commercials as discussed via their individual comments and the small group discussions.

Our thematic analysis of the written and oral comments provided by the focus group participants was guided by three criteria outlined by Owen (1984): repetition, recurrence, and forcefulness. As such, the texts generated via the written comments and larger group discussions were reviewed for preliminary themes. Subsequently, eight preliminary themes were reviewed until a smaller number of core themes emerged that we believe captured the essence of the participants' comments. Through this interpretative reduction process, three specific thematic insights that enhance our critical analysis of the "Whassup?!" guys were identified. Each of these is explicated in the remaining sections of this essay.

Relating to the "Experience"

Almost without exception, the participants found the "Whassup?!" ads to be highly creative, unique, and entertaining. In fact, bursts of audible laughter filled the room while the commercials were being shown. Initial written descriptions, as well as subsequent group discussions, displayed a general consensus that the "Whassup?!" guys had "hit a comedic nerve" with mass audiences. However, a deeper level of scrutiny in terms of why participants felt the ads were so funny reveals some interesting patterns.

Analysis of written responses provides insight into differences between non-African Americans and African Americans. Nearly every African American woman and man perceived the "Whassup?!" commercials as targeted at young African Americans in general, and young African American males in particular. Several commented specifically on the use of an all-black cast, while others pointed to the ways in which the ads featured "the common language of black men." Without question, African Americans responded favorably to the ads because of the "authentic" ways in which black culture was represented. The black students tended to conclude that most non-African Americans would not relate to the content of the commercials. One African American explained in no uncertain terms that:

> This ad, in particular, is [targeted] at young Black men. The reason [why I say this] is because of the language and the style of the commercial . . . these are not things that a man 35+ would do or phrases that a man 35+ would use. They are things that young Black men do.

What the African American participants did not anticipate, however, were the powerful ways in which non-African Americans also identified with the depiction of the "Whassup?!" guys. For example, only one European American commented on how the ad targeted the African American community:

> I've never seen these commercials before, but I've heard so much about them. I think that Budweiser is trying to appeal to the African American community because it has been known in the past as sort of a "hill-billy, ol' boy brew." These commercials bring BUD out of being just a "white man's beer" . . . Trust me, I used to cocktail waitress—it is!!!

It is significant that out of all of the European, Latino, and Asian American participants she was the *only* non-African American to perceive the "Whassup?!" guys as targeting the black community. Contrary to African American perceptions, nearly all other racial/ethnic group members perceived the ad as representative of male life experiences. Reflecting on our earlier discussion of how "authenticity" functions, it became apparent that non-African American men related to the images of "guys"—not necessarily "Whassup?!" guys—doing "guy things." One European American man shared that:

> [I] had seen the commercials before and found [them] highly comical because I could relate to the experience of having a beer and watching a game with my friends acting silly . . . The target audience of the commercial is clearly men in their early-late twenties.

By and large, non-African Americans focused on the "universal" nature of male bonding and sports. One Asian American male agreed that the target audience was "anyone from the ages of 18–30 who drink beer," but added, "yes, the 'what's up' guys are all black, but I don't think that blacks are the target audience because everyone loves those commercials." European American women were also quick to point out the lack of cultural specificity in the behaviors of the "Whassup?!" guys. The quotation below is representative of several similar comments.

> I had never seen those actual commercials but I had heard about them . . . all of my male friends acted like the men on the video a lot last year. My initial reaction is that it was just a bunch of burly men (weird) . . . Guys always have an inside joke or way of showing off to their buddies.

The contrast between how different racial/ethnic groups perceived the target audience of the "Whassup?!" commercials is of particular significance given Anheuser-Busch's explicit objective to create a campaign that would be appealing to predominately white audiences. How, then, was it also able to sell the "Whassup?!" guys to African American audiences who yearned for media displays of black culture? The basic principles related to spectacular consumption provide a schemata that makes available answers to this lingering question. As explicated in the next thematic section, we argue that marketing strategists are able, ironically, to negotiate such tensions by emphasizing the cultural "authenticity" of the "Whassup?!" guys.

(Re-)Emphasizing Cultural Authenticity

As stated earlier, responses to the initial "Whassup?!" ads were overwhelmingly positive. However, when participants were asked to comment on their perceptions of two spoof commercials, their reactions were quite varied and significantly different than those based on the initial ads. Specifically, many commented on how the ads "didn't make sense." "I really don't know what the intent of these two commercials were," shared one biracial woman. Some, but certainly not all, of the African American participants felt that the change in actors reflected a different target audience. This makes sense given that the general consensus was that the initial ads that featured the "Whassup?!" guys were targeted at young African Americans. Many didn't know how to perceive the spoof ads: "These characters don't fit the voices. The voices are very African American; the faces on the screen are very WHITE." However, one African American articulated how the ad did, in fact, continue to target African Americans. She concluded that these two ads "were a cool, creative way to target blacks . . . I still believe the intent is to attract African Americans by subliminally making fun of Whites."

In comparison, non-African Americans saw these ads as extensions of earlier "Whassup?!" commercials. One European American woman described the spoofs as:

> . . . really funny! They are different because you've got these "white" people trying to be "black" . . . That's the perception I got anyway. I also think that that's why they were so funny—because it was outrageous in that you never should see that.

Another European American woman extended these comments and implicated associations of stereotypical behaviors and subsequently connected them to the perceived target audience:

> They are funny because they took two groups: Superhero cartoons and elderly white women who don't normally talk LOUD and made them do the same dialogue. Neither of the two groups were the target audience: The target audience remained the same.

As had the African American participants, several of these European Americans understood how these parodies extended earlier attempts to make use of the "authentic" to attract a large audience. Interestingly, it appears that non-African Americans continue to identify with the "universal" appeal of the "Whassup?!" guys in direct relation to seeing how absurd it could be when "uncool" people try to imitate them. In other words, "we" (those of us who are "cool") can continue to relate—or even strengthen our relationship— to the "Whassup?!" guys because of the perceived distinction between "us" and those who are spoofed.

Several key ideas emerge as central to the way the spoofs reinforce the original advertisements. First, from the perspective of non-African Americans, the spoof ads appear to strengthen the "universal" appeal of the "Whassup?!" guys; this is accomplished by featuring the absurdity of attempting to reproduce its "aura" with different faces and in different settings. Second, for African American viewers the spoof ads strengthen the "authentic" nature of the "Whassup?!" guys for a very similar reason: the ads hint that white (un-hip) characters can't "really" imitate black culture. As described earlier, one of the basic tenets associated with spectacular consumption is that the pleasure of consuming otherness is advanced by the Other's uniqueness. Perhaps these spoof ads help to reestablish the unique nature of the "Whassup?!" guys by parodying attempts to serialize the authentic. This point is best captured in another spoof ad that was never aired but is available at the AdCritic.com website where it frequently is listed in the top ten. This commercial features a group of young European American friends who attempt to use "Whassup?!" as a means to display their "coolness" at a summer gathering. Despite their continued efforts, though, they are never able to capture correctly the authentic greeting. Again, this spoof enhances the "Whassup?!" aura by illustrating that the coolness associated with it, and with black culture generally, is virtually impossible to replicate. In this way, the commodity value of the image that is already "owned" increases by virtue of its "uniqueness."

An Unconsciousness of Commodification

The final questions posed to participants in our focus groups related to their perceptions of the marketing strategies that manufactured the "Whassup?!" ads. Most participants felt that the advertising campaign was highly effective, with African Americans focusing on the inclusion of the black community, and non-African Americans applauding the use of "humor [that could be] enjoyed across racial barriers." Across racial and ethnic groups, however, several participants questioned what the "Whassup?!" ads had to do with selling beer. One African American woman commented that "the strategy was humorous and attention-getting, but the product could have been emphasized more." What seemed to be just below the level of consciousness for some participants was the idea that the "product" was not the beer, but the "authenticity" of the "Whassup?!" guys. This critical understanding, however, was not lost on all participants. Several participants discussed the increased exposure that the company got in light of the commercials' popularity and effective use of humor in associating their product with the "in-crowd." In fact, one Korean/American woman applauded Anheuser-Bush's marketing creativity:

> Budweiser knows how to capture their audience's attention by using humor. I think [the ads] are effective because they're catchy and people are always talking about their commercials. As to how much beer they sell, I'm not sure because I don't drink; however, I think because people think the commercials are cool, they might think their beer is too.

While some participants made this connection, only one person talked specifically about the historical pattern of the dominant culture co-opting black cultural artifacts for profit. Consequently, comments that focused on the "Whassup?!" guys (e.g., "they are hilarious!!!") were few; more significant attention was paid to the "genius" of Anheuser-Busch. In this regard, it was the corporate marketing team—and not the "Whassup?!" guys—that was given most of the "credit" for the success of the ads. One African American woman, for instance, praised "the folks at BUD [for] using an everyday phrase for some and turn[ing] it into a million dollar commercial." Comments lauding Anheuser-Busch's ability to use humor to market their products were consistent. Interestingly, the "Whassup?!" guys—despite the central role that Charles Stone played in the development of the ads—were seen as pawns strategically deployed by corporate culture. Consistent with the operations of spectacular consumption, the focus groups believed that the "authenticity" of the "Whassup?!" guys was at once "real" and manufactured for mass consumption.

One final point of critical analysis crystallizes the powerful ways in which the "Whassup?!" guys were commodified by mass mediated marketing. Within his written responses, one biracial man (Filipino/European American) described his reaction to the ads in relation to a previous Budweiser advertising campaign:

> I've seen these ["Whassup?!"] ads before. My initial response to these was that they were pretty funny. When I see them now, I still can't help but laugh. These ad wizards at Budweiser out-did themselves this time. I love these guys—a lot better than the frogs. The marketing strategy is GENIUS. I am a Bud man. It is the King of Beers. They've won my vote.

This comment is especially didactic as it unwittingly brings to the surface the paradox of spectacular consumption. The commodification of the "Whassup?!" guys is perceived from the perspective of other Budweiser fabrications. The realization that, philosophically speaking, a fabrication cannot be "authentic" in the way that the focus groups articulated is discouraged by the simultaneous replication of the "aura." This contradiction can be apparently maintained, in part, because "real life" social relations are themselves always already mediated in the spectacle.

CONCLUSIONS

Throughout this essay we have argued that the "Whassup?!" ad campaign is constitutive of an ambivalence in the white imagination regarding "authentic" blackness. Idealism concerning racial comity interpenetrates racial pessimism in such a way as to produce discursive tensions within cultural artifacts that seek to sell "race." In the "Whassup?!" campaign, this stress is actualized within the discursive contours of "authenticity." In terms of denoting "universalism" or "sameness," the ad campaign is perceived as delivering a male-bonding ritual with which "everyman" can identify. Conversely, "authenticity" also implicates distinctive black style and culture. The "True" ads explicitly reference a notion of realism that holds in tension differences associated with how spectators see the "authentic" as either colorless or colorful. Moreover, we contend that the operations of spectacular consumption replicate and amplify this ambivalence because the anxiety inscribed in it enhances the market value of black imagery.

Our focus group analysis demonstrates how white consumers overtly recognize the "universal" character of the "authentic" masculine ritual while tacitly appreciating the ads as (black) ultra-hip. We posit that this cultural dissociation is a sign of how the white imagination appropriates blackness as commodity while denying such appropriation. Blackness here intensifies the pleasure of "eating the other" (hooks, 1992, p. 21) and brokers an escalation of the commodity value of the "Whassup?!" guys. Such "pleasure" is a symptom of ambivalence. But also white ambivalence toward "true" blackness forces a *suppression* of the character of such consumption precisely because its conscious recognition would turn the white gaze upon itself. That is, white consumers would be compelled to interrogate the reasons why consuming Otherness as a historically cultivated taste is predicated on white supremacy. Since this sort of public deliberation may reduce the angst white people experience when faced with blackness, spectacular consumption seeks to prefabricate the conditions in which such denial is an effect of public consumption itself. This is why the replication of white ambivalence toward blackness becomes a central facet of these consumptive processes. Endorsing the "universality" of "colorless" male bonding pays tribute to American idealism about race relations but it cannot (and is not meant to) displace the significance of distinctive black culture. In the white imagination, such a tribute is replicated just as carefully and consumed just as voraciously as the "authentic" blackness that it obscures.

Our textual analysis of the original "Whassup?!" commercial demonstrated how the ad is made up of competing consumptive impulses. Stone's script is itself a strategic response to the operations through which he and his friends were being commodified. The ad vectors in two directions at once; it satiates and mollifies white desires and fears regarding "real" black brotherhood by turning the greeting into a cartoon version of itself. It also gestures toward a site of cultural integrity beyond the shouts and shrills of the corporate sign of "Whassup?!" In the first and third acts of the commercial, Stone and Williams "have a Bud" and observe how the spectacular game is played. Their subjective and consumptive acts help reshape the conditions of their commodification because they serve as a narrative frame for the second hyperbolic scene. Understood from this perspective, the ad begins and ends with a commentary on how to "keep it real" while playing the "game."

The game continues. While there have been several interesting "Whassup?!" spin offs, the "True" ad that appeared during the 2001 Superbowl critically dramatizes the problem that spectacular consumption poses for critics who seek to conceive of "reality" and "power" in conventional terms. As a replica of the original commercial, the ad reintroduces us to notions of cultural authenticity and surveillance. This ad, however, features two white guys and their brown friend and represents the inversion of cultural cool.

The phone rings. "Brett," looking rather stiff while watching TV, answers the phone:

"This is Brett."
"What are you doing?"
"What are *you* doing?"
"Just watching the market recap, drinking an import."
"That is correct. That is correct!"

A knowing audience is immediately clued into the fact that this conversation is "lame" and even strange compared to the familiar rhythm of the "Whassup?!" guys. Indeed, the fact that these new friends are drinking imported beer signifies a kind of *foreignness*. "Chad" (who is brown) enters carrying a tennis racket and exclaims "what are you doing?" and "Brett" directs him to "pick up the cordless." The friends exchange their cumbersome greeting with comedic gusto. Despite the fact that the scene is silly, we would like to note some serious implications. Viewers who are knowledgeable about "Whassup?!" cool are encouraged to ridicule the "What are you doing" guys. Although signifying economic privilege, they are marginalized as un-hip (and, perhaps, un-American) "wannabes." Moreover, the "What are you doing" guys seem unaware that their cultural performance is out of fashion. At the end of the commercial, Fred Thomas and Paul Williams are shown having a Bud and watching the "wannabes" on TV. Here, the ad characterizes the black male gaze as central and authoritative as the "Whassup?!" guys look at each other with facial expressions that say, "these guys can't be for real"; their capacity to sit in judgment over the "wannabes" places "authentic" black culture in a position of cultural commodity privilege. But popular culture dominance is not the only significant issue. While the "Whassup?!" guys are watching their imitators fail, the "What are you doing" guys are keeping an eye on fluctuations in the value of consumer culture in general; they are "watching the market recap."

Such competing visions of "authenticity" and power are provocative; in spectacular consumption, "real" cultural value is produced through both perspectives. An audience familiar with the "Whassup?!" guys can share in their repose even as it identifies with the "What are you doing" guys' focus on capital investment. Critics are encouraged to see that the ad, in part, represents the notion that spectacular consumption itself is cool. After all, as arbiters of good taste the "Whassup?!" guys are transfixed by the other guys' spectacle. Thus, their consumptive habits stand in for ours and culminate in increased market value for "authentic" black culture and any of its manufactured opposites. This process is also paradoxical because it relies on the notion of cultural essentialism (like "true" blackness) even as cultural boundaries become more permeable and lived experiences become more malleable.

But this dialectic brings up the character of white American ambivalence once again. The "Whassup?!" guys' consumptive gaze is energized by representing the "What are you doing" guys as "inauthentic" and "foreign" laughing stocks. In so doing, however, the ad constitutes "authentic" blackness as authoritative and, thus, perpetuates the threat. So, not only does the ad's humor help to alleviate such angst, but the ad seems to mediate this danger by placing the "What are you doing" guys' economic power over against the cultural allure of the "Whassup?!" guys. The discursive space of white capitalist power (despite the fact that "Chad" is brown) is tacitly maintained by the reproduction of this ambivalence.

The schemata of spectacular consumption not only allows us to explore how image value is manufactured and magnified, but also to perceive how persons and life worlds are transformed in terms of values generated by their public consumption. Hence, the critic is steered away from an overemphasis on forms of autonomy, individual or cultural; such autonomy is not wholly denied, but symbolic forms are understood as constitutive of substances and of relations that are shaped by the character of public consumption. From this perspective, the culture industry does not dictate forms of consumption; nor does an agent determine her own image; they are both altered by the ways that forms are consumed. The relations among the industry, the life worlds of persons, and cultural forms cannot be adequately understood as characterized by *exchanges* of meaning and value; they are more precisely meaning and value *transfusions*. And so, we contend that the "True" character of the "authentic" in the land of spectacular consumption is neither an ontological given nor a semiotic project. Rather, it is a decentralized and localized achievement based only in part on one's lived experience, now understood as a function of how ways of life are commodified and consumed.

REFERENCES*

Adande, J. A. (2000, January 31). Couch potatoes capture a mood. *Los Angeles Times,* D1.

Allen, R. L. (1990). *Black awakening in capitalist America.* Trenton, NJ: Africa World Press.

Baudrillard, J. (1984). The precession of simulacra. In Wallis, B. (Ed.), *Art after modernism* (pp. 253–281). New York: The Contemporary Art Museum.

Benjamin, W. (1984). The author as producer. In Wallis, B. (Ed.), *Art after modernism* (pp. 297–310). New York: The Contemporary Art Museum.

Best, S. & Kellner, D. (1997). *The postmodern turn.* New York: Guilford Press.

Cassidy, M. & Katula, R. (1995). The black experience in advertising: an interview with Thomas J. Burrell. In Dines, G. & Humez, J. M. (Eds.), *Gender, race, and class in media* (pp. 93–98). Thousand Oaks, Ca.: Sage Publications.

Debord, G. (1983). *Society of the spectacle.* Detroit: Black and Red Press.

Entman, R. & Rojecki, A. (2000). *The black image in the white mind: Media and race in America.* Chicago: University of Chicago Press.

Ewen, S. (1988). *All consuming images: The politics of style in contemporary culture.* New York: Basic Books, Inc.

Farhi, P. (2000, March 14). Whassup? Glad you asked; Budweiser's ads tap into male bonding rituals. *Washington Post,* C1.

Franklin, C. (2000, June 1). Letter to the Editors. *Advertising Age,* 6.

Garfield, B. (2000a, June). Budweiser has all Cannes asking whasssuppppp? *Advertising Age.* Available: www.advertisingage/adreview.com.

Garfield, B. (2000b, January). Superbowl ad standout? Whatever.com. *Advertising Age.* Available: www.advertisingage/adreview.com.

Gruner, C. R. (1997). *The game of humor: A comprehensive theory of why we laugh.* New Brunswick, NJ: Transaction Publishers.

Hall, S. (1995). The whites of their eyes: Racist ideologies in the media. In Dines, G. & Humez, J. M. (Eds.) *Gender, race, and class in media* (pp. 18–22). Thousand Oaks, Ca.: Sage Publications.

Heller, K. (2000, March 19). "Whassup?" A new career; Budweiser ads turn four black friends into major pop icons. *Houston Chronicle,* 11.

hooks, b. (1992). *Black looks: Race and representation.* Boston: South End Press.

Jhally, S. (1995). Image-based culture: Advertising and popular culture. In Dines, G. & Humez, J. M. (Eds.), *Gender, race, and class in media* (pp. 77–87). Thousand Oaks, Ca.: Sage Publications.

Kennedy, D. (2000). Marketing Goods, marketing images: The impact of advertising on race. *Arizona State Law Journal, 32,* 615.

Lusane, C. (1994). *African Americans at the crossroads: The restructuring of black leadership and the 1992 elections.* Boston: South End Press.

Madhubuti, H. R. (1990). *Black men: Obsolete, single, dangerous?* Chicago: Third World Press.

Majors, R. & Billson, J. (1992). *Cool pose: The dilemmas of black manhood in America.* New York: Lexington Books.

McGuire, J. M. (2000, June 28). Whassupp?! You ask? *St. Louis Post-Dispatch,* El.

Owen, W. (1984). Interpretive themes in relational communication. *Quarterly Journal of Speech, 70,* 274–287.

Procter, D. E. (1990). The dynamic spectacle: Transforming experience into social forms of community. *Quarterly Journal of Speech, 76,* 117–133.

Watts, E. K. (1997). An exploration of spectacular consumption: gangsta rap as cultural commodity. *Communication Studies, 48,* 42–58.

West, C. (1994). *Race matters.* New York: Vintage Books.

---

*Editor's note: Citations for Graham and for McCarthy were not given in the original publication.

14

"IN A CRISIS WE MUST HAVE A SENSE OF DRAMA"
Civil Rights and Televisual Information

Sasha Torres

THE BURDEN OF LIVENESS

Rather than locating the dominating tropes of African American televisual representation in a set of stock characters or "stereotypes," in this chapter I look instead to the historical relationship between African American political struggles and televisual institutions and, more particularly to a particular historical coincidence: the simultaneous rise of the southern civil rights movement in the wake of the Montgomery Bus Boycott, and of television news as an authoritative force in American public life. To complicate the now-dominant historical understanding that TV borrowed its tropes of blackness from a variety of representational sites all more or less indebted to the traditions of minstrelsy, I will argue that the period roughly from 1955 to 1965 was a crucial moment in the establishment of extremely durable ideological, rhetorical, and institutional procedures for the depiction of African American persons and politics on television, and that these procedures had less to do with black social subservience than with an emergent black political agency. For . . . , American television has—and always has had—a liberal tradition of African American representation, and it is the representations comprising that tradition that are my central focus. One of the stock elements of such representations has been a certain documentary or ethnographic impulse, an imperative to "authenticity" in depictions of African Americans. Television's concern with "realism" in such representations has been at least as durable as its tendency to create black subjects out of whole cloth.

At least as durable, and perhaps also as dangerous: José Muñoz has called the imperative that people of color ceaselessly perform our own authenticity "the burden of liveness."[1] Noting that "the minoritarian subject is always encouraged to perform, *especially* when human and civil rights disintegrate," Muñoz further elaborates "the burden of liveness" as the "mandate to 'perform' for the amusement of the dominant power bloc." In other words, Muñoz collates the widely shared Western tendency to privilege live over recorded performance with a fetishizing racist or imperial gaze on bodies of color.

Thus Muñoz turns the more usual use of the term "liveness"—to describe a representational mode specific to television—on its head in productive ways. For both television

Reprinted from Sasha Torres, *Black, White, and in Color: Television and Black Civil Rights* (Princeton, NJ: Princeton University Press, 2003).

scholars and for the medium itself, liveness has generally referred to the fact of television's capacity to transmit images more or less in real time (as opposed to film, which must be developed in order to signify). Among television scholars, liveness refers as well to the corresponding and specious assertion that television representation has a privileged claim to immediacy and transparency.[2] Television's claim to be "live" has been central to its self-promotion and reception since its beginnings. But the medium's relation to its own liveness is a fraught one; indeed, television's constant and anxious insistence on its own liveness can only betray its fear of becoming technologically or culturally dead. Muñoz's notion of the "burden of liveness" suggests that it's not enough for television to *be* live: the medium needs as well to represent "authentic" persons of color, stockpiling *their* liveness to be borrowed back in times of political or representational crisis.

The "burden of liveness" as a "mandate" to perform for "the amusement of the dominant power bloc"—amusement, yes, but also horror. For television's African American spectacles have persistently been characterized not only by black performance as "entertainment" but also as "information," to employ one of the medium's own favorite binaries. And black performances in information genres have most often been deployed, by African Americans themselves as well as by both cynical and well-meaning whites, to product outrage, trepidation, and alarm.

Part of my project here is to speculate on the underpinnings of the tendency for certain kinds of informational liveness to infiltrate even contemporary entertainment genres featuring black performance. . . . [The] persistence of burdensome liveness as a structuring element of African American televisual representation has been produced not only by the medium's obsessive, anxious, and incessant claims to be (a)live, but also by specific historical circumstances arising in the 1950s that produced a set of lived practices of journalism and publicity. These practices coimplicated the movement and television information workers in a set of overlapping and common interests. In this respect, Muñoz's characterization of liveness as a "burden" evokes both Martin Luther King's understanding of the project of the civil rights movement—to persuade blacks to embrace the redemptive promise of suffering on their own behalf and on that of future generations—and his customary figuration of that project in terms of bearing a burden, usually a cross.[3] Taking up the burden of liveness—of producing televisual immediacy via black performances of physical suffering and political demand—was a primary focus of the movement and a crucial key to its success.

"Pictures Are the Point of Television News"

The civil rights movement played a crucial role in the emerging production practices and self-understanding of network information workers—the makers of news, documentary, and public affairs programming—during the 1950s. The fates of the movement and information genres in their formative periods were intertwined with each other not merely by temporal coincidence, or by what J. Fred MacDonald has called "the simultaneous emergence of the civil rights movement and television."[4] This convergence resulted also from a quite specific, if also quite fortuitous, collation of needs and resources. Telejournalism, obviously, needed vivid pictures and clear-cut stories; less obviously, it also sought political and cultural *gravitas*. For its part, the civil rights movement staked the moral authority of Christian nonviolence and the rhetoric of American democracy to make a new national culture; to succeed, it needed to have its picture taken and its stories told.

Although few take civil rights coverage as their explicit subject, the memoirs of television information workers who began their careers in the medium's early days provide clues to how the movement was understood within the emerging culture of telejournalism.[5] For example, former NBC News president Reuven Frank's memoir, *Out of Thin Air: The Brief Wonderful Life of Network News,* situates civil rights as the domestic issue on which NBC News cut its teeth.[6] "Television news began," he writes, in the book's inaugural sentence, "with the 1948 political conventions."[7] And the 1948 political conventions made interesting coverage, Frank claims, largely because of the battle among the Democrats over the party's civil rights plank. Here is Frank's description of that battle, quoted at some length:

> The party platform, the heart of the fight that was tearing the Democratic party apart, was scheduled for presentation Tuesday, the next day. For the first time in its young life, television would be present at a watershed event in history. The party's factions could not agree on a compromise position on civil rights, and the presentation of the platform was delayed all day. All day Tuesday and all that night, the arguing, the conciliating, the posturing, and the dealing continued. . . .

> Then the television audience saw a historical event unfold spontaneously before its eyes, two days of conflict and resolution that changed the course of the country, the struggle to commit one of America's major parties to redress by law the disabilities that enshackled Negro Americans. In one form or another, the issue was to dominate American society for the rest of the century, but never was the issue so clear as it was at that convention, or seen so clearly as by the people who saw it covered live on television.[8]

I am less interested in the evident falsity of Frank's claims about the capacity of live television to impart "clarity" on "the issue" than I am in the fact that he makes them at all. Civil rights serves in this passage as television news's origin(al) story: "For the first time in its young life, television would be present at a watershed event in history," "the struggle to commit one of America's major parties to redress by law the disabilities that enshackled Negro Americans."[9] Here and elsewhere in the book, Frank situates television as the medium best suited to cover civil rights, and situates civil rights as a particularly apt story for television news. These reciprocal claims, I think, rely on what Frank understands to be the unique contribution of television journalism—its visuality. "Pictures," he insists, "*are* the point of television news."[10] The putative hypervisibility of racial difference—and racial violence as well—grants race privileged status in Frank's account of why television news "mattered more" than print journalism.[11] Frank elucidates these links in his description of a package on "the country's most important segregationist," Mississippi Senator James Eastland, which he produced for the NBC news program *Outlook:*

> [Eastland] was asked about repressive practices against Negroes in his state and his hometown. He indignantly rejected the imputation as incredible, because it would be illegal, a crime. He paused, then slowly and more quietly he said, "That is, if you could get the grand jury to indict."
>
> He pronounced it "indaht" and we let it hang there. He smiled. His round face beamed and his wire-rimmed spectacles shone as the smile persisted. It was another of those small occasions that justify the existence of television. Eastland clearly knew what he was saying; he was playing games with us. In a newspaper report, the smile would not have been

visible, and he knew that. But like so many in those days, even politicians, he had yet to learn about television. So he smiled as he said it. Inferring smugness or hypocrisy from that smile in a newspaper account would have been considered bad journalism. We could have cut the film at Eastland's last word, as though his words mattered but how he said them did not. Television news people who have no feel for television, in time the majority, would have done it that way. On television, we were able to follow his last word with a few milliseconds of smile, because pictures differ from words, and how they differ is not in degree but in kind.[12]

This passage's repetitions of the word "smile" indicate a certain self-aware strain here, marking its incapacity to describe adequately that which "a few milliseconds" of television can signify with ease: the smug performance of a sectionally marked whiteness, its corruption and privilege, its ill-conceived excess. Thus Frank's description of this moment clarifies the necessity of the imbrication of television with race trouble: on one hand, race and racial conflict fed the new medium's enormous appetite for visual spectacle; on the other, the mere fact of television's coverage served paradoxically to render racism visible in new ways, and to new audiences. But if Frank provides an account of why television covered the movement, the question of why television generally covered the movement *sympathetically* remains to be answered.

As Michael Curtin has observed, . . . early television journalists often looked to the storytelling conventions of Hollywood, slotting televisual information into recognizable entertainment genres to garner audiences.[13] Like the reporting of the Cold War—the other big story of the fifties—coverage of the civil rights movement often played like the westerns on offer in the cinemas of the period, in which the distinctions between good and evil were sharply drawn. To put it another way, reporters in the South often ignored the journalistic imperative to neutrality. This can be attributed in part to the moral authority commanded by movement participants, who acted with remarkable courage in the face of the violent reprisals and economic deprivations that accompanied their activism. As movement stalwart John Lewis observes, the journalists covering Mississippi in 1964

> tried to remain objective, but there was no question that . . . [they] became very sympathetic to the movement. They couldn't help it. Day in and day out, going into those backwoods communities as well as to the more visible towns and cities of that state, watching people singing and praying from the bottoms of their souls, seeing the sorts of conditions these people were living in, with nothing for a front step but an old metal bucket turned upside down, with front porches that were nothing but a couple of planks nailed over dirt and mud, with no plumbing or electricity or decent clothes for their children or themselves, just pure and utter poverty—these reporters *had* to be moved.[14]

The accretion of detail in Lewis's last, long sentence here begins to suggest something of how the process he describes worked in practice: constant exposure to the everyday life of the movement won the press over.

The press's widespread abandonment of "balance" can be attributed as well to the self-evident bankruptcy of the segregationist position, motivated as it was by brutal and obvious self-interest on one hand and irrational hatred on the other. The assessment of Paul Good, who covered the 1964 movement in Saint Augustine for ABC news, is typical:

> Reporters are supposed to revere objectivity. . . . I tried to tell both sides as far as there were sides to tell. But how would you report a Dachau or a Buchenwald? By faithfully

expounding Hitler's thesis of the Jewish problem, so much space for the international con-
spiracy of World Zionism, so much for descriptions of mothers leading children into gas
chambers? . . . The contrast was not so extreme in Saint Augustine, unless inhumanity to
man is everywhere and always the same degree of mortal sin, but it was vivid enough.[15]

The difficulties Good describes here were compounded by the fact that segregationists
were unable to articulate their position to journalists in ways that would gain the sympa-
thies of audiences outside the South; their arguments about states' rights, which were perhaps their best hope rhetorically, were so transparently euphemistic for their underlying
fears of lost political power that they rung false virtually from the moment *Brown v. Board
of Education* was handed down. Faced with a public relations crisis of ever-increasing
proportions, many segregationists blamed press coverage for "the South's problem with the
Negro," and many chose to counter their bad press with intimidation of and violence
against reporters.[16] Faced with bat-wielding, camera-smashing segregationists advocating
the perpetuation of American apartheid on one side and with nonviolent civil rights workers seeking to redeem the promises of American democracy on the other, it is not particularly surprising that journalists tended to empathize with the latter.

Howard K. Smith's memoir, *Events Leading up to My Death,* provides an extended
meditation on the question of objectivity in coverage of the movement. In 1961, Smith and
his crew went south to shoot the CBS documentary "Who Speaks for Birmingham?" Before
they left, Smith's producer, David Lowe, issued a warning that seems to self-destruct on
utterance: As Smith represents this moment, "Lowe summed up our mission, 'You know
how this report is going to turn out. However balanced we try to keep it, the Establishment
is going to look awful because its position is awful. So we have to work harder than ever to
give it *a form of balance.*'"[17] This imperative, however half-hearted, to "balance" became
even more difficult to realize when Smith and his crew, tipped off by a publicity-hungry
Klan leader, found themselves at Birmingham's bus terminal the day the first Freedom
Riders arrived. Smith and his cameras witnessed a melee carefully planned by Birmingham
Police Commissioner, Bull Connor, in concert with local Klansmen, in which

> the riders were being dragged from the bus to the station. In a corridor I entered they were
> being beaten with bicycle chains and blackjacks and steel knucks. When they fell they
> were kicked mercilessly, the scrotum being the favored target, and pounded with baseball
> bats.[18]

Ultimately, the "form of balance" Lowe and Smith gave "Who Speaks for Birmingham"—
which ended with Smith calling on President Kennedy to "restate" the laws of the land to
recalcitrant southerners—got Smith fired from CBS in a conflict with William Paley over
the meaning, precisely, of "balance." ("The Civil Rights issue was not one over which reasonable minds might differ," Smith later wrote.[19]) But I would argue that Smith's dismissal
merely imposed a limit on what was already standard operating procedure with respect to
the treatment of civil rights by television journalism, rather than ruling it out of court. This
suggestion is borne out by the fact that Smith was almost immediately hired by ABC,
where he continued to advocate for SCLC-style civil rights throughout the 1960s.[20]

If television journalists risked the authority generally accruing to "balance," this gesture must be read as the product not only of the contingencies of the movement, but also
as a self-interested one, both for news organizations and for the networks of which they
were a part. For news workers, civil rights reporting promised—and delivered—precisely

the cultural capital the new medium needed. Because publicity was such a crucial part of the movement's strategies, and because public opinion was such an important element in the disposition of particular civil rights struggles, coverage of the movement allowed network news not only to report, but also to intervene in, national culture and political discourse. The networks' response to the 1957 integration crisis in Little Rock is an important case in point.

Taylor Branch has called the events in Little Rock "the first on-site news extravaganza of the modern television era" and indeed Little Rock was the perfect story for network news.[21] It was oversaturated with dramatic images, and it satisfied television's craving for moral absolutes. On September 4, for example, the day Arkansas governor Orval Faubus ordered the National Guard to bar nine black students from entering Central High School, viewers witnessed the mob's rage, its violence (including, famously, the attack on black journalist Alex Wilson, who was beaten with a brick on camera), and in stark contrast, the almost uncanny composure of Elizabeth Eckford, one of the black students, who had gotten separated from the others and had to walk alone through a mass of threatening whites. And on September 25, after Eisenhower reluctantly sent units of the 101st Airborne Division to Little Rock to protect the students, viewers watched the "Little Rock Nine"— linked visually with federal authority and the rule of law—walking into school surrounded by soldiers armed with fixed bayonets.

Little Rock was not only the right story for television news; it was the right story at the right time. The crisis materialized as the regionally uneven distribution of affiliates and television households (more on which to follow) was subsiding, and as television's penetration into American homes was almost complete. As Thomas Leonard has pointed out, "Little Rock's troubles reached a viewing public that dwarfed the television audience when the ['50s] began: eighty-five percent of all homes were watching for five hours a day."[22] Thus a large and newly national audience followed the story intently, and coverage was unrelenting: NBC led with John Chancellor's reports from Arkansas every night for a month.[23] As one journalist put it, the collective nightly ritual came to resemble "a national evening séance."[24] For the networks, that séance conjured new legitimacy and influence for television news, affording them restored prestige as it afforded their news divisions political clout: by framing the story as they did, reporters not only helped to forge, but also participated in, the public opinion that eventually forced Ike's hand.

With so much at stake in network reportage, it is not surprising that the civil rights beat was a highly desirable one among reporters, and it is no accident that covering the movement made the reputations of many of the major figures of television journalism— including John Chancellor, Peter Jennings, Dan Rather, Harry Reasoner, Howard K. Smith, Sander Vanocur, and Mike Wallace. But the stakes in civil rights coverage were high as well in network precincts other than the news division, for the profitability of the networks required the elaboration of a new national consensus on race.

"We Have Shut Ourselves Off from the Rest of the World"

While TV always aspired to a national address, the early expansion of television, with respect to the numbers both of television stations and of homes with television sets, was very uneven across the country. The medium grew most rapidly in the Northeast and most slowly in the deep South.[25] This uneven development was exacerbated by the FCC's freeze on the licensing of new stations from 1948 to 1952, while it tried to resolve a number of technical issues having to do with channel separation and the UHF band.[26] The freeze left Arkansas, Mississippi, and South Carolina completely without television at least until 1953.[27]

The unevenness of television's national penetration had crucial implications for network/affiliate relations during the second half of the 1950s. During this period, the completion of coaxial cable and relay links to the networks marked the full incorporation of southern affiliates into the networks; in addition the South offered a growth market for programmers and advertisers, as southern viewership continued to grow after the rest of the country had been saturated with both stations and sets. At the same time, to complicate matters further, network/affiliate relations were under considerable governmental and regulatory scrutiny. As the number of television stations increased after the freeze, station owners, many of whom had been located in one- or two-station markets and were thus able to affiliate with more than one network, lost much of their bargaining power in negotiating with the networks, particularly NBC and CBS. At issue were station compensation fees (the station's share of advertising revenues from the network's sale of time in the local market) and option time (network access to affiliate airtime). Option time served to guarantee that the networks would have high "clearance" rates, or, in other words, that a high percentage of affiliates would broadcast, or "clear," network programming, thus allowing the networks to charge the highest possible rates for advertising. Concerned about antitrust issues, a number of congressional committees spent considerable effort during the second half of the 1950s studying the question of whether option time was analogous to the block booking that had been outlawed by the Paramount decision. Though the FCC ultimately declined to address option time during the 1950s, these hearings served to keep the imperative to high clearance rates firmly in the networks' view.[28]

By the late '50s, the economic and regulatory climate combined with the political climate in the South to produce a quandary for the industry. For a number of reasons, it was in the networks' interest to strengthen ties to their southern affiliates during this period, but the percolating race trouble in the South threatened those ties. More specifically, disparate sectional assumptions about what counted as acceptable racial representation on television produced conflicts between the networks—northern both in location and temperament—and their southern affiliates. These disparities had been submerged during television's early years: when audiences were concentrated in the Northeast, programmers could afford to be somewhat experimental in their deployment of black performance in both entertainment and information genres.[29] White southern audiences, however, were likely to balk at black performance in *any* genre, and this tendency—which in some cases grew as the civil rights movement continued—threatened clearance rates. The industry made certain concessions with respect to entertainment programming: *The Nat King Cole Show* was cancelled in 1957 when it failed to garner a national sponsor due to advertisers' reluctance to "offend" southern audiences, and CBS served up the remarkable series *The Gray Ghost,* about a heroic confederate general, just as the battle of Little Rock was raging.[30] But, for the reasons I've suggested, the stakes with respect to information programming were too high for the networks to concede to southern tastes. As the civil rights movement was enticing television information workers, many southern affiliates were systematically refusing to clear news and documentaries about civil rights produced by the networks.

On a May 26, 1963 episode of Howard K. Smith's *News and Comment,* black Birmingham attorney Charles Morgan discussed this policy with respect to network documentaries:

> [Birmingham] is a city where for any number of years we have shut ourselves off from the rest of the world. . . . For instance . . . I believe "Walk in My Shoes" was a program produced by ABC. But the people here [in Birmingham] didn't see "Walk in My Shoes" because locally the television station didn't want to show it to them. They didn't see "Who Speaks for the South." They didn't see the *NBC White Paper* on the sit-ins.[31]

Morgan's assertions are borne out by television historian Steven Classen's research on one of the local stations in Jackson, Mississippi, WLBT. Classen notes that "in Jackson, [the] mediated omission of African American images and perspectives was nearly complete . . . and extended well into the sixties."[32] He elaborates:

> [T]he station staff was careful not only regarding what to include, but also what to exclude from the schedule—most notably programming that showcased articulate African Americans, such as NBC's *Nat King Cole Show,* or offerings that explicitly addressed southern race relations. For example, of the seven regularly scheduled NBC network "public affairs" programs that occasionally discussed racial integration and were offered to affiliates during approximately fourteen months between 1962 and 1963, WLBT chose to regularly air only the *Today Show,* and even then allegedly omitted "pro-integrationist" portions of that program (86).

While WLBT is an infamous case—African American activism against the station's persistently racist practices prevented its relicensing in 1969—the kinds of practices Classen describes here were widespread among southern affiliates, whose managers often viewed network-produced racial representation as integrationist propaganda. Anti-network sentiment ran high in many precincts: John Chancellor recalls that the networks were known, in some quarters at least, as "the Nigger Broadcasting Company (NBC), the Communist Broadcasting System (CBS) or the Asshole Broadcasting Company (ABC)."[33]

In the late 1950s and early 1960s, then, the television industry was faced with a number of competing factors constraining the representation of African Americans, their culture, and their political struggles. On one hand, the civil rights movement served network news organizations well in the various ways I've described; on the other, some southern affiliates threatened clearance rates by refusing to air network news viewed by southern station managers as critical of segregation. On one hand, television wanted to exploit the visuality and topicality of race trouble in both news and entertainment programming; on the other, network bosses wanted to avoid alienating southern audiences and provoking southern affiliates.[34] At the heart of these conflicts were sectionally specific understandings of the meanings and functions of race; these specificities threatened television's self-constitution as a properly national form addressing an audience assumed to share certain core ideological assumptions about the privileges of citizenship and the rule of law, and thus threatened the profits to be garnered from selling such an audience to advertisers. In this regard, the networks shared common cause with the movement, which sought to produce precisely such a national consensus. No wonder, then, that network programming tended to ease the achievement of movement goals.

"That Cycle of Violence and Publicity"

For their part, the key organizations of the southern civil rights movement—the Southern Christian Leadership Conference (SCLC), the Congress of Racial Equality (CORE), and the Student Nonviolent Coordinating Committee (SNCC)—all understood the importance of television in placing southern violence and intransigence on the national agenda, though each group's media-relations strategies were slightly different. Generally, nationally broadcast television news served the movement in two crucial if contradictory ways: on one hand, it tended to modulate segregationist violence against civil rights workers in the field; on the other, it captured and amplified the violence that movement demonstrations occasionally sought, replacing it within a national, rather than regional, context, in which it carried very different meanings.[35]

Television cameras provided a kind of safety net for those in the movement, who mention them frequently in oral histories and movement memoirs. Ruby Hurley, for example, the veteran Birmingham activist who opened the first NAACP office in the deep South, observes that "to me the fifties were much worse than the sixties. When I was out there by myself, for instance, there were no TV cameras with me to give me any protection. There were no reporters traveling with me to give me protection, because when the eye of the press or the eye of the camera was on the situation, it was different."[36] Andrew Young recalls objecting to SNCC's plans for Freedom Summer; in his view the project was recklessly dangerous, because "the presence of national media was virtually the only inhibitor of official violence, and you simply could not get that kind of attention for people in dozens of towns in Mississippi."[37] Albert Turner, commenting on why the 1965 demonstration in Marion, Alabama, became so violent, claims that

> one of the major reasons that thing was so bad that night, they shot the [cameramen's] lights out, and nobody was able to report what really happened. They turned all the lights out, shot the lights out, and they beat people at random. They didn't have to be marching. All you had to do was be black. And they hospitaled fifteen or twenty folks. And they just was intending to kill someone as an example, and they did kill Jimmie Jackson.[38]

Willie Bolden, an SCLC worker who was also in Marion, notes that "in filming, in many cases, they missed a lot of it because if the shit was gonna *really* go down, those folk tried to get those cameras out of the way first. And many times even after they were able to put the camera back into motion, much of the real *bloody* part of these marches was all over."[39]

These comments point out the doubleness of the effects that cameras could have on the day-to-day life of the movement. Their presence afforded movement workers a measure of protection against their segregationist opposition by signaling the capacity to broadcast southern race trouble nationally, to an audience unschooled in the traditional regional interpretations of racial terrorism. But, as I've suggested, cameras also tended in themselves to aggravate racist rage and violence, precisely by marking the extent to which the perpetuation of southern race relations was increasingly out of southern hands. The result was a delicate balance between provocation and restraint that was difficult for movement leaders to control precisely. Journalists and civil rights historians agree, though, that achieving and wielding such control was an explicit aim of SCLC: as Adam Fairclough argues in his history of the organization, "By carefully selecting its targets, SCLC . . . publicized white repression to its fullest possible effect. It contrived to do this, moreover, while keeping white violence to a minimum: SCLC's very presence, accompanied as it was by a phalanx of reporters and cameramen, inhibited white officials and restrained them in their use of violence."[40]

In the rest of this section I will discuss SCLC's media strategy, drawing from archival sources, movement memoirs, and critical studies of the organization. Narrowing the focus to SCLC inevitably produces some distortions, the most important of which is the risk of reproducing mainstream media's own obsession with King and their tendency to cover him to the exclusion of other movement leaders. And, given that the SCLC media strategy always concentrated on major media outlets, my observations here will certainly obscure strategies like SNCC's, which sought as well to facilitate local blacks in making their own media documenting the movement's activities and in using the licensing process to protest racist broadcasting by southern media outlets.[41] Nevertheless, I've chosen to concentrate on SCLC because that organization—particularly in its production of King as a media figure—clearly did the best job among major movement groups in using television to advance its aims, and because materials relating to SCLC's media strategy are more readily available than corresponding materials related to other groups. After a brief discussion of the Montgomery Bus Boycott, the context in which King and the movement discovered the importance of being mediated, I will consider two of the organization's most successful campaigns, those in Birmingham (1963) and Selma (1965), in order to illustrate how SCLC deployed the visuality of black performance in confrontations with segregationist power.

In Montgomery, King and the other leaders of the Montgomery Improvement Association (MIA) ran head-on into the problem of media representation almost immediately. David Garrow describes an early meeting of the boycott's organizers, in which

> Reverend Wilson reported that press photographers would be at the rally, and some ministers seemed reluctant to volunteer as speakers in light of that fact. E. D. Nixon angrily rebuked them. "Somebody in this thing has got to get faith. I am just ashamed of you. You said that God has called you to lead the people and now you are afraid and gone to pieces because the man tells you that the newspaper men will be here and your pictures might come out in the newspaper. Somebody has got to get hurt in this thing and if you preachers are not the leaders, then we have to pray that God will send us some more leaders."[42]

"Somebody has got to get hurt." Nixon's words indicate his assent to Reverend Wilson's premise that mediated visibility will indeed entail risk, possibly mortal risk. Indeed, the fact of being publicly identified as an organizer of the boycott might well have killed Nixon himself, as his home, along with King's, was bombed during the eleven-month protest. And being known by sight as well as by name would certainly increase the likelihood of harassment and attack. Nonetheless, something crucial in the history of the movement's relation to publicity happens in this moment: the terrifying leap of faith Nixon asks his colleagues to take here is precisely what allows King and his circle eventually to appreciate the uses to which having one's picture "come out in the newspaper" might be put.

Perhaps Nixon, an associate of A. Phillip Randolph and a longtime organizer, was thinking of Emmett Till, lynched the previous year in the Mississippi delta for allegedly addressing a white woman without observing the strict southern rules governing interracial speech. Till's murder provided a significant precedent for the Montgomery movement in two ways. First, Mamie Till Mobley, Till's mother, brilliantly insisted on iconizing the abused body of her son, demanding an open casket past which mourners in Chicago streamed for four days, and allowing *Jet* to use an image of Till's battered face, bloated and misshapen from river water, on its cover.[43] It would not be going too far to say that Mobley thus invented the strategy that later became the SCLC's signature gesture: literally *illustrating* southern atrocity with graphic images of black physical suffering, and disseminating those images nationally.[44] In addition, although Till's murderers, Roy Bryant and J. W. Milam, were acquitted of the crime, Till's trial provided the occasion for a coalescence of reporters covering a new beat: civil rights.[45] These reporters, many of whom worked for northern papers, provided abundant critical commentary on southern racial mores during the trial, thus signaling to astute black readers that they had a new ally in this national press corps.

Whether Nixon had Till in mind or not, he was proved correct in his assessment that, in addition to increasing black activists' vulnerability to racial terrorism, media attention could serve to protect them from it, as well as providing strategic information to local blacks. And despite the specter of "pictures in the newspapers" that loomed over the early MIA meeting, print media were not the only important sources of information in Montgomery, as the following anecdote, from Garrow, suggests:

> Just as Nixon had hoped, Sunday morning's *Advertiser* featured an Azbell story headlined NEGRO GROUPS READY BOYCOTT OF CITY LINES. . . . The prominent news story had two immediate effects. First, Montgomery's white community was informed of the blacks' challenge. City Police Commissioner Clyde Sellers, a rabid racist, went on local television to denounce the effort and to say that Montgomery policemen would stand ready on Monday to assist those black citizens who wanted to ride the buses. . . . Second, the *Advertiser* story, plus Sellers' television pronouncement, reached many of Montgomery's black citizens, including some who had missed both the door-to-door leaflets and the Sunday morning announcements in most black churches. Nixon, who returned Sunday morning from his train run, and the other organizers were overjoyed at the unwitting assistance the whites had given them.[46]

Both television and the movement were new enough that Montgomery whites apparently didn't think to censor televised representations of the protest. Thus, throughout the boycott, local television played a crucial and unusual role by breaking the local newspapers' monopoly on information.[47] Both papers were owned by the same company; the less racist, the *Advertiser,* covered the movement only reluctantly and disparagingly. But, according to David Halberstam, news director Frank McGee, at Montgomery's NBC affiliate WSFA-TV, sympathized with the protesters' demands. Perhaps more to the point, he understood that he had a very good story on his hands, and covered it assiduously. Once the boycott became a national story, NBC agreed, often including McGee's reports from Montgomery on the network news.[48] Bridging local and national audiences, then, McGee's coverage allowed protesters to see themselves represented as social agents, both within Montgomery and within much larger struggles for human rights in the U.S. and internationally.[49] The capacity to *see* themselves—both figuratively and literally—as political actors was something long denied black activists in the South, where local papers generally refused to cover black protest.[50] Television coverage of the boycott thus helped bolster the boycotters' growing audacity in the face of racist retaliation and break the immobilizing fear of terrorist violence that had for decades prevented mass protest among southern blacks. As that fear dissipated, Fairclough notes, "the ministers began to enjoy their new role. By early 1956, the protest was attracting national and international publicity. . . . [I]nitially cagey about revealing their identities, they now enjoyed the prestige conferred by media coverage."[51]

None enjoyed that prestige more than King. He got the most of it, and there is wide consensus among both participants in and chroniclers of the movement that he was extremely savvy in its deployment.[52] Montgomery made him a national media star of sufficient magnitude that he continued to garner coverage even as SCLC struggled to find an agenda, a method, and an administrative structure during the late '50s. During this period, King continued to polish his on-air skills and to think about television's potential uses for the movement, imagining a weekly television show and a Billy-Graham-style "Crusade for Citizenship" that would "arouse the conscience of the nation through radio, TV, newspapers and public appearances of southern leaders as to conditions that exist, progress being made, and the responsibility of the entire nation to help ensure for Negro citizens these elementary rights."[53] In fact, the Crusade for Citizenship went forward, under the direction of Ella Baker, but had only marginal effects. It was not until the apex of the Birmingham movement, in 1963, that the various ingredients enabling the movement's effective use of television would be collected.[54] Montgomery had yielded a number of these: the further consolidation of the civil rights press corps first assembled to cover the Till case; a telegenic leader; and a strategic understanding of the uses to which nonviolent protest and the self-iconization of black suffering might be put. The rest had yet to be assembled.

The first of these was well-organized press outreach, which was coordinated in Birmingham by Wyatt Walker, then SCLC's executive director. Walker held daily briefings for the press and helped journalists meet their deadlines by organizing the demonstration schedule around the time-consuming process of getting film from Birmingham to New York in time to air that night.[55] He also had a flair for the dramatic and clearly understood his task as producing spectacular racist violence against nonviolent black demonstrators. Thus he was not above expressing regret over Bull Connor's restraint early in the campaign, trying to provoke the Public Safety Commissioner's retaliation, and expressing delight at Connor's eventual decision to employ fire hoses and police dogs against marchers. As Fairclough notes, "the dogs and hoses were SCLC's best propaganda. Walker recalled how he told [James] Bevel 'to let the pep rally go on a while and let these firemen sit out there and bake in the sun until their tempers were like hair triggers.' According to James Forman of SNCC, when Walker watched the ensuing scenes replayed that evening on television, he jumped up and down in elation."[56]

Another of the ingredients in SCLC's successful deployment of television in Birmingham was a staff member with production experience in TV, and a thorough understanding of the medium's constraints and requirements. Before moving to Atlanta to work with SCLC, during his tenure at the National Council of Churches, Andrew Young had become interested in the power of visual media like film and television to influence by "control[ling] the image that appeared in the viewer's mind." Spurred by this interest, he became involved in the making of a weekly series produced jointly by the NCC and CBS called *Look Up and Live.* Young worked both behind and in front of the camera, learning that "television was demanding and unforgiving." He recalls, "We had sixty seconds to open and close the program. In that time, we had to get across the main point. . . . It couldn't be sixty-two seconds and it shouldn't be fifty-eight seconds."[57]

Young's training in formulating a visual message economically and efficiently contributed crucially to SCLC's campaign in Birmingham and its subsequent efforts. In particular, he refined the organization's publicity efforts and focused them more clearly on the needs of television news crews by inventing what later came to be known as the "sound-bite." In his words,

> At the Dorchester [planning] meeting [for the Birmingham campaign], I had impressed upon Martin the importance of crafting a message that could be conveyed in just sixty seconds for the television cameras. Martin picked it up right away, reciting to me a favorite saying of Dr. Benjamin Mays, President of Morehouse College:
>
> > One tiny little minute
> > Just sixty seconds in it
> > I can't refuse it
> > I dare not abuse it
> > It's up to me to use it
>
> . . . [W]hen I emphasized the need to have a message that we could convey in a matter of seconds, Martin would smile and say "One tiny little minute, just sixty seconds in it."[58]

There is little question that King was a receptive student of Young's media-relations pedagogy, or that the student could teach a few lessons of his own. King was keenly aware of the importance of the press to SCLC's success in Birmingham, going to jail on Good Friday to spark national interest in the campaign and agonizing over the movement's inability to generate coverage prior to movement stalwart James Bevel's innovation of the children's crusade.[59] King's phone conversation with Coretta Scott King from the Birmingham jail provides an excellent index of his preoccupation with keeping the movement in the news. As scholars of King note unfailingly, his primary interest was in ensuring that his wife told Walker that President Kennedy had called her to express concern over King's welfare in jail, so that Walker could tell reporters.[60]

The final ingredients contributing to the movement's successful use of television in Birmingham were supplied by James Bevel. As a college student in Nashville, Bevel had, with Bernard Lafayette, John Lewis, Diane Nash, and others, participated in the nonviolent sit-ins that desegregated the city's restaurants. In that capacity, he was one of the "stars" of the *NBC White Paper,* "Sit In." . . . Bevel's experience with "Sit In" produced certain insurgent knowledges about television that were extremely useful in Birmingham. First, as one of the earliest performers in the emerging genre of civil rights TV, Bevel understood well the mechanisms of political dramaturgy involved in "staging" a protest. And this understanding no doubt contributed to Bevel's audacious and risky conception of the children's marches. Faced with a shortage of adults willing or able to go to jail, Bevel was first among his cohort to imagine the practical and spectacular uses to which a mass performance of infantile citizenship might be put, in crowding Birmingham's jails and America's field of vision at the same time.[61] In addition, Bevel was able to imagine a television spectatorship comprised of to-be-mobilized blacks who would be recruited to the movement and prepared for nonviolent protest by televisual representation. He used "Sit In" as a training film in Birmingham (and elsewhere), thus routing black performance to potential black political agents through the medium of network television.

Clearly, the various innovations of Birmingham with respect to media relations reinforced each other in effecting a major shift in the culture of SCLC. During and after Birmingham, Walker, Young, Bevel, and King collaborated in elaborating innovative publicity techniques that placed the press, and particularly television, at the center of the organization's planning and strategies. SCLC operatives, though, knew enough to downplay the media's role in the movement. Noting that such an admission "likely would have made the movement, and Dr. King, appear considerably more 'calculating' than they wanted to seem," Garrow emphasizes that King's writing and speeches contain virtually no mention of media, save for allegorical references to visibility or light, "as when King spoke of 'the light of day' or the 'spotlight' that illuminated the evils of racist brutality."[62]

Despite its strategic silence about its publicity efforts, though, SCLC's 1965 Selma campaign dispels any doubts as to the media-centeredness of the organization's efforts.[63] The organization chose Selma not only because of the well-known intransigence of the Dallas County registrars with respect to registering black voters, but also because of the famously short fuse of Dallas County Sheriff Jim Clark and the proximity of Selma to network affiliates in Montgomery.[64] SCLC planners hoped that the combination would prove fortuitous. In Andrew Young's words, "The movement did not 'cause' problems in Selma. . . . [I]t just brought them to the surface where they could be dealt with. Sheriff Clark had been beating black heads in the back of the jail for years, and we're only saying to him that if he still wants to beat heads he'll have to do it on Main Street, at noon, in front of CBS, NBC, and ABC television cameras."[65]

In fact, the SCLC was sufficiently focused on its goal of providing the networks with Clark's racist performances that the staff decided, after the sheriff behaved mildly at the first demonstration, that they would move on to another town if he didn't react as expected the following day.[66] They needn't have worried. Clark returned to form the next day in a contretemps with veteran local activist Amelia Boynton in front of television cameras. In John Lewis's recollection, "Mrs. Boynton apparently moved too slowly for his tastes, and the next thing you knew he was manhandling her, really shoving and roughing her up. . . . You could hear the news photographers' cameras clicking, and I knew that now it was starting, that cycle of violence and publicity and more violence and more publicity that would eventually, we hoped, push things to the point where something—ideally, the law—would have to be changed."[67] Lewis's account suggests how thoroughly, by the time of the Selma campaign, his understanding of the movement's progress had become imbricated with his awareness of the coverage it garnered: what the memoirist recalls, many years later, is not finally the violence of this moment, but the moment's initiation of "that cycle of violence and publicity" that might force change.

Movement workers were elated: at the mass meeting that night, Ralph Abernathy, before a cheering crowd, proclaimed the sheriff an "honorary" civil rights worker for his service to the cause.[68] Abernathy's quip underscores the attention being paid to the coverage by the highest levels of the SCLC, attention further demonstrated by King's notes to Andrew Young from jail after his arrest on February 1, which read as though written by an accomplished public relations operative. The instructions King gave Young on February 2, titled "Do following to keep national attention focused on Selma," read, in part, "Keep some activity alive every day this week." Other points included "Follow through on suggestion of having a congressional delegation to come in for personal investigation. They should also make an appearance at mass meeting if they come"; "Seek to get big name celebrities to come in for moral support"; "Consider a night march to the jail protesting my arrest (an arrest which must be considered unjust). Have another night march to court house to let Clark show true colors."[69] In other words, King provides Young with specific examples of movement-generated content for the press—the congressional visit to Selma, the "big name celebrities," the night marches, and "Clark show[ing his] true colors"—even as he proposes a frame for the story with the parenthetical "an arrest that must be considered unjust."

On February 3, King laid out the next day's schedule for Young: "If all goes well get us out at 1:00 P.M. tomorrow. We will go directly to Federal Building to see Congressmen. Set press conference for 2:30. Prepare the kind of statement that I should read to press on release from jail. When it is definite that we are coming out let the press know the time so they will be on hand at the jail for our release." The stops on King's itinerary—coming out of jail, meeting the congressional delegation, and the press conference—would provide photo opportunities and thus satisfy King's demand for political showmanship: at the close of the note, King urges Young, "Also please don't be too soft. We have the offensive. It was a mistake not to march today. In a crisis we must have a sense of drama."[70]

King's concern with "drama" was a value that, by Selma, had clearly saturated the SCLC's political culture, a fact that is evidenced by C. T. Vivian's February 16 encounter with Jim Clark while leading a demonstration at the Dallas County courthouse. It was raining that day, and Vivian asked that those waiting to sign the Registrar's "appearance book" be allow to stand inside, out of the rain. When Clark refused, Vivian continued to bait him, comparing him to Hitler and his deputies to Nazis, all the while urging the television cameras across the street to capture the escalating confrontation.[71] The reporters became players in the scene when a cameraman switched on a light and Clark's anger was momentarily directed toward him; Selma historian Charles Fager reports that Clark yelled "Turn out that light or I'll shoot it out!"[72] When Clark could stand no more of Vivian's heckling, and with deputies trying to restrain him, he hit Vivian in the face in full view of the cameras and then went after the cameramen and reporters with a billy club.[73] When Vivian regained his feet, cameras recorded him exclaiming triumphantly, blood dripping from his mouth, "We're willing to be beaten for democracy, and yet you misuse democracy in these streets!" As Fager observes dryly, "This encounter made vivid television"[74] (Figures 14.1 and 14.2).

If Clark deserves coproducer credit with Vivian for their courthouse showdown, his own sense of drama may have overtaken the movement's during the encounter with marchers on the Edmund Pettus Bridge on "Bloody Sunday," March 7. I have found no evidence that movement strategists anticipated the intensity of the violence that Alabama state troopers and Clark's "posse"—the deputized racists who did much of the sheriff's dirty work—would visit on the protesters. Trapped by the line of troopers in front of them, with the Alabama River to their left and right, blacks were chased by mounted possemen, beaten bloody and broken by billy clubs, trampled by fleeing comrades, and blinded by tear gas.

FIGURE 14.1 Sheriff Jim Clark threatens a network reporter with a billy club.

FIGURE 14.2 Reverend C. T. Vivian, just after being hit by Clark.

But Clark (and George Wallace, who dispatched the troopers) had intended this to be a live performance only: officials on the scene had pushed the cameras back far enough from the action that they, apparently unfamiliar with telephoto lenses, thought that the newsmen couldn't get "good" pictures. I will have more to say on the question of "good" pictures in a moment; I will merely note here that the pictures were good enough, at least, for ABC to interrupt its premiere broadcast of *Judgement at Nuremberg* with footage from Selma, confusing many viewers about the difference between the American South and Nazi Germany and setting a number of them on the road to Alabama.[75] They were good enough that SCLC lawyers entered the CBS footage into evidence at the hearings held by federal district court Judge Frank Johnson to adjudicate the legality of the Selma to Montgomery march and that the screening immediately preceded Johnson's ruling in favor of the SCLC.[76] They were good enough for then-Selma Mayor Joseph Smitherman to muse in retrospect, "I did not understand how big it was until I saw it on television."[77] And they were good enough, according to the CBS correspondent covering Selma, Nelson Benton, that "the word started going around, around the [Alabama] statehouse, middle of the week, and the phrase was 'There was too much film.' You know, that was the phrase that the governor's people [were] using. 'Just too much film. Too much film.'"[78]

"The Vehemence of a Dream"

I have argued that, for reasons of its own, network television made common cause with the civil rights movement in its quest for a national audience. I have argued as well that civil rights strategists, particularly those associated with King's SCLC, proved remarkably adept both at providing visually dramatic and narratively coherent stories designed with the networks in mind, and at streamlining the logistics of the networks' incorporation of those stories into their narrative flows. In the process, I have attempted to disrupt the origin story that claims that African American representation on television derives solely from the stock types of minstrelsy and to begin to explain another kind of televisual traffic in black performance, one that usually fancies itself antiracist and tends to be marked by the generic admixture of information and entertainment forms.

I have tried to suggest as well some of the counterhegemonic uses to which the burden of liveness might be put by black subjects. For despite the falsity of liveness's promise of unmediated access to an extra-televisual real, liveness by its nature opens a space through which the occasional kernel of history sometimes propels itself, landing in the lap of the unsuspecting home viewer, if not unmediated then at least incompletely processed by television's narrative-making apparatus. Viewers are then left, briefly, to make their own narratives; on Bloody Sunday, the stories some of them told forced them out of their houses, onto buses or planes, or into cars, and on to Selma.

There is a good deal of discussion about the quality of the film shot by television cameras on the Edmund Pettus Bridge. Andrew Young notes, "After the beating on the bridge everyone knew about Selma, and for a very good reason: the brutality was fully captured by television news cameras on the other side of the bridge. The newsmen were situated behind the mass of troopers, and while the troopers had moved them back to where they thought they could not get good pictures, the scenes they captured were vivid."[79] Nelson Benton recalls, "I was pressing for more [air]time . . . because, under the criteria that we use, it was a hell of a good piece of film."[80] While Young is certainly correct that the footage was "vivid," Benton's claim is more puzzling because it is so obviously false. The film from Selma was not good film by the usual standards of television news, which tend to favor clarity and legibility: the respectful long shot of the President getting off a plane; the close-up of the neighbor amazed that the man living next door turns out to be a serial killer; or the witness at the scene of the accident describing the squeak of tires and the half-seen license plate. George B. Leonard came closer to the truth. As he described it at the time for the *Nation,* "The pictures were not particularly good. With the cameras rather far removed from the action and the skies partly overcast everything that happened took on the quality of an old newsreel. Yet this very quality, vague and half silhouetted, gave the scene the vehemence and immediacy of a dream."[81]

Like the Rodney King video, . . . the Selma footage is *not* good footage by the standards of television news, but it is exemplary footage by the standards of the privileged form of liveness that Mary Ann Doane had called crisis coverage.[82] Crisis coverage, like that from Selma, is marked narratively by ongoing conflicts, often political ones; it is marked visually by long static shots of nothing much happening, replaced suddenly by frenzied, oddly-framed or blurry images once the crisis begins to unfold (Figure 14.3). These visual markers, which often add up to one or another kind of illegibility, are in fact the formal markers of the political process that is unraveling before our eyes: the loss of

FIGURE 14.3 Crisis coverage in Selma.

the camera's control of the image is one of the things that tells the audience that political control, too, is up for grabs. In the process, the television narrator's drive to tell the story of the pictures is confounded and we find ourselves momentarily able to tell our own, and, in some cases, to dream a vehement dream.

NOTES

1. José Muñoz, *Disidentifications: Queers of Color and the Performance of Politics* (Minneapolis: University of Minnesota Press, 1999), 182ff.
2. Thus the term "liveness" can be meaningfully deployed to denote kinds of television that are not *technically* live at all, but that promise something similar to what liveness promises: putatively immediate or transparent representation, perhaps, or a close temporal proximity to the event depicted. Network news coverage of civil rights movement activities, for example, were shot on film that was rushed by plane to New York for processing and editing. But such coverage still managed to claim to be more "real" than its print counterparts.
3. See, for example, the various epigraphs, all from King, to David Garrow's *Bearing the Cross: Martin Luther King, Jr., and the Southern Christian Leadership Conference* (New York: Vintage, 1988).
4. J. Fred MacDonald, *Blacks and White TV: African Americans in Television since 1948,* 2nd ed. (Chicago: Nelson Hall, 1992), 81.
5. See, for example, Harry S. Ashmore, *Hearts and Minds: The Anatomy of Racism from Roosevelt to Reagan* (New York: McGraw-Hill, 1982) and *Civil Rights and Wrongs: A Memoir of Race and Politics, 1944–1994* (New York: Pantheon, 1994); David Brinkley, *11 Presidents, 4 Wars, 22 Political Conventions, 1 Moon Landing, 3 Assassinations, 2,000 Weeks of News and Other Stuff on Television and 18 Years of Growing Up In North Carolina* (New York: Knopf, 1995); Paul Good, *The Trouble I've Seen: White Journalist/Black Movement* (Washington, D.C.: Howard University Press, 1975); Dan Rather and Mickey Herskowitz, *The Camera Never Blinks: Adventures of a TV Journalist* (New York: William Morrow, 1977); and Howard K. Smith, *Events Leading up to My Death: The Life of a Twentieth Century Reporter* (New York: St. Martin's, 1996).
6. Reuven Frank, *Out of Thin Air: The Brief Wonderful Life of Network News* (New York: Simon & Schuster, 1991).
7. Ibid., 7.

8. Ibid., 21.
9. Harry Reasoner apparently shares Frank's sentiment (though he disagrees with his periodization). He is quoted by Ashmore in *Hearts and Minds* as saying that Little Rock was "where television came to influence, if not to maturity" (269).
10. Frank, *Thin Air,* 41; original emphasis.
11. Ibid., 50.
12. Ibid., 94.
13. Michael Curtin, *Redeeming the Wasteland: Television Documentary and Cold War Politics* (New Brunswick: Rutgers University Press, 1995), 177–96.
14. John Lewis, with Michael D'Orso, *Walking with the Wind: A Memoir of the Movement* (New York: Simon & Schuster, 1998), 267–68.
15. Good, *The Trouble I've Seen,* 95.
16. On the southern tendency to scapegoat the press, see Good, *The Trouble I've Seen,* 53; Robert Patterson, founder of the Citizen's Council, interviewed in Howell Raines, *My Soul Is Rested: Movement Days in the Deep South Remembered* (New York: Penguin, 1983), 297–303; Lewis, *Walking with the Wind,* 111. Violence against journalists in the South during the civil rights movement has been widely documented. See, for example, Adam Fairclough, *To Redeem the Soul of America: The Southern Christian Leadership Conference and Martin Luther King, Jr.* (Athens: University of Georgia Press, 1987), 240; David Halberstam, *The Children* (New York: Random House, 1998), 503; Thomas C. Leonard, "Antislavery, Civil Rights, and Incendiary Material," in *Media and Revolution: Comparative Perspectives,* ed. Jeremy D. Popkin, Jr. (Lexington: University Press of Kentucky, 1995), 115–35; Lewis, *Walking with the Wind,* 158, 268; the various journalists interviewed by Raines in *My Soul Is Rested;* Rather and Herskowitz, *The Camera Never Blinks,* 74ff.; Reese Schonfeld, "The Unsung Heroes of TV News," *Channels* (March/April 1983); Andrew Young, *An Easy Burden: The Civil Rights Movement and the Transformation of America* (New York: HarperCollins, 1996), 293.
17. Smith, *Events,* 269–70 (emphasis added).
18. Ibid., 271.
19. Ibid., 275.
20. Ibid., 283ff. See as well the transcript for Smith's *News and Comment* of 26 May 1963, Shuttlesworth, KLA, box 3, folder 8.
21. Taylor Branch, *Parting the Waters: America in the King Years, 1954–1963* (New York: Simon & Schuster, 1988), 223.
22. Leonard, "Antislavery, Civil Rights, and Incendiary Material," 125–26.
23. Frank, *Thin Air,* 124.
24. Daniel Schorr, quoted in David Halberstam, *The Fifties* (New York: Villard, 1993), 679.
25. For information on the licensing of television stations by state, see "Communications," *Statistical Abstracts of the United States* (Washington, D.C.: GPO, 1948–60); for information on the percentages of homes with television sets broken down by region, see U.S. Bureau of the Census, *Housing and Construction Reports,* Series H-121 (Washington, D.C.: GPO, 1955–60).
26. William Boddy, *Fifties Television: The Medium and Its Critics* (Urbana and Chicago: University of Illinois Press, 1990), 42–62.
27. In *Blacks and White TV,* MacDonald, states that "[g]iven the freeze on licensing new stations by the Federal Communications Commission, not until 1953 was the South able to redress this imbalance. Until that date, there were no operative TV transmitters in Mississippi, Arkansas, or South Carolina" (74). Steven Classen, in "Broadcast Law and Segregation: A Social History of the WLBT Case" (Ph.D. diss., University of Wisconsin, Madison, 1995), confirms MacDonald's dates, listing January 1953 as the date that Mississippi's first station, WJTV in Jackson, went on-air, with the infamous WBLT going on-air in December 1953. *Statistical Abstracts of the United States,* however, indicates that Mississippi and South Carolina had no

stations in 1953, and four and nine respectively in 1955. Inexplicably, *Statistical Abstracts* contains no data for 1954.

28. My discussion of "the economics of networking" here is heavily indebted to Boddy's chapter of the same name in *Fifties Television,* 113–31.

29. MacDonald identifies an early "promise" on the part of the early television industry to be "bias-free" and argues that television reneged on this promise in part because of the growth of southern audiences. While I read early industry policy-statements on race rather more suspiciously than MacDonald does, I agree that the penetration of television into the deep South necessitated a renegotiation of earlier representational conventions. See *Blacks and White TV,* chapters 1 and 6.

30. MacDonald, *Blacks and White TV,* 68, 82.

31. Transcript of Howard K. Smith's *News and Comment,* 26 May 1963, Shuttlesworth, KLA, box 3, folder 8. Morgan refers here to three well-known civil rights documentaries: ABC's "Walk in My Shoes," *Bell and Howell Close-Up* 19 September 1961 (in the collections at MTR and UCLA); "Who Speaks for the South?" *CBS Reports* 27 May 1960; and "Sit-In," *NBC White Paper,* 20 December 1960 (MBC).

32. Classen, "Broadcast Law and Segregation," 88.

33. John Chancellor, quoted in David Halberstam, *The Children,* 489. Frank confirms Chancellor's recollection: "Some NBC affiliates in the South chose not to carry us at all, believing, but never saying, that the New York-based networks were in favor of integration. We were particularly suspect because of all those stories on *Outlook.* The grapevine quoted jokes about the Nigger Broadcasting Company" (*Thin Air,* 117).

34. Indeed, we might see the controversial series, *The Gray Ghost,* the story of a Confederate general, which debuted during the Little Rock crisis in 1957, as an index of these conflicting desires.

35. I am indebted here to Thomas C. Leonard's assertion, in "Antislavery, Civil Rights and Incendiary Material," that "when media play a role in revolution, the reason is often that leaders manage to force new readings of news and draw legitimacy for these interpretations. . . . [W]ords and pictures that once seemed safe become infuriating in a new context" (115).

36. Raines, interview with Ruby Hurley, *My Soul is Rested,* 136.

37. Young, *An Easy Burden,* 303. For a fascinating and detailed account of SNCC's efforts to maintain the press's attention during Freedom Summer, see Mary King, *Freedom Song: A Personal Story of the 1960s Civil Rights Movement,* 1st ed. (New York: Morrow, 1987).

38. Interview with Albert Turner, in Raines, *My Soul is Rested,* 189.

39. Interview with Willie Bolden, ibid., 193.

40. Fairclough, *To Redeem the Soul of America,* 8.

41. On local campaigns against racist broadcasters, the best source is Classen, "Broadcast Law and Segregation," though the efforts he discusses were not led by SNCC. For clues to SNCC's media strategy, see King, *Freedom Song,* as well as the various policy statements on communications in the SNCC records, KLA: "Toward a Theory for Communications," box 24, folder "Communications Department n.d."; "Radio and Television Programming and Editorializing," box 33, folder "Correspondence, n.d."; "Press Procedures," box 36, folder "Staff Memos 1964"; "Memo to SNCC Field Staff re Efficient Press System," box 36, folder "Staff Memos 1964"; "A Story About SNCC Communications," box 153, folder 8.

42. Garrow, *Bearing the Cross,* 23. On the Montgomery movement, see also Stewart Burns, *Daybreak of Freedom: The Montgomery Bus Boycott* (Chapel Hill: University of North Carolina Press, 1997); David Garrow, ed., *The Walking City: The Montgomery Bus Boycott, 1955–1956* (Brooklyn: Carlson, 1989); Jo Ann Gibson Robinson, *The Montgomery Bus Boycott and the Women Who Started It: The Memoir of Jo Ann Gibson Robinson* (Knoxville: University of Tennessee Press, 1987); and Roberta Hughes Wright, *The Birth of the Montgomery Bus Boycott* (Southfield, Mich.: Charro, 1991).

43. The standard account of the Till lynching and its aftermath is Stephen J. Whitfield's *A Death in the Delta: The Story of Emmett Till* (Baltimore: Johns Hopkins University Press, 1991). For an extremely useful discussion of the visuality of the Till case, see Jacqueline Goldsby, "The High and Low Tech of It: The Meaning of Lynching and the Death of Emmett Till," *Yale Journal of Criticism* 9, no. 2 (1996): 245–82.

44. The latter point is crucial. As Leonard points out, southerners made their own images—lynching photography—but as long as those photographs circulated only within racist communities they had no incendiary value for blacks. Such images must be taken out of the context in which they exemplify a kind of racial common sense in order to signify progressively ("Antislavery, Civil Rights, and Incendiary Material," 125). On the role of visuality in the Till case and in 1950s culture generally, see also Goldsby, "The High and Low Tech of It."

45. Halberstam, *The Fifties*, 440–41.

46. Garrow, *Bearing the Cross*, 19–20.

47. Halberstam, *The Fifties*, 559.

48. Ibid., 561–62.

49. Garrow notes that press comparisons of King to Gandhi began quite early in the boycott; these would have enabled the framing of the events in Montgomery as "international" (*Bearing the Cross*, 66).

50. On the blacking out of movement coverage by local newspapers in the South, see Halberstam, *The Fifties*, 557ff; interview with Ed Gardner in Raines, *My Soul Is Rested*, 139–45.

51. Fairclough, *To Redeem the Soul of America*, 18.

52. See, for example, Robert J. Donovan and Ray Scherer, *Unsilent Revolution: Television News and American Public Life, 1948–1991* (Cambridge: Cambridge University Press, 1992), 15; Fairclough, *To Redeem the Soul of America*, 28.

53. In regard to the television show, Branch quotes a letter from Stanley Levinson to King: "All we need is a sponsor to give us a half hour weekly. We already have the star" (*Parting the Waters*, 225). King quoted in Garrow, *Bearing the Cross*, 97.

54. On the Birmingham campaign, see Glenn T. Eskew, *But for Birmingham: The Local and National Movements in the Civil Rights Struggle* (Chapel Hill: University of North Carolina Press, 1997); Andrew Michael Manis, *A Fire You Can't Put Out: The Civil Rights Life of Birmingham's Reverend Fred Shuttlesworth* (Tuscaloosa: University of Alabama Press, 1999); and William A. Nunnelley, Bull Connor (Tuscaloosa: University of Alabama Press, 1991).

55. Young, *An Easy Burden*, 226.

56. Fairclough, *To Redeem the Soul of America*, 126.

57. Young, *An Easy Burden*, 111–12.

58. Ibid., 207.

59. Fairclough, *To Redeem the Soul of America*, 122; Garrow, *Bearing the Cross*, 247.

60. Fairclough, *To Redeem the Soul of America*, 123; Branch, *Parting the Waters*, 736; Garrow, *Bearing the Cross*, 244–45.

61. The phrase "infantile citizenship" is Lauren Berlant's. For a rich account of the vicissitudes of the infantile citizen, see her *The Queen of America Goes to Washington City: Essays on Sex and Citizenship* (Durham: Duke University Press, 1997).

62. David Garrow, *Protest at Selma: Martin Luther King, Jr., and the Voting Rights Act of 1965* (New Haven: Yale University Press, 1978), 227, 226.

63. On the Selma movement, see J. L. Chestnut, Jr., *Black in Selma: The Uncommon Life of J. L. Chestnut, Jr.* (New York: Farrar, Straus and Giroux, 1990); Charles E. Fager, *Selma, 1965* (New York: Scribner, 1974); Stephen L. Longenecker, *Selma's Peacemaker: Ralph Smeltzer and Civil Rights Mediation* (Philadelphia: Temple University Press, 1987); Mary Stanton, *From Selma to Sorrow: The Life and Death of Viola Liuzzo* (Athens: University of Georgia

Press, 1998); and Sheyann Webb et al., *Selma, Lord, Selma: Girlhood Memories of the Civil Rights Days* (Tuscaloosa: University of Alabama Press, 1980).

64. Halberstam, *The Children,* 487, 490. See also Fager, *Selma, 1965,* 34.

65. Young, quoted in Fairclough, *To Redeem the Soul of America,* 226–27.

66. Fager, *Selma, 1965,* 31; Garrow, *Bearing the Cross,* 379; Fairclough, *To Redeem the Soul of America,* 230.

67. Lewis, *Walking With the Wind,* 310; compare with Fager, *Selma, 1965,* 33.

68. Accounts differ as to whether Clark was initiated into the Dallas County Voter's League or the SCLC. See Fager, *Selma, 1965,* 34; Garrow, *Bearing the Cross,* 379.

69. Garrow, *Bearing the Cross,* 383.

70. King's notes made in Selma Jail, 1–5 February 1965, MLK, KLA, Box 22, Folder 6.

71. My account of this incident is based on Fager, *Selma, 1965,* 70; Halberstam, *The Children* 501–2; Garrow, *Bearing the Cross,* 391; and "1965: Bridge to Freedom," *Eyes on the Prize: America's Civil Rights Years* (Turner Home Entertainment/PBS Home Video, 1995). Because of the difficulty of gaining access to tapes and images from network archives, the images of Selma in this chapter have been taken from *Eyes on the Prize.*

72. Fager, *Selma, 1965,* 70.

73. Fairclough, *To Redeem the Soul of America,* 237. In *Bearing the Cross,* King biographer David Garrow writes, "Only years later did Vivian admit that it was one of Clark's deputies who had punched him. 'Clark didn't, but he wanted to take credit for it,' and Vivian had no reason to contest it. 'He was the symbol, not the guy standing beside him'" (391). Later accounts of the incident (Fairclough, Halberstam) have returned to the earlier version of the story; I have done so based on my viewing of some of the news footage, which indicates quite clearly, I think, that it was Clark who hit Vivian.

74. Fager, *Selma, 1965,* 70.

75. Fager, *Selma, 1965,* 98; Garrow, *Bearing the Cross,* 399; Lewis, *Walking With the Wind,* 331; Young, *An Easy Burden,* 358. Fairclough notes, "Many of the clergymen [who came to participate in the Selma to Montgomery march] were old supporters of the civil rights movement, but most, like the scores of lay people present, had traveled to Selma on impulse after viewing the graphic television film of the attack on Pettus Bridge" (*To Redeem the Soul of America,* 243).

76. See Halberstam, *The Children,* 516, and Lewis, *Walking With the Wind,* 337.

77. Halberstam, *The Children,* 515.

78. Nelson Benton, quoted in Raines, *My Soul is Rested,* 386.

79. Young, *An Easy Burden,* 358.

80. Benton, quoted in Raines, *My Soul is Rested,* 386.

81. George B. Leonard, quoted in Garrow, *Protest at Selma,* 84.

82. Mary Ann Doane, "Information, Crisis, Catastrophe," in *Logics of Television,* ed. Patricia Mellencamp (Bloomington: Indiana University Press, 1990), 235–38.

REFERENCES

Ashmore, Harry S. *Hearts and Minds: The Anatomy of Racism from Roosevelt to Reagan.* New York: McGraw-Hill, 1982.

———. *Civil Rights and Wrongs: A Memoir of Race and Politics, 1944–1994.* New York: Pantheon, 1994.

Berlant, Lauren. *The Queen of America Goes to Washington City: Essays on Sex and Citizenship.* Durham: Duke University Press, 1997.

Boddy, William. *Fifties Television: The Medium and Its Critics.* Urbana and Chicago: University of Illinois Press, 1990.

Branch, Taylor. *Parting the Waters: America in the King Years, 1954–1963.* New York: Simon & Schuster, 1988.

Brinkley, David. *11 Presidents, 4 Wars, 22 Political Conventions, 1 Moon Landing, 3 Assassinations, 2,000 Weeks of News and Other Stuff on Television and 18 Years of Growing up in North Carolina.* New York: Knopf; Distributed by Random House, 1995.

Burns, Stewart. *Daybreak of Freedom: The Montgomery Bus Boycott.* Chapel Hill: University of North Carolina Press, 1997.

Chestnut, J. L. *Black in Selma: The Uncommon Life of J.L. Chestnut, Jr.* New York: Farrar, Straus and Giroux, 1990.

Classen, Steven. "Broadcast Law and Segregation: A Social History of the WLBT Case." Ph.D. diss., University of Wisconsin, Madison, 1995.

Curtin, Michael. *Redeeming the Wasteland: Television Documentary and Cold War Politics.* New Brunswick: Rutgers University Press, 1995.

Doane, Mary Ann. "Information, Crisis, Catastrophe." In *Logics of Television,* edited by Patricia Mellencamp, 222–39. Bloomington: Indiana University Press, 1990.

Donovan, Robert J., and Ray Scherer. *Unsilent Revolution: Television News and American Public Life, 1948–1991.* Cambridge: Cambridge University Press, 1992.

Eskew, Glenn T. *But for Birmingham: The Local and National Movements in the Civil Rights Struggle.* Chapel Hill: University of North Carolina Press, 1997.

Fager, Charles E. *Selma, 1965.* New York: Scribner, 1974.

Fairclough, Adam. *To Redeem the Soul of America: The Southern Christian Leadership Conference and Martin Luther King, Jr.* Athens: University of Georgia Press, 1987.

Frank, Reuven. *Out of Thin Air: The Brief Wonderful Life of Network News.* New York: Simon & Schuster, 1991.

Garrow, David J. *Protest at Selma: Martin Luther King, Jr., and the Voting Rights Act of 1965.* New Haven: Yale University Press, 1978.

———. *Bearing the Cross: Martin Luther King, Jr., and the Southern Christian Leadership Conference.* New York: Vintage, 1988.

———, ed. *The Walking City: The Montgomery Bus Boycott, 1955–1956.* Edited by David J. Garrow. Brooklyn: Carlson, 1989.

Goldsby, Jacqueline. "The High and Low Tech of It: The Meaning of Lynching and the Death of Emmett Till." *Yale Journal of Criticism* 9, no. 2 (1996): 245–82.

Good, Paul. *The Trouble I've Seen: White Journalist/Black Movement.* Washington, D.C.: Howard University Press, 1975.

Halberstam, David. *The Fifties.* New York: Villard, 1993.

———. *The Children.* New York: Random House, 1998.

Hughes Wright, Roberta. *The Birth of the Montgomery Bus Boycott.* Southfield, Mich.: Charro, 1991.

King, Mary. *Freedom Song: A Personal Story of the 1960s Civil Rights Movement.* New York: Morrow, 1987.

Leonard, Thomas C. "Antislavery, Civil Rights, and Incendiary Material." In *Media and Revolution: Comparative Perspectives,* edited by Jeremy D. Popkin, Jr., 115–35. Lexington: University Press of Kentucky, 1995.

Lewis, John, with Michael D'Orso. *Walking with the Wind: A Memoir of the Movement.* New York: Simon & Schuster, 1998.

Longenecker, Stephen L. *Selma's Peacemaker: Ralph Smeltzer and Civil Rights Mediation.* Philadelphia: Temple University Press, 1987.

MacDonald, J. Fred. *Blacks and White TV: African Americans in Television since 1948.* 2nd ed. Chicago: Nelson Hall, 1992.

Manis, Andrew Michael. *A Fire You Can't Put Out: The Civil Rights Life of Birmingham's Reverend Fred Shuttlesworth.* Tuscaloosa: University of Alabama Press, 1999.

Muñoz, José. *Disidentifications: Queers of Color and the Performance of Politics.* Minneapolis: University of Minnesota Press, 1999.

Nunnelley, William A. *Bull Connor.* Tuscaloosa: University of Alabama Press, 1991.

Raines, Howell. *My Soul Is Rested: Movement Days in the Deep South Remembered.* New York: Penguin, 1983.

Rather, Dan, and Mickey Herskowitz. *The Camera Never Blinks: Adventures of a TV Journalist.* New York: Morrow, 1977.

Robinson, Jo Ann Gibson. *The Montgomery Bus Boycott and the Women Who Started It: The Memoir of Jo Ann Gibson Robinson.* Knoxville: University of Tennessee Press, 1987.

Schonfeld, Reese. "The Unsung Heroes of TV News." *Channels* (March–April 1983).

Smith, Howard K. *Events Leading Up to My Death: The Life of a Twentieth Century Reporter.* New York: St. Martin's, 1996.

Stanton, Mary. *From Selma to Sorrow: The Life and Death of Viola Liuzzo.* Athens: University of Georgia Press, 1998.

Webb, Sheyann, Rachel West Nelson, and Frank Sikora. *Selma, Lord, Selma: Girlhood Memories of the Civil-Rights Days.* Tuscaloosa: University of Alabama Press, 1980.

Whitfield, Stephen J. *A Death in the Delta: The Story of Emmett Till.* Baltimore: Johns Hopkins University Press, 1991.

Young, Andrew. *An Easy Burden: The Civil Rights Movement and the Transformation of America.* New York: HarperCollins, 1996.

15

BLACK CONTENT,
WHITE CONTROL

Darnell M. Hunt

On May 28, 1999, an article appeared in the *Los Angeles Times* that would have a profound impact on the politics of prime time. Television beat reporter Greg Braxton revealed that the four major television networks—ABC, CBS, NBC, and Fox—planned to introduce twenty-six new situation comedies in the fall 1999 season. Incredibly, however, not one of the new programs would feature a minority in a lead role. "A White, White World on TV's Fall Schedule," as the story was headlined, seemed brazenly out of sync with a society that was more than 30 percent minority and becoming more diverse by the minute. Not long after this revelation, public discussions of the profound disconnect between the nation's demographic makeup and prime-time representational practices reached a feverish pitch.[1]

By the end of that summer, the networks had reacted quickly to quell the public rancor by adding minority characters to the previously all-white casts. As at least one content analysis of the 1999 season would later suggest, however, these eleventh-hour additions were largely window dressing, tokens that facilitated the business-as-usual, white world of prime-time television to continue largely unscathed.[2]

Indeed, a month later the National Association for the Advancement of Colored People (NAACP) anchored a nineteen-member "grand coalition" created to press for the diversification of network television.[3] The NAACP, as we saw in Chapter 1, had been committed since its inception to promoting black media representations that facilitated racial integration. Most often this work had entailed using the legal system or public condemnation to challenge demeaning and stereotypical portrayals of black Americans, representations that the civil rights organization felt retarded efforts to integrate blacks into a white-controlled society. A highly publicized NAACP report on industry diversity would later explain how the coalition—now operating in the racial order of twenty-first century America—focused its efforts on increasing minority *employment* in the industry as a means to the age-old end of more progressive representations:

> The current initiative has focused primarily on the greater inclusion of racial minorities in the broadcast network television industry. Although the accurate depiction of minorities in front of the camera continued to be a critical consideration, the impetus behind the current initiative was the belief that once integration took place behind the camera in executive and decision-making positions, the proper portrayal of the American public would naturally evolve.[4]

Following the coalition's threat of network and advertiser boycotts, a Fifty-first Annual Emmy Awards program in which a few of the virtually nonexistent minority award winners criticized the lack of industry diversity,[5] and the employment guilds' public pledge to join this latest push for increasing minority employment in the industry,[6] voluntary agreements were signed between the coalition and each of the networks. The nonbinding documents stipulated, among other provisions, that the networks would strive to increase minority casting, create programs to develop young writers, develop plans to increase purchases from minority vendors, and appoint network diversity executives responsible for implementing the other plans.[7]

By the end of 2003, the diversity agreements—which some critics had described as "lacking teeth"—had been in place for nearly four years. A quartet of black women had been appointed by the networks to occupy the all-important diversity executive positions,[8] and periodic reports by industry watchdog groups revealed the possible signs of progress, albeit amid considerable industry inertia.[9] But the coalition itself, to the delight of industry insiders, had largely fallen apart.[10] Member advocacy groups had begun to feel the tug of group-specific interests, prompting them to issue separate report cards on industry efforts to diversify. Latino, Native American, and Asian American evaluations of the industry were generally negative, while a 2003 NAACP report was cautiously optimistic about the progress made in network television. Meanwhile, a conservative-controlled Federal Communications Commission (FCC) moved forward with its plans to further deregulate the media industry, a development that would most likely retard efforts for meaningful diversification by further consolidating media ownership in a few hands, thereby reducing the points of access for those traditionally excluded from industry participation.[11]

Little of the concern surrounding minority exclusion from the industry was new, of course. A series of studies by the U.S. Commission on Civil Rights in the late 1970s had documented the insular nature of the television industry, showing how the absence of minorities behind the camera was intimately connected to representational problems in front of it.[12] The commission had also revisited the issue in the early 1990s, during a public hearing on racial tensions held in Los Angeles. In his hearing testimony, the head of entertainment at CBS echoed a common industry refrain—while much work remains to be done, an industry commitment to diversity has resulted in meaningful progress:

> I think that there are and have been some successes and there are things that the industry, I think, still has a lot of work to do on. I think that certainly one of the great successes is that there is much more awareness and concern about the problem. I don't think there's a development session that I attend or a casting session that I go to where the issue of minority representation and portrayal is not discussed.[13]

Meanwhile, other witnesses were less optimistic about the prospects for meaningful industry change. An official for the Writers Guild of America, West—an industry labor union whose own membership was only about 4 percent minority at the time—suggested that the talk of "progress" was little more than an attempt at public relations. Reports documenting the involvement of minority writers, he noted, showed only "miniscule incremental advances":

> I mean, we're sitting here going over and playing this numbers game. If you look at the last two reports that preceded this one [a prominent guild study on industry diversity], you could see some really miniscule incremental advances in certain areas for certain groups.

Over the years, a discernible political pattern concerning the industry diversity issue has emerged, defined by five basic moments connected in a circular chain: (1) periodic circulation of outrageously insensitive and offensive representations of minorities (usually black Americans, as other nonwhites were virtually invisible), (2) public outrage and/or pressure, (3) the release of depressing statistics about minority exclusion from the industry, (4) token or symbolic industry diversity initiatives designed to appease critics, and, (5) a return to business-as-usual practices, which virtually guaranteed the conservation of a radically insular industry under white control.

The preceding chapters in this volume have collectively documented how comedic, dramatic, sports, and news representations of black Americans have shifted over the years with changes in America's racial landscape. They have shown how "positive" black characterizations have increasingly circulated alongside more "negative" ones, evoking in both black and white Americans a profound ambivalence about the images of blackness circulated on the small screen. But despite these representational twists and turns, the hegemonic project of white supremacy has held sway in America, largely in the background in recent years, negotiating the tensions and contradictions inherent in channeling blackness on television. In a meaning-making process marked by continual adjustment and adaptation, white control has remained a compelling constant. This final chapter explores the links between black content on television and white control by considering in-depth case studies of the 2001 and 2002 fall prime-time television schedules. How do market concerns, industry structures, and racial realities combine to produce the patterns in black representation we see on the small screen? What do these patterns tell us about race in twenty-first-century America?

RACIAL REFLECTIONS

When television was widely introduced in the United States following World War II, the nation's population was starkly rendered in black and white. Data from the 1950 U.S. census, for example, present a nation divided between a hulking white majority (89.3 percent) and a marginalized black minority (9.9 percent). Other-raced groups, which together accounted for less than 1.0 percent of the population,[14] were largely absent from official representations of the nation.[15]

Network television—a medium devised to sell audience attention to advertisers—reflected this popular image of the nation from the beginning. In a period of legalized racial segregation, U.S. commercial television was carefully crafted into a tool to service the amusement needs of the dominant, white majority, which also happened to be the largest, most affluent market segment. Indeed, early television programmers were mindful to circulate images and themes the white audience would find comforting. In practical terms, this meant that television portrayals of race had to reflect a racial order with which the white audience was familiar: whites on top, blacks on bottom.

Toward this end, early popular shows like *Amos 'n' Andy* (CBS) and *Beulah* (ABC) portrayed blacks in either comical or subservient terms, either as buffoons unequipped for equal participation in society or as servants who seemed content to cater to the needs of their white masters. The NAACP, as we saw in earlier chapters, argued that these images were damaging to the growing movement for racial integration and thus it played a key role in CBS's cancellation of *Amos 'n' Andy* in 1953, at the height of the show's popularity. But black Americans had by then been established as the prototypical racial "Other" in prime time, a status that would endure throughout the unfolding history of the medium.

Subsequent decades witnessed network television make adjustments to the racial ethos of the times. In reaction to the social movements and racial reforms of the 1960s, for example, television moved to present "respectable" images of blacks that more closely reflected America's newfound sense of racial morality. Thus "assimilationist" shows like *I Spy* (NBC) and *Julia* (NBC), to borrow Herman Gray's nomenclature (see Chapter 9), introduced novel black characters whose accomplished middle-class lifestyles positioned them, unfortunately, as tokens in a white world disconnected from the realities of the rest of the black community. The societal tensions laid bare by the 1960s urban uprisings that concerned the National Advisory Commission on Civil Disorders (see Chapter 2), for example, were virtually nonexistent in the world of small-screen fiction.

During the 1970s, by contrast, a series of black-oriented situation comedies emerged on network television that confronted the gritty realities of inner-city urban life—albeit with much humor and comic relief. But while period shows like *Sanford and Son* (NBC), *Good Times* (CBS), and *The Jeffersons* (CBS) were set firmly in the black world and populated with black characters, they were controlled by white producers to appeal to the largely white television audience. Some critics questioned whether the medium had regressed back to the buffoonish portrayals of the 1950s. Reviewing the 1974 television season, the National Black Feminist Organization had this to say on the matter:

1. Black shows are slanted toward the ridiculous with no redeeming counter images;
2. Third World peoples are consistently cast in extremes;
3. When blacks are cast as professional people, the characters they portray generally lack professionalism and give the impression that black people are incapable and inferior in such positions;
4. When older persons are featured, black people are usually cast as shiftless derelicts or nonproductive individuals.[16]

These observations, it seems, prefigured a refrain that continues to characterize exclusionary practices in the industry: the more things have changed, the more they stay the same.

The 1980s proved a pivotal period for network television. By the beginning of the decade, the network share of the television-watching audience began a dramatic slide from more than 90 percent to the 50 percent figures that marked the turn of the century. Cable television and other technologies (e.g., the VCR) were becoming an alarming threat to the three largest networks (ABC, CBS, and NBC). Ironically, it was during these troubling times, in 1985, that Fox Broadcasting Company established a fourth major network. Meanwhile, the 1980 census had recorded a significant jump in the population of "other" race Americans (from 1.3 percent to 2.3 percent) and announced for the first time that "Hispanic origin" individuals made up 6.4 percent of the population.[17] The black-and-white rendering of America was becoming more complicated at the same time that Reagan-era politics heralded the declining significance of race.

So it is not surprising that *The Cosby Show* (NBC) exploded in popularity after it was introduced in 1984 (see Chapters 1, 6, 7, 8, and 9). Consciously engineered by its black creators to counter earlier black stereotypes with "positive" images, it had the unintended effect of nicely resonating with regressive racial politics. The white audience embraced the sitcom, research revealed (Chapter 6), largely because the comfortable lifestyle of the fictional Huxtable family seemed to confirm the popular idea that America had finally moved beyond race. That is to say, in exchange for inviting the black family into their homes every Thursday night, white viewers could feel more secure in their own racial morality, even as they supported terminating programs that were instituted during the civil rights era to combat racism.

The decade of the 1990s was marked by a number of important developments and trends: the debut of two new networks (UPN and the WB in 1995) and the increasing segmentation of the television audience; an alarming consolidation of media ownership; the continuing invisibility of Other-raced groups in prime time and a corresponding overrepresentation of black Americans (about 16 percent of all characters, compared with about 12 percent of the U.S. population); and a significant rise in the number of black-oriented sitcoms. Indeed, by the first few years of the twenty-first century, the most prominent[18] black characters on prime-time television were ghettoized on the two least-watched networks (UPN, and to a lesser degree the WB), on certain nights of the week, and in a handful of black-oriented sitcoms.[19]

Figure 15.1 presents a longitudinal graph of new television shows featuring black Americans in prominent roles, from the beginning of the widespread availability of television in 1950 to 2003. The graph compares trends in the introduction of new shows, that are "black-themed"—that is to say, shows with predominately black casts or in which a black character is *the* central character (bottom line)—with trends in the introduction of new

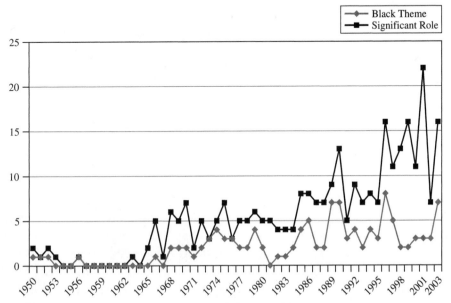

FIGURE 15.1 New TV shows featuring blacks, by year and type.

shows that merely feature a black character or two in significant roles (top line). Several observations emerge from the graph. First, without exception, black-themed programs (bottom line) are less prevalent than "mainstream" programs that happen to incorporate a black character or two (second line). Second, the gaps between the two lines—which may be interpreted as a barometer of industry conventional wisdom about the viability of integrating representations of blackness into the mainstream as opposed to channeling them to black-specific media spaces—are biggest between the late 1960s and early 1970s, in the mid-1980s, and from the late 1990s onward. Third, a clustering of a few black-themed and significant-role programs is introduced in the early 1950s, followed by a virtual absence of programs featuring blacks until the mid-1960s; toward the end of the 1960s there is a relative explosion in the programs featuring blacks that reaches a localized crescendo in the mid-1970s, before declining a bit in the early to mid-1980s; and from the mid-1980s to 2003 there is a general upward trend in the introduction of new fictional programming that features black Americans.

Table 15.1 attaches program names to the bottom trend-line; it provides a decade-by-decade listing of new black-themed programs, by program type (Sitcoms versus Other). With the exception of the 1950s and 1960s, when the introduction of black-themed programs of any type was extremely rare, new black-themed *sitcoms* greatly outnumber other types of black-themed programs. This pattern is particularly evident in the 1990s, a decade in which new black-themed sitcoms outnumbered other types of black-themed programming by nearly eight to one.

Figure 15.2 graphs new black-themed programs by network and decade. It documents the more than fivefold increase in new black-themed shows on ABC, CBS, and NBC between the 1950s/1960s and the 1970s. By the 1980s, however, a decline in new black-themed programs is evident on the three major networks, which is more than offset by the emergence of new black-themed programs on the upstart Fox, UPN, and WB networks

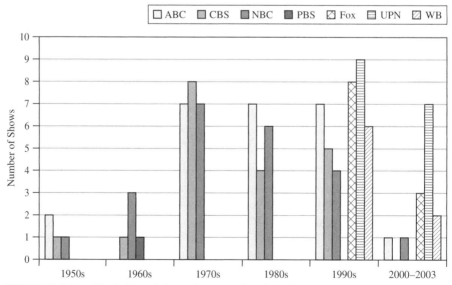

FIGURE 15.2 New black-themed shows, by network and decade.

TABLE 15.1 Black-Themed Network Television Shows, by Decade

	Sitcoms	Other
1950s	*Beulah* (ABC), 1950–1953 *Amos 'n' Andy* (CBS), 1951–1953	*Billy Daniels Show* (ABC), 1952–1952 *Nat "King" Cole Show* (NBC), 1956–1957
1960s	*Julia* (NBC), 1968–1971 *The Bill Cosby Show* (NBC), 1969–1971 *Leslie Uggams Show* (CBS), 1969–1969	*Sammy Davis Jr. Show* (NBC), 1966–1966 *Black Journal* (PBS), 1968–
1970s	*Barefoot in the Park* (ABC), 1970–1971 *Sanford and Son* (NBC), 1972–1977 *The New Bill Cosby Show* (CBS), 1972–1973 *That's My Mama* (ABC), 1974–1975 *Get Christie Love!* (ABC), 1974–1975 *Good Times* (CBS), 1974–1979 *The Jeffersons* (CBS), 1975–1985 *Grady* (NBC), 1975–1976 *What's Happening!* (ABC), 1976–1979 *Cos* (ABC), 1976–1976 *Sanford Arms* (NBC), 1977–1977 *Baby, I'm Back* (CBS), 1978–1978 *Diff'rent Strokes* (NBC), 1978–1986 *Benson* (ABC), 1979–1986 *Harris and Company* (NBC), 1979–1979	*The Flip Wilson Show* (NBC), 1970–1974 *Roll Out* (CBS), 1973–1973 *Shaft* (CBS), 1973–1973 *Tenafly* (CBS), 1973–1973 *The Richard Pryor Show* (NBC), 1977–1977 *The Lazarous Syndrome* (ABC), 1979–1979 *Paris* (CBS), 1979–1979
1980s	*Sanford* (NBC), 1980–1981 *The New Odd Couple* (ABC), 1982–1983 *Webster* (ABC), 1983–1989 *One in a Million* (ABC), 1980–1980 *The Cosby Show* (NBC), 1984–1992 *Charlie & Co.* (CBS), 1985–1986 *227* (NBC), 1985–1990 *Amen!* (NBC), 1986–1991 *He's the Mayor,* 1986–1986 *Melba,* 1986–1986 *A Different World* (NBC), 1987–1993 *Frank's Place* (CBS), 1987–1988 *Robert Guillaume Show* (ABC), 1989–1989 *Family Matters* (CBS), 1989–1998	*Fortune Dane* (ABC), 1986–1986 *Sonny Spoon* (NBC), 1988–1988 *Gideon Oliver* (ABC), 1989–1989 *A Man Called Hawk* (ABC), 1989–1989 *Snoops* (CBS), 1989–1990
1990s	*New Attitude* (ABC), 1990–1990 *Sugar & Spice* (CBS), 1990–1990 *True Colors* (Fox), 1990–1992 *Roc* (Fox), 1991–1994 *The Royal Family* (CBS), 1991–1992 *Hangin' with Mr. Cooper* (ABC), 1992–1997 *Here & Now* (NBC), 1992–1993	*Gabriel's Fire* (ABC), 1990–1992 *Brewster Place* (ABC), 1990–1991 *In Living Color* (Fox), 1990–1994 *M.A.N.T.I.S.* (Fox), 1994–1995

(Continued)

TABLE 15.1 (*Continued*)

	Sitcoms	Other
	Rhythm & Blues (NBC), 1992–1993	
	Martin (Fox), 1992–1997	
	Living Single (Fox), 1993–1998	
	Thea (ABC), 1993–1994	
	704 Hauser (CBS), 1994–1994	
	South Central (Fox), 1994–1994	
	Me and the Boys (ABC), 1994–1995	
	In the House (NBC), 1995–1999*	
	The Wayans Brothers (WB), 1995–1999	
	The Parent'Hood (WB), 1995–1999	
	Moesha (UPN), 1996–2001	
	Malcolm & Eddie (UPN), 1996–2000	
	The Jamie Foxx Show (WB), 1996–2001	
	The Steve Harvey Show (WB), 1996–2002	
	Sparks (UPN), 1996–1998	
	Goode Bahavior (UPN), 1996–1997	
	Homeboys in Outer Space (UPN), 1996–1997	
	Cosby (CBS), 1996–2000	
	Smart Guy (WB), 1997–1999	
	Between Brothers (Fox), 1997–1999	
	The Gregory Hines Show (CBS), 1997–1998	
	Arsenio Hall (ABC), 1997–1997	
	The Secret Diary of Desmond Pfeiffer (UPN), 1998–1998	
	The Hughleys (ABC), 1998–2002*	
	The Parkers (UPN), 1999–	
	The PJs (WB), 1999–2001	
2000–2003	*Girlfriends* (UPN), 2000–	*Cedric the Entertainer Presents* (Fox), 2002–2003
	My Wife and Kids (ABC), 2001–	*The Twilight Zone* (UPN), 2002–2003
	The Bernie Mac Show (Fox), 2001–	*Platinum* (UPN), 2003–2003
	One on One (UPN), 2001–	*Steve Harvey's Big Time* (WB), 2003–
	Half & Half (UPN), 2002–	
	Wanda at Large (Fox), 2003–2003	
	Eve (UPN), 2003–	
	Whoopi (NBC), 2003–	
	Tracy Morgan Show (NBC), 2003–	
	All of Us (UPN), 2003–	
	Like Family (WB), 2003–	
	All About the Andersons (WB), 2003–2004	

Note: "Black-themed" shows are defined as those with majority black casts and settings or shows where a black character is *the* central character.

*Moved to UPN in subsequent seasons.

during the 1990s. Indeed, the relatively small Fox, UPN, and WB networks accounted for nearly 60 percent of new, 1990s black-themed programs. The four-year period of 2000 to 2003 witnessed a sharpening of this pattern: nearly 86 percent of all new black-themed programs appeared on the upstart networks, particularly on UPN, which alone accounted for an incredible 50 percent of these shows.

As Table 15.2 shows, most of these black-themed sitcoms were among the lowest-rated, least-watched programs on television in 2003. Viewership figures for the UPN and WB black-themed shows, in particular, paled in comparison to those for the top television shows—by a factor of nine at the extremes.

The virtual disappearance of new black-themed programs from the major networks (ABC and NBC introduced only one new program each, while CBS introduced none), combined with the explosion of new black-themed programs on the smaller networks, raised interesting questions about the role of racial considerations in programming practices. Was the total disappearance of all new black-themed programs from Viacom-owned CBS during this period and the concomitant escalation of these new shows on Viacom-owned UPN, for example, a harbinger of things to come? Would audience segmentation practices increasingly channel prominent black representations to the lesser-watched networks, away from the "mainstream"? What does the apparent "ghettoization" of prominent black representations in prime time tell us about the contemporary meaning of blackness in America?

TABLE 15.2 Rankings and Viewers of Black-Themed Sitcoms Versus Top Shows, Fall 2003

	Show	Network	Average Ranking	Average Viewers (millions)
Top Shows	*CSI*	CBS	1.3	26.4
	Survivor	CBS	3.0	21.2
	ER	NBC	3.3	21.1
	Friends	NBC	5.5	19.7
Black-Themed Shows	*My Wife and Kids*	ABC	39.8	11.1
	Bernie Mac	Fox	49.0	9.3
	Whoopi	NBC	55.0	9.1
	Tracy Morgan Show	NBC	56.5	8.7
	Girlfriends	UPN	91.3	4.3
	Eve	UPN	94.5	4.1
	The Parkers	UPN	97.0	3.8
	Half and Half	UPN	98.3	3.7
	All of Us	UPN	98.8	3.8
	Steve Harvey's Big Time *	WB	99.7	3.4
	One on One	UPN	101.0	3.3
	Like Family	WB	106.7	2.9

Note: Figures were computed by averaging Nielsen data from the following four weeks: September 22–28, October 27–November 2, November 10–16, and December 1–7. On average, there were 111 programs ranked.

*Steve Harvey's Big Time is a variety show hosted by black comedian Steve Harvey.

CASE STUDY: BLACK TELEVISED REPRESENTATIONS AT THE NEW MILLENNIUM

The remainder of this chapter focuses on a two-year longitudinal study of (1) the on-screen presence of black Americans in prime-time network television and (2) issues pertaining to behind-the-scenes control. The first component, a study of the 2001 fall prime-time season, is based on a content analysis of 224 episodes of 85 sitcoms and dramas airing on ABC, CBS, NBC, Fox, UPN, and WB during three selected weeks between October 14 and November 17, 2001. The second component, an analysis of the 2002 fall season, examines 234 episodes of 85 fictional series airing on the same six networks during three weeks between October 13 and November 16, 2002.[20] The resulting samples each consisted of nearly two hundred hours of programming and included coding for 3,544 and 3,656 characters, respectively.

Representing the Nation, 2001

Figure 15.3 reveals that the black-and-white rendering of America remained alive and well on prime-time television in 2001. Both white and black Americans were overrepresented on the screen, accounting for about 76 percent and 16 percent of all "featured"[21] characters, respectively ($n = 3,544$). Together, these two groups represented 92 percent of all prime-time characters, while comprising only 81 percent of the nation's population. These figures, the chart shows, closely resemble those from a comparable study of the 1999 fall season.[22]

In contrast, Latinos were greatly underrepresented in prime time (only 2 percent of all characters), while Asian Americans approached proportionate representation (about

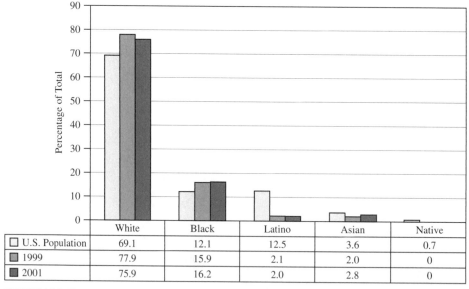

	White	Black	Latino	Asian	Native
☐ U.S. Population	69.1	12.1	12.5	3.6	0.7
▣ 1999	77.9	15.9	2.1	2.0	0
▪ 2001	75.9	16.2	2.0	2.8	0

FIGURE 15.3 Representation, TV versus population, by race and year (2000).

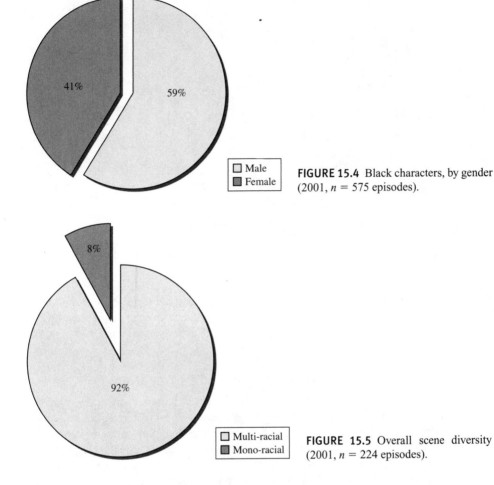

FIGURE 15.4 Black characters, by gender (2001, *n* = 575 episodes).

FIGURE 15.5 Overall scene diversity (2001, *n* = 224 episodes).

3 percent of all characters), and Native Americans remained invisible (0 percent of all characters).[23]

When gender is considered, Figure 15.4 shows that black men significantly out-numbered black women on the screen, the former accounting for nearly 60 percent of all prime-time characters for the group. The gender breakdown for white characters was identical.

Figure 15.5 presents the share of episodes (*n* = 224) that were coded as "multi-racial" or "mono-racial." That is to say, the chart expresses a global determination of whether any characters of other racial backgrounds appear in an episode, either as "featured" characters or in the background (e.g., "extras"). Consistent with the increasing diversity of American society, about 92 percent of all episodes were "multi-racial." But as the racial breakdown for "featured" characters revealed earlier (see Figure 15.1), most of these episodes attained "multi-racial" status because Other-race characters were typically included as "props" in the background—not because they were centrally located in the story line.

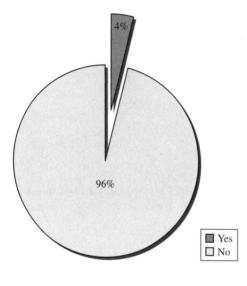

4%

96%

Yes
No

FIGURE 15.6 Explicit reference to race (2001, $n = 224$ episodes).

Finally, Figure 15.6 suggests that race was rarely addressed *explicitly* in prime time. While many of the episodes exhibited the undercurrents of race through either their settings or casts of characters, only about 4 percent directly acknowledged race as a key narrative theme.

Marketing, Segmentation, and Segregation

Conventional programming wisdom holds that audience members naturally gravitate toward characters with whom they can identify and relate. In racial terms, this has meant that programmers assume the largely white audience prefers programs primarily populated by white characters in the more central roles. But because black audience members also prefer to see themselves represented on the screen, A. C. Nielsen reports have shown that the Top 20 most popular television programs for white and black Americans scarcely overlap.[24] While more recent reports have heralded a convergence in black and white viewing tastes due to the emergence of some prominent overlaps,[25] significant differences remain that underscore the importance of racial identification in the television experience. To be sure, this experience is marked by the episodic nature of most prime-time programs, which (unlike films) depend upon viewer identification with central characters to bring back viewers week after week.

Although it is rarely admitted publicly,[26] network programmers select and schedule programs with this truism in mind, and advertisers buy airtime according to the resulting racial demographics. One consequence of these practices is an increasing segregation of prime time, whereby most programming is designed to efficiently garner the attention of *either* white or black Americans—rarely both.[27]

Indeed, a 1999 study of prime time revealed that black characters were largely ghettoized by network, by day of the week, and by show type (i.e., concentrated in sitcoms).[28] It should be noted here that programmers have long known that black Americans watch a disproportionate share of television, about 45 percent more than whites in 2002 (seventy-seven

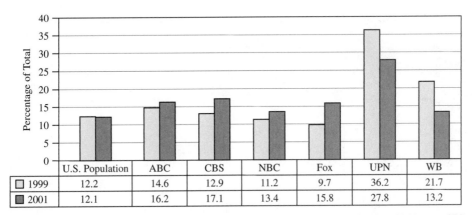

	U.S. Population	ABC	CBS	NBC	Fox	UPN	WB
☐ 1999	12.2	14.6	12.9	11.2	9.7	36.2	21.7
■ 2001	12.1	16.2	17.1	13.4	15.8	27.8	13.2

FIGURE 15.7 Black characters, by network and year (1999, $n = 988$ episodes; 2001, $n = 575$ episodes).

hours a week versus fifty-three).[29] It is also known that black Americans spend a larger share of their disposable income on the types of consumer items marketed in television commercials.[30] While it was beyond the scope of this study to formally analyze prime-time commercials, anecdotal evidence from the 2001 and 2002 seasons suggests that these all-important product pitches also exhibit the racial demographics of the anticipated audience.

Figure 15.7 presents findings on the black presence by network from a study of the 1999 fall season and compares it with data for the 2001 fall season. In 1999, black characters were clearly concentrated on the two least-watched networks (UPN and WB), accounting for about 36 percent and 22 percent of all characters on each network, respectively. Indeed, more than half of all black characters appearing in the sampled episodes that season did so on the two fledgling networks. Two seasons later, however, black characters continued to account for a hugely disproportionate share of UPN characters (about 28 percent), but the remainder were more evenly distributed across the other networks, at levels not too divergent from the black proportion of the U.S. population.

When the black presence by night of the week is examined, however, a pattern emerges that resembles earlier findings of ghettoization. Figure 15.8 reveals that Monday and Saturday were "black" nights during the fall 2001 season, accounting for nearly 40 percent of all black characters in prime time. (In 1999, Monday and Friday nights combined for more than 50 percent of all black characters.[31])

This figure becomes more compelling when it is noted that Saturday is the least-watched night of network television[32] and that the sampled episodes from Saturday were populated by only about 4 percent of the total number of characters in prime time. Two Saturday programs on CBS—*Early Edition* (a drama set in a large metropolitan newspaper) and *The District* (a law and order drama set in the nation's capital)—featured casts that were largely black, 76 percent and 62 percent, respectively.

Meanwhile, Monday night featured three of the four programs with the highest percentage of characters that were black—*Girlfriends* (89 percent), *One on One* (88 percent), and *The Parkers* (79 percent). Each of these black-oriented sitcoms aired on UPN,

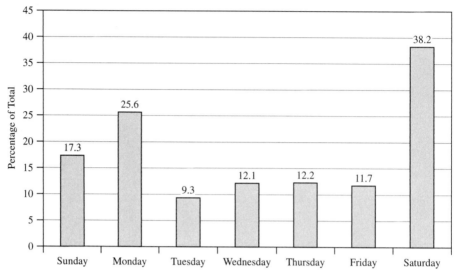

FIGURE 15.8 Black characters as a percentage of all characters, by night of the week (2001).

TABLE 15.3 Top Five and Bottom Five Shows in Terms of the Percentage of Characters That Were Black

	Program	Format	Black Characters
Top Five Shows	1. *Girlfriends* (UPN)	Sitcom	89%
	2. *One on One* (UPN)	Sitcom	88%
	3. *My Wife and Kids* (ABC)	Sitcom	83%
	4. *The Parkers* (UPN)	Sitcom	79%
	5. *Early Edition* (CBS)	Drama	76%
Bottom Five Shows	1. *Just Shoot Me* (NBC)	Sitcom	0%
	2. *Dharma and Greg* (ABC)	Sitcom	0%
	3. *Three Sisters* (NBC)	Sitcom	0%
	4. *Dawson's Creek* (WB)	Drama	0%
	5. *Sabrina* (WB)	Sitcom	0%

combining for a sizable share of the fledgling network's disproportionately large pool of black characters. Table 15.3 presents the top five and bottom five shows for 2001 in terms of the percentage of black chararacters.

Finally, Figure 15.9 reveals that black characters were less concentrated in sitcoms during the fall 2001 season than in 1999. About 61 percent of all black characters appeared in dramas in 2001, compared with only about 50 percent in 1999. Nonetheless, compared with whites (31 percent), Latinos (23 percent), and Asians (21 percent), black characters (39 percent) were still the most likely to appear in sitcoms.

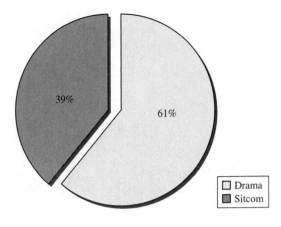

Drama
Sitcom

FIGURE 15.9 Black characters, by genre (2001, $n = 575$ episodes).

TABLE 15.4 Occupations of Black Characters

Other	36.5%	Criminal	2.8%
Unclear	29.9%	Doctor	2.6%
Student	10.4%	Nurse	2.2%
Police officer	7.8%	Secretary	2.2%
Attorney	3.7%	Teacher	1.9%

Note: n = 539 episodes.

Representations of Black Life

A recent study of entertainment television found that black characters, like white characters, now are more likely than their counterparts in the real world to occupy high-status lifestyles.[33] While this finding suggests that the binary-based stereotyping of black Americans so prevalent in earlier periods may no longer control prime time, it also raises concerns about the unintended consequences of overly "positive" representations of black life. As audience research on *The Cosby Show* revealed (see Chapter 6), perhaps unrealistically rosy renderings of black life on television worked to mask the continuing disadvantages faced by the group, thereby relieving whites of the moral obligation to acknowledge and share more of their group-based privilege.

Table 15.4 reveals that the occupations of black characters in prime time were largely inconclusive on this score. The largest single category, representing about 37 percent of all characters, was labeled "other" because none of the thirty or so distinct occupations forming the category was present to any appreciable degree in the sample. The next largest category, about 30 percent of all characters, was coded as "unclear" because occupation could not be determined from the relevant episode. With the exception of "criminal" (about 3 percent of all black characters), the remaining occupations were all suggestive of middle-class to upper-middle-class lifestyles: student (10.4 percent), police officer (7.8 percent), attorney (3.7 percent), doctor (2.6 percent), nurse (2.2 percent), secretary (2.2 percent), and teacher (1.9 percent).

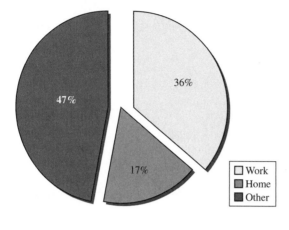

FIGURE 15.10 The first appearance of black characters, by location (2001, $n = 553$ episodes).

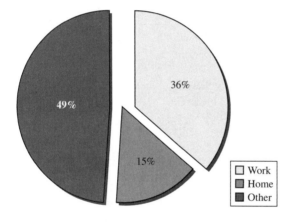

FIGURE 15.11 The second appearance of black characters, by location (2001, $n = 363$ episodes).

One indicator of the degree to which black life is integrated into the mainstream may be how frequently television takes us inside the black home. In the past, critics of prime time have argued that when black characters appear on the screen, they often do so primarily to complement white characters who are more central to the story line. Rarely did black characters appear as central characters in their own right, whose family connections were explored in any meaningful way.[34] Figure 15.10 suggests that despite the overrepresentation of blacks in prime time, relatively few images are provided of life inside the black home. When a black character first appeared in an episode, she or he was most likely seen at some place "other" (47 percent) than "home" (17 percent) or at "work" (36 percent).

If the same character appeared a second time, Figure 15.11 shows that the likelihood she or he would be seen in any one of the locations was about the same: 49 percent of characters appeared at some "other" place, 36 percent at "work," and only 15 percent at "home." Moreover, most of the at-home appearances of black characters in 2001 can be attributed to a handful of black-oriented sitcoms.

UPN and Black Prominence

The finding of black overrepresentation in prime time during the 2001 season does not necessarily mean that the black characters appearing on the screen did so in any meaningful way. In order to better understand the centrality of black characters in prime time, we must consider two important indicators of character *prominence:* series regular status and screen time.

"Series regulars" are those central characters around whom a prime-time program revolves. The names and/or faces of the actors who portray these characters appear in the opening credits. They are the primary characters with whom audience members connect when they tune in week after week. Figure 15.12 shows that when black series regulars are examined by network, a pattern emerges that is similar to but more pronounced than the one observed earlier for all black characters. That is to say, the percentage of UPN series regulars who are black (37 percent) was even higher than the network's figure for black characters (28 percent), and it is about three times the black American share of the overall U.S. population. On Fox, CBS, NBC, and ABC, black series regulars were present in proportions that are close to the group's actual population proportion (about 17 percent, 15 percent, 14 percent, and 10 percent, respectively). On the WB, however, black series regulars accounted for less than 7 percent of the series regulars appearing on the network.

But all series regulars are not equal, and series regular status alone may give an incomplete picture of how important a given black character is to an episode's story line. Observing how long black characters appear on the screen provides us with another, complementary measure of prominence.

Consistent with the high concentration of black characters and black series regulars on UPN, Figure 15.13 reveals that the black characters appearing on the network in 2001 were

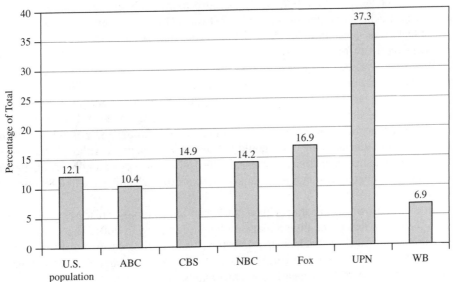

FIGURE 15.12 Black series regulars as a percentage of all series regulars, by network (2001).

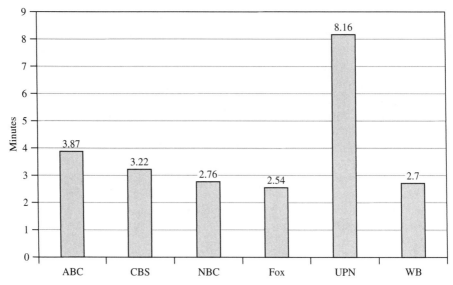

FIGURE 15.13 Mean screen time for black characters, by network (2001).

typically on the screen for much longer durations than their counterparts on the other networks. The mean screen time per hour of programming for black characters on UPN was 8.16 minutes, compared with only 3.87 minutes for ABC, 3.22 minutes for CBS, 2.76 minutes for NBC, 2.7 minutes for WB, and 2.54 minutes for Fox. Indeed, more than half (52 percent) of all black characters with screen times exceeding 10 minutes—arguably *the* most important black characters to their respective story lines—appeared on UPN. These findings mirror those from a 1999 study that also found UPN exhibiting a significantly larger mean black screen time than the other networks (14.01 minutes).[35] Findings further suggest that mean screen time for black characters has decreased somewhat for each of the networks over the two-year period.

When we consider mean screen time by night of the week, findings support the earlier characterization of Monday as a "black night" in prime-time 2001. The mean screen time for black characters on Monday night (6.61 minutes per hour of programming) was nearly double the mean across all nights (3.68 minutes). When we consider mean screen time by show type, it appears that findings about the possible declining concentration of blacks in sitcoms should be treated with caution. Although 61 percent of all black characters appeared in dramas in 2001, the more *prominent* black characters were still concentrated in sitcoms (mean screen times of 2.61 minutes and 4.89 minutes, respectively).

In short, an analysis of series regular status and screen time for black characters reinforces the notion that prime time remained highly segregated in 2001. That is to say, the most prominent black characters in prime time were ghettoized on the least-watched network (UPN), in situation comedies, and on Monday nights. With a few notable exceptions,[36] the black characters appearing on other nights, other networks, and in dramas were much less prominent.

A Year Later: The 2002 Season

Despite the ever-increasing diversity of American society, prime time continued to depict a largely black-and-white world in 2002. Findings from the year 2 analysis revealed that both black and white Americans were still overrepresented in prime time, with whites accounting for about 74 percent of all characters, compared with only about 69 percent of the U.S. population. Blacks accounted for about 16 percent of all characters, compared with about 12 percent of the population (see Figure 15.14).

The television figures for blacks had held steady since at least 1999 (when the Screen Actors Guild released a study on race in prime time), while those for whites had decreased slightly from about 78 percent in 1999.[37] Combined, whites and blacks constituted 90 percent of all prime-time characters in 2002, a number not significantly different from the 92 percent figure observed in the first year of the study.

Latinos accounted for only about 3 percent of all characters in prime time, compared with nearly 13 percent of the U.S. population. This more than four-to-one representation gap seemed particularly anomalous given public discussions in 2002 about the emergence of Latinos as the nation's largest minority group. Some observers have accounted for this representation gap by pointing to the presence of Spanish-language media in the United States, which they argue may better serve the needs of Latino audience members and the advertisers interested in reaching them. In other words, some have argued that prime-time network television underrepresents Latinos because it is less profitable to target them as viewers (i.e., to cast shows with Latino characters) than it is to target white or black Americans. While this logic is rooted in findings suggesting that viewers tend to prefer programs populated with characters resembling them, it is silent on the possible social and political implications of Latino underrepresentation in prime time. Another explanation for

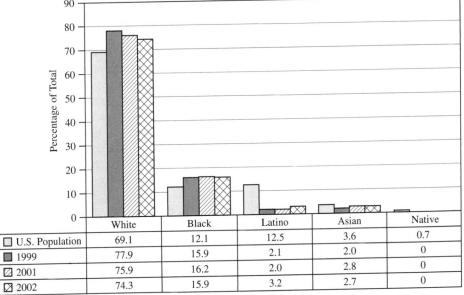

	White	Black	Latino	Asian	Native
☐ U.S. Population	69.1	12.1	12.5	3.6	0.7
■ 1999	77.9	15.9	2.1	2.0	0
▨ 2001	75.9	16.2	2.0	2.8	0
⊠ 2002	74.3	15.9	3.2	2.7	0

FIGURE 15.14 Representation, TV versus population, by race and year (2000).

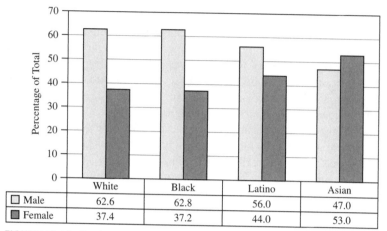

FIGURE 15.15 Gender breakdown of characters, by race (2002).

the gap holds that the white male–dominated industry has a hard time imagining Latino characters as anything other than maids and gardeners, which severely restricts narrative (and casting) opportunities for Latinos in prime time. (I explore this explanation later, when character occupations are examined.) Combined with the continued overrepresentation of black and white characters, however, the Latino gap also seemed to underscore the steady significance of the binary as a representational anchor in the American racial order.

Asian Americans accounted for about 3 percent of all characters in prime time during the 2002 season, compared with nearly 4 percent of the U.S. population. In this sense, Asian Americans, unlike Latinos, appeared to be closing the gap between their on-screen presence and their actual presence in the nation's population. On the other hand, relatively few of these Asian American characters were "series regulars," the central characters around whom a prime-time program revolves and with whom audience members identify. Indeed, not a single prime-time network series in 2002 featured an Asian American as *the* central character. The other groups (with the exception of Native Americans) had at least one series in which a member of the group was featured as the primary character.

Finally, not a single Native American character could be identified out of the 3,656 characters coded in the 2002 study. This finding was consistent with findings from the first year of the study, as well as a 1999 study of minority representation in prime time.[38]

Figure 15.15 presents a gender breakdown of characters by race. For both whites and blacks, nearly 63 percent of all characters were male during the 2002 season (the figure for both groups was a similar 60 percent in 2001). For Latinos, the figure was 56 percent, while females outnumbered males only among Asian Americans (about 53 percent to 47 percent).

Among high-status occupations like "doctor" and "lawyer" (see Figures 15.16 and 15.17), white and black Americans were portrayed similarly in prime time. That is to say, white characters were slightly more likely than black ones to be portrayed as doctors (4.9 percent to 4.1 percent), while black characters were slightly more likely than white ones to be portrayed as lawyers (3.6 percent to 2.6 percent). While there were no clearly identified Asian American lawyers in the sampled programming, Asian American characters were

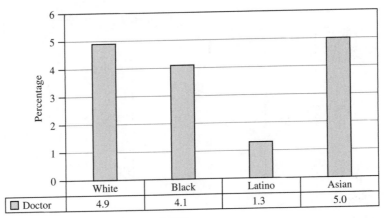

	White	Black	Latino	Asian
☐ Doctor	4.9	4.1	1.3	5.0

FIGURE 15.16 Doctors, by race (2002).

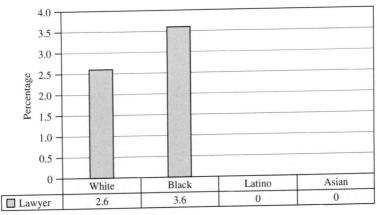

	White	Black	Latino	Asian
☐ Lawyer	2.6	3.6	0	0

FIGURE 15.17 Lawyers, by race (2002).

more likely than those from any other group to be portrayed as doctors (5 percent). Latino characters were the least represented among these high-status occupations, with just 1.3 percent of the characters portrayed as doctors and none clearly portrayed as lawyers. This latter finding may lend some credence to the argument discussed earlier that the white males who dominate industry decision making tend to imagine Latino characters primarily in low-status occupations.

Figures 15.18 and 15.19 present a racial comparison of characters portrayed as "police officers" and "criminals," respectively. Police officer was one of the most popularly portrayed occupations across the groups, with the exception of Asian American characters who—despite the model minority stereotype—were more likely to be portrayed as criminals than characters from any other group (11.7 percent). Meanwhile, black characters were more likely to be portrayed as police officers than characters from any other group (11.8 percent), followed by Latino characters (10.1 percent), white characters (6.8 percent), and Asian American characters (1.7 percent). Black characters were slightly more

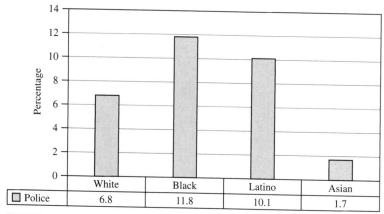

FIGURE 15.18 Police, by race (2002).

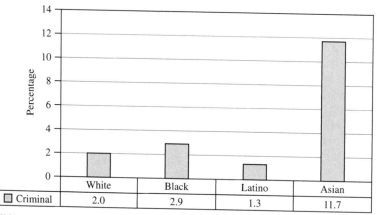

FIGURE 15.19 Criminals, by race (2002).

likely than white or Latino characters to be portrayed as criminals (2.9 percent, compared with 2.0 percent and 1.3 percent, respectively).

"Student" was another popularly portrayed occupation in prime time (see Figure 15.20). Latino characters were more likely than characters from any other group to be portrayed as students (24.1 percent), followed by black characters (15.7 percent), white characters (14.2 percent), and Asian American characters (8.3 percent). It should be noted, however, that the apparent popularity of this occupational portrayal was likely due to a coding rule that identified all children of school age as "students."

The largest occupational category across the groups was "unclear" (see Figure 15.21). Consistent with narrative conventions in prime time, the occupations of characters were often not discussed or even identified in a given episode.[39]

In addition to examining *screen time* for black characters, the 2002 analysis also considered the total amount of time white, Latino, and Asian American characters appeared on the screen in their respective shows (see Figure 15.22). The data revealed that white

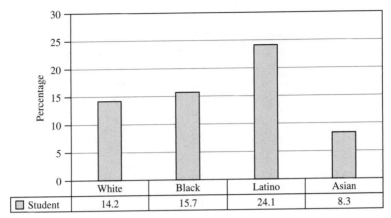

FIGURE 15.20 Students, by race (2002).

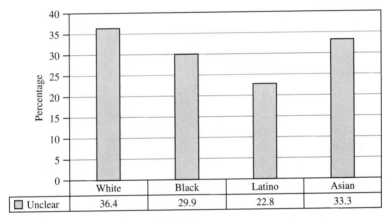

FIGURE 15.21 Unclear, by race (2002).

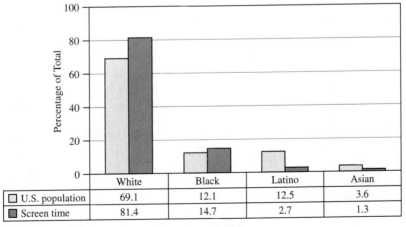

FIGURE 15.22 Share of screen time, by race (2002).

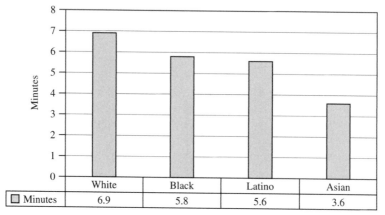

FIGURE 15.23 Mean screen time, by race (2002).

characters continued to dominate prime time not only in terms of the number of characters, but also in terms of the *prominence* of the characters in their respective shows' narratives. That is to say, white characters accounted for 224.4 hours of screen time—about 81 percent of the total screen time of 275.8 hours for characters of all groups. Black characters accounted for 40.5 hours of screen time, or about 15 percent of the total.

Meanwhile, Latino and Asian American characters accounted only for 7.4 hours and 3.6 hours of screen time, respectively. In other words, both Latino and Asian Americans were significantly underrepresented in terms of screen time, accounting for only about 3 percent and 1 percent of total screen time, respectively. *Mean* character screen times by group were as follows: white characters, 6.9 minutes; black characters, 5.8 minutes; Latino characters, 5.6 minutes; and Asian American characters, 3.6 minutes (see Figure 15.23).

Previous studies of race in prime time suggest that black and white characters have been largely segregated by network and night of the week. Findings from the 2002 season reveal that white Americans are most overrepresented on the WB and NBC, where they accounted for about 83 percent and 81 percent of all characters, respectively (compared with only about 69 percent of the U.S. population). Blacks, in contrast, continued to be most overrepresented on UPN, where they accounted for 31 percent of all characters, despite making up only about 12 percent of the U.S. population (see Figure 15.24). Other minority characters appeared so infrequently in prime time during the 2002 season that the patterns were not as pronounced as the ones for blacks and whites.

As we saw earlier, studies of prime time have documented the absence of black television dramas and noted that black characters were more likely to be concentrated in situation comedies than characters from any other racial group. In the past, this finding raised concerns that prime time might be primarily portraying black Americans in binary terms, as buffoonish characters ill-equipped for meaningful contribution to the larger society.[40] Figure 15.25 shows that for the 2002 season, this pattern was not evident. While it is likely that the most *prominent* black characters continued to be concentrated in situation comedies (e.g., those from UPN's Monday night lineup, discussed next), black characters in general were twice as likely to appear in television dramas (66.6 percent versus 33.4 percent). The figures for white characters were similar—73.8 percent in dramas,

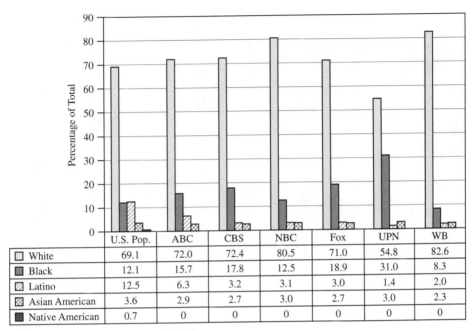

	U.S. Pop.	ABC	CBS	NBC	Fox	UPN	WB
☐ White	69.1	72.0	72.4	80.5	71.0	54.8	82.6
■ Black	12.1	15.7	17.8	12.5	18.9	31.0	8.3
▨ Latino	12.5	6.3	3.2	3.1	3.0	1.4	2.0
⊠ Asian American	3.6	2.9	2.7	3.0	2.7	3.0	2.3
■ Native American	0.7	0	0	0	0	0	0

FIGURE 15.24 Race, by network (2002).

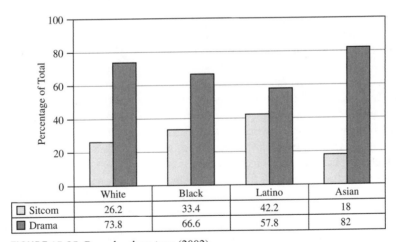

	White	Black	Latino	Asian
☐ Sitcom	26.2	33.4	42.2	18
■ Drama	73.8	66.6	57.8	82

FIGURE 15.25 Race, by show type (2002).

compared with just 26.2 percent in situation comedies. A higher percentage of Latino characters appeared in situation comedies than of characters from any other group (42.2 percent). In contrast, Asian Americans had the smallest representation in situation comedies (18 percent).

While not as pronounced as in previous years, UPN's Monday night situation comedies continued to account for a disproportionate share of prominent black characters in

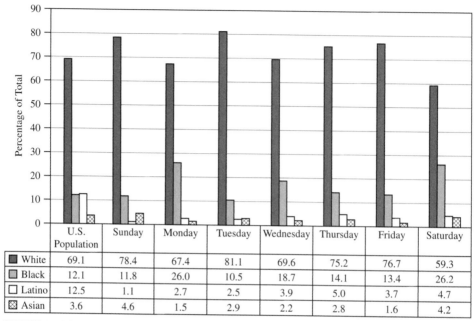

	U.S. Population	Sunday	Monday	Tuesday	Wednesday	Thursday	Friday	Saturday
■ White	69.1	78.4	67.4	81.1	69.6	75.2	76.7	59.3
■ Black	12.1	11.8	26.0	10.5	18.7	14.1	13.4	26.2
□ Latino	12.5	1.1	2.7	2.5	3.9	5.0	3.7	4.7
⊠ Asian	3.6	4.6	1.5	2.9	2.2	2.8	1.6	4.2

FIGURE 15.26 Race, by night of the week (2002).

2002 (see Figure 15.26). That is to say, 112 of the 125 black characters appearing on Monday night did so on UPN (90 percent). Although these 112 characters represented only about 19 percent of all black characters in prime time ($n = 580$), they accounted for nearly 30 percent of total black screen time (about 12.2 hours out of a total of 40.5 hours). Moreover, four of the five shows with the highest percentage of characters who were black—*The Parkers* (76.7 percent), *Half and Half* (76.0 percent), *Girlfriends* (70.4 percent), and *One on One* (65.6 percent)—constituted the network's Monday night lineup. The fifth show, *My Wife and Kids* (72.4 percent) is a black-oriented sitcom that appeared on ABC. Saturday—the least-watched night for prime-time television—was another prominent night for black characters, where they accounted for more than 26 percent of all characters. The four series airing that evening all featured casts in which black Americans were overrepresented. Three of the series aired on CBS—*The District* (50 percent), *Touched by an Angel* (18 percent), and *The Agency* (15 percent)—while the remaining series, *Law & Order* (20.2 percent), aired on NBC. Fox, UPN, and WB did not air original series on Saturday evenings.

Not surprisingly, the top shows for black American viewers in 2002 were black-themed programs with predominantly black casts, four of the top five appearing on UPN (see Table 15.5). The three exceptions to this rule, *Monday Night Football, Fastlane,* and *CSI: Crime Scene Investigation,* nonetheless featured prominent black representations.

In the final analysis, the findings from 2002 are mixed. Prime time continued to present a largely black-and-white world. The industry continued to be driven by business logics that divide the nation into market segments based on race, where the large but declining white segment reigned supreme. Programs designed to reach the other, smaller

TABLE 15.5 Top Ten Shows Among Black Households, 2002

1. *Cedric the Entertainer Presents* (Fox)	6. *My Wife and Kids* (ABC)
2. *One on One* (UPN)	7. *The Bernie Mac Show* (Fox)
3. *Girlfriends* (UPN)	8. *Monday Night Football* (ABC)
4. *Half and Half* (UPN)	9. *Fastlane* (Fox)
5. *The Parkers* (UPN)	10. *CSI: Crime Scene Investigation* (CBS)

Source: Initiative Media Agency study, reported in *Jet*, May 19, 2003.

racial niches were relegated to a night or two, and often concentrated on the smaller networks, if at all. Integrated programming featuring characters of different races that interact with one another—and that share equitable degrees of prominence—was the exception rather than the rule.

On the other hand, prime time 2002—as reflected in character occupations—depicted an American landscape where minorities are more prevalent in high-status occupations than they are in the real world. While these representations may provide minorities with high-status role models and contradict some of the meanings of blackness associated with the binary and its chains of equivalence, they also constitute a representational double-edged sword that presents American society as more open than it really is. This development, as we saw in the case of *The Cosby Show* (see Chapters 1, 6, 7, and 9), poses deleterious consequences for social justice in a hegemonic racial order such as our own. While the picture painted in prime time over the two-year study period arguably reflects the complex reality of today's racial order with startling clarity, it also works to reinforce that reality by splintering the diverse cultural forum that might otherwise re-imagine it.

White Control

When Sidney Poitier became the first black American to win a best actor Oscar in 1963, Hollywood paced the nation on matters of racial inclusion. As the nation's political establishment slowly responded to the demands of the civil rights movement, prominent white members of the entertainment industry quietly supported efforts for a more sweeping transformation. Some of these Hollywood insiders even provided behind-the-scenes financial support for militant organizations like the Black Panther Party.[41] Even though the whites who controlled the entertainment industry were generally seen as left of center,[42] the escapist fare of 1960s television favored the medium's conservative, commercial imperatives over the growing movements for racial justice.

Over the next several decades, America was locked in a cycle of progress and retreat on matters of racial inclusion. Affirmative action programs had been instituted in the early 1970s to open up white-controlled institutions to previously excluded minority groups. These programs, many had pointed out, most directly benefited middle-class minorities and were thus no panacea for the nation's deeper structural inequities. Supporters had nonetheless hoped that the resulting trickle of minorities into key institutional positions would slowly begin to transform the institutions from within.

But an increasing white backlash, inaugurated by the election of President Ronald Reagan in 1980,[43] effectively diagnosed affirmative action as terminally ill. The patient soon took a turn for the worse as the conservative president stacked the U.S. Supreme Court with justices in his own political image. Many pronounced her as all but dead when California voters passed Proposition 209 in 1996, banning the use of race as a criterion for admissions, hiring, and/or the awarding of contracts in state public institutions. Officially and popularly, America was "color-blind."

But the television establishment was clearly out of touch with this "fact."

While conservatives invoked the little progress made since the 1960s to proclaim that America was "beyond race," white control of network television remained frozen in time. Network television, like the rest of Hollywood, continued to be a highly insular industry in which white decision makers reproduced themselves by hiring other whites who shared similar experiences and tastes. In Chapter 1, I noted that white males occupy nearly all of the industry "green-lighting" positions—the positions from which it is decided what projects will be made, with what kind of budget, and by whom. This near monopoly includes the all-important "showrunner" positions—the executive producers who manage the development and day-to-day production of television programs. Once these producers succeed in developing a hit program, they can generally rely upon a revolving door of opportunities to develop other programs. In contrast, only a handful of minorities have actually been assigned to run a show. And because the credential of having a hit series to one's credit has been the surest way to show running assignments, few minorities have been seriously considered for them when opportunities arose. Indeed, black showrunners could be identified for only five of the eighty-five shows analyzed from 2001 (5.9 percent), and all but one of these five shows were black-oriented sitcoms.[44] Figure 15.27 graphs black showrunners from 1950 to 2003. It shows that the first black showrunner does not appear until 1969 (Bill Cosby for *The Bill Cosby Show*[45]) and that the numbers—which begin to rise after 1990—remain between zero and five throughout the fifty-three-year period. It is worth noting that the modest increases in black showrunners after 1990 can be attributed largely

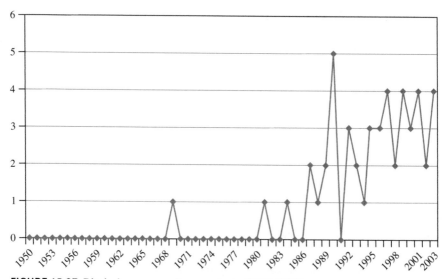

FIGURE 15.27 Black showrunners for new shows (1950–2003).

to the dramatic rise in black-oriented sitcoms on Fox, UPN, and the WB during the 1990s and beyond.

We also saw in Chapter 1 that white males have traditionally dominated the ranks of television directors. Although white males made up only about 34 percent of the U.S. population in 2000, they accounted for 80 percent of the television directors from the Top 40 shows in the 2000–2001 season. Women (composed primarily of white women) accounted for 11 percent of the television directors; all other minorities—31 percent of the U.S. population—combined for only 6 percent (3 percent black, 2 percent Latino, and 1 percent Asian).[46]

In 2001, minorities were similarly underrepresented among prime-time television writers, combining for only 9 percent of the total (6.2 percent black, 1.4 percent Latino, 1.3 percent Asian, 0.1 percent Native American). Although black writers, like black actors, were more prevalent in prime time than their Latino, Asian, or Native American counterparts, they were still woefully underrepresented in the writing corps. They were also concentrated in situation comedies and ghettoized by network. That is to say, fifty-five of the eighty-three black writers worked on sitcoms (66 percent), and thirty-eight of the writers worked on UPN (46 percent). Indeed, 30 percent of all writers on UPN were black; no other network had a writing corps that was more than 8 percent black.[47] In short, most black writers wrote for black-oriented situation comedies, most of which appeared on the least-watched network, UPN.

A year later in 2002, the minority share of television writing positions had increased to 13 percent (see Figure 15.28). But white writers continued to dominate, accounting for 94 percent of all writers on nonethnic sitcoms (see Figure 15.29), 88 percent of all writers on television dramas (see Figure 15.30), and more than half of all writers on ethnic sitcoms (see Figure 15.31). At the same time, more than 24 percent of the writers on UPN programs were black, again underscoring the degree to which black self-representation was concentrated on the least-watched network. Black presence on writing staffs for the other networks—particularly the larger ones—was only a fraction of this figure: 6.4 percent for ABC; 3.8 percent for CBS; 6.7 percent for Fox; 5.3 percent for NBC; and 1.2 percent for the WB.[48]

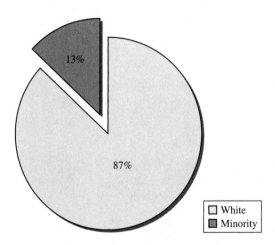

☐ White
■ Minority

FIGURE 15.28 TV writers, by race (2002).

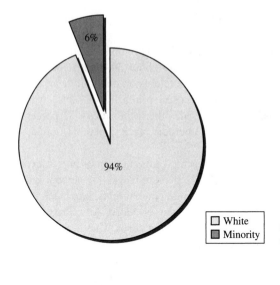

FIGURE 15.29 Writers on nonethnic sitcoms, by race (2002).

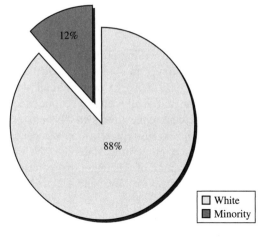

FIGURE 15.30 Writers on TV dramas, by
race (2002).

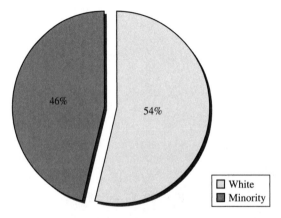

FIGURE 15.31 Writers on ethnic sitcoms,
by race (2002).

Rights, Profits, and Responsibilities

Apologists for prime-time practices have typically resorted to three basic arguments to explain the racial conditions chronicled in this chapter: the "First Amendment, creative rights" argument; the "small-talent-pool" argument; and "the bottom-line" argument.

The First Amendment, creative rights argument maintains that the constitutional right of free speech extends to the creators of television programs, artists who would be best left alone to enrich the marketplace of ideas by following their own inspirations. Diversity cannot be engineered, the argument follows, without somehow damaging this creative process and the long-term integrity (and commercial value) of television programs.

But what this line of reasoning fails to consider is that the very artists who are uniquely situated to create fresh and diverse takes on standard television fare are the ones who are seldom hired to do so. The corps of television writers, as we have seen, is overwhelmingly white (91 percent white for the 2001–2002 season and 87 percent white for the 2002–2003 season). These writers typically write from their own experiences, which tend to differ from and obscure the experiences of people of color. Indeed, when these writers attempt to portray minority experiences in their work, the results are often implausible at best and stereotypical at worst. Rarely do we see minority experiences portrayed in prime time with the kind of artistic sensitivity often invoked to insulate the craft from diversity demands.

A common refrain among those who control the industry is that the minority talent pool is not very extensive. This "fact," the small-talent-pool argument contends, explains why whites continue to occupy a disproportionately large share of key industry positions year after year. In an attempt to appease those who demand more diversity in prime time, key industry decision makers have traditionally relied upon devices such as the minority training program or the minority hiring fair.

But at best, these public relations programs constitute a lottery system that provides one or two opportunities for the hundreds of talented minorities competing for them. At worst, these programs result in much training and exposure, but no minority hiring; they effectively become fig leaves covering business-as-usual hiring practices. Minority under representation in prime time has had little to do with the availability of minority talent. It has had much to do with the availability of opportunities, with the decision of those who control the industry not to share them. In this sense, minority underrepresentation in the industry reflects with startling clarity broader exclusionary practices at work throughout America's twenty-first-century racial order.

The bottom-line argument has served as the final line of defense for those who support the prime-time status quo. After all, this argument reminds us, prime-time television is first and foremost a business faced with important profit-making imperatives. To be sure, as we saw in Chapter 1, the five media conglomerates that own the broadcast networks (Disney/ABC, Viacom/CBS/UPN, General Electric/NBC, NewsCorp/Fox, and AOL Time Warner/WB) controlled vertically integrated, global operations in 2001, combining for more than $240 billion in revenues.[49] The decisions made by network executives are conditioned by the earnings expectations of these giant corporations—nothing more and nothing less. If higher ratings and advertising revenues were produced by different prime-time practices (i.e., more diversity among decision makers, writers, and programming), the argument continues, then basic business logic would eventually lead to their use.

But this argument fails on two accounts. First, it is hard to demonstrate the degree to which more diverse practices would increase ratings and revenues because these practices have not been tried on any meaningful scale. Instead, the traditional institutional arrangement is simply presumed to be the only viable one, despite the fact that it has a rather lackluster track record: more than 70 percent of all new shows fail to be renewed for a second season.[50]

Second, and more important, the argument assumes that profit, and the underlying property right claimed by the corporate entity, is the most salient value in this matter. This assumption is dubious at best, but has endured because competing values have been effectively excised from the public discourse about television. That is to say, early understandings about public ownership of the airwaves and the responsibilities of broadcasters to serve the public interest have all but disappeared.[51] Indeed, the Federal Communications Commission—created by legislation to protect this public interest[52]—essentially became a booster for the industry in the early years of the twenty-first century.

AFFIRMING RACE IN "RACELESS" TIMES

Scholars of prime-time television have long recognized the links between televised representations of blackness and the changing dynamics of race in American society. As Marlon Riggs's award-winning, 1991 documentary on prime-time images of blackness so graphically demonstrates, television has made constant "adjustments" to the racial ethos of the times.[53] Writing in the early 1990s, television scholar J. Fred MacDonald identified four distinct periods that seemed to match particular representational practices with shifting political imperatives. He labeled these periods as follows: "The Promise Denied" (1948–1957), a period marked by the general exclusion of prominent black images from television; "Blacks in TV in the Age of the Civil Rights Movement" (1957–1970), a period defined by a society-wide push for racial integration and an industry focus on circulating "positive" black images; "The Age of the New Minstrelsy" (1970–1983), a period marked by the rise of "gritty," "relevant," and "authentic" inner-city sitcoms that critics accused of circulating "negative" black images akin to those associated with early black shows like *Amos 'n' Andy;* and "Blacks in the New Video Order" (1983 and beyond), a period marked by the decline of network audience shares, a trend away from *broad*casting toward *narrow* casting, and a concomitant rise in opportunities for the circulation of black representations, albeit to smaller audiences.[54] A more recent study by television scholar Donald Bogle presents an epochal model of black prime-time representations and racial politics that maps closely onto MacDonald's, despite being organized by decade: "Scraps" (1950s); "Social Symbols" (1960s); "Jokesters" (1970s); "Superstars" (1980s, distinguished by the rise of *The Cosby Show*); and "Free-For-Alls" (1990s).[55]

In contrast, sociologist Herman Gray (see Chapter 9) and media scholar Todd Boyd identify distinct *styles* in the practice of racial representation that—while their roots may be traced to specific historical moments—transcend the various periods, waxing and waning in dominance over time. Gray defines three such stylistic practices, each based on a particular racial discourse: *assimilationist* (e.g., 1960s programming like *I Spy* and *Julia*); *pluralist or separate-but-equal* (e.g., the 1950s sitcom *Amos 'n' Andy,* 1970s sitcoms like *Sanford and Son,* and 1990s sitcoms like *Living Single*); and *multiculturalist/diversity* (e.g., short-lived shows from the late 1980s and early 1990s like *Frank's Place* or *South Central*). Boyd focuses on a shorter time frame, but also posits three distinctive styles: the "race man," exemplified by the "positive," "acceptable" (to whites) image of Bill Cosby; the "new black aesthetic," composed of "authentic" yet highly commodified representations of blackness produced by middle-class black artists and intellectuals; and "the Nigga," in-your-face representations of blackness produced by (predominantly male) ghetto-based artists who profess little concern with white standards or white reactions. While a detailed textual analysis of prime-time programming is beyond the scope of this study, anecdotal evidence supports the existence of these practices during the study period. Mixtures of Boyd's so-called Nigga style (which I would relabel as "ghetto" to underscore its class dimension *and* avoid minimizing black female contributions), his "new black aesthetic" style, and Gray's "pluralist" discursive approach indeed appear to frame many black-themed sitcoms, particularly the ones concentrated on UPN and WB. Meanwhile, observations of black representations on the larger networks suggest that they may be shaped more by Gray's "assimilationist" discursive approach, and to a lesser degree his "multiculturalist/diversity" discursive approach.

In an early twenty-first-century racial order predicated on racial inequality amid official denials of race, television has become a white-controlled cultural forum that offers a little of something for everyone. Industry executives dress enduring racial assumptions and imperatives in the garb of race-neutral, market-based rhetoric, channeling blackness in ways that segment the audience along racial lines and simultaneously support the myth of an America beyond race. To be sure, most of the programs in prime time—particularly the top-rated shows that appear on the larger networks—remain a white place in which whites can affirm the universality of whiteness in raceless times. In this discursive space, white characters lead and nonwhite characters follow. White characters dominate not only in terms of the on-screen population but also in terms of *time* on the screen. Black characters are typically the coworkers of more prominent white characters, who unlike black characters from earlier periods, enjoy relatively affluent lifestyles. These television blacks seem content to blend into the (white) mainstream, often abandoning family and community for honorary inclusion in this happy realm. The specter of race rarely emerges as an explicit concern in these narratives. When hints of the "ghetto" style surface—for example, on popular law and order shows like *The District*—they do so as implicit threats to (white) order that invoke the binary and its related chains of equivalence. These threats, of course, are contained by show's end at the hands of the (white) lead, likely feeding an enduring white ambivalence toward blackness and generating considerable audience pleasure.

Meanwhile, prime-time practices during this period still provided black viewers with increased opportunities to affirm cultural community—albeit at the margins. The upstart Fox network had cut its teeth on several programs that featured black characters and themes, attracting significant black audiences in the process. Fox's marketing strategy, no doubt, was at least partially motivated by the long-standing realization that black Americans form a disproportionately large share of the television audience. The WB and UPN would soon follow suit, targeting black viewers with black-themed sitcoms that were never meant to catch on among whites. Indeed, Nielsen data from 2002 reveal that black viewers made up nearly 80 percent of the audience for the black-themed sitcoms on the smaller networks.[56] It is interesting to note, as we saw earlier, that nearly all of these shows were either run by blacks or created by them and featured creative staffs with a critical mass of black writers. The racial tables are turned in these programs. Blacks generally lead and whites follow. Black homes and communities are given center stage, while black characters dominate both in terms of on-screen population and time on the screen. Moreover, these programs often combine "problematic" or "negative" representations of blackness, such as those inspired by the "ghetto" style, with more "positive" or "acceptable" ones to craft complicated, "insider" narratives that black viewers likely embrace as familiar and endearing. Sitcoms such as *Girlfriends, Eve,* and *The Parkers* come to mind here. These *self*-representations, of course, are not as attractive to white viewers, who gravitate toward shows on the larger networks that feature representations of a more contained blackness.

Supporters of the prime-time status quo might invoke any number of democracy tropes to address the patterns just described. For example, some might claim that audience segmentation along racial lines is the benign result of consumer choice. Others might suggest that differences between the readings of black *self*-representations and the readings of similar black representations circulated in a more mainstream context underscore the primacy of polysemy—a reality that supports the possibility, if not the existence, of "semiotic democracy."[57] If American society were truly race-neutral, then these arguments might be reasonable. But American society, as we have seen throughout this book, is profoundly raced. Since its introduction nearly sixty years ago, television has adjusted to America's evolving racial order in ways that permit the privileged to have their representational cake and eat it too. The early twenty-first century is a time when white supremacy thrives in a climate of color-blind ideology. The apparent "anomaly" of black overrepresentation in prime time during this period, when considered in the broader scheme of things, is not so anomalous after all. Black overrepresentation in color-blind times serves the critical need of stabilizing the binary in racial formation processes, and in so doing, framing the popular discourses through which other nonwhite groups are situated in the racial order. Against a backdrop of increasing racial diversity, a white-controlled industry continues to channel blackness in ways that affirm whiteness, while at the same time promoting the fiction of an America beyond race.

NOTES

1. Portions of this chapter are excerpted from Darnell M. Hunt, "Prime Time in Black and White: Making Sense of the 2001 Fall Season," *CAAS Research Report* 1, no. 1 (2002), and "Prime Time in Black and White: Not Much Is New for 2002," *Bunche Research Report* 1, no. 1 (2003), Ralph J. Bunche Center for African American Studies at UCLA.
2. Darnell M. Hunt, *The African American Television Report: Progress and Retreat,* Screen Actors Guild, June 2000.
3. *Los Angeles Times,* September 11, 1999, F2.
4. National Association for the Advancement of Colored People, *Out of Focus—Out of Sync: Take 3,* November 2003, 7.
5. *Los Angeles Times,* September 13, 1999, F13.
6. *Los Angeles Times,* October 27, 1999, F1.
7. For example, see *Los Angeles Times,* January 6, 2000, A1; *Los Angeles Times,* January 7, 2000, A1; *Los Angeles Times,* January 12, 2000, A1.
8. One of the women was replaced by a man.
9. Throughout the period, a number of studies were produced by the employment guilds (e.g., the Screen Actors Guild, the Writers Guild of America, West, and the Directors Guild of America), advocacy groups (e.g., Children Now, the Asian Pacific Media Coalition, the National Latino Media Council, and the NAACP), and other research organizations (e.g., the Bunche Center for African American Studies at UCLA) that chronicled lackluster industry progress on the diversity front.
10. See *Los Angeles Times,* October 14, 2003, C2.

11. See William T. Bielby and Denise D. Bielby, "Controlling Primetime: Organizational Concentration and Network Television Programming Strategies," *Journal of Broadcasting and Electronic Media,* forthcoming.

12. U.S. Commission on Civil Rights, *Window Dressing on the Set: Women and Minorities in Television,* U.S. Government Printing Office, 1977.

13. Testimony of Jeffrey Sagansky, President, CBS Entertainment, Hearing Before the United States Commission on Civil Rights, "Racial and Ethnic Tensions in American Communities: Poverty, Inequality, and Discrimination—Los Angeles Hearing," June 15–17, 1993.

14. For purposes of census enumeration during this period, the Hispanic/Latino population was classified as "white." Today, of course, the U.S. government officially considers "Latino" or "Hispanic" as an "ethnic" category, and a large portion of people who identify as being of Latino or Hispanic *ethnicity* classify themselves as *racially* "white."

15. U.S. Bureau of the Census, *The American Almanac: Statistical Abstract of the United States,* 1994–1995, Table 12 (Austin, TX: The Reference Press, 1994).

16. National Black Feminist Organization, quoted in *Window Dressing on the Set.*

17. As scholars have noted, changing census figures for certain populations do not necessarily reflect objective changes in the sizes of the groups. Racial and ethnic categories are often added, deleted, or redefined between censuses. The resulting numbers, however, do reflect official and popular understandings at the time they are released.

18. By "prominent," I mean the characters that are most central to a program's narrative, characters that tend to be series regulars and are present on the screen for significant amounts of time.

19. Hunt, *The African American Television Report.*

20. These weeks were selected to correspond to the weeks selected in the 2001 benchmark year, which also coincide with the initial airings of new fall programming and include two important programming environments in the sample (sweeps versus non-sweeps). Trained researchers viewed tapes of the programming and coded the data in accordance with a standard codebook. An agreement level of greater than 90 percent was achieved in a training test, as well as in 10 percent post-test sampling. Certain variables were dropped from the analysis and others were recoded to subsequently increase the effective level of inter-coder reliability.

21. "Featured" characters were defined as those with speaking lines or as those who were directly referenced by other characters with speaking lines.

22. Hunt, *The African American Television Report.*

23. Percentages do not sum to 100 due to the observation of "unclear" race characters.

24. For example, see A. C. Nielsen Company, *Black American Study,* May 1991.

25. For example, see *USA Today,* "TV's Big Black-White Divide Narrows," April 15, 2003.

26. Indeed, personal interviews with network executives in February and March 1993 revealed that they are reluctant to explicitly talk about race when describing audience demographic goals. More recent public statements by network executives are notable for their lack of reference to race or racial considerations.

27. Popular exceptions to this rule included dramas like *The District* (CBS), *Early Edition* (CBS), and *Boston Public* (Fox).

28. Hunt, *The African American Television Report.*

29. These findings come from an Initiative Media Agency study, reported in *Jet,* May 19, 2003. The Nielsen Media data on which the study is based come from the fourth quarter of 2002.

30. "Black households continue to outspend white households on key consumer products," *Target Market News,* February 13, 1999, http://www.targetmarketnews.com/trends.htm.

31. Hunt, *The African American Television Report.*

32. Indeed, neither Fox, UPN, nor WB aired original programming on Saturday nights. Instead, a substantial portion of the black characters from the larger networks was relegated to this least-watched night.

33. See Robert Entman and Andrew Rojecki, *The Black Image in the White Mind: Media and Race in America* (Chicago: University of Chicago Press, 2000).

34. Hunt, *The African American Television Report.*

35. Ibid.

36. Some of the more prominent examples were identified earlier.

37. Hunt, *The African American Television Report.*

38. Ibid.

39. The popularity of this occupational portrayal (or lack thereof) can also largely be attributed to a coding rule—one that demanded explicit reference to or signs of a given occupation *in the specific episode* in order to warrant coding for the occupation.

40. Hunt, *The African American Television Report.*

41. Personal interview with David Hilliard, May and June 2002.

42. See Robert S. Lichter, Linda S. Lichter, and Stanley Rothman, *Watching America: What Television Tells Us About Our Lives* (New York: Prentice-Hall, 1991).

43. See Michael Omi and Howard Winant, *Racial Formation in the United States: From the 1960s to the 1990s* (New York: Routledge, 1994).

44. The sitcoms included *The Parkers* (UPN), *One on One* (UPN), *Bernie Mac* (Fox), and *My Wife and Kids* (ABC); *Philly* (ABC) was the lone drama.

45. See Donald Bogle, *Prime Time Blues: African Americans on Network Television* (New York: Farrar, Straus and Giroux, 2001).

46. Directors Guild of America, "DGA Report Reveals Lack of Diversity in Hiring Practices on Top Forty Prime Time Drama and Comedy Series," January 30, 2002, http://www.dga.org/news/pr_expand.php3?232.

47. Data from Writers Guild of America, West.

48. Ibid.

49. In addition to CBS and UPN, Viacom owned thirty-six television stations, MTV, Nickelodeon, VH1, Showtime, BET, and nearly two hundred radio stations. AOL Time Warner owned WB, CNN, HBO, TBS, TNN, Cartoon Network, and dozens of record labels. Disney owned ABC, twenty-seven radio stations, and 80 percent of ESPN. NewsCorp owned Fox and thirty-three television stations (it purchased DirecTV in late 2003). GE owned NBC, thirteen television stations, AMC, and Bravo. Data from company annual reports and literature, 2001.

50. *New York Daily News,* Friday, May 10, 2002, sports final edition.

51. For a detailed discussion of the relationship between media ownership and the public interest, see Robert W. McChesney, *Corporate Media and the Threat to Democracy* (New York: Seven Brothers Press, 1997).

52. See the testimony of Chon Noriega before the U.S. Commission on Civil Rights, in *Racial and Ethnic Tensions in American Communities: Poverty, Inequality, and Discrimination—Los Angeles Hearing,* June 15–17, 1993. See also Robert L. Hilliard, *The Federal Communications Commission: A Primer* (Boston: Focal Press, 1991).

53. Marlon Riggs, "Color Adjustment," California Newsreel, 1991.

54. See J. Fred MacDonald, *Blacks and White TV: African Americans in Television Since 1948,* 2nd ed. (Chicago: Nelson-Hall, 1992), vii–viii.

55. See Bogle, *Prime Time Blues.*

56. *USA Today,* "TV's Big Black-White Divide Narrows," April 15, 2003.

57. For a discussion of this controversial idea, see John Fiske, 1988, *Television Culture* (New York: Routledge, 1988).

INDEX

An index entry for a note (e.g., 297n49) directs the reader to the page that contains the in-text citation for that note, with the actual text of the note appearing at the end of that respective chapter.